Heritage

Identification, Conservation, and Management

Graeme Aplin

OXFORD

UNIVERSITY PRESS

OXFORD
UNIVERSITY PRESS

253 Normanby Road, South Melbourne, Victoria 3205, Australia
Oxford University Press is a department of the University of Oxford.
It furthers the University's objective of excellence in research, scholarship,
and education by publishing worldwide in

Oxford New York

Auckland Bangkok Buenos Aires Cape Town Chennai
Dar es Salaam Delhi Hong Kong Istanbul Karachi Kolkata
Kuala Lumpur Madrid Melbourne Mexico City Mumbai Nairobi
São Paulo Shanghai Singapore Taipei Tokyo Toronto

and an associated company in Berlin

OXFORD is a trade mark of Oxford University Press
in the UK and in certain other countries

© Graeme Aplin 2002

First published 2002

National Library of Australia
Cataloguing-in-Publication data:

Aplin, G. J. (Graeme John).
Heritage identification, conservation, and management.

Includes index.
ISBN 0 19 551297 9.

1. Cultural property. 2. Cultural property, Protection of. 3. Historic preservation.
4. Historic Sites—Conservation and restoration. 5. Historic buildings—
Conservation and restoration. 6. Nature conservation. 7. Conservation of natural
resources. 8. Environmental protection—Management. I. Title.

363.690994

Edited by Katie Barnett
Text and cover designed by Racheal Stines
Typeset by Racheal Stines
Printed through Bookpac Production Services, Singapore

CONTENTS

Plates   xi

Figures   xviii

Tables   xx

Boxes   xxi

Acknowledgments   xxiv

Abbreviations   xxv

Introduction: Heritage and Its Components   1

1   The Nature of Heritage   7

    1.1   What is 'heritage'?   7

    1.2   Heritage as a concept   13

    1.3   History, heritage, and commodification   15

    1.4   The role and uses of heritage   16

            Identity and belonging—Political uses—Economic uses

    1.5   Heritage significance and criteria for identification   18

    1.6   Differences between Australian and European approaches   23
            to heritage

    1.7   Conclusion   27

2   Interpretation and Presentation of Heritage: 30
    Attaching and Conveying Meaning

    2.1   Heritage as social construct   30

    2.2   What is interpretation?   30

            Interpretation by whom?—Interpretation for whom?

    2.3   Uses of interpretation   34

            *Public awareness—Encouraging visitors—Adding value—Building
            identity—Specific education—General education—Management*

    2.4   Interpretation principles   39

            *Research the subject and strive for accuracy—Research the
            audience—Carefully devise methods—Balance detail and
            brevity—Entertain as well as educate—Provide context*

    2.5   Interpretation and presentation: some practical issues   42

            *Signs—Guides—Printed material—Audio-visual aids—Web
            sites and other IT media—Visitor centres*

    2.6   Further discussion   47

3   Tourism and the Economics of Heritage Management   **49**

3.1   Whose heritage? Who pays?   49

3.2   Public vs private interests—costs concentrated, benefits dispersed?   50

3.3   Can heritage be made to pay its way?   52

3.4   Valuing heritage   53

3.5   Public financing of heritage preservation and conservation   55
Direct public sector management—Grants for preservation and conservation—Tax relief and other incentives—Conditions attached to public assistance

3.6   Commodification and commercialisation   56
User-pays principle—Commercial uses of heritage sites

3.7   Tourism, recreation, and heritage   59
Ecotourism, cultural tourism, and heritage tourism—The 'pros' and 'cons' of tourism

3.8   Marketing heritage   65

4   Some General Principles of Conservation and Management   **67**

4.1   Definitions   67
Place—(Cultural) Significance—Fabric—Conservation—Maintenance—Preservation—Restoration—Reconstruction—Adaptation and compatible uses

4.2   Identifying and documenting heritage values   74

4.3   Published guidelines for managing heritage   75

4.4   Heritage plans   75

4.5   Who manages, and for whom?   76

4.6   Visitor management   76

4.7   Private owners' rights and obligations   78

4.8   Management principles   79
Information base—Goals and objectives—Outcomes and evaluation—Flexibility and monitoring—Awareness of societal context—Building community support—Doing as little as possible—Dealing with change—Balancing competing goals—Managing visitor pressure—Funding and budgetary issues

4.9   Conclusion   82

5   Natural Heritage and Its Management   **83**

5.1   Natural heritage—an introduction   83
General comments—World Heritage definitions

5.2   Reasons for conserving ecosystems and landscapes   85
Overview—Environmental services—Biodiversity Conservation—Non-material values

5.3   Protecting endangered species and ecosystems   87
What should be preserved?—Geographical distribution of reserves—Size and shape of reserves

5.4   Wilderness—a contested concept   94

5.5   Preservation outside reserves   96

5.6   Managing protected natural areas   97
       *Specific environmental problems within reserves—Environmental
       effects of reserves on surrounding land—Management practices to
       counter visitor pressure—Public involvement*

5.7   Management plans   102
       Some examples—Conclusion

5.8   Australian Natural Heritage Charter   107

5.9   Recreation and tourism uses of the natural environment   108
       Multiple uses including recreation and tourism—Ecotourism

5.10   Conclusion   110

6   Cultural Heritage and Its Management   113

6.1   Definitions and scope   113

6.2   Application of criteria to cultural heritage   115
       Architectural significance—Associational significance

6.3   Listing cultural heritage items   120
       Data required—Statement of significance

6.4   Significance of context and contextual significance   121
       *Curtilages—Grouped heritage items—Heritage precincts and
       urban conservation areas—Historic towns and villages—
       Landscape conservation areas*

6.5   Cultural heritage sites other than historic buildings   127
       *Gardens and parks—Cemeteries—Archaeological sites—
       Industrial archaeology—Shipwrecks*

6.6   Dealing with change: alterations and additions   129
       *How original is original? How authentic is authentic?—
       Organic change and realistic expectations*

6.7   Management of cultural heritage   131
       *Who manages, and for whom?—The Burra Charter—
       The conservation plan—Practical management issues*

6.8   Adaptive re-use   134

6.9   Outdoor museums or heritage theme parks?   137

6.10   Commodification and commercialisation   138

7   Indigenous and Minority Heritage and Its Management   140

7.1   Introduction   140

7.2   National and minority heritage   140

7.3   Context and significance   142

7.4   Ownership and involvement   143
       *Research, listing, and planning—Interpretation and presentation—
       Planning and managing heritage—Appropriation—Advantages
       and disadvantages of heritage exploitation—Active conservation
       and maintenance*

7.5	Indigenous tourism and Australian Aboriginal cultures	151
7.6	An integrated view of heritage	152

8   Global Heritage: The World Heritage Convention and Other Treaties   **154**

8.1	The concept of world heritage	154
8.2	The World Heritage Convention	154
8.3	Identifying, assessing, and managing World Heritage	163

Defining World Heritage—Identifying and assessing World Heritage—Role of non-government organisations—National responsibilities—Global coverage and representativeness—Global Strategy

8.4	List of World Heritage in Danger	172
8.5	Other international initiatives	176

Biosphere Reserves—Ramsar sites—Convention on Biological Diversity

8.6	Conclusion	178

9   Regulatory Frameworks and Approaches to Heritage: Commonwealth of Australia   **181**

9.1	Australia: a federation	181
9.2	Historical and cultural influences	182

Australian history and perceptions of heritage—Developmentalism—Administrative categorisation of heritage

9.3	The Federal Government and its agencies	185

The role of the Federal Government—Environment Australia—Australian Heritage Commission—Register of the National Estate—Natural Heritage Trust

9.4	Australian World Heritage properties	190

South-western Tasmania—Kakadu National Park—Management of World Heritage properties

9.5	Other Commonwealth legislation and related reserves	204
9.6	New and proposed legislation, 1998–2001	205

Indigenous heritage—World Heritage and natural heritage—National heritage and cultural heritage

10   Regulatory Frameworks and Voluntary Organisations: Australian States and Territories   **211**

10.1	Introduction	211
10.2	New South Wales	211

Administrative and legislative framework—Built heritage: complementary roles of state and local government—Natural and indigenous heritage—Summary and conclusion

10.3	Other Australian states and territories	221

Australian Capital Territory—Northern Territory—Queensland—South Australia—Tasmania—Victoria—Western Australia

10.4   Local government authorities   231

10.5   Voluntary and community organisations   232

      The National Trust—Other local and voluntary involvement

10.6   Conclusion   237

**11   Regulatory Frameworks and Approaches to Heritage: 239
Some European Countries**

11.1   Introduction   239

11.2   United Kingdom   241

      *Introduction—Cultural heritage—Natural heritage—National
Trusts—World Heritage properties in the United Kingdom*

11.3   France   255

      *Introduction—Cultural heritage—Natural heritage—French
World Heritage properties*

11.4   Italy   266

      *Introduction—Cultural heritage—Natural heritage—Italian
World Heritage properties*

11.5   Spain   279

      *Introduction—Cultural heritage—Natural heritage—Spanish
World Heritage properties*

11.6   Ireland   290

      *Introduction—Cultural and natural heritage—Irish World
Heritage properties*

11.7   The European Union   294

**12   Regulatory Frameworks and Approaches to Heritage: 296
Some Other Countries**

12.1   Introduction   296

12.2   New Zealand   296

      *Background—Heritage management—New Zealand World
Heritage properties*

12.3   United States of America   304

      *Background—Cultural heritage—Natural heritage— Example
of heritage management at the state level: California—United
States World Heritage properties*

12.4   South Africa   320

      *Background—New legislation of 1999—Cultural heritage—
Natural heritage—South African World Heritage properties*

12.5   Thailand   330

      Background—Heritage management—Thai World Heritage properties

12.6   China   334

      Background—Heritage management—Chinese World Heritage properties

12.7   Conclusion   347

**13 Heritage: Conserving the Best of the Past and   349
    Present for the Future**

  13.1 What is heritage?   349
  13.2 Whose heritage?   352
  13.3 Scale revisited: local to global significance   353
  13.4 Conservation and management   354
  13.5 Final conclusions   357

**Appendix 1 Key to World Heritage criteria used in the   359
    tables in this book**

Appendix 2 Relevant web sites   361

Index   366

Plate 1.1	Dolmen in vineyards outside village of St-Fort-sur-Né, Charente, France	8
Plate 1.2	Cathédral Notre-Dame, Chartres, Eure-et-Loire, France	8
Plate 1.3	The byre (cow shed) dwelling in the Bunratty Folk Park, Co. Clare, Ireland	9
Plate 1.4	The village of Burnsall, Wharfedale, North Yorkshire, within the Yorkshire Dales National Park, England	10
Plate 1.5	Grampians National Park, Victoria	11
Plate 1.6	A magnificent crimson waratah (*Telopea speciosissima*), growing in the Muogamarra Nature Reserve, NSW	11
Plate 1.7	Scotch Whisky Heritage Centre, Castle Hill, Edinburgh, Scotland	12
Plate 1.8	Irish band performing in the Oliver St John Gogarty Hotel, Dublin, Ireland	13
Plate 1.9	Banks of the River Seine, Paris, France	27
Plate 2.1	Wheelchair access, Echidna Aboriginal engraving site, Ku-ring-gai Chase National Park, NSW	33
Plate 2.2	French brochures publicising a range of sites covering many different forms of cultural heritage	34
Plate 2.3	Sign outside the Ling Yin (Soul's Retreat) Buddhist temple, Hangzhou, Zhejiang Province, China	34
Plate 2.4	Sign at Kanangra–Boyd National Park, NSW	35
Plate 2.5	An official Chinese Tourist Office guide at Hangzhou, China	36
Plate 2.6	Explanatory signs in shelter at entrance to Bunjil's Cave Reserve, east of the Grampians National Park, Victoria	36
Plate 2.7	Sign at Port Campbell National Park, Victoria	37
Plate 2.8	Model of monastic site in the Glendalough Visitor Centre, Co. Wicklow, Ireland	46
Plate 3.1	Bunratty Castle, Co. Clare, Ireland	53

Plate 3.2   Sign indicating the many levels of govern-   55
ment involved in financing conservation
works at the Pont du Gard World Heritage
property in the Gard Département,
Languedoc-Rouisillon, France

Plate 3.3   Commercial marina operation at Akuna   58
Bay, within the Ku-ring-gai Chase
National Park, NSW

Plate 3.4   Château de Versailles, south of Paris,   60
France

Plate 4.1   Room with period furnishings in the   68
Treaty House, Waitangi, Northland,
New Zealand

Plate 4.2   Treaty House, Waitangi, New Zealand,   69
lathe and plaster wall

Plate 4.3   Forest-floor debris in a moist section of   70
Bulahdelah State Forest, Mid-North
Coast, NSW

Plate 4.4   Mirror Lake, Yosemite National Park,   70
California

Plate 4.5   Restoration work on the Pont Neuf, over   72
the River Seine, Paris, France

Plate 4.6   Reconstructed replica of the original   73
Shakespearean Globe Theatre on the
South Bank of the Thames, London

Plate 4.7   Northern side of Charlotte Square, built   77
in the 1790s, in the New Town district of
Edinburgh, Scotland

Plate 4.8   Signs warning of the crocodile danger and   77
the management practices used to reduce
the hazard, Kakadu National Park,
Northern Territory

Plate 4.9   The Piazza dei Miracoli, Pisa, Italy   81

Plate 5.1   View over the wilderness areas of the   85
Kanangra–Boyd National Park, NSW

Plate 5.2   Inland semi-arid scrubland, near King's   90
Canyon, in Watarrka National Park,
Northern Territory

Plate 5.3   Landcare and Land for Wildlife signs,   97
Grampians Pioneer Cottages, just outside
Grampians National Park, Victoria

Plate 5.4   Old eroded track and new boardwalk near   98
The Balconies, Grampians National Park,
Victoria

Plate 5.5   Steel mesh walkway between the   101
Crackenback Range and Mt Kosciuszko,
Kosciuszko National Park, NSW

Plate 6.1   Glanum Visitors' Centre, St-Rémy-de-   114
Provence, Bouches-du-Rhône, France

Plate 6.2   Sydney Opera House, Sydney, NSW   117

Plate 6.3   Malachi Gilmore Hall, Oberon, NSW   117

Plate 6.4   Fitzgerald's Hotel, Avoca, Co. Wicklow, 118
Ireland

Plate 6.5   Drummond Street, Carlton, Melbourne,   125
Victoria

Plate 6.6   Gaskill Street, the heart of the Canowindra 125
Urban Conservation Area, Canowindra,
NSW

Plate 6.7   Street scene in the historic town of Maldon, 126
Victoria

Plate 6.8   Formal gardens, Powerscourt, Ireland   127

Plate 6.9   Smelters at abandoned copper mines,   128
Chillagoe, Queensland

Plate 6.10 Musée du Louvre, Paris, France   130

Plate 6.11 Kircaldie and Staines Building, Wellington, 135
New Zealand

Plate 6.12 Musée d'Orsay, Paris, France   137

Plate 6.13 Reconstructed village street, Beamish, 137
The North of England Open Air Museum,
Co. Durham, England

Plate 7.1   Monument Valley Tribal Park, Navajo   144
Nation, USA

Plate 7.2   Uluṟu (Ayers Rock) in the Uluṟu–Kata 145
Tjuṯa National Park, Northern Territory

Plate 7.3   Sign at Basin Aboriginal Engraving Site, 146
Ku-ring-gai Chase National Park, north of
Sydney, NSW

Plate 7.4   A large engraving of an emu, Elvina   148
Aboriginal Engraving Site, Ku-ring-gai
Chase National Park, north of Sydney,
NSW

Plate 7.5   Bunjil's Cave, in the Black Range east of 148
the Grampians National Park, Victoria

Plate 7.6   Protective fencing to prevent visitor damage 149
at Red Hands Cave (Manja Shelter) in the
western section of the Grampians National
Park, Victoria

Plate 7.7	Basin Aboriginal Engraving Site, Ku-ring-gai Chase National Park, north of Sydney, NSW	149
Plate 7.8	(A) Rock engraving of male and female human figures, Basin Site, Ku-ring-gai Chase National Park, NSW; (B) reproduction of these figures outside the Kalkari Visitors' Centre, Ku-ring-gai Chase National Park, NSW	149–50
Plate 8.1	Annexe to the Nunnery, a late-Classical Mayan building at Chichén Itzá in Yucatán, Mexico	164
Plate 8.2	Marktplatz, Goslar World Heritage town, Germany	164
Plate 8.3	Stonehenge, England	164
Plate 8.4	Château de Chambord, Loire Valley, France	166
Plate 9.1	Post office, Bendigo, Victoria	186
Plate 9.2	Aboriginal paintings at Ubirr (Obiri Rock), Kakadu National Park, Northern Territory	195
Plate 9.3	Barramundie Gorge, in the southern section of Kakadu National Park, Northern Territory	195
Plate 9.4	Kata Tjuṯa (The Olgas), Uluṟu–Kata Tjuṯa National Park, Northern Territory	196
Plate 9.5	Banks of the Gordon River, in the Franklin–Gordon Wild Rivers National Park, south-western Tasmania	196
Plate 10.1	Unique cave formations, Jenolan Caves, NSW	218
Plate 10.2	Captain Cook's Landing Place, Kurnell, Sydney, NSW	219
Plate 10.3	King's Canyon, Watarrka National Park, Northern Territory	223
Plate 10.4	Wilpena Pound, Flinders Ranges National Park, South Australia	225
Plate 10.5	Sign outside the Old Melbourne Gaol, Melbourne, Victoria	227
Plate 10.6	Distant view from Mount Hotham, Victoria	228
Plate 10.7	The Bungle Bungles, Purnululu National Park, Western Australia	231
Plate 10.8	National Trust of Australia (NSW) head-quarters, Observatory Hill, Sydney, NSW	234

Plate 10.9	Rippon Lea, Elsternwick, Melbourne, Victoria	234
Plate 10.10	Interior of the Castlemaine Market Hall, Castlemaine, Victoria	234
Plate 10.11	Historic Engineering Marker, Jenolan Caves, NSW	236
Plate 11.1	Gordes, Vaucluse Département, Provence, France	240
Plate 11.2	Arcaded footpaths, cobbled roadway and city gate, Bern, Switzerland	240
Plate 11.3	Half-timbered buildings, Chester, England	242
Plate 11.4	Conwy Castle, Conwy, North Wales	243
Plate 11.5	Excavated remains of granaries at House-steads Roman Fort, the best-preserved site on the Hadrian's Wall World Heritage property, Northumberland, England	247
Plate 11.6	Valley on the western side of the main valley of Glen Coe, Scotland	249
Plate 11.7	Formal garden and garden front of Waddesdon Manor, Buckinghamshire, England	255
Plate 11.8	Drum Castle, Aberdeenshire, Scotland	255
Plate 11.9	Ruins of Roman town of Glanum, near St-Rémy-de-Provence, Bouches-du-Rhône, France	257
Plate 11.10	St-Etienne-du-Mont, place Ste-Geneviève, Paris, France	257
Plate 11.11	View north from Col de Guéry in the Monts Dore, Puy de Dôme Département, France	259
Plate 11.12	Pont du Gard, Gard Département, Languedoc-Roussillon, France	266
Plate 11.13	Mont-St-Michel, Normandy, France	266
Plate 11.14	Chiesa di Santa Croce, Florence, Italy	268
Plate 11.15	The Colosseum, Rome, Italy	270
Plate 11.16	Street in Pompeii, Campania, Italy	272
Plate 11.17	Siena, Tuscany, Italy	272
Plate 11.18	Monasterio de la Oliva, Navarra, Spain	279
Plate 11.19	Palacio de la Alfajería, Zaragoza, Aragon, Spain	280
Plate 11.20	House in the Parc Güell development (1910–14) designed by Antoni Gaudí, Barcelona, Spain	282

Plate 11.21	Castletown House, Celbridge, Co. Kildare, Ireland	291
Plate 11.22	Drombeg Stone Circle, Co. Cork, Ireland	292
Plate 11.23	Limestone pavement, The Burren National Park, Co. Clare, Ireland	293
Plate 12.1	Old Parliament House (1876), Wellington, New Zealand	298
Plate 12.2	First Presbyterian Church (1868–73), Dunedin, Otago, New Zealand	298
Plate 12.3	Hochstetter Icefall, on the east face of Mount Tasman, Mount Cook National Park, South Canterbury, New Zealand	300
Plate 12.4	Franz Josef Glacier, Westland National Park, Westland, New Zealand	301
Plate 12.5	Harpers Ferry National Historic Park, West Virginia, USA	306
Plate 12.6	The Alamo, San Antonio, Texas, USA	307
Plate 12.7	Mount McKinley, Denali National Park, Alaska, USA	311
Plate 12.8	Reconstructed interior of a miner's hut, Columbia State Historic Park, California, USA	314
Plate 12.9	Corner of 2nd and K Streets in Old Sacramento, California, USA	314
Plate 12.10	Independence Hall, Philadelphia, Pennsylvania, USA	315
Plate 12.11	Grand Canyon, Grand Canyon National Park, Colorado, USA	316
Plate 12.12	Fynbos vegetation below Table Mountain, Cape Town, South Africa	327
Plate 12.13	Wat Phra Keo, adjacent to the Royal Palace, Bangkok, Thailand: (A) Temple or Chapel Royal (*bot*) of the Emerald Buddha; (B) mural panel	330
Plate 12.14	Head of Buddha surrounded by roots of tropical trees, Ayutthaya, Thailand	331
Plate 12.15	Wat Phra Si Sanphet, Ayutthaya Historical Park World Heritage property, Thailand	334
Plate 12.16	Grounds of Ling Yin (Soul's Retreat) Buddhist temple complex, Hangzhou, Zhejiang Province, China	337

Plate 12.17   The Bund, Shanghai, China, with mainly 1920s and 1930s commercial and government buildings   337

Plate 12.18   The central lake of the Garden of the Humble Administrator, Suzhou, Jiangsu Province, China   341

Plate 12.19   The Summer Palace, Beijing, China   341

Plate 12.20   The Gate of Supreme Harmony at the Forbidden City or Palace Museum, Beijing, China   341

Plate 13.1   Memphis and its Necropolis with the Pyramid Fields, Egypt   351

Plate 13.2   Street scene in Orcival, Puy de Dôme Département, France   351

Plate 13.3   Claude Monet's house and garden, Giverny, Eure, France   354

Plate 13.4   Porte Narbonnaise and medieval city ramparts, Carcassonne, Aude, France   355

Plate 13.5   17th-century Moulin de Cierzac, Cierzac, Charente, France   356

Plate 13.6   Relocated general store, Beamish, the North of England Open Air Museum, north of Durham, England   357

Figure 1.1	Major environmental philosophies	18
Figure 1.2	The three major dimensions or criteria used in heritage evaluation	21
Figure 5.1	Distribution of major vegetation types in NSW prior to European settlement	89
Figure 5.2	Distribution of national parks and other major reserves, NSW, 2000	91
Figure 5.3	Size and shape considerations in planning natural reserves	93
Figure 5.4	Criteria used to define wilderness areas in a recent study covering eastern Victoria	95
Figure 5.5	Conservation practice implied in the *Australian Natural Heritage Charter*	108
Figure 6.1	Wallsend Civic Precinct, Newcastle, NSW	124
Figure 6.2	The basic elements and the sequence of steps in a conservation plan	133
Figure 8.1	Numbers of State Parties to the World Heritage Convention and number of State Parties with World Heritage properties inscribed, 1975–2000	155
Figure 8.2	Number of World Heritage properties inscribed each year from 1978 to 2000, showing number of cultural, natural, and 'mixed' inscriptions	162
Figure 8.3	World map of World Heritage property distribution by nation	171
Figure 9.1	Organisational diagram of the relevant sections of Environment Australia	186
Figure 9.2	Map showing Australian World Heritage properties, Ramsar Wetlands of International Importance, and Biosphere Reserves	194
Figure 9.3	Two alternative proposals for the Gordon-below-Franklin hydroelectricity scheme and the ultimate Franklin–Gordon Wild Rivers National Park	198
Figure 9.4	Zoning in Kakadu National Park	200

Figure 11.1	United Kingdom national parks and World Heritage properties	248
Figure 11.2	French national parks and World Heritage properties	260
Figure 11.3	Italian national parks and World Heritage properties	271
Figure 11.4	Spanish national parks and World Heritage properties	281
Figure 11.5	Irish national parks and World Heritage properties	292
Figure 12.1	New Zealand national parks and World Heritage properties	302
Figure 12.2	United States national parks and World Heritage properties in the forty-eight contiguous states	312
Figure 12.3	South African national parks and World Heritage properties	326
Figure 12.4	Thai national parks and World Heritage properties	333
Figure 12.5	Chinese Biosphere Protection Zones, Nature Reserves, and World Heritage properties	339

TABLES

Table 3.1	Short-term overseas visitor arrivals in Australia for the 1990s and forecasts to 2008	60
Table 3.2	Conflict between conservation and recreation and tourism	63
Table 3.3	'Hard' and 'soft' tourism development strategies	64
Table 5.1	Multiple use zoning in the Solitary Islands Marine Park, NSW	104
Table 6.1	List of styles in Australian architecture	119
Table 6.2	Re-use of old buildings: some Australian examples	136
Table 8.1	Status of World Heritage State Parties and type and number of sites as at March 2001	155
Table 8.2	List of the World Heritage in Danger, March 2001	173
Table 9.1	Australian World Heritage properties	191
Table 11.1	United Kingdom World Heritage properties	251
Table 11.2	French World Heritage properties	261
Table 11.3	Italian World Heritage properties	273
Table 11.4	Spanish World Heritage properties	283
Table 11.5	Republic of Ireland World Heritage properties	293
Table 12.1	New Zealand World Heritage properties	303
Table 12.2	United States World Heritage properties	317
Table 12.3	South African World Heritage properties	329
Table 12.4	Thailand's World Heritage properties	335
Table 12.5	People's Republic of China World Heritage properties	342

BOXES

Box 1.1	The French village of Oradour-sur-Glane, Haute-Vienne	16
Box 1.2	A call for increased 'ethnic' content in the 'official' state heritage of NSW	17
Box 1.3	Items from a section of the south-west of Victoria listed on the Register of the National Estate, 1980	19
Box 1.4	Criteria for the Register of the National Estate (Australia)	21
Box 1.5	Samples of National Trust of Australia (NSW) statements of significance for sites in Newcastle, NSW	22
Box 2.1	Results from a visitors' survey at Jenolan Caves, NSW	40
Box 3.1	The Rocks, Sydney	50
Box 3.2	'Redleaf', Wahroonga, Sydney	51
Box 3.3	Placing values on heritage—major approaches to valuing non-economic factors	54
Box 3.4	The Code of Environmental Practice of the Australian Tourism Industry Association	61
Box 5.1	Wollemi pine	84
Box 5.2	Federal–state politics and land clearing in Queensland	92
Box 5.3	The 1994 IUCN objectives for management of wilderness areas	95
Box 5.4	Criteria for judging effectiveness of alternatives in 'Draft Yosemite Valley Plan'	106
Box 5.5	Code of Practice of the Ecotourism Association of Australia	110
Box 6.1	Proposals for more detailed criteria and state themes for the NSW State Heritage Inventory Program	115
Box 6.2	Guide to assessing buildings	120
Box 7.1	Ku-ring-gai National Park rock engravings	150
Box 7.2	Key indigenous tourism principles and sensitive issues	152

Box 8.1	'Summary of Provisions' of the World Heritage Convention	162
Box 8.2	Greater Blue Mountains World Heritage nomination	167
Box 9.1	Process for listing places on the Register of the National Estate	189
Box 9.2	Key features of Plan of Management, Kakadu National Park, 1991	201
Box 9.3	Summaries of the recommendations of the UNESCO Mission to Kakadu National Park and the Australian Government's response	202
Box 9.4	Purpose and Principles of the National Heritage Strategy, April 1999	207
Box 10.1	The ten stages of a local heritage study	215
Box 10.2	Forms of reserves in South Australia, Tasmania, and Western Australia	221
Box 10.3	Grampians National Park—background and park management	228
Box 10.4	The National Trust and the redevelopment of the Sydney Conservatorium of Music	232
Box 10.5	Royal Australian Institute of Architects (NSW) Heritage Committee nominations—October 2000	236
Box 11.1	Courtauld House, London	243
Box 11.2	The Royal Commission on the Ancient and Historical Monuments of Scotland	244
Box 11.3	Yorkshire Dales National Park Authority and its planning documents	246
Box 11.4	Management of the Hadrian's Wall World Heritage property	247
Box 11.5	Le Parc naturel régional de Camargue	259
Box 11.6	Italian protected natural heritage areas	269
Box 12.1	Westland/Tai Poutini National Park—Draft Management Plan	299
Box 12.2	United States National Parks Service—System Units	304
Box 12.3	Some examples of US National Monuments, National Historic Sites, and National Historic Parks	307
Box 12.4	United States National Trust for Historic Preservation Main Street Program	310

Box 12.5   Yellowstone National Park—World Heritage in Danger   320

Box 12.6   Definition of the South African National Estate   322

Box 12.7   Private wildlife parks in South Africa   328

Box 12.8   Thailand's National Marine Parks   332

Box 12.9   Historic buildings of Shanghai   336

Box 12.10   History of protection of the classical Suzhou gardens   338

ACKNOWLEDGMENTS

My enthusiasm for heritage issues was given a huge boost by my involvement over many years with the National Trust of Australia (New South Wales), and I warmly acknowledge the opportunities the Trust gave me in the early to mid-1990s. It is an association I wish to renew once retirement gives me the time and energy required. As a direct result of my experience with the Trust, I introduced a third-year unit in the Department of Human Geography at Macquarie University, 'Heritage and Conservation'. This book, in part, results from teaching that unit, but it is much more than a tertiary text, and is aimed at all people interested in heritage, as well as those whose enthusiasm is yet to be kindled.

Preparing the manuscript for this book has involved an enormous amount of research, even if this has been of a type unfamiliar to bureaucrats in Canberra and some people at Macquarie. It has involved gathering a vast amount of information from a wide range of sources, and I thank all those authors and webmasters whose work has inspired me and has made my research on heritage so much easier and more fulfilling. It has also required considerable, and extremely enjoyable, fieldwork in many nations, and I certainly appreciate the chances Macquarie University has provided for the time and travel involved. My wife, Carolyn, has supported me throughout this project and her company made the fieldwork so much more enjoyable. Thank you Carolyn.

Above all, I wish to heartily thank all the students I have interacted with in teaching my heritage unit at Macquarie over a number of years. Their reaction has been very positive and generally enthusiastic and they have fed many ideas and much information to me. Their contributions cannot be acknowledged individually, and in many cases are not even consciously known to me, as they are part of the dialectic of enjoyable teaching and mutual-learning experiences. I also wish to thank those of my colleagues in the Department of Human Geography who have supported and encouraged me in both teaching and writing on heritage matters. Special thanks are due to Bob Fagan, a particularly tolerant head of department.

The enthusiasm of those around me is reflected in the long list of those who have so kindly allowed me to use their photographs: my relatives—Richard Aplin, Stephanie Aplin, and Don Johnston; former students—Jane Chandler, Helen Dimas, Monica Green, and Robert Wells; colleagues—Peter Curson, Margaret Dudgeon, Kevin McCracken, and Carolynne Paine; and Katie Barnett and Diane Callender. The maps and diagrams were all very professionally drawn by Judy Davis, who also cheerfully, and often at short notice, helped with digital photos and preparing material to send to the publishers. Finally, this book would not have appeared at all without the marvellous assistance from three wonderful women at Oxford University Press. Jill Henry has always encouraged me to see the project through, despite my feeling from time to time that it was just too daunting a task. Katie Barnett is a firm, but also flexible and understanding, editor. She has been incredibly thorough in her approach and has vastly improved the final work: while the content is chiefly mine, there is a little of Katie there, too. The book has been very professionally designed by Racheal Stines, who worked closely with Katie throughout in a commendable show of teamwork.

Despite all of the assistance from others, there will still be errors and shortcomings in this book. Those remain my responsibility alone.

ABBREVIATIONS

ACT	Australian Capital Territory
AHC	Australian Heritage Commission
AHCA	*Australian Heritage Commission Act 1975* (Cth)
AH Council	Australian Heritage Council
ANCA	Australian Nature Conservation Agency
ANHC	Australian Natural Heritage Charter
An Taisce	An Taisce—The National Trust for Ireland
BA	Building Application (NSW)
Cal-Parks	California State Parks (USA)
CHB	Cultural Heritage Branch (TPWS) (Tas)
CHL	Commonwealth Heritage List (Australia)
CITES	Convention on International Trade in Endangered Species
CNC	Cape Nature Conservation (South Africa)
CNMHS	*Caisse Nationale des Monuments Historiques et des Sites* (National Fund for Historic Monuments and Sites—France)
CNP	Council for National Parks (UK)
COHP	California Office of Historic Preservation (USA)
CPP	Community Partners Program (NTHP, USA)
DA	Development Application (NSW)
DEA&T	Department of Environmental Affairs and Tourism (South Africa)
DEPA	Department of the Environment Protection Agency (Qld)
DLA	Designated Landscape Area (Qld)
DNRE	Department of Natural Resources and Environment (Vic)
DOC	Department of Conservation (NZ)
DoE	Department of the Environment (UK)
DUAP	Department of Urban Affairs and Planning (NSW)
Dúchas	Dúchas—The Heritage Service (Ireland)
EC	European Community
EPAA	*Environmental Planning and Assessment Act 1979* (NSW)
EPBCA	*Environment Protection and Biodiversity Conservation Act 1999* (Cth)
ERISS	Environmental Research Institute of the Supervising Scientist
EU	European Union
FEC	*Fondo Edifici di Culto* (Religious Properties Fund—Italy)
GIS	Geographic Information Systems
HBC	Historic Buildings Council (Vic)
HEC	Hydro-Electric Commission (Tas)
ICCROM	International Centre for the Study of the Preservation and Restoration of Cultural Property
ICO	Interim Conservation Order (NSW)
ICOMOS	International Council on Monuments and Sites
IUCN	International Union for the Conservation of Nature and Natural Resources

KRSIS	Kakadu Regional Social Impact Study (NT)
KZNNCS	KwaZulu-Natal Nature Conservation Services (or *Ezemvelo KZN Wildlife*) (South Africa)
LCA	Landscape Conservation Area (NSW)
LEP	Local Environmental Plan (NSW)
LGPEA	*Local Government (Planning and Environment) Act 1990* (Qld)
LWHD	List of World Heritage in Danger
MAB	Man and the Biosphere Programme
NFP	National Forest Park (China)
NGO	non-government organisation
NHL	National Heritage List (Australia)
NHRA	*National Heritage Resources Act 1999* (South Africa)
NHT	Natural Heritage Trust (Australia)
NLC	Northern Land Council (NT)
NPCA	National Parks Conservation Association (USA)
NPS	National Park Service (USA)
NPWS	National Parks and Wildlife Service (NSW)
NRHP	National Register of Historic Places (USA)
NSCAB	National Strategy for the Conservation of Australia's Biodiversity
NSW	New South Wales
NT	Northern Territory
NTHP	National Trust for Historical Preservation (USA)
NTS	National Trust for Scotland (UK)
NZ	New Zealand
NZHPT	New Zealand Historic Places Trust
OPW	Office of Public Works (Ireland)
PA	Parks Australia
PCO	Permanent Conservation Order (NSW)
QLD	Queensland
RAIA	Royal Australian Institute of Architects
RCAHMS	Royal Commission on the Ancient and Historical Monuments of Scotland
RCAHMW	Royal Commission on the Ancient and Historical Monuments of Wales
RCHME	Royal Commission on the Historical Monuments of England
RMA	*Resource Management Act 1991* (NZ)
RNE	Register of the National Estate (Australia)
SA	South Australia
SAHRA	South African Heritage Resources Agency
SANP or SANPARKS	South African National Parks
SCN	*Servizio Conservazione della Natura* (Nature Conservation Service—Italy)
SCRA	Sydney Cove Redevelopment Authority (NSW)

SEPP	State Environmental Planning Policy (NSW)
SHR	State Heritage Register (NSW)
SMR	Sites and Monuments Record (England and Wales)
SNH	Scottish Natural Heritage (UK)
Tas	Tasmania
TFAD	Thai Fine Arts Department (Thailand)
TPWS	Tasmanian Parks and Wildlife Service
UCA	Urban Conservation Area (NSW)
UCBAAAS	*Ufficio Centrale per i Beni Architettonici, Archeologici, Atristici e Storici* (Central Office of Architectural, Archaeological, Artistic and Historical Properties—Italy)
UCBAP	*Ufficio Centrale per i Beni Ambientali e Paesaggistici* (Central Office of Environmental and Landscape Properties—Italy)
UNCED	United Nations Conference on the Environment and Development
UNEP	United Nations Environment Programme
UNESCO	United Nations Educational, Scientific and Cultural Organization
US(A)	United States (of America)
VHR	Victorian Heritage Register
Vic	Victoria
WA	Western Australia
WHB	World Heritage Bureau
WHC	World Heritage Convention
WHCom	World Heritage Committee
WHF	World Heritage Fund
WHL	World Heritage List
YDNP	Yorkshire Dales National Park (UK)
ZICO	*Zone Important pour la Conservation des Oiseaux* (France)

Heritage and Its Components

We are all products of our personal and collective pasts, including those of our forebears and of local, ethnic, religious, and other groups to which we belong. We are also products of our present physical, social, and cultural environments. Not surprisingly, we each identify and value *our heritage* according to our backgrounds and experiences. Our heritage is made up of existing 'things' that often, but not always, have historical associations, for example, important buildings, landscapes, plant and animal species, and less tangible cultural features. Furthermore, we value the components that make up our heritage for a wide range of reasons, and at many different scales, from personal through to local, regional, national, and global. The one common element is that we identify items in our heritage as worth preserving and sharing with present and future generations. At the most intimate level, heritage is an intensely personal concept. But it also helps define the various groups of which we are part, including nations and, ultimately, humanity. Not surprisingly, then, heritage can also be intensely political as well as intensely personal.

Heritage is frequently, but generally artificially, divided into *natural* and *cultural* components. In Australia, and in some other nations, a third sub-division is often added, one that is even more artificial: *indigenous* heritage. There are historical and contemporary reasons for this separate treatment, some of which will be explored in Section 1.6, Chapter 7, and Section 9.2. More commonly indigenous heritage is integrated as part of cultural heritage, which is in my view a much healthier and realistic approach. Cultural and natural heritage are also more commonly and more successfully integrated in heritage management systems in many other nations than they are in Australia (see Section 1.6, Chapters 9 to 12). However, despite personal misgivings relating to the artificiality of such divisions, for pragmatic reasons there are separate chapters on natural, non-indigenous cultural, and indigenous cultural heritage. This book attempts to embrace all aspects of what might be called *immoveable* heritage—landscapes, places, sites, buildings—regardless of whether they are natural, cultural, or specifically indigenous. Most often they will be a mix of two or more of these types.

Moveable and *non-material* heritage are not dealt with except in passing, and in as much as they are frequently associated with immoveable heritage items. Examples of moveable heritage include works of art, furniture, books,

1

and many smaller artefacts. While such things are often preserved in historic buildings or on-site museums, they are also kept in off-site museums, libraries, and other collections. The preservation of objects in the former case falls within the scope of this book, but the preservation of the latter does not. Furthermore, forms of non-material heritage such as music, dance, food, and folklore are only treated in as much as they are related to, or give meaning to, immoveable heritage items. Moveable and non-material heritage are, nonetheless, vitally important parts of our heritage.

Main aims and themes of the book

This book has a number of aims, briefly introduced by the following seven themes. While each of these themes may not be specifically and transparently addressed in every section of the book, the themes are reflected upon throughout and it is worth bearing them in mind as you read each chapter.

1   *To understand the multiple and contested meanings of heritage and the implications for the conservation and management of heritage.*

A recurrent theme of heritage management, already introduced here, is that we all have different perceptions and definitions of heritage, which are keenly contested. Hence, priorities in heritage management and funding to preserve heritage items are exceedingly controversial and political matters. Each of us sees different things as being important and worth preserving, and groups and individuals each contest their definitions of heritage, setting different priorities. In particular, minority groups often contest the set of priorities put forward by the dominant group. As heritage is both personal and political, and often intimately involved in the self-image of an individual or a group, debate can become heated.

2   *To stress the crucial importance of scale considerations in any definition of heritage.*

Scale is absolutely critical in any attempt to define heritage or to identify specific heritage items. What is important locally may or may not be important nationally or internationally. Hence there is an implied hierarchy of heritage 'lists'. In most cases, of course, something as important as global heritage will also be seen as important on the national and local scales, although not always. The scale at which heritage sites are considered of importance affects the way protection and presentation are administered, financed, and carried out.

3   *To analyse the contribution of heritage issues to our understanding of the human–environment relationship, of the inter-relatedness of various aspects of the broadly defined environment, and of our social and cultural history.*

Studying how groups perceive heritage, including both cultural and natural heritage, illuminates many aspects of attitudes towards history, present social conditions, and the environment. If, for example, we consider indigenous peoples' heritage, then increased understanding may lead to an appreciation of a more benign approach to human-environment interactions than those common in 'western' societies. Heritage often provides material evidence of the history of ourselves and others, complete with both the triumphs and the disasters. Understanding other cultures and peoples is often the first step towards genuine acceptance and true tolerance. A broad inclusiveness in our definition of national heritage is likely to lead to more tolerance of other groups in society, rather than domination and imposition of particular views. The destruction of Buddhist statues by the Afghani Taliban in early 2001 reflects an intolerance of massive proportions. On the other hand, many other nations are willing to incorporate in their heritage aspects of history that are certainly not pleasant memories. In some cases, these aspects are greatly at odds with the modern political and cultural context.

4 *To understand current debates in the heritage professions about the relationship between heritage managers and other stakeholders, especially 'the community'.*

In this context, *stakeholders* are all people with an interest in heritage generally, or in a specific heritage property. In the latter case they might include owners, occupiers, neighbours, various users, the local council, and many interest groups. Reconciling these interests, which often conflict, is one of the most difficult tasks to confront heritage managers, as well as legislators and bureaucrats when they are framing policy. There are also more specific debates among heritage professionals, such as debates about conservation as opposed to preservation, the related questions of originality and authenticity, and adaptive re-use, among others.

5 *To understand the range of possible statutory frameworks in which heritage and conservation are managed.*

As a result of the complexity of the situation, there does need to be a considerable body of *legislation* and *regulation* relating to heritage issues, as well as a *bureaucratic structure*, often spanning several levels of government, to administer heritage matters. This book, especially in its second half, introduces examples of these frameworks from a number of nations and at scales ranging from local councils to the World Heritage Committee (WHCom).

6 *To introduce the economics of heritage, its marketing and its presentation to visitors where appropriate.*

Economic considerations need to be taken into account in any heritage proposal or management plan. Someone has to pay to preserve heritage. In some cases, this may be a reasonable cost for the taxpayers of a nation, through their government, to bear. In others, heritage items may need to be self-financing in some way, or to be used for private or corporate ends, such as a home or office. In that case, should there be a public contribution to maintenance, or is it wholly the responsibility of the private owner? If a heritage site is to generate income, what uses and revenue-raising techniques are acceptable? And do all citizens have a right to have access to certain heritage sites, regardless of their ability to pay? If other benefits, such as the development of a site, are foregone, who should bear that cost?

7   *To showcase heritage investigation, assessment, conservation, and management techniques in a variety of settings, with an emphasis on the human dimension of heritage management, and on a small number of sets of guidelines.*

Heritage items do not look after themselves. They need to be *managed* by someone, whether it be a private owner, a commercial operator, a non-government organisation, or a government instrumentality. Before they can be properly managed, however, they must be investigated, assessed, and documented. A *management plan* is essential, and there are some sets of guidelines to help accomplish successful management. And, crucially, if a site is open to visitors, *visitor management* becomes as important as site management.

Why conserve heritage?

If conserving heritage is likely to be both expensive and difficult, why should we do it? There are many reasons. Natural heritage areas, for example, can provide a wide range of environmental services and help preserve the world's biodiversity. Cultural heritage can preserve aspects of our culture and history and add to our sense of belonging and group identity. All forms of heritage can help define and maintain a sense of identity at local, regional, national, and global scales. In fact, heritage items are part of the context that makes us human.

We need more than just material goods if we want to do better than merely survive in physical terms. Each one of us exists in a complex web of meanings, some of which are derived from our heritage. Heritage can thus play a major role in maintaining and defining the context in which we live, assisting us to locate ourselves in the world and in society, past and present. Without such a context, our personal lives are diminished, and so, too, is national life. Along with the spiritual side of life, however understood, heritage gives life meaning and raises us above animal survival level. These two factors also, very importantly, add a dimension other than the purely economic and materialistic to individual and group existence.

While we all recognise pieces of heritage that we would like to see preserved, some people are much more materialistic and development-oriented than others. This does not mean, however, that they are necessarily more future-oriented; in many cases, such people are mainly living for the present day, and are not overly concerned for either the past or the future. On the other hand, while people who are most concerned with preserving heritage may be nostalgic, they are also frequently very future-oriented. In fact, they see a continuity between past, present and future, and recognise that preserving key items, ideas, and practices adds meaning to that continuity, and to people's lives within it. Hence those who work for heritage preservation, generally speaking, are not stuck in the past at all, but simply have a particular vision of the future that includes elements from the past and present.

Heritage is also a vital component of that which defines either a social group, or a place or locality. Shared heritage allows us to see ourselves as members of a group or society, not just as an individual in a sea of individuals. It helps impart a sense of a group in the minds of both group members and others; in other words, it helps define both internal self-image and external images held by others. It also contributes in a major way to the *sense of place* studied by geographers, among others. This sense of place is defined by both natural and cultural features and, crucially, by interactions between the two. Similarly, heritage, through the conservation of historic sites and districts, helps provide a *sense of time* to illustrate past stages in history. Both locals and visitors use heritage items, among other things, to build an image or perception of any particular place. Heritage thus helps differentiate group from group, and place from place. Just as we each have a personal definition of heritage, so heritage helps define our personalities, our places of residence, work and play, and the groups to which we belong.

Why study heritage?

The study of heritage is valuable in a number of ways. First, and most generally, it helps increase awareness of heritage values and the ways in which heritage can contribute to a richer life in a more meaningful society. Secondly, it can increase interest in actively taking part in heritage identification, assessment, conservation, and management on a voluntary or paid basis. Thirdly, it may help some pursue careers in heritage management. Finally, anything that is valued by society, or parts of society, is worth studying. Whether individuals admit it or not, heritage is a part of and enriches our lives.

Structure of the book

This book could be structured in many ways. Divisions between topics, and hence between chapters, are often fluid, and could be identified in a multiplicity of ways. There is so much inter-relatedness between topics that many 'chicken-and-egg' decisions had to be made, while some divisions between chapters (especially Chapters 5–7) are purely for convenience. While the structure seems to work well, readers should feel free to read the chapters in whatever order suits them. Frequent cross-referencing between sections and chapters should facilitate such flexibility; these connections are necessary in order to fully appreciate the richness of heritage as a concept and the complexity of heritage conservation and management.

The first chapter further develops the nature and definitions of heritage, partly through introducing a selection of 'official' definitions and sets of criteria, but also by posing questions that challenge readers to think about their own perceptions. Chapters 2 to 4 then introduce some concepts and techniques with common applicability to all types of heritage. Chapter 2 deals with the interpretation and presentation of heritage and the ways in which meaning is conveyed to the public; Chapter 3 with economic considerations, including the relationship between tourism and heritage; and Chapter 4 with some common management issues. Chapters 5 to 7 then further develop these definitions and criteria in relation to the three artificial divisions of natural, cultural, and indigenous heritage. The wide variety of regulatory frameworks employed to define, protect, and manage heritage is introduced in Chapters 8 to 12, covering international treaties and World Heritage (Chapter 8), and the laws, regulations, and bureaucratic frameworks in Australia (Chapters 9 and 10) and in a number of other countries (Chapters 11 and 12). Discussion of the roles of local communities and voluntary or non-government organisations is integrated into these chapters where appropriate. This second half of the book also introduces a large number of examples and practical applications of the themes and concepts from earlier chapters. Finally, the short concluding chapter, using the author's personal experiences, revisits the broad themes and concepts introduced in this introduction and in later chapters.

One final comment is pertinent. The subject matter of this book is exceedingly visual and demands a large number of illustrations. It is hoped that these and their often extensive captions significantly add to the value of the book. Coloured versions and further illustrative examples available on the web site associated with this publication will further enhance its value, so please use that site extensively. Other useful and relevant web sites are also listed at the end of the book, while a limited number of key works for further reading are listed at the end of each chapter.

CHAPTER 1

The Nature of Heritage

1.1 What is 'heritage'?

The aim of this section is to set you thinking about heritage and your perceptions of it, something you may never have done specifically before. To start with, try answering the following questions:

- What is your heritage? What things would you include?
- What would you include in the heritage of each of the various groups to which you belong or have belonged in the past?
- Would other people's heritage be different?

Try to be quite specific and name particular places, buildings, landscapes, and other items, rather than generic types. You were probably quick to name a few key items for your personal heritage list, then found it harder to add further items. What associations did you use? To what extent do you think your list is idiosyncratic? Would you, in fact, find it difficult to explain some items to other people, and to justify their inclusion? When it comes to considering the heritage of groups, think of schools, universities, church or other religious groups, local neighbourhoods, sporting groups, social clubs—you might be surprised at the number of groups with which you have some relationship, not necessarily as a formal member. The heritage of such groups is closely bound to their traditions, and many groups stress the importance of maintaining those traditions in one way or another.

Each individual belongs to a different set of overlapping and interacting groups; each of us has a life and a personality reflecting, and reflected in, our membership of such groups; and each of us assembles the 'pieces' of group associations in a unique way. So it should come as no surprise that we each have our own, idiosyncratic perception of what is important in heritage terms, and what should be preserved for future generations. There are thus no 'correct' answers to any of the questions listed. They almost certainly raise even more questions in your mind.

Here are some more questions:

- Is an ancient cave painting or grave site (Plate 1.1) part of your heritage, even if it is in France or Spain? Is it part of some global human heritage?
- Is a Gothic cathedral (Plate 1.2) part of European heritage? Is it part of your heritage, even if you were born in Australia of European ancestry? What if

Plate 1.1

Dolmen (prehistoric grave site) in vineyards outside village of St-Fort-sur-Né, Charente, France.

Photo: Graeme Aplin

Plate 1.2

Main west front of the Cathédral Notre-Dame, Chartres, Eure-et-Loire, France. Begun in 1020, it was largely destroyed by fire in 1194, although the west front and the south tower (right) survived. Very few alterations occurred after 1250, with the exception of the Flamboyant Gothic north tower (left) added c.1500. Chartres was inscribed on the World Heritage List in 1979.

Photo: Graeme Aplin

you were of non-European ancestry and/or non-Christian? Are some buildings of global heritage importance?

- Is a typical peasant farmer's cottage (Plate 1.3) part of Irish heritage? Even if, as in this case, it has been rebuilt in a historic theme park? Is its importance more obviously local than in the case of the cathedral?
- Is a beautiful landscape, even if largely farmland (Plate 1.4), part of English (or any other) heritage? Is it reasonable to have landscapes that have been so

obviously culturally altered in national parks? Or is there some more appropriate means of protecting them?

- Alternatively, must 'national' parks be 'natural' parks (Plate 1.5)? Must national parks be as 'unspoilt' and as close as possible to a state of wilderness? Are there any true wilderness areas left anywhere in the world?
- Are native flora and fauna part of a nation's heritage (in this case, Australia's) (Plate 1.6)? And are there other reasons for conserving flora and fauna?
- Is the use of the word 'heritage' in Plate 1.7 a legitimate one? Are our food and drink part of our heritage?
- And are such things as art, crafts, dance, and music part of a nation's heritage (Plate 1.8)?

Again, there are no correct answers, but I will make some comments that help to expand on the concept of heritage.

The dolmen or prehistoric grave site in western France (Plate 1.1) has survived for thousands of years while agricultural life has been introduced around it. Large numbers of such sites, many more visually impressive (see Plate 8.3), remain in Europe and elsewhere. How many should be preserved? How do we choose which ones? Other prehistoric sites are perhaps more obviously worth preserving; for example, the Lascaux Caves and others in south-western France, and still others in Spain, contain what is perhaps the earliest human art discovered and reliably dated. The caves are key sources of information about an important stage in the development of the human species. In that sense, we can all claim them to be part of our heritage, and they are, indeed, recognised on the World Heritage List (WHL) (see Chapter 8 and Section 11.3). In fact, what visitors see at Lascaux is a reconstruction of the most important parts of the cave system—an exact and extremely authentic replica, but not the original. The effects of humans so rapidly damaged the precious paintings that visitors had to be barred, but the paintings are so important to human heritage that it was recognised that some viable alternative was needed. Later chapters, particularly Chapters 3 and 4, deal with this difficult conflict between preservation and accessibility, and the related questions of originality and authenticity.

Plate 1.3

The byre (cow shed) dwelling in the Bunratty Folk Park, Co. Clare, Ireland is an example of a building from Co. Mayo occupied by both a farming family and their milking cows. A pigsty is adjacent.

Photo: Graeme Aplin

A Gothic cathedral in France, especially if it is as architecturally and historically significant as Chartres Cathedral (Plate 1.2), is certainly of heritage importance in that country and, by extension, to many people elsewhere who consider themselves part of the Western European cultural tradition and the Christian religious tradition. If you are not part of those traditions, however, you may well not consider the cathedral to be in any way part of your heritage; unless, that is, you agree that it is so significant that it, too, is part of the global heritage. This 13th-century architectural masterpiece, with its remarkable thirty-seven-metre-high nave and world-renowned 12th–13th century stained glass is also a World Heritage Site (see Chapter 8, Section 11.3) because there is something so important about it that it transcends religious barriers, as do the Historic City of Ayutthaya in Thailand (see Section 12.5, Plates 12.14 and 12.15), the Historic Sanctuary of Machu Picchu in Peru, and the Mayan ceremonial site of Chitzén Itzá in Mexico (Plate 8.1). Very different cultural and religious traditions are involved, but all four sites are important enough to be recognised as part of our World Heritage.

The farmer's cottage (Plate 1.3) introduces two different aspects of heritage, the local and the representative (rather than the unique). Such a cottage represents something important in local and maybe even national history and culture. It is not only the grandiose or outstanding that contribute to our heritage; after all, much of most people's lives is mundane, not outstanding. And ordinary people are of major importance in any local, regional, or national cultural evolutionary process, while quite ordinary-looking landscapes, ecosystems, and buildings are crucially important. Heritage professionals have tended until quite recently to concentrate on the 'grand mansion and magnificent scenery' view of heritage, neglecting less spectacular, but more typical, examples. As for relocation, well, it is almost always best to leave heritage items *in situ*, but there are two reasons for taking the 'theme park' approach: to save items, usually buildings, that cannot be retained on their original site and would otherwise be lost completely; and to present a collection of buildings that is more likely to be accessible to, and visited by, the public than a number of isolated examples spread over the countryside. The latter is,

Plate 1.4

The village of Burnsall, Wharfedale, North Yorkshire, is within the Yorkshire Dales National Park, England. The National Park Authority was set up in 1954 and strict planning controls have been in place since then to severely restrict development and intrusion of out-of-keeping 20th-century change.

Photo: Graeme Aplin

Plate 1.5

The Grampians National
Park, sometimes known by
its Aboriginal name of
Gariwerd, is in south-
western Victoria. Much of
its 167 000 hectares is
rugged forested country
accessible only to walkers,
as shown in this view from
The Balconies, with only
the unknown visitor
intruding.

Photo: Graeme Aplin

Plate 1.6

A magnificent crimson
waratah (*Telopea
speciosissima*), growing in
the Muogamarra Nature
Reserve, on the sandstone
country north of Sydney
and just south of the
Hawkesbury River, NSW.

Photo: Graeme Aplin

of course, as much an educational and entertainment reason as a heritage
reason for taking the drastic relocation step, but, then, education about
heritage is of major importance (see Chapter 2).

We admire many landscapes, and the majority of them have been very
obviously altered by human activity. There is virtually nowhere in Europe, in
particular, that is not at least partly a cultural artefact, as well as a natural
landscape. European nations regularly include landscapes replete with farms
and villages in their national parks; Yorkshire Dales National Park (YDNP), for
example, has a resident population of approximately 18 000 and 8.3 million
visitor days were spent there in 1994 (Plate 1.4; see also Section 11.2).
Distinctions between natural and cultural heritage are frequently meaningless
and almost always blurred, but Australians, along with practitioners and the
public in some other 'new world' countries, have the desire to keep national

parks as 'natural' and as free from obvious human impact as possible (Plate 1.5). *National parks* are thus defined in those places in a very conservative manner, with other designations being used for the more clearly culturally determined landscapes of note (see Chapters 9 and 10 for Australian examples). Australia tends to have a similarly strict definition of *wilderness*, in the extreme case insisting that there be no sign of human intervention. This begs the question of the status of Aboriginal Australians and Torres Strait Islanders, who have inhabited and used every part of the continent, and now wonder how they are viewed in relation to their 'country' (see Chapters 5, 7, and 9, which all touch on this debate).

Native flora and fauna (Plate 1.6) are seen as part of national and regional heritage in many parts of the world. Notable plants and animals, often endemic species, are closely identified with particular places and, by association, with particular human communities. Furthermore, as discussed at some length in Section 5.2, there are other reasons for conserving biodiversity and ecosystems. Indeed, the present level of biodiversity with its myriad species of all types can be considered one of the most important of all elements of our global heritage.

There are many aspects of our heritage that are moveable or even non-material, in addition to the sites, buildings, and landscapes on which this book mainly focuses. Many Scots see Scotch whisky as part of their heritage (as do many people elsewhere!). In the case of the Scots, it is probably a legitimate heritage item, identified with their nation, as are various other foods and beverages associated with other nations, regions, and ethnic groups. So, too, are forms of music, dance, art, literature, and crafts. All these things are certainly heritage items, but fall largely outside the scope of this book. Having said that, the use of the word 'heritage' on the building in Plate 1.7 has as much to do with capturing the tourist pound as it does with preserving heritage; but a great deal of heritage is now commodified and marketed to some degree or other (see Chapter 3). One could similarly argue that the pubs of Dublin (Plate 1.8) are about both preserving heritage (Irish folk music and, perhaps, the building), and attracting tourists with the income they bring.

Plate 1.7

Scotch Whisky Heritage Centre, Castle Hill, Edinburgh, Scotland, in the former Castle School building.

Photo: Graeme Aplin

Plate 1.8

Irish band performing in the Oliver St John Gogarty Hotel, located in the rejuvenated Temple Bar area of Dublin, Ireland.

Photo: Graeme Aplin

1.2   Heritage as a concept

Heritage is defined by the *New Shorter Oxford Dictionary* as:

> **1** That which is or may be inherited; *fig.* the portion allotted to a specified person, group, etc. **b.** Property consisting of land etc. that devolved on the heir at law as opp[osed] to the executor. **2** The fact of inheriting; hereditary succession. **3** A gift which constitutes a proper possession… **4** Inherited circumstances or benefits.

None of these definitions is particularly helpful, but 'heritage', in our present context, certainly implies a gift for future generations and benefits for the community. These definitions may, perhaps, reflect a 'western' preoccupation with economic rationalism, and a view that land and material possessions are to be used for generating wealth, either now or in the future, through speculation or investment. The entry, however, continues to consider 'attributive uses and combinations':

> In the senses 'forming part of a national or cultural heritage', as *heritage highway, train,* etc.; 'concerned with the conservation and use of the national or cultural heritage', as *heritage group, industry,* etc. Special combs., as *heritage coast* a section of the UK coastline designated as aesthetically or culturally important and therefore protected from development; *heritage trail* a route linking places of historic interest.

While presenting a number of valid examples of the use of the word 'heritage', this still does not really give a suitable definition. The same dictionary defines *patrimony* in similar vein, this and its variants being the term used in some European countries:

> **1 a** The estate or property belonging by ancient right to an institution etc… **b** Property or estate inherited from one's father or ancestors…an estate inherited from one's father or ancestors; a heritage, an inheritance.

There is at least a hint of something more than the mere bequest and inheritance of property in this definition—ancestors are a broader, more nebulously defined group, and it implies the endowment of a group in society, or of a socially and voluntarily constituted organisation. It is interesting to note that the main French organisation concerned with the conservation and preservation of what we might term *cultural heritage* is the 'Direction du Patrimoine' of the Ministère du Culture (see Section 11.3). In Australia, the notion of a patrimony, in the sense of an estate to be passed down through the generations, was implied federally in the Register of the National Estate (see Section 9.3), while in Australia and elsewhere the National Trusts have promoted such a concept (see Section 10.5 and Chapters 11 and 12).

In fact, the definition of what constitutes heritage is an individual, subjective matter that depends on a person's background, life experiences, and personality, although groups of people, perhaps with a common socio-economic, cultural, or ethnic background, may share many aspects of their perceptions. In similar fashion, the definition of heritage in any particular country depends on local historical, social, and cultural circumstances. Within any one nation, the 'official' or 'accepted' definition is frequently that of the dominant group. In other words, the concept of heritage is appropriated as a further manifestation of the group's dominance in politics and national debate. Ownership of at least part of the officially recognised heritage of a country is important to many groups in order to help manufacture and maintain their group identity. Examples of these groups are indigenous peoples, migrant groups, religious denominations, and local communities. The acceptance by others of the legitimacy of their group's heritage is equally important.

What is included in a nation's heritage? It follows from the discussion in the previous paragraph that this is contested by various groups in a particular nation, and there is thus a large degree of fluidity, with changing fashions as well as an evolving understanding. However, there is likely in any nation to be a set of core features that are commonly accepted as elements of the national heritage. In all nations, both cultural and natural items are included, although natural heritage features often are administered by separate departments. It seems that natural items are often not easily or universally incorporated under the umbrella term 'heritage', which is reserved for cultural items, including both individual artefacts and built environments, as well as, frequently, such non-material things as language, folk song, crafts, and dance. In some nations, usually more recently settled ones, the heritage of indigenous peoples is also seen, and perhaps administered, as a separate category. So, the three categories of *cultural* heritage, *indigenous* heritage, and *natural* heritage are integrated conceptually and administered together to various degrees and in various combinations in different countries, as shown in Chapters 9 to 12. Purely for convenience, and with serious misgivings on the author's part, the three categories are dealt with in separate chapters (Chapters 5 to 7).

Heritage is thus a complex concept that can be defined in many ways. The New South Wales (NSW) Heritage Office (see Section 10.2) defines cultural heritage in two ways. Firstly, it defines cultural heritage through heritage items:

> Heritage items, which include landscapes, buildings, structures, relics, places and other works, are valuable cultural resources that are not renewable and are becoming increasingly scarce.

And, secondly, it defines the concept through the meaning of heritage items to people:

They inspire present and future generations and therefore need careful consideration by owners, managers and the community.[1]

Graeme Davison and Chris McConville note the changing meaning of 'heritage' in Australia when they write:

Only in very recent times, however, and especially since the 1970s, has heritage acquired its present more specialised usage as the name we give to those valuable features of our environment which we seek to conserve from the ravages of development and decay.[2]

Two sets of ideas—heritage as a set of ideals, and heritage as things—merged in the 1960s so that heritage now refers to things that represent ideals. Heritage therefore says a lot about who we think we are, as the things we save from change make certain ideals real and reinforce our identity. This 'we' can operate at a variety of geographical scales or political levels, and sometimes the ideals and identities constructed at different levels are contradictory. Although relating in the first instance to cultural heritage, the statements in this paragraph are also applicable to natural heritage.

1.3   History, heritage, and commodification

Gregory Ashworth makes a clear distinction between history and heritage, while identifying the political nature of both. First, he claims that:

History, that is the occurrences of the past, is widely used to fulfil a number of major modern functions, one of which is shaping socio-cultural place-identities in support of particular state structures.[3]

Secondly, he outlines history's contemporary uses in shaping socio-cultural place-identities: history satisfies our (individual and societal) psychological needs 'so that the comfort of the past may anchor the excitement of the future'.[4] History provides the resources, not only for cultural or heritage tourism, but also as a broader amenity resource base for a wide range of high-order economic activities. According to Ashworth, heritage is a product or commodity reliant on the resource-base of history. He is, of course, referring specifically to historical or cultural heritage. (We return to the concept of commodification of heritage later, particularly in Section 3.6.) Ashworth further identifies *interpretation* as the process that converts historical resources (and, one might add, cultural, biological, landscape, and other resources) into heritage, the commodity (see Chapter 2). However, history is no less reliant on interpretation, than is heritage. History and heritage both have the potential to be appropriated by particular groups and to be commodified. Perhaps the key difference between them is that heritage is a selection of items (but not necessarily material 'things') that represents our individual and group histories. Interpretation often involves making the connection between heritage and history, and this is by no means a one-way relationship. And then there are heritage items, most frequently natural heritage items, that have little or no relationship to history, that represent perhaps our geographies, places, and cultures, rather than our histories. You could argue, then, that we commodify our cultures and our environments, just as we do our histories, most obviously in the context of tourism (see Section 3.7).

1.4   The role and uses of heritage

Heritage is not something that simply exists. It is, as we have seen, culturally constructed and frequently politically motivated. It is also useful to individuals and societies in a number of ways.

Identity and belonging

We gain comfort from being able to relate to the past, not only through the sometimes trivial (or trivialised) concept of nostalgia, but also in deeper and more meaningful ways. We need connections with both place and time to locate our present lives geographically and historically; heritage helps in both the temporal and spatial sense. It also helps us locate ourselves socially, in the sense that it is one of the things that binds communities and nations, giving a sense of group identity to both insiders and outsiders. Australian heritage, for example, is a large part of what makes Australians distinct from other nationalities. It is generally true that the more an individual identifies with that heritage, the more 'Australian' she or he feels. That is why the desire to preserve heritage often increases during periods of rapid change, or when there is some feeling of real or perceived national decline. Wars and natural disasters can bring communities together (Box 1.1), and may well increase identification with a group's shared heritage.

Box 1.1   The French village of Oradour-sur-Glane, Haute-Vienne

Intense French Resistance activity during World War II in the Limousin region led to severe reprisals against local people by the occupying German army. On 10 June 1944, 200 German SS troops entered the village of Oradour-sur-Glane, near Limoges, in the Limousin region of France. The troops closed all exits from the village and ordered the entire population of 650 to assemble in the village square. The men were all either machine-gunned or burned to death in barns, while the women and children were locked in the church, which was set alight for those inside to burn alive. Of the entire population of 650, only about eight managed to escape alive. The ruins of the previous village have been kept intact, left exactly as they were on that day, as a shrine, and a new village has been built adjacent to them. Other vivid reminders of the events of that day include the cemetery, a small museum with a few of the former inhabitants' personal effects, and a sign in German saying 'Do not forget'. As well as being of great local heritage importance, the ruins are a memorial to French resistance against the invading Nazi armies, and, as such, they form an important heritage component of modern French national identity.

Source: adapted from *Eyewitness Travel Guides: France*, Dorling Kindersley, London, revised edition 1996, p. 346.

Political uses

National heritage is sometimes used by a government or dominant group in society as a concept to legitimise the state, to help define it, and to advance individuals' identification with it. Heritage is a political concept in that the state appropriates things and feelings that are perhaps traditionally regarded as personal. Psychological or spiritual ownership, as well as private or material ownership, can be involved. Heritage can also be used to reinforce the standing and power of a hegemonic group, by helping to more closely align the group self-image with the national image. On the other hand, the extent to which the heritage of less powerful, perhaps minority, groups in a nation are accepted or suppressed can greatly affect the extent to which non-dominant groups feel included or excluded (Box 1.2). Heritage is a crucial part of group identity; it can be used politically to either strengthen or weaken a group's sense of identity and the feeling that they have part-ownership of the national heritage.

Box 1.2   A call for increased 'ethnic' content in the 'official' state heritage of NSW

The Ethnic Communities Consultation Program was established by the NSW Heritage Office in 1997. The aims were to:
- develop an awareness within ethnic (mainly migrant) communities of the heritage system in NSW and how it works;
- encourage those communities to identify and celebrate places important to the history of their settlement in the state; and
- assist with the listing of places of particular importance to those communities.

Initial focus was on the Italian and Chinese communities. Project officers were employed to work with the communities and professional historians were commissioned to write histories of their settlement in NSW. Potential heritage items were identified through these processes. The Chinese community nominated important cultural items, such as the Yiu Ming Temple in Alexandria, Chinese Market Gardens at La Perouse, and the Wing Hing Long Store in Tingha, all of which were added to the State Heritage Register in 1999. The Italian community, on the other hand, set up groups in key centres to identify and assess heritage properties. A conservation management plan is being prepared for the settlement of New Italy in northern NSW prior to its nomination to the Register.

One element of the 2000–2005 strategic plan of the Heritage Council and Heritage Office is an aim to 'encourage listing nominations from ethnic and Aboriginal communities and specialist heritage groups'. Furthermore, the relevant Minister, in his Heritage Week Directions Statement for 2000, declared that he would be 'devoting a lot of attention to indigenous and multicultural heritage over the next three years'. More specifically, he said that he was 'setting the recognition, the exploration, the celebration of our multicultural heritage as [a] key priority', and that he wanted 'the State Heritage Register to reflect our exciting cultural diversity'.

Source: adapted from various sections of the Heritage Office of NSW web site: http://www.heritage.nsw.gov.au/about/abus_2_2.htm and http://www.heritage.nsw.gov.au/about/abus_5_7.htm, accessed 1 December 2000.

Economic uses

Heritage is important economically in two major ways. First, if we are to preserve our heritage, there are obvious economic costs involved, while benefits are not always as clearly identifiable in economic terms, often being more subtle, diffuse, and psychological. Secondly, there is now a thriving heritage 'industry', most obviously in terms of heritage tourism. Heritage tourism can sometimes become a growth industry in declining localities, bolstering local economies. It can also, of course, give additional impetus to already thriving economies. Less directly, promoting a heritage ambience can provide a strong regional or community image and hence encourage investment from both internal and external sources. For example, Sydney's built heritage and its physical setting provide a high level of amenity, attractive to overseas companies considering locating in Australia, as well as to potential tourist visitors. Indeed, one of the lasting benefits of the Sydney 2000 Olympic Games will be the worldwide television coverage of those attractions. Chapter 3 includes a discussion of the direct and indirect economic costs and benefits of heritage protection.

1.5   Heritage significance and criteria for identification

There are some unique management issues in heritage, different from those faced by other socially constructed resources. Ashworth notes the distinct role of managers in the heritage process:

> … the necessity for deliberate selection is implicit at each stage of the process. In part, this is performed by the vagaries of time, which have determined what has survived either physically or in human memory, but deliberate choice from such survivals actually determines what is used … [i]t is thus intrinsically a planned system; the question of who plans, for what purposes, remains open, not the necessity for intervention as such.[5]

People may have many different perceptions of any particular environmental or heritage issue, partly based on their philosophies. Figure 1.1 presents an overview of attitudes to the environment generally, but it can also be applied to heritage. It is possible to translate this diagram into heritage terms: the top left corner would represent people prepared to take extreme levels of action to save heritage sites; the bottom left corner would represent less actively involved, but nonetheless keen and committed, heritage conservationists; the top right corner stays as it is, representing people committed, above all else, to development and redevelopment of sites regardless of their heritage values; and the bottom right represents people who insist that heritage has to survive unaided in the market place. If we want to conserve or preserve a heritage item, of whatever sort, we have to justify it over other forms of land use and development. Keeping a heritage item always has a cost—if nothing else, the opportunity cost of other uses foregone.

Figure 1.1

Major environmental philosophies

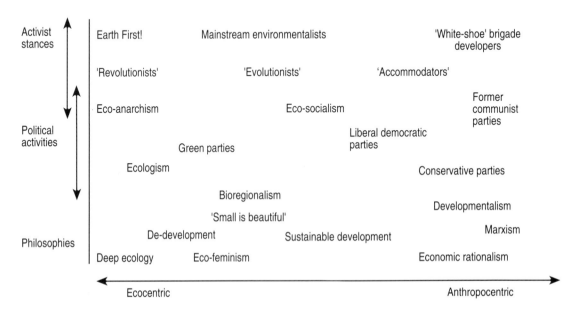

Source: G. Aplin, *Australians and Their Environment: An Introduction to Environmental Studies*, Oxford University Press, Melbourne, 1998, p. 130.

Any statement of justification for retention of a heritage item or site involves an exploration of the concept of *significance* and of the criteria used to establish it. Establishing significance is also a key part of the very practical process of completing a listing proposal, a crucial element in the successful nomination of an item for inclusion on any heritage register (discussed in Chapter 4 and Section 6.3, with specific examples in Box 1.5). First, though, it is worth looking at some examples, drawn from the Australian Register of the National Estate (RNE), to see just how broad a range of items can be included. Box 1.3 presents a briefly annotated list of items on the register for a small portion of south-western Victoria. It illustrates the typical breadth of coverage, including natural, cultural, and indigenous heritage items, listed for a wide variety of reasons. Significance can thus be of many kinds and at many levels. Not surprisingly, perceptions of an item's significance will vary from group to group, and from individual to individual.

Box 1.3   Items from a section of the south-west of Victoria listed on the Register of the National Estate, 1980*

Belfast Shire

'Woodbine' Farmhouse (two-storey house with separate kitchen and stabling, 1845–46, 'an excellent example of Georgian vernacular architecture'); Commercial Hotel, Yambuk (built 1870–71, an important roadside stopping place); Lady Julia Percy Island State Faunal Reserve (important seabird and Australian fur seal breeding area); Armstrong Bay Area (extensive surface and midden deposits in coastal dunes, dated at c.6000 yrs old); The Craigs Area (multiple-layered Aboriginal midden deposits, c.2300 yrs old).

Dundas Shire

'Glenisla' Homestead via Cavendish (a well-preserved 1873 homestead, 'important for its association with the long established Carter family); 'Murndal' Homestead, near Merino (largely dating from 1845–50, with landscaped garden and outbuildings); 'Monivae', near Hamilton (a two-storey Classical bluestone mansion, c.1878); Pastor Hiller's House, Hamilton (former Lutheran Church Manse, 1865–66, single-storey brick); 'Gazette Estate', Penshurst (single-storey stuccoed brick residence, Victorian Italianate/Edwardian, c.1899); Mount Napier Homestead, via Penshurst (Edwardian brick house of 1906 and original 1853 vernacular stone structures); The Grampians (partly in another LGA, comprising all contiguous Reserved Forest and Crown Land in the area, rugged sandstone ranges, important flora and fauna habitats, some endemic and/or endangered species [see Plates 1.5, 5.4, and 7.6, and Box 10.3]); Camp of the Emu's Foot, Cave of Fishes, Glenisla Area, and Cave of Hands (Grampians, rock shelters with Aboriginal cave paintings—Figure 7.6); Macarthur Area, Byaduk (pre-contact and post-contact Aboriginal sites, including remnants of stone houses).

Minhamite Shire

Sheep yards and sheep wash, Bessiebelle Station (built of basalt dry-stone walls); The Turkish Bath House, 'Dunmore' Homestead, near Hawkesdale ('an idiosyncratic monument to [a] prominent pastoralist'); Mount Eccles National Park (rugged volcanic area, scoria cone with crater filled by Lake Surprise, representative vegetation, tiger cat habitat); The Stones State Faunal Reserve, Heywood (volcanic 'stony rise' topography, manna gum woodland, endangered tiger cats); Lake Condah Area (Aboriginal fish traps, stone houses and cairns).

Mount Rouse Shire

'Chatsworth House', near Chatsworth (built 1859–59, 'prototype of the Western District mansion of the 1870s'); 'Devon Park' Homestead, near Dunkeld (two-storey Classical Revival bluestone residence, 1882–83);

'Kolor' Homestead, Penshurst ('one of the most picturesque mansions in far western Victoria, and one of Joseph Reed's most successful residential designs'); Former 'Kolor' Woolshed, Penshurst (basalt and timber, 'remarkable for both general design and detailing'); Mount Rouse Shire Hall, Penshurst (bluestone, built in two harmonious sections, 1865 and 1887); 'The Gums', Penshurst (two-storey Classical stucco-faced mansion designed in 1876 by Joseph Reed, important historical associations with William Ross); Nareeb Nareeb Declared Archaeological Area (sandstone outcrops with axe-grinding grooves); Hopkins River Area (partly in another LGA; earth mounds with Aboriginal artefacts, greenstone quarries).

Port Fairy Borough

Port Fairy Conservation Area (initially an early whaling station, the town has many buildings from the 1840s and 1850s, the following being registered separately: Former Customs House; St John's Church of England; Former Merrijig Inn; ANZ Bank; 'Seacombe House'; 'Emoh'; Court House; Captain John Mill's House; Methodist Church; Caledonian Hotel; 'Seaview'; Office of Port Fairy Gazette; Star of the West Hotel; Mott's Cottage; Post Office); Cottages, 64–68 Campbell St (three representative vernacular cottages in a 'notable and related group'); Powder Magazine (built in 1860, heavily buttressed structure); 'Girteen' (a limestone rubble Georgian cottage, 1855, with Regency interior); St Patrick's Roman Catholic Church ('a notable example of Gothic Revival style', from 1857); 'Talara' (two-storey stone house, c.1855, 'well preserved and has a fine interior'); Former St Andrew's Presbyterian Church (rectangular, gabled church with an austere facade with long and established associations with the early settlement of Port Fairy, particularly in the years prior to 1862); Lighthouse, Griffith Island (erected in 1857–58, characteristic of lighthouse architecture in Victoria in the 1850s).

Note: * Local Government Areas (LGAs) in Victoria have been significantly reorganised since 1980.

Source: *The Heritage of Australia: The Illustrated Register of the National Estate*, Macmillan/Australian Heritage Commission, Melbourne, 1981, pp. 3/89–3/112.

Figure 1.2 shows the three main dimensions or criteria that are important in establishing significance:
- *scale*—something may be important to a local community, to a region, to a state or other administrative unit, to a nation, or globally
- *importance*—how important is it at the appropriate scale, and why (examples are given in the detailed themes proposed for the NSW State Heritage Inventory, referred to in Box 6.1)
- either *uniqueness* or *representativeness*

The last point obviously contains a contradiction, but something can be significant either because it is a unique case (perhaps the last remaining case), or because it is a representative example of a type. Box 1.4 sets out the basic criteria used for the RNE, while a more detailed assessment of the criteria used in different jurisdictions is given in Chapters 8 to 12.

A statement of significance addressing the relevant set of criteria is an essential element of any listing proposal and ultimate justification for a listing on a register; Box 1.5 gives examples of actual statements. We need, above all else, a clear statement as to why each particular item is an important piece of our heritage, and thus why it must be kept. After all, we are often trying to convince hard-nosed developers, politicians, and economists of the need to preserve heritage items, even if short-term economic benefits are foregone as a result.

Figure 1.2

The three major dimensions or criteria used in heritage evaluation

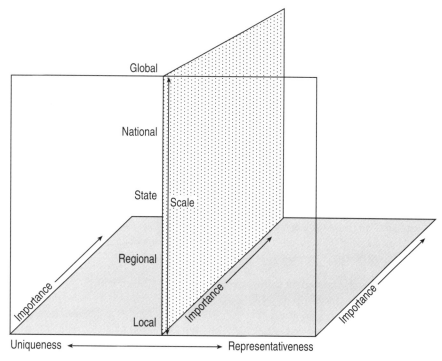

Source: G. Aplin, *Australians and Their Environment: An Introduction to Environmental Studies*, Oxford University Press, Melbourne, 1998, p. 195.

Box 1.4   Criteria for the Register of the National Estate (Australia)

Criteria to be considered in assessing items for inclusion on the Register of the National Estate.
(1a) Without limiting the generality of subsection (1), a place that is a component of the natural or cultural environment of Australia is to be taken to be a place included in the national estate if it has significance or other special value for future generations as well as for the present community because of any of the following:

a   its importance in the course, or pattern, of Australia's natural or cultural history;

b   its possession of uncommon, rare, or endangered aspects of Australia's natural or cultural history;

c   its potential to yield information that will contribute to an understanding of Australia's natural or cultural history;

d   its importance in demonstrating the principle characteristics of:
  i   a class of Australia's natural or cultural places; or
  ii   a class of Australia's natural or cultural environments;

e   its importance in exhibiting particular aesthetic characteristics valued by a community or cultural group;

f   its importance in demonstrating a high degree of creative or technical achievement at a particular period;

g   its strong or special association with a particular community or cultural group for social, cultural or spiritual reasons;

h   its special association with the life or works of a person, or group of persons, of importance in Australia's natural or cultural history.

Source: *Australian Heritage Commission Amendment Act 1990*, Section 4, p. 3.

Box 1.5   Samples of National Trust of Australia (NSW) statements of significance for sites in Newcastle, NSW

Former David & Cohen Warehouse Facade, 48–50 Bolton St, Newcastle.
One of the best examples of a Federation-era warehouse to be found anywhere in Australia. Designed by the distinguished Newcastle architect Menkens and regarded as his finest commercial essay in brick design based on the functionalist tradition. The building affords a spectacular street element of cityscape scale and is a fitting reminder of the once bustling warehouse and shipping office quarter of Newcastle.

Toll Cottage (also known as Rose Cottage), behind 57 Bolton St, Newcastle.
This simple Georgian cottage is a reminder of Newcastle as it was before the development of the latter part of the 19th century. It is likely that it is the last remaining dwelling in the inner area of the city that can be linked with the early days of the settlement. It is a good example of the first buildings in the town.

'Minumbah', 88 Church St, Newcastle.
A well preserved example of a 19th-century Gothic Revival dwelling, restored inside and out and largely unaltered. The house has been wallpapered and furnished with Victorian period pieces. 'Minumbah' is one of the showpieces of the Hill district of Newcastle, a major contributor to the Church St townscape. It is not built out on any side by later development and relates well to the Harbour behind it.

Christ Church Cathedral Cemetery, Church St, Cooks Hill.
This is the earliest burial ground remaining in Newcastle and probably contains the earliest monuments in the Newcastle region, and represents the importance of the church as the diocesan centre after relocation from Morpeth. It includes unusual examples of masons' work, including fine Neo-Gothic and Georgian styles.

David Jones Building (formerly Scotts Ltd), 169–185 Hunter St, Newcastle.
The building is one of the few remaining examples in NSW of an architecturally significant Federation-period department store. It has great importance to the streetscape, having a dominant scale and position on a corner site at the end of Hunter Street Mall. It is interesting evidence of the development of the complex under different architects, while retaining a sympathetic scale and character.

The Bogey Hole (The Commandant's Baths), King Edward Park, Newcastle.
The only surviving man-made structure (except Macquarie Pier) in Newcastle from the days of its earliest settlement as a penal colony. It is therefore probably Newcastle's earliest man-made structure extant. A unique item, being a convict-constructed baths hewn out of a rock face. A link with a famous historical figure from the early period of white settlement in Australia (Major James Morisett).

Civic Railway Workshops Group, Newcastle.
A handsome group of industrial buildings in generally sound condition in the heart of Newcastle City. Although somewhat neglected in recent years, the buildings have important links with Australian railway history. They are a fine example of 19th-century railway yards, and they form an important part of the Newcastle City landscape. [Note: these buildings have since been very well restored and are now used for craft markets, artists' studios, and the like.]

Carrington Hydraulic Power Station Facade, Cowper St, Carrington.
The building is Carrington's most significant architectural landmark. Its exterior is in basic good order—brickwork dirty but in excellent state of preservation. Superb decorative stonework. Building is of unusually high architectural merit considering its original purpose. As well, it is of considerable significance to industrial archaeologists. It is one of the few important remnants of Newcastle's romantic past as a port. The future of this building is a matter of concern because of possible redevelopment of area on which it is sited.

Technical College Annex (formerly part of the Castlemaine Brewery), Wood St, Newcastle.
This imposing building is a fine example of an architecturally designed late-Victorian brewery that lends itself to sensitive rehabilitation for many other functional uses. It is a rare building of its type in Australia, rarer still in Newcastle, and possessing an interesting history connected with the City's growth and commerce. [Note: well restored and sympathetically adapted to its new use.]

Richmond Vale Railway.
Part of the Richmond Vale Railway System is believed to be Australia's oldest operating [note: in 1984] railway. Its Act of Parliament was passed in 1854 and coal haulage began immediately. The first steam loco ran in 1856. The complete Richmond Vale railway from Hexham to Pelaw Main represented one of the most important privately owned railways in Australia. Its construction was a major undertaking by John Brown, pioneer of the coal industry in the Hunter region. ... The line retains many original features and its coal loading and operating techniques are extinct elsewhere in Australia.

'Cartrefle', 79 Howe St, Lambton.
'Cartrefle' is an excellent example of Federation-period architecture with characteristic detailing, and is among the best examples of this style in Newcastle. The intact nature of the interior, detailing and furnishings, and the complementary garden setting, identify this house as an excellent example of the style even in a state-wide context. The prominent corner location treatment provides a significant contribution to the streetscape of the area.

St Luke's Anglican Church, Brown St, Wallsend.
This building is a fine example of a simple Neo-Gothic church, several of which have been demolished in the Wallsend area, leaving no buildings of similar character or constructed of mudstone. The carved stone font and cedar pews, rails, chairs, altar, lectern, etc., enhance the whole.

Revival House (formerly School of Arts), 69 Cowper St, Wallsend.
The building has a finely decorated Italianate facade which is outstanding in the local context. Its historical association with the School of Arts is important evidence of the former widespread nature of that institution. The building makes a significant contribution to a tree-lined streetscape in the historic centre of Wallsend.

Source: Registration cards of the National Trust of Australia (NSW).

1.6 Differences between Australian and European approaches to heritage

If perceptions of heritage differ between ethnic groups, genders, socio-economic classes, and age groups, then one would expect there to be discernible national differences in how heritage is perceived, and in how it is managed and used. A brief, if personal, look at some of these differences will highlight the contested nature of heritage, its intensely political nature, and the complexity implied in the question: 'What is heritage?' The comparison that follows is limited to countries that are either European or are dominated by relatively recent European settlers and their descendants (ex-European colonies). Even greater differences might be expected if other nations were also included. The present intent is to further illustrate many of the points already raised in this chapter and in the Introduction; Chapters 9 to 12 deal with individual nations in much greater detail.

In nations which today have ethnically European ruling groups, national histories and the relative length of European settlement have had a noticeable impact on definitions of, and practical approaches to, heritage. As a result, heritage has a decidedly political dimension. 'New World' heritage perceptions are generally markedly Eurocentric, reflecting the hegemonic positions of the European settlers and the relative lack of recognition of indigenous cultures. In some cases, any references to past historical events that reflect badly on the dominant group are largely absent from heritage inventories—almost completely in the case of Australia, and somewhat less so in the USA. In the latter case, battle sites tend to celebrate European victories, rather than remind the nation of adverse effects on the American Indians, or they relate to intra-European-American battles (see Plate 12.5). In Europe itself, all peoples from prehistoric times to the present seem to be woven into a continuous fabric of cultural heritage. Thus, in France and Spain, for example, prehistoric cave paintings, and ancient grave and ceremonial sites (see Plates 1.1 and 8.3) are seen as part of the cultural heritage in the same sense as later castles and cathedrals. In Australia, on the other hand, prehistoric art sites (see Plates 7.3 to 7.8 and 9.2) are seen as part of indigenous heritage, somehow separate from other aspects of national heritage. Perhaps this is at least partly because Aboriginal culture is still a living culture, noticeably different from the dominant European culture. Aboriginal culture is also seen as something of a threat, whereas the prehistoric peoples of Europe represent a past stage in the development of the present hegemonic populations. Reconciliation between Aboriginal and non-Aboriginal Australians must include consideration of heritage issues and a generally increased recognition and valuing of Aboriginal heritage, but not an appropriation of it by non-Aborigines. (Chapter 7 deals with this issue at length.)

Another aspect of indigenous heritage that is worrying to many Australians is the coupling of it with natural heritage and national parks. In some state jurisdictions, indigenous heritage administratively falls within the ambit of natural heritage organisation, which gives the impression that Aboriginal Australians are part of the natural landscape, or another animal in the ecosystem, rather than part of the cultural environment. There are undoubtedly practical reasons for the coupling; in NSW, for example, most relatively undisturbed and undesecrated Aboriginal sites are in national parks and other comparatively protected areas that are 'unused' by Europeans (see discussion in Sections 9.2 and 10.2). But there are also other reasons, including the desire, at least until very recently, to avoid the recognition of sites on land where it might hinder development or the property rights of European Australians, together with a distinct feeling of cultural superiority on the part of many such people.

Prehistoric monuments in Europe, like Stonehenge in England (see Plate 8.3), Drombeg (see Plate 11.22) or Newgrange in Ireland, or Lascaux, Carnac, and thousands of minor sites (see Plate 1.1) in France, are considered part of a continuous cultural heritage dating from many thousands of years BC to the present. The people who built or painted such monuments are more or less direct forebears of the modern inhabitants of the areas in which they are located, though most likely other groups have since settled or invaded the areas, too, and have interbred. It is certainly true that there is no separate, extant group responsible for those particular heritage items. It is thus easier to absorb prehistoric heritage into the general cultural heritage than it is in

Australia, where there was a sudden influx or invasion by an alien cultural group and hence a clear discontinuity. In addition, because Aboriginal Australians still maintain a vibrant culture, their spiritual and cultural sensitivities need to be taken into account, whereas the prehistoric peoples of Europe are not around to have any say in how their sites are managed, used, and interpreted.

Similarly, European nations are often able to recognise the heritage value and historical significance of unsavoury or painful episodes in their histories and the physical reminders of them. For example, much of the built heritage in the Republic of Ireland represents the English occupation and the unconscionable suffering and oppression it involved (see Section 11.6). On the other hand, while Australia has only quite recently recognised the importance of buildings and sites associated with its convict heritage, it has not, generally speaking, recognised those connected with conflicts between Europeans and Aboriginal Australians. The particular heritage of migrant groups has only recently been recognised as important by the mainstream heritage community (see for example Box 1.2). In somewhat similar vein, minority groups fighting for cultural and political recognition, such as the Basques in both France and Spain, and the Welsh in the United Kingdom, have gradually had their particular heritage recognised as being part of the national heritage. One could argue that all aspects of national history and heritage make important contributions to a sense of national identity that is an honest representation and involves all citizens.

Because of the short non-Aboriginal history of Australia, many Australians feel that there is little non-indigenous cultural heritage worth preserving as nothing is very old by, say, European standards. There is also a clear disjunction between the very ancient cultural heritage of Aboriginal Australians, and the recent cultural heritage of non-Aboriginal Australians, as alluded to above. Furthermore, the widespread philosophy of developmentalism has led to a mania for demolition and major redevelopment, made easier by the perception that little is old enough to worry about preserving.

European nations, on the other hand, have both a greater awareness of the richness of their heritage, and a massive infrastructure of buildings, services, and town plans that would be extremely expensive to replace, and less expensive, though certainly not inexpensive, to adapt and use (see Chapter 11). European cityscapes and rural landscapes have evolved over many centuries. In fact many buildings, such as castles and cathedrals, also evolved, being built, rebuilt, refurbished, restored, adapted to other uses, and otherwise altered over and over again (see Plate 11.10). Some late 20th-century heritage practitioners seem to be saying that change must be stopped wherever possible and the present state frozen for ever to maximise both *authenticity* and *originality* (concepts dealt with again in Section 6.6). This is specially so in Australia where European built environments are so new by comparison with Europe that there is an urge to get things back to a state that is as old or as original as possible. Similarly, there is an urge to remove many cultural features from natural areas to better meet strict definitions of national parks and wilderness areas, as discussed later in this section. For similar reasons re-use of heritage buildings and sites, either for new uses, or involving adaptation, is also more readily accepted, it seems, in Europe than in Australia.

European governments at all levels seem more ready to provide funds for non-government organisations and individuals to restore and maintain heritage buildings and sites than do Australian governments, although there are clear exceptions. Perhaps there is a more obvious return from tourism in Europe. Perhaps there are so many heritage sites and buildings there that it is almost inevitable that many are maintained at least partly at the expense of the community. Or perhaps individuals and organisations care more about their heritage and are more ready to act jointly with government, while, conversely, taxpayers are happier to see government money help restore and maintain private heritage sites. The separation between public and private conservation efforts certainly seems to be less clear in Europe than it is in Australia, but there is also a greater recognition of the need for government involvement.

Europeans also have more experience at managing heritage-based tourism and the pressures it places on heritage sites. But they have not always come up with the best answers and I am not sure how local people react to the hordes that invade their villages and countryside. Tensions certainly do show from time to time.

Where natural heritage is involved, differences between Europe and Australia are perhaps more difficult to see, as history and culture play less of a role. However, definitions of *wilderness* have been problematic in Australia, as they usually imply a lack of human interference with a natural landscape. Aboriginal Australians and Torres Strait Islanders argue that by this definition no part of Australia is wilderness. If the same definition were applied in Europe, there would certainly be no wilderness there. In fact, European national parks, unlike their Australian counterparts, often include extensive human occupation, including farmland and complete villages (see Plate 1.4). The nearest Australian equivalent to this type of area is variously called a *landscape protection zone* or *conservation zone*, in which the amalgam of human and natural features has special significance, including, in many cases, aesthetic significance. Australian national parks may contain limited cultural features, but they are usually historical, rather than currently operative, or are used as tourism-related commercial ventures. The major exception is indigenous cultural features, which brings us back to the dichotomy outlined earlier.

Not surprisingly, when nations are compared, the relative importance of cultural and natural heritage in World Heritage listings reflects much about the history and attitudes of the particular nation (see Chapters 8, 9, 11, and 12). 'New World' nations generally have many more natural areas listed, whereas European nations have very few such areas, and cultural sites dominate. Australia has no areas of European cultural heritage listed, although the Sydney Harbour area including the Opera House (see Plate 6.2) and the Harbour Bridge may soon be nominated as an assemblage analogous with the Seine assemblage in Paris (Plate 1.9). A spatially discontinuous group of convict sites is also being considered for nomination. Australia does, however, have a number of sites for which both cultural (in this context, indigenous) and natural values have been important criteria for World Heritage inscription (see Chapter 8).

Finally, Australian governments have been, and are at the start of 2001, generally more aggressively in favour of progress and development than are many governments elsewhere. Conserving heritage sites does often preclude development and change, with obvious economic consequences. The balance

Plate 1.9

Banks of the River Seine,
Paris, France, with the Ile
de la Cité and the Pont
Neuf ('New Bridge',
actually the oldest in Paris,
finished in 1607). A large
area along the Seine,
including the Louvre (see
Plate 6.10), the Eiffel
Tower, the Cathédral
Notre-Dame and the broad
boulevards designed by
Haussmann are included in
a World Heritage property.
Yet it is also a 'working'
river, as shown by the
barges in the foreground.

Photo: Graeme Aplin

in Australia is more towards change than it is in Europe, though that certainly is not to say that European heritage is safe from attack, or that much has not been lost, or that there are not some weird and awful juxtapositions of the old and the new. Perhaps there is simply so much European heritage that a lot seems to survive.

1.7   Conclusion

Our heritage is an important part of our broader physical and cultural environment, and of our society and community. Management of heritage is thus a key element in both environmental management and political activity. Active management of heritage is essential, too, as it does not simply look after itself. Even if we want to keep something exactly as it is, unchanging and unused, there will be so many external forces impacting on it that management remains crucial. Much of the remainder of this book focuses on this management. While it concentrates almost entirely on *in situ* conservation and management, we should not forget that heritage includes much more than buildings and sites, and that there is an important place for museums, galleries, libraries, archives, and other collections in preserving the moveable and non-material elements of our heritage. Documentation of our heritage is also crucial, but again largely beyond the scope of this book, although touched on in many places, notably in Section 11.2 and in Box 11.2.

Finally, it is worth stressing again that heritage is both contested and culturally constructed, which inevitably makes it a highly political topic and one with a scarcity of clear-cut definitions or answers. Different people, both individually and in groups, define their heritage, and the manner in which it is to be preserved and used, in different ways. This chapter will, it is hoped, have led you to think deeply about your own perceptions of heritage.

J. E. Tunbridge and Gregory Ashworth state that:

> Surviving buildings and objects … are inevitably the heritage of governments and social elites, whereas everyday heritage is discernible only in the predispositions, habits, attitudes and behaviours of the common people.[6]

While there is some political truth in this statement, the distinction drawn is, in fact, largely artificial and rarely clear-cut. Tunbridge and Ashworth also discuss three objections to the heritage process: some people say it cannot be done; more argue that, although it is done, it should not be, for various reasons; and the largest number of people accept what is occurring, but would do it differently. Much of what follows in this book is about how to overcome, or at least be aware of and allow for, the dissonances implied. It is largely about how to 'do heritage'. An inherent assumption is that it can, and should, be done.

Notes

1   Heritage Office and Department of Urban Affairs and Planning, (1996) *NSW Heritage Manual*, HO/DUAP, Sydney, p. 1.

2   Davison, G. & McConville, C. (1991) *A Heritage Handbook*, Allen & Unwin, Sydney, p. 1.

3   Ashworth, G. J. & Larkham, P. J. (1994) *Building a New Heritage: Tourism, Culture and Identity in the New Europe*, Routledge, London, p. 13.

4   Lynch, K. cited in Ashworth, G. J. & Larkham, P. J. (eds) (1994) *Building a New Heritage: Tourism, Culture and Identity in the New Europe*, Routledge, London, p. 14.

5   Ashworth, G. J. & Larkham, P. J. (1994) *Building a New Heritage: Tourism, Culture and Identity in the New Europe*, Routledge, London, p. 18.

6   Tunbridge, J. E. & Ashworth, G. J. (1996) *Dissonant Heritage: The Management of the Past as a Resource in Conflict*, Wiley, Chichester, p. 1.

Further Reading

Ashworth, G. J. & Larkham, P. J. (eds) (1994) *Building a New Heritage: Tourism, Culture and Identity in the New Europe*, Routledge, London, pp. 13–30.

Australian Heritage Commission (1990) *A Sense of Place: A Conversation in Three Cultures*, Australian Government Publishing Service, Canberra.

Australian Heritage Commission (1998) *Protecting Local Heritage Places: A Guide for Communities*, AHC, Canberra.

Davison, G. & McConville, C. (eds) (1991) *A Heritage Handbook*, Allen & Unwin, Sydney.

Furze, B., De Lacy, T. & Birckhead, J. (1996) *Culture, Conservation and Biodiversity: The Social Dimension of Linking Local Development and Conservation through Protected Areas*, Wiley, Chichester.

Garden, G. & Nown, G. (1985) *A Sense of the Past*, Ward Lock, London.

Hall, C. M. & McArthur, S. (eds) (1996) *Heritage Management in Australia and New Zealand: The Human Dimension*, Oxford University Press, Melbourne.

Jacobs, J. (1996) *Edge of Empire: Postcolonialism and the City*, Routledge, London.

Keith, M. & Pile, S. (eds) (1993) *Place and the Politics of Identity*, Routledge, London.

Lowenthal, D. (1998) *The Heritage Crusade and the Spoils of History*, Cambridge University Press, New York.

Massey, D. & Jess, P. (eds) (1995) *A Place in the World: Places, Cultures and Globalization*, Oxford University Press, Oxford.

Pearson, M. & Sullivan, S. (1995) *Looking After Heritage Places: The Basics of Heritage Planning for Managers, Landowners and Administrators*, Melbourne University Press, Melbourne.

Tunbridge, J. E. & Ashworth, G. J. (1996) *Dissonant Heritage: The Management of the Past as a Resource in Conflict*, Wiley, Chichester.

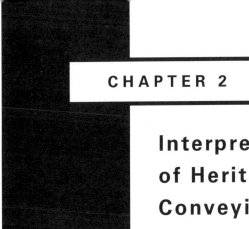

CHAPTER 2

Interpretation and Presentation of Heritage: Attaching and Conveying Meaning

2.1   Heritage as social construct

As we saw in Chapter 1, heritage is far from being a fixed, objectively defined phenomenon. Different people perceive and define heritage very differently, depending on their educational background, previous experiences, beliefs, and philosophy of life. While perception of heritage is ultimately an individual matter, groups defined on socio-economic, ethnic, religious, or other bases frequently share a common group perception of heritage, not surprisingly, since their backgrounds and philosophies are likely to have much in common. There are also commonly accepted local, regional, national, and even global heritage items brought together in lists such as the WHL (see Section 8.3) and Australia's RNE (see Section 9.3). But the items that are included in such commonly accepted lists are still interpreted in individual ways, and have widely varying meanings for different groups and individuals.

2.2   What is interpretation?

Interpretation is taken here to include any form of presentation of factual material and interpreted meaning about a site or other heritage item, whether on site or off site. Brochures, web sites, media coverage, and advertising campaigns all involve interpretation according to this definition. It should be noted that even in the presentation of a small number of 'facts', in whatever form, interpretation is involved, as these 'facts' have been selected by someone, and presented in a chosen form using particular words and graphics. Thus no presentation of material is objective or value-free.

Heritage items gain *meaning* through an interpretation that is often our own. However, we do not always have the knowledge-base to provide our own interpretation, or our knowledge and experience limit our ability to consider a range of possible interpretations of a particular site or artefact, and we rely on the interpretation provided by others. There is, of course, normally more than one possible interpretation, although different interpretations will usually all be based on a single body of 'factual' information, such as dates, names of people associated with the item, species lists, and former uses. These 'facts' and

one or more possible interpretations are often generated by heritage experts and presented to the public. Heritage professionals, however, have their own knowledge- and experience-bases, as well as their own prejudices, and thus it is crucial to be aware of who is doing the interpreting. It is also crucial for the interpreter and the visitor to be aware of the target audience for the interpretation, as interpretation does, and should, differ to accommodate the needs of different audiences.

The remainder of this chapter concentrates on what we might term 'official' or 'institutional' interpretation presented to visitors either at a site, or in literature relating directly to the site or an artefact. If individuals wish to hone their own interpretation, they need to obtain as much information as possible from diverse sources. They need information not only about the item under consideration, but also information about the contexts in which it originated and later evolved. They also need to be aware of the fact that much of this information, particularly if it is in published form, will have been already interpreted by someone else. In that case, the following discussion will still be relevant, although it will be one step removed.

Interpretation by whom?

Most 'official' interpretation is carried out by professionals, though not necessarily by professional interpreters. Inevitably, professionals working within a given national and institutional framework tend to have a particular group background and philosophy underlying their individual backgrounds and philosophies. Political imperatives and bureaucratic policies will have a great influence on the interpretation, in both its general content and its detail. As a result, the majority of 'official' interpretations strongly reflect the beliefs and philosophies of the dominant group in society, and, whether as a result of conscious decisions or not, more often than not they reinforce the dominant perceptions of the hegemonic group. The perceptions and personal interpretations of members of minority groups are likely to be relegated to the background, if they are mentioned at all, unless a conscious effort is made to include alternative interpretations.

Those involved in interpretation may be divided into three broad groups: those responsible for policy and decisions covering choice of content and orientation at a general level (*the message*); those responsible for detailed content (*the detail*); and those responsible for determining issues relating to how the material is presented (*the means*). There is, of course, frequent overlap between these rather artificial categories. When an interpretation specialist is involved, their input will be largely in the third area, as the message will often be either explicitly dictated by management or government, or will be required to fall within implicit guidelines set by political or corporate culture. The detail will usually be supplied by experts such as ecologists, marine scientists, architectural historians, and industrial archaeologists. Unless a conscious effort is made to ensure otherwise, none of the members of these groups is likely to share the background and life experiences of any group other than the dominant socio-economic and political group. Indeed, heritage interpretation is often quite clearly used as a political tool, reinforcing the beliefs and stances of the hegemonic group, which is clearly shown in the use of national monuments and icons, and in the very visible place they occupy in national heritage lists. However, efforts often have been made, for example, to include the perspectives of indigenous peoples and to allow for the needs of those with various disabilities.

It is worth spending just a little longer on the use of heritage interpretation as political and religious propaganda. Given that a dominant political system or religion spends so much effort reinforcing its position and trying to ensure adherence to it—by means ranging from censorship and subtle, if sometimes unintentional, misinformation to, in extreme cases, physical coercion—it should come as no surprise if a dominant group also orients heritage information in such a way as to reinforce its dominance, occasionally reaching the extremes of the wanton destruction of non-hegemonic heritage, which took place in Afghanistan in early 2001. Sometimes this may be unintentional; a group in a position of power is often simply unaware of other points of view, or of other groups. But closed minds and blinkered vision can lead to the same result as purposeful propaganda. Furthermore, some people believe that there should be one national heritage interpreted in one way for all citizens, regardless of individual and group differences. Heritage is seen by them as yet another tool to help mould national character and create cohesion by assimilating all groups. Others see strength in diversity and in a broadening of the inclusiveness of the concept of heritage. Heritage is one of the key elements of the policy of multiculturalism as espoused in Australia (see Box 1.2), albeit sometimes half-heartedly or in a tokenistic way.

Interpretation for whom?

If most heritage interpretation is done by professionals who more often than not belong to the dominant group in society, there is a clear danger that the interpretation will be done for that same group, or, at the very least, will be, by default, most accessible and meaningful to that group. After all, the originator and the consumer have a shared background and philosophy, and have the same priorities in their definitions of heritage. Making heritage interpretation accessible and meaningful to others, then, requires a conscious effort on the part of the professional interpreter to get 'outside' their own social context and 'inside' someone else's.

Any nation contains a wide range of different groups, sub-groups, and individuals, no matter how much a central authoritarian government tries to homogenise its population. Even if political and religious differences are minimised, and deviations from the norm are ignored or suppressed, differences in gender, age, and geographical context can still greatly affect perceptions of heritage and of the suitability of different styles of interpretation. Individual interests, including occupational and leisure interests, also lead to different heritage priorities. When interpreting heritage all of these differences are important, perhaps none more than the geographical context. An urban dweller's perception of heritage may be very different from that of a rural person; for example, preserved farm buildings may need little or no explanation for a local person but might require a great deal of background for an urban visitor to enable them to appreciate their significance. Likewise, overseas tourists will need explanations of aspects of Australian history and folklore that locals take for granted—just think of the inclusion of Ned Kelly figures, Victa mowers, Mambo symbols, and Hills hoists in the opening and closing ceremonies of the Sydney 2000 Olympic Games, the meanings of which were undoubtedly lost on most overseas television viewers. Furthermore, Anglo-Saxon Australians will need considerable, sensitive explanation of Aboriginal and Asian cultural traditions in order to appreciate related heritage items.

There are also more obvious barriers to access to, and appreciation of, heritage, even within otherwise fairly homogeneous populations. Age and level of education are examples of factors that can make a particular form of interpretation suitable for some, but not for others. It is not simply a matter of how far people have taken their education, as someone with a strong historical education will need a different form of interpretation for a historic building than will someone with little knowledge of, or interest in, history. The same applies to different levels of education in ecology when it comes to natural heritage sites, while people from different socio-economic backgrounds may well require quite different interpretations of housing styles and of various productive and leisure activities. Disabilities can also demand particular approaches; for example, some effort is now being made to provide heritage experiences for the visually impaired, as well as access for people in wheelchairs (Plate 2.1), with lifts where possible. Language can be a barrier, too, although this applies more to communities with migrant and ethnic minority groups and, more and more importantly, to those acting as hosts to overseas tourists.

Interpretation is also inextricably linked to the promotion, advertisement, and marketing of heritage sites. Managers of sites must increasingly meet at least part of their operating costs using income generated through visitors (see Sections 3.6 and 3.7). To do this successfully, they need to be able to target actual or potential audiences, often identified through visitor surveys (see Section 2.4). It then becomes necessary to identify the interpretation needs of various groups for economic reasons, as well as educational ones. If it is not possible to separately target a number of groups (perhaps because overall visitor numbers are too small, and a series of distinct interpretation efforts is too costly) attempts may be made to compromise with a 'one size fits all' approach. The danger is that this approach may not fit anyone particularly well.

Plate 2.1

Echidna Aboriginal engraving site, Ku-ring-gai Chase National Park, just north of Sydney, NSW, showing wheelchair access (see also Plate 7.3).

Photo: Graeme Aplin

2.3 Uses of interpretation

Public awareness

Interpretation, and especially off-site interpretation through brochures (Plate 2.2), web sites, and media coverage, can be used to increase public awareness of a particular heritage site or item, or as part of a broader exercise to raise general awareness of heritage values and the need to protect them. On-site signs can also have broader educational value extending beyond the particular site (Plates 2.3 and 2.4), an issue dealt with later in a discussion of 'general education'. Site-specific interpretation is obviously closely related to public relations and advertising, by involving the presentation to the public of key features and values to raise the site's image. This can certainly increase visitor numbers, but, just as importantly, it can change the public perception of the site, and perhaps

Plate 2.2

French brochures publicising a range of sites covering many different forms of cultural heritage. All the sites included are listed on the *Caisse Nationale des Monuments Historiques et des Sites* (see Section 11.3).

Photo: Graeme Aplin

Plate 2.3

Sign outside the Ling Yin (Soul's Retreat) Buddhist temple, Hangzhou, Zhejiang Province, China, exhorting citizens to value and care for heritage items. This sign is a model of brevity.

Photo: Graeme Aplin

Plate 2.4

Sign at Kanangra–Boyd National Park, NSW, erected at the edge of the proclaimed Wilderness Area to explain the concept and value of wilderness areas, along with conservation and safety issues. While the sign is very detailed with small text and complex maps, it is located on the main track as it enters the area and visitors could reasonably be expected to pause for some minutes to read it carefully.

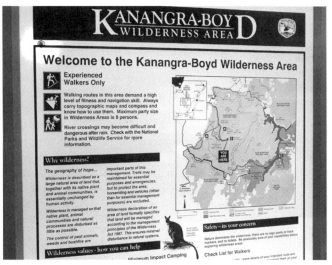

Photo: Graeme Aplin

increase pressure on the government to manage and protect the site adequately. Site-specific interpretation can be a key weapon in promoting the presence of management to politicians and bureaucrats, and in increasing public pressure on those people by gaining public support for the sites. It may also help in enlisting public involvement on a voluntary basis with running the site, and the cooperation of, for example, owners of adjoining land. All of these ends, among others, can be achieved partly through enhancing the appreciation of the particular heritage item or site, even if the people reached never visit it.

Encouraging visitors

Heritage conservation can be justified on several grounds associated with abstract value systems and people will be happy simply knowing items have been protected. But in most cases the public will want the opportunity to actually visit sites. First-hand experience reinforces the appreciation of the heritage item and can serve to increase the pressures for conservation, as mentioned above. Increasingly, visitors are also needed for revenue-raising reasons, as detailed further in Chapter 3. In this context, interpretation is partly image promotion (that is, advertising), but it should also be factually based. It will, hopefully, whet appetites for further knowledge of sites, as well as for the sheer enjoyment of personally experiencing them.

Adding value

Once visitors are on site, interpretation is a key tool in adding value to visitor experiences, in both educational and entertainment terms (Plates 2.4 to 2.7). Anyone can, up to a point, enjoy a heritage experience without outside help. But we enjoy the experience much more if our attention is directed to the most notable and interesting features; if we are informed as to their significance and have them put in context; if we learn about the processes and personalities related to those features and to the site as a whole; and if we are kept safe and relatively comfortable.

Differences between individuals will mean that some will want to be as safe and comfortable as possible, while others will wish to be challenged. In the former case, interpretation may involve giving information to maximise safety and comfort, while subtly pointing out why a little discomfort and effort might be necessary to enhance the experience. In the latter case, interpretation may involve explaining why certain limits have to be set on visitor activities for the protection of heritage values and the individual's safety. Furthermore, some visitors will already have a great deal of relevant knowledge and require minimal extra interpretation, and may even become annoyed at being given too much. Others will have very little prior knowledge, but a great curiosity and desire to learn. Still others will simply want to enjoy a day out and whatever entertainment the site offers, and not be bothered with learning about it.

Plate 2.5

An official Chinese Tourist Office guide at Hangzhou, China, who informed, entertained, and assisted our Australian tour group.

Photo: Graeme Aplin

Plate 2.6

Explanatory signs in shelter at entrance to Bunjil's Cave Reserve, east of the Grampians National Park, Victoria (see also Plate 7.5). A considerable amount of information is given on both the natural environment and the Aboriginal occupation and significance of the site to prepare visitors for what they are about to see.

Photo: Graeme Aplin

Plate 2.7

Sign giving basic information without overwhelming the visitor, Port Campbell National Park, Victoria. The sign explains formation of cliffs, off-shore rock stacks—such as the Twelve Apostles— and other coastal formations. Note the indication of a series of markers to follow.

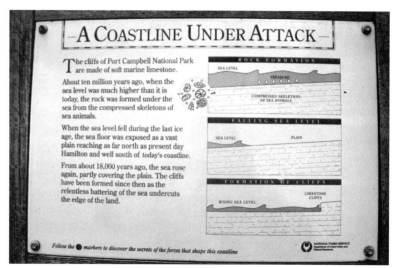

Photo: Graeme Aplin

Information and values can be conveyed through entertainment, too. It is often the subtle, carefully packaged (or 'sugar-coated') presentation of information that is most successful. Those out to enjoy their day with never a thought of actually learning about the place they are visiting can still learn through carefully prepared interpretational material. Once a visitor's interest and involvement have been gained, entertainment can also be used to communicate more explicitly information-oriented material and activities.

Building identity

Interpretation can be used to promote the use of heritage to help build national, regional, and community identities. There are two elements to this: one covert and the other overt. The covert aspect involves relating the specific heritage item to a broader context and to a generally accepted body of heritage at the appropriate geographic scale. Visitors or, in the case of off-site material, readers are then left to make the connections, and to perhaps experience changed perceptions of both the particular heritage item and their group heritage more generally. I suspect that many United States (US) visitors to the Washington Mall react in this way. Overt propaganda can also be included in heritage interpretation material to bolster the heritage perception favoured by the dominant group in society, or by the government of the day. This is often seen as a way to meld a cohesive society that shares a group ethic and belief system, buttressed by heritage elements relating to some 'glorious past'. Heritage items become national or regional icons.

Heritage interpretation can also be used in minority groups to bolster a sense of identity, with the self-assurance that goes with it. Provided that the minority group's culture is presented in a sensitive, positive, and culturally appropriate manner, rather than being trivialised, misinterpreted, or, at worst, mocked, it can help reawaken interests in minority cultures and lifestyles, both within the group itself and in the broader community. If the broader community comes to better appreciate the culture of a minority group, their cohesion and confidence will be enhanced, and a sense of identity and purpose renewed. Entertainment has a place in this context, too, but should be treated with extra care.

Specific education

Many visitors want to learn about the places they visit. Learning about a place usually leads to a more rewarding experience and often forms part of personal education and development in a more general sense. Interpretation can convey factual material about, for example, the history of a building or the ecology of a wetland. It can convey information of both a general and a more detailed and specialised nature about, for example, architectural styles, building techniques, industrial processes, geologic formations, or mammal breeding cycles (see Plates 2.4, 2.6, and 2.7). Information can relate to a type of feature more generally, as well as to the particular example; information on water-powered flour milling at one restored mill will probably contain information on milling in general, in addition to more site-specific information. Similarly, information will normally situate the example in a broader historical, social, and biophysical context in a way that helps the visitor slot the specific knowledge into their broader knowledge-base. Heritage interpretation can thus be a powerful informal source of education for the community.

General education

Interpretation can convey broader community education messages, including those designed to influence general attitudes to heritage and the environment (see Plates 2.3 and 2.4). A demonstration of the need to conserve, manage, and care for one site can translate into a better understanding and a stronger acceptance of the need to conserve heritage in general. Feelings of continuity with the past can be nurtured through interpretation of particular historic buildings, and recognition of the need to preserve biodiversity can be fostered through the interpretation of nature reserves and national parks. Overall concern for environmental issues and behavioural change favouring environmental health may result from carefully constructed interpretation at the few sites actually visited by any individual.

Management

Site management can be greatly assisted by interpretation. It is usually more effective to explain the reasons behind directions and prohibitions than to enforce them in a heavy-handed way; for example, certain behaviours may be suggested, requested, or insisted upon to ensure the safety of visitors, the enjoyment of the site by others, or the preservation of heritage values (see Plate 4.8). Entry to certain areas may be undesirable because of problems with trampling of vegetation, erosion of slopes, or disturbance of nesting birds. It will almost always be cheaper to explain the reasons for preventing entry to these areas in brochures or on signs than it would be to erect fences or other barriers. The latter solution may well be too intrusive, at any rate. Prohibitions without explanations are rarely received favourably, even if they are complied with, so a mixture of education and visitor control is preferable.

2.4 Interpretation principles

Research the subject and strive for accuracy

While there will more often than not be an element of entertainment in the interpretation and presentation of heritage, accuracy remains crucial. The items being interpreted need to be researched in detail, unless results of reliable research are already available. Even where detailed information is available, it may have been obtained for a different purpose and may need recasting to make it more suitable for a general audience. If information is not available, original research will be necessary. This need not be an additional burden, as all conserved heritage items should be documented as fully as possible for management purposes, whether or not they are accessible to the public and interpreted for visitors. Formal documentation will not, however, contain the entertainment element often present in visitor-oriented material, and may well be too detailed, obscure, and 'dry'. The basis of good interpretation, however, will often already be in the archives. Having said that, fact should be carefully separated from myth or popular but unverified stories; the myths and stories can still be presented, and often add to the entertainment value of interpretation, but should be clearly identified for what they are.

Research the audience

Different audiences or market segments require different forms of interpretation. One crucial, but ultimately unachievable, goal is to cater for the needs of all such segments. Usually, the best an interpreter can do is to bear in mind the needs of the major groups and meet them as closely as possible; compromise is, however, the order of the day. Needs differ according to just about every factor imaginable, and only a few of them can be briefly alluded to here.

Age and gender differences are important as they often affect the life experiences that visitors can draw on. Age also affects the educational and intellectual levels of visitors; it is important to engage children and young adults, as well as older people. This is not only a matter of equity: young people who grow up with pleasant and fulfilling memories of heritage sites and a firmly ingrained perception that heritage is important will assist immeasurably with heritage protection in the future, not only by ensuring the continuation of official heritage organisations, but also by creating positive attitudes to heritage on the part of private owners and occupiers. It is to everyone's advantage to have heritage education as a key part of formal and informal education, and this can, in part, be achieved by sound interpretation that is accessible to children at various stages of their development.

Educational background and current interests are other key variables. Some visitors may already have detailed knowledge of, for example, architectural history or wetlands ecology, and will want to learn more about these in the context of a specific site. Most visitors, however, will need a much more fundamental explanation of just a few of the most relevant points related to the site. Furthermore, some visitors will be totally uninterested in topics that absolutely fascinate others. Some will have a much better grasp of fundamental scientific principles than others. Foreign visitors, or even those from other parts of the same country, may need brief explanations of historical or other background that local people take for granted.

Language is another obvious point of difference between groups of visitors. In many nations, local minority or immigrant groups are sizeable and speak a language other than the official or major national language. Foreign tourists often speak yet other languages. In the case of Australia, even if tourists have basic conversational or phrase-book English, this may not be adequate for the more specialised explanations often necessary in heritage interpretation.

Finally, in this non-exhaustive treatment, interpreters need to be aware of, and, where possible, allow for those with *disabilities*. Catering for the needs of the disabled frequently involves responses of a physical, structural nature. Interpretation, however, may need to provide alternative experiences and associated explanatory material, rather than just relying on the mainstream material.

The variety of needs of the major groups described poses major problems for interpreters. Should they try to find a 'middle-of-the-road' approach that attempts to meet the needs of all? Or should they provide alternatives? For people who speak a foreign language or have a visual disability, the only possibility is the latter. While provision of multiple signs, brochures and guided tours might be possible in heavily visited sites, it will not be feasible in smaller, less-visited ones. There are thus two balancing acts involved: balancing the needs of the various identifiable groups; and achieving a balance between visitor needs and realistic expectations in terms of finances and personnel. A knowledge of the characteristics of actual or potential visitors is fundamental to any attempt to provide interpretation for different groups, or even to provide a single suitable interpretation. Visitor surveys are used for marketing purposes to determine the target audience(s) for interpretation, and to assess performance success in interpretation and other aspects of site management. Chapter 3 deals with such surveys at greater length, but Box 2.1 outlines some of the results of a visitor survey conducted at Jenolan Caves, NSW.

Box 2.1   Results from a visitors' survey at Jenolan Caves, NSW

A total of 100 visitors visiting the Jenolan Caves Karst Conservation Reserve, now a part of the newly listed Greater Blue Mountains World Heritage property, completed a detailed questionnaire in mid-2000. While this was first and foremost part of the research for an Honours thesis at Macquarie University, it was carried out with the full cooperation of the Trust managing the reserve. Survey results and recommendations made in the thesis were made available to the Caves management.

Cave tours are of utmost importance, providing the bulk of the interpretation received by visitors of the underground features of the reserve. The overall quality of the caves experience was rated as 'outstanding' by half of the visitors, and 'above average' by most of the remainder. Complaints related to overcrowding in caves (that is, too many people in the group), the cost of tours, the limited time available for tour coach groups (not really a Caves Trust issue), and screaming babies among visitors. The more tightly focussed question relating to the guides' presentation on the tours elicited responses almost entirely of 'above average' (52 per cent) or 'outstanding' (44 per cent). One free response described the two guides as 'lively', 'informative', 'patient', and 'careful'. Respondents were, however, slightly less positive about the information content of the guides' presentations. The researcher felt that this reflected the fact that content, apart from some warnings and information about appropriate visitor behaviour, is determined by each guide, and that there is no formal guide training program in place. The guides also found some difficulty in rapidly assessing each group and adapting for age, education, language proficiency, and other variables (this was backed up by interviews with some of the guides). It is interesting to note that 80 per cent of visitors questioned said that they would have liked more information on the Aboriginal history of the area. Finally, it is likely that the 6 per cent of visitors who found the information difficult to understand came from among the 27 per cent of visitors who were from outside Australia. While providing tours in languages other than English is obviously desirable, it would be extremely difficult to implement.

By contrast, visitors were generally not favourably impressed by the standard of above-ground *signs* in the reserve. It was felt that signs needed updating because they looked 'scrappy' and they should better cater for non-English speaking tourists (this is much more feasible than providing guided tours in other languages). *Brochures* were also felt to be of a relatively poor standard. It was generally felt that they should be better illustrated and presented, and some respondents felt there should be brochures specifically for children. The Visitors' Centre was felt to be of a very poor standard and inadequate for its purpose; some of the staff even regarded it as 'a joke'.

The Caves tours, then, are of a high standard due to committed but under-trained guides. Other aspects of interpretation and presentation at Jenolan Caves could, however, be greatly improved.

Source: J. Chandler (2000) 'Interpretation at the Jenolan Caves Reserve', unpublished BA(Hons) thesis, Department of Human Geography, Macquarie University, Sydney.

Carefully devise methods

There are many ways of presenting an interpretative message once its content has been agreed on. There is also a two-way relationship between message and form of presentation, and it is important to find a suitable match. As well as deciding on the major form of interpretation—signs, brochures, guided tours, audio-visual presentations—there are many more detailed decisions to be made. Most importantly, managers and interpreters need to have a clear idea as to their goals in using interpretation, and of the messages to be conveyed. The mix of purposes, and especially the desired balance between providing entertainment and information, is a central issue to be addressed. It is good to be able to 'think beyond the circle' and to be innovative, too. Sensitivity is needed in dealing with information relating to indigenous groups and others, such as former owners and occupants of historic buildings and those connected with, for example, battle or disaster sites.

Balance detail and brevity

Yet another balancing act, already referred to above, is that between detail and brevity (see Plates 2.3, 2.4, 2.6, and 2.7). Generally speaking, interpretative material will need to be relatively brief, leaving out much that the experts may see as important. Signs need to be concise and to the point; they quickly lose their impact as they become more cluttered. The same applies to brochures and leaflets; if they are to be made available free of charge, either on site or off site, they have to be small and cheap to produce. Guides, too, can only provide a certain amount of information in the time available and do not want to be talking non-stop during a tour. Apart from anything else, visitors need time to understand things in their own way and to make their own interpretations, rather than being 'spoon-fed' or overwhelmed with excessive information. On the other hand, some visitors will want more information and will want to delve beyond the necessarily superficial coverage of most interpretation. To cater for this need more detailed booklets can be available for sale, more detailed briefing notes loaned for self-guided tours, or separate 'advanced' tours could be made available. Of course, all of these additional, alternative forms of interpretation are much easier to provide at large, well-visited sites than at small, less-visited ones.

Information technology offers another possible solution to this dilemma. Computerised databases and CD-ROMs can provide alternate pathways and linkages for the exploration of available information. Access to such materials in a visitor centre might provide for those with special or more advanced interests, as well as allowing for alternative versions of the standard material for different age groups or in different languages. Nevertheless, the most memorable experiences are likely to be out in the field, not indoors in the visitor centre, so information technology approaches are likely to be supplementary or complementary, not a substitute.

Entertain as well as educate

Many exponents of interpretation emphasise that it is necessary to entertain as well as to inform. Entertainment can certainly capture the visitor's interest and set the scene for information acquisition, and the possibility that interpretation could convey meaning about a site to visitors primarily interested in entertainment and enjoyment is seen by managers as a bonus. While entertainment might be the 'spoonful of sugar that helps the medicine go down', one hopes that heritage information is not seen as a nasty form of medicine. It should be possible to paint such information in a positive light and impart it without overt attempts at pure entertainment, provided the visitor's interest is gained and maintained. Information should certainly not be too dry and boring, but any associated entertainment should avoid trivialising the heritage values or conveying misinformation. Perhaps interpretation does, however, involve *infotainment*, to use a horrible late 20th-century term.

Provide context

Finally, interpretation should constantly provide context to heritage, both within the site and beyond. Parts or aspects of a heritage site should be placed in the context of the whole, and the various features and processes involved should be related to each other. Furthermore, the heritage site as a whole should be placed in a broader ecological or societal context, and its significance at various geographical scales and political levels should be explained. In some cases, this may involve placing the item alongside others of its type in a comparative sense.

2.5   Interpretation and presentation: some practical issues

This section is certainly not a 'how-to' guide to interpretation and its presentation. (By 'presentation', I mean the act of conveying the interpretative material to visitors, and the practical means by which this is done.) It raises questions, rather than answering them. There are many good theoretical and practical guides to interpretation available if you need more of the 'nuts and bolts'. (See the 'Further Reading' section at the end of this chapter for a few examples.)

Signs

On-site signs can be important tools for both site and visitor management, and for giving information. They need to be well placed, eye-catching, attention-grabbing, and attention-holding (see Plate 2.3). As for any form of interpretation or presentation, there is a need to achieve a balance between brevity and detail. As lettering and graphics generally need to be of a size easily read from at least one metre away, signs have a strictly limited capacity in terms of the information they can convey. Cluttered signs are ineffective, especially in crowded areas where large numbers of people gather around them. In many cases, graphics can carry much of the information burden, but they often need some text and some key-word labelling on or next to the diagrams, maps, and photographs, and this ancillary text also needs to be large enough for easy reading (see Plates 2.4, 2.6, and 2.7). Information-giving signs work best, in most cases, when they are positioned so that the object they relate to can also be seen, making the relationship between sign and heritage feature easier for visitors to establish. Signs with a larger amount of information are more appropriate in an introductory role, preparing the visitor for what is to come (see Plates 2.4 and 2.6).

The concepts involved in heritage interpretation are often complex, whether they relate to natural processes or cultural ones. Signs should, perhaps, be seen as the 'front-line' of information; printed material, audio-visual and computer presentations, and guides, as appropriate and practical, add further information. At any rate, many visitors will only want a minimal amount of guidance, so signs should probably be directed at them, and the provision of any additional detail should be made through other media aimed specifically at the groups that want to know more. Given that many (perhaps most) visitors seek entertainment and enjoyment as much as knowledge, most visitors do not want to be overwhelmed by signs.

Carefully conceived and well-designed signs are a key management tool for keeping visitors on designated routes and out of sensitive areas (see Plate 4.8), for promoting heritage-friendly behaviour, and for preventing damage and injury. A brief explanation of the reasons behind the message is often appropriate, and frequently makes a sign more effective than would be a straight-out prohibition or admonition. Giving such reasons also adds an educational dimension to a primarily management tool.

Guides

Trained professional or voluntary guides, usually accredited in some way, are used at many heritage sites to give an on-the-spot commentary outlining the main features of the site and also providing, in many cases, a degree of entertainment (see Plate 2.5). There are a number of advantages to using guides. First, they can provide information as one moves around a site, something that would otherwise require a large number of signs which, at times, would be too intrusive—in caves, for example. Secondly, experienced guides can adapt the content of their presentation to each group they lead, according to the age–sex composition, geographical origin, and specialised interests of the group. In some cases, guides can use a language other than the local majority language. In other cases, guides can be assigned in advance to pre-booked groups with special requirements. Thirdly, guides, by their mere presence and official standing, can influence visitor behaviour and dissuade harmful, dangerous, or disruptive activities, and, when necessary, explicitly comment on behaviour and request compliance. In this way, they act as management as well as interpretation personnel. Fourthly, visitors can question guides if they require further information; the best guides provide interactive interpretation *par excellence*.

What, then, makes the best guides? They need to be interested in the visitors and tolerant of their foibles, including their lack of knowledge. Above all, they need to be thoroughly knowledgeable about the site, and to have and display an enthusiasm and affection for it. A good guide never gives the impression of 'just doing their job', however difficult it might be to avoid that impression, given personal circumstances, environmental conditions, and visitor pressures. Guides need to present the basic information clearly and concisely, reserving detail for answers to specific questions. They certainly need to remain interesting so that visitors maintain their engagement with the guide and the information presented, rather than 'switching off' and letting their minds wander to other things. Guides should also, at least in part, entertain, which is another way of maintaining visitors' interest.

Guides are often accredited and are almost invariably trained, although enthusiastic amateurs are invaluable in smaller, more local sites lacking the finances and infrastructure for paid staff and training. Amateurs with enthusiasm almost always have the desire to be as knowledgeable as possible about a site, frequently to the extent of carrying out their own research. In Australia, some guides are accredited by the Australian Ecotourism Association. Other countries run different systems: in South Africa, for example, there is a three-tiered accreditation system.

Printed material

Printed material of various kinds is a traditional medium for interpretation, and is used to convey both on-site and off-site information. It can come in many different forms and with many different levels of information, sometimes with elements of entertainment.

Brochures and leaflets can be used either as advertising to draw visitors to the site (see Plate 2.2), or to provide a brief introduction for visitors at the site. These two aims may result in quite different types of brochure. On-site brochures can often provide more information than is presented on signs, although their content is still strictly limited. They can be carried around the site and referred to as necessary, especially if features are numbered or named using signs. Usually they can be retained as souvenirs of the visit, although sometimes site managers provide leaflets or single sheets, often laminated for weather protection, that visitors are asked to return when they leave. This is mainly due to budget constraints, but many visitors do not want or need the printed material beyond their visit and so waste is also minimised. Ideally, sites should cater for the purchase of material by those who want to retain it.

Brochures and leaflets are, by their very nature, brief, and the comments made about brevity, clarity, and eye-catching layout in relation to signs also apply to this type of printed material.

There is also a place for more extensive printed material for those wishing to have greater detail, or a more permanent record of their visit. Books, booklets, postcards, and the like are expensive to provide, and often impossible for small and infrequently visited sites to make available. When available, they are almost always for purchase, and are frequently provided by commercial entities other than the site management or the agency it represents. Having such outside providers may mean a loss of control over content, but management should attempt to reach a cooperative agreement to ensure accuracy and maintain a positive image of the site. A graded range of printed material, perhaps in several languages, is a good way of providing for the diversity of visitor needs. Printed materials also cater for non-visitors who have an interest in the site.

Audio-visual aids

Many sites around the world provide some form of audio guide, although financial constraints mean that this is more common at the large, heavily visited sites. In Australia, few heritage sites have followed suit, with the exception of some museums and art galleries. There are a number of variants on the theme. Simple *audio-cassette recorders* may be lent or hired to visitors, who play the recording while walking around the site and stopping at designated points to listen to the tape and view a point of interest. A much more advanced form used in many places, including the Shanghai Museum in China, is a handset the size of a large mobile phone. The visitor keys in a number that is referred to at the exhibit or site feature where she or he stands, and receives the appropriate portion of the commentary. Another form used in the United States of America (USA) many years ago, specifically at Suttor's Fort outside Sacramento, involved a series of *low-power transmitter loops* that broadcast the commentary for each feature. Visitors would hire headsets and, as they moved through the site, they would move out of the range of one commentary and enter the range of the next. All of the audio-visual methods mentioned here allow time flexibility for the visitor, and the last two also allow route flexibility. None of them involves intrusive loudspeaker commentaries audible to all, whether they are interested or not.

Again, accuracy and a mix of entertainment and information are essential. Different ages and backgrounds can also be catered for if required, and where practical. Simple audio tapes can be made available in different languages and the handsets used at the Shanghai Museum also provide the commentary in a variety of languages. In the future, handsets could also contain video screens showing graphics relating to the features at each stop. For example, short video loops or diagrams could be used to explain building techniques or animal behavioural patterns. Visitors could also view a particular location in different seasonal or weather conditions, or a particular aspect of a historical site as it was in the past. Like signs, such material may mean more to a visitor when it is experienced first-hand on location than when viewed in a visitor centre or off site.

Web sites and other IT media

Web sites are an exceptionally powerful off-site medium for interpretative information relating to heritage sites (as well as advertising, of course). Many museums, art galleries, and heritage sites now have comprehensive web sites offering 'virtual tours'. This facility allows many more people to experience the actual site, even if they live on the other side of the world. Web sites can offer versions in multiple languages, and the best ones allow users to navigate their way around the site in their own time and in whatever sequence they choose. These web sites, often in the form of intranet on-site versions, can be used to allow visitors to access much more detailed information than can be conveyed on signs or in most printed material. They allow each visitor to choose the level of information they wish to access. *CD-ROMs* can also provide similar experiences, both on site and off site.

There are a number of problems with the use of information technology such as web sites. Cost is the obvious one, and once again large, well-patronised sites can do much more than others. Electronic equipment is difficult to make weatherproof and will almost always be housed in visitor centres, although computers housed in sheltered kiosks, and with touch-screen or voice-recognition capabilities, rather than keyboards, may overcome this limitation. And, most importantly, visitor frustration must be minimised. There need to be enough machines to cater for peak visitor periods, equipment must work, and when it does not it should be rapidly repaired.

Visitor centres

A *visitor centre* can bring together all types of interpretations and presentations mentioned above, along with additional static and dynamic displays. These centres also normally house food outlets, toilets, a shop selling related literature (and often tacky souvenirs!), and guides or other staff to answer visitors' questions. The atmosphere should be relaxed, to the extent that visitor numbers allow, and the centre should provide a comfortable place, protected

Plate 2.8

Model of monastic site in the excellent, modern Glendalough Visitor Centre, Co. Wicklow, Ireland. The model gives visitors an overall impression of the extensive site before they begin to walk around it. The visitor centre also has displays of artefacts, static 'poster' displays, and an audio-visual theatre.

Photo: Graeme Aplin

from the weather, in which visitors can wait for others and find information. This may take place prior to their on-site visit, or after it, to add to their information or simply to allow them to reflect on it. One of the major management decisions will be the size and visitor capacity of the centre. It should not appear crowded at any but the busiest times, yet it will inevitably be an expensive place to build, maintain, and staff, and will be underutilised for much of the time. Siting and design are also crucial; the former, as it relates to natural heritage areas, is addressed in Section 5.6. A visitor centre can be a crucial part of a visitor's experience at any heritage site, as an introduction and a showcase (Plate 2.8; see also Plate 6.1).

2.6   Further discussion

Interpretation used in advertising and visitor attraction, and visitor surveys will be discussed further in the next chapter, which deals with economic aspects of heritage preservation and management. Particular examples involving interpretation and its uses will also arise in Chapters 5, 6, and 7 in the context of natural heritage sites, non-indigenous cultural heritage sites, and indigenous heritage sites respectively, and in later chapters dealing with specific countries.

Further Reading

Ballantyne, R., Leverington, F. & Sutherland, L. (eds) (1997) *Big Ideas… Small Budgets: Proceedings of the Sixth National Conference of the Interpretation Australia Association*, IAA, Melbourne.

Beckmann, E. & Hull, S. (eds) (1994) *Interpretation Attached to Heritage: Papers Presented at the Third Annual Conference of the Interpretation Australia Association*, IAA, Melbourne.

Beckmann, E. & Russell, R. (eds) (1995) *Interpretation and the Getting of Wisdom: Conference Papers of the Fourth Annual Conference of the Interpretation Australia Association*, IAA, Melbourne.

Department of Environment & Heritage (Qld) (1996) *The Art of Interpretation Workbook*, DEH, Brisbane.

Department of Natural Resources & Environment (Vic) (1999) *Best Practice in Park Interpretation and Education: A Report to ANZECC Working Group on National Park Management Benchmarking and Best Practice Program*, NRE, Melbourne.

Hall, C. M. & McArthur, S. (eds) (1996) *Heritage Management in Australia and New Zealand: The Human Dimension*, Oxford University Press, Melbourne, selected chapters.

Ham, S. H. (1992) *Environmental Interpretation: A Practical Guide for People with Big Ideas and Small Budgets*, North American Press, Golden, CO.

Harrington, J. (ed.) (1995) *Historic Environment: Meaning, Method and Madness— Heritage Interpretation in the 1990s*, Australia ICOMOS, Vol.11. No.4.

Machlis, G. E. & Field, D. R. (1992) *On Interpretation: Sociology for Interpreters of Natural and Cultural History* (revised edn), Oregon State University Press, Corvallis, OR.

Mackenzie, K. (ed.) (1996) *Interpretation in Action: Fifth Annual Interpretation Australia Conference*, IAA, Interpretation Australia Association, Melbourne.

Tilden, F. (1977) *Interpreting Our Heritage* (3rd edn), University of North Carolina Press, Chapel Hill, NC.

Uzzell, D. L. (1989) *Heritage Interpretation. Volume 1: The Natural and Built Environment*, Belhaven, London.

Uzzell, D. & Ballantyne, R (eds) (1998) *Contemporary Issues in Heritage and Environmental Interpretation*, Stationery Office, London.

Vererka, J. (1994) *Interpretive Master Planning*, Falcon Press, Helena, MN.

CHAPTER 3

Tourism and the Economics of Heritage Management

3.1   Whose heritage? Who pays?

It is all very well to say that key heritage items should be documented, preserved for posterity, and interpreted so that the public can enjoy and learn from them. But heritage conservation and management entails considerable costs that someone has to bear. Who should it be? Whose heritage is it, after all? To what extent should heritage sites be financially self-sufficient? Should they be adapted for commercial use? Should heritage be viewed as a commodity? Not surprisingly, these are all contentious, political questions.

As we saw in the Introduction and Chapter 1, heritage items can be deemed significant at various geographical scales or political levels from local to global. The scale at which an item is significant partially determines the level at which financial responsibility falls. National governments normally bear the primary responsibility for heritage deemed significant at the global and national levels. It is possible to receive grants towards caring for World Heritage items from the United Nations Educational, Scientific and Cultural Organisation (UNESCO) and other international organisations, especially in the case of low-income nations that find it difficult, if not impossible, to internally fund less-essential items such as heritage (see Sections 8.2 to 8.4). Having said that, it should be noted that even the poorest nations often have cultural and religious reasons, as well as ones related to national pride and identity, for preserving key heritage sites. Within any nation, regional or state governments, and local or municipal governments, are usually responsible for heritage significant at the regional and local scales. Responsibility and funding may, of course, be shared between the various levels of government, and this occurs frequently (see Plate 3.2 and Chapters 11 and 12 for examples).

Particular examples of bureaucratic structures and the mechanisms for sharing responsibility are highlighted in Chapters 9 to 12. It is common to have a hierarchy of heritage bodies or departments taking responsibility at various levels. Natural heritage areas might include national parks administered by the national government (although this is partly contrary to Australian usage of the term *national park*), regional or provincial parks, and local parks and reserves administered by departmental or municipal governments. The exact structure varies, as do the administrative structures of nations. Australia, unlike most nations—even other federations such as the

USA and Canada—has few truly 'national' parks, but it has numerous so-called national parks administered by state governments, an indication of both the recency of federation (1901) and the strength of the states' rights movement (see Chapter 9).

While major heritage sites may be publicly owned and managed, a large proportion of significant sites are in private ownership, including family homes, business premises, and farmlands. Is it reasonable to expect private owners to bear the entire cost of conservation and management? Is it reasonable to expect them to accept constraints on their use of the site and their activities because of the heritage values of the property? Should government at the appropriate level contribute towards the direct costs and compensate for foregone opportunities?

3.2   Public vs private interests— costs concentrated, benefits dispersed?

On the surface, it seems entirely reasonable to argue that the benefits of heritage conservation should be shared by the whole community, whether this be a local, state, or national community. Everyone, or at least an identifiable sub-section of the population, shares the benefit of knowing that an important part of their heritage is safe and well maintained. Such knowledge may have important positive impacts on a sense of community, among other things. Heritage buildings or landscapes preserved by private owners can be seen and appreciated by the public, at least from a distance. These sites may make key contributions to larger streetscapes or rural landscapes. They may, in fact, be elements within large listed historic precincts or landscape conservation zones, in which the whole is much more than the sum of the parts (see Section 6.4). If the community benefits from the preservation of these sites, even if people do not normally have access to them, should not the community contribute to the costs involved? This is in fact the case with The Rocks in Sydney (Box 3.1).

Box 3.1   The Rocks, Sydney

The Rocks area was important in the early history of Sydney, and hence that of NSW and Australia more generally. The rugged, hilly, and rocky landscape that gave the district its name is still evident. The official Rocks Conservation Area includes the suburban area of Millers Point, west of the Sydney Harbour Bridge approaches, as well as the area more specifically known as The Rocks east of those approaches. In the 19th century much of the area was devoted to activities related to the waterfront, or provided housing for those who worked there. Like many waterfront areas, it was in parts a rough place, with many hotels or pubs, brothels, and low-class accommodation houses. Some of the housing, especially on the higher areas and in Argyle Place, was of good quality, but other areas could only realistically be termed slums.

The bubonic plague hit the area in 1900, brought by rats jumping ship at the wharves surrounding the peninsula on three sides. The NSW government took control of the area, handing it over to the Sydney Harbour Trust, which proceeded to demolish the worst of the housing in sections of Millers Point, and to clean up rubbish and fumigate other properties. Wharves were redeveloped over ensuing years and waterside worker housing was built in High Street and Windmill Street, along with shops and even a hotel for the workers. Some historians see this as a thinly disguised push for government control over the waterfront rather than a necessary public health measure.

By the 1960s the area was again rather run down, at a time when Sydney was experiencing a business, property, and construction boom. The Askin Coalition Government established the Sydney Cove Redevelopment Authority (SCRA) in 1968 with plans to demolish all but a very few existing historic buildings, and to replace most of the buildings with high-rise residential and commercial tower blocks. Local residents fought against the proposal and unionists, led by Jack Mundey and the Builders' Labourers Federation, placed 'green bans' on work in The Rocks, partly because of the disruption that would be caused to long-term residents (mainly working-class people), and partly because they saw value in preserving the historic nature of the district. Support also came from those interested in heritage conservation.

As a result, the word 'redevelopment' was quietly dropped from SCRA's title and, particularly after a Labor government was elected and the *Heritage Act 1977* (NSW) was passed, its remit became to conserve the historic values of the district, but in a way that was self-financing. Sydney City Council actively supported this change of emphasis with a rezoning scheme and a register of heritage sites. The renamed Sydney Cove Authority (now the Sydney Harbour Foreshore Authority) has undertaken comprehensive conservation of many buildings, leasing them once completed to existing residents at pegged rents, to new residents at higher rents, or to commercial concerns. Much of the commercial activity has become tourist-oriented. Adaptive re-use and a limited amount of generally sympathetic new development has also occurred, but under strict guidelines, and high-rise development has been limited to the area south of the Cahill Expressway and a line extending from it to the west. The mainly 19th-century heritage value of The Rocks has been recognised and its commercialisation and commodification used to pay for its conservation. It is now one of Sydney's key tourist attractions.

A private owner may also benefit from a heritage listing. In many cases, property values will be enhanced and owners will gain prestige, either in the area where they live (social prestige) or where they conduct business (commercial prestige, translating into increased business). Many people also quite obviously gain immense self-satisfaction from taking on the role of a guardian of heritage. They feel good about caring for a historic building or a wetland, even if it costs them a considerable amount of time and/or money to do so. Owners often willingly take on the tasks of caring for a heritage site for a mixture of reasons and frequently see it as a way of putting something back into their community while still gaining personal rewards. Box 3.2 introduces a currently controversial case in suburban Sydney, in which owners are seeking to redevelop part of a site to offset the costs of preservation. This example illustrates the complexity of issues involved in this whole area of ownership and finance.

Box 3.2   'Redleaf', Wahroonga, Sydney

'Redleaf', in the upper socio-economic Sydney suburb of Wahroonga, is a heritage-listed grand mansion on a spacious block of land, and is home to the Moran family who have made their fortune in the Australian health care industry. The house was built in the 19th century and has, in recent years, won an award for heritage conservation work on its restoration. Owners of properties like 'Redleaf' claim that they are being forced to sell or subdivide because of the large land tax bill owing to the NSW State Government (over A$1 million in extreme cases). Mr Moran wishes to build ten townhouses on a section of the property under the State Environmental Planning Policy (SEPP) 5, which provides for housing for the aged and disabled. Properties built under this policy must be close to public transport and local shops, and 'Redleaf' fulfils this requirement, being situated close to Wahroonga Station and shopping centre. Such a development would defray the land tax costs and possibly provide further funds for maintaining the property, an expensive proposition for any private owner, however wealthy. There is no suggestion of demolishing or altering the house itself, but its curtilage (see Section 6.4) will be severely compromised.

The property is in the Ku-ring-gai municipality, and the municipality's Deputy (and Acting) Mayor is quoted as saying that any alterations to the estate would mar its heritage significance. Indeed, the estate is not large and at least some of the ten townhouses would inevitably be quite close to the main house and would impact visually on its immediate surrounds. Houses such as 'Redleaf' are designed to have quite extensive gardens, sweeping drives and outbuildings, and not to be hemmed in by other unassociated buildings. However, the Deputy Mayor also states that, although the proposed development is inappropriate in his view, it probably meets the criteria of SEPP 5, and if Council refused the application an appeal to the Land and Environment Court would most likely be upheld.

Who, then, should bear the cost of the upkeep of such a property? Should its curtilage be protected? If so, should the land tax burden be reduced because of the estate's heritage value to the community? Should this occur even if it remains entirely a private home only open for public inspection once or twice a year, as has been the case in recent years?

Source: partly based on J. McMillan (2000) 'Outcry over SEPP 5 plan', *North Shore Times*, 13 October, p. 4.

'Redleaf', Wahroonga,
Sydney, NSW.

Photo: Graeme Aplin

The 'bottom line' is that someone has to pay for heritage conservation. Because of the very nature of heritage items, especially historic buildings (see Chapter 6), they usually require considerable repair work and they are expensive to maintain, frequently relying on old and now uncommon materials and skills. They may also require upgrading of fire prevention and safety features. Finding the most appropriate mixture of public and private funding is difficult. Some ways in which private owners can be assisted are outlined below.

3.3   Can heritage be made to pay its way?

One solution to the cost of heritage conservation is to find ways for items and sites to directly pay for their own maintenance and preservation. One of these ways has already been mentioned: the prestige, location, or other values of the property may lead to higher rentals or other payments by private tenants or owners. Hence many historic buildings are adapted for uses other than their original ones, often with modifications to the building fabric to enable this to occur (see Section 6.8). In other words, whether or not public agencies are involved, non-heritage benefits subsidise or completely cover the costs of heritage protection.

The other major way in which heritage can 'pay its way' is through *commodification* and *commercialisation*. These processes are dealt with at greater length in Section 3.6, and both imply the identification and sale of heritage as a commodity in its own right. Money is made from the heritage value of a site, and then at least some of the income is put towards maintaining the site (Plate 3.1). This implies marketing heritage, a concept that some purists still find difficult to accept. As with so many aspects of heritage management, each individual case has to be evaluated to find the most suitable approach. Some sites, such as the Australian War Memorial in Canberra, or the Pantheon in Paris, may have such universal community significance, possibly with deep symbolism, that it seems unacceptable to charge entry fees. Religious buildings often also fall into this category as they are seen as being distinct from the material world, and an essential part of the local social fabric that should be freely available, at least to local people. However, there has been an increasing realisation that visitors interested in heritage values, rather than worship, should be willing to contribute to the upkeep of the building or site.

Plate 3.1

Bunratty Castle, Co. Clare, Ireland. This impressive 15th-century castle is one of Ireland's most popular tourist attractions. The castle was derelict when bought by its present owner in the 1950s, but has since been well restored to its original state, with the interior much as it was in the early 17th century. Tourists can view the interior, medieval banquets are regularly held in the Main Guard (soldiers' quarters), and a Folk Park has been established in the grounds (see Plate 1.3).

Photo: Graeme Aplin

3.4   Valuing heritage

We probably all agree that heritage values are real, and they may or may not be tangible. But can we put a monetary value on heritage, aside from obvious real estate values? What value does heritage add to (or subtract from) those real estate values? And how can we calculate a value for the intangible aspects of heritage? Answers to such questions become important when heritage values are involved in processes such as benefit–cost analyses and environmental impact assessments. A means of assessing the value of returns from conservation work is also required for programs that administer grants (see Section 3.5) and for distributing funds from the budgets of heritage agencies.

There are a number of methods for giving at least an approximate monetary value to factors and characteristics with no obvious market value, as briefly outlined in Box 3.3. In some cases, it may be sufficient to argue that the heritage values of a particular site are so important that they should be saved at (almost) any cost. Other sites may be placed in priority order by means of similarly subjective, even emotive arguments or non-monetary value judgments. Frequently, however, hard-nosed politicians and bureaucrats, as well as hip-pocket-sensitive taxpayers, demand a more quantified answer, and a budget showing costs (many of which are easily quantified) balanced against benefits (normally much less easily quantified). This is yet another way in which economics enters into heritage deliberations.

Box 3.3   Placing values on heritage—major approaches to valuing non-economic factors

---

A   Market-value approaches

1   *Change in productivity*—To what extent is the output from a productive process affected by the proposed action?
2   *Change in income*—How are incomes affected by the action?
3   *Replacement costs*—What expenditure is needed to replace an environmental resource, for example, lost or damaged through the action?
4   *Preventative expenditure*—How much would it cost to prevent the adverse effects of an action?
5   *Relocation costs*—What would it cost to relocate an affected asset or activity?

B   Approaches involving surrogates

6   *Travel costs*—Can costs incurred in travel to, for example, a national park, give a measure of the values people place on it?
7   *Wage differentials*—Do wage differentials between locations reflect environmental quality differences?
8   *Proxy goods*—Is there a good or service that is a substitute for the uncosted one?
9   *Contingent valuation*—What are people willing to pay for, or accept compensation for the loss of, an environmental value?
10   *The trade-off game*—Trade-offs between alternatives are used to gain an idea of values.
11   *Contingent ranking and rating*—Several alternatives are ranked in order of preference and values inferred; alternatives include the environmental effect under consideration, substitutes for it, and items that do have market values.
12   *Priority evaluation*—This approach simulates choices in a market and a hypothetical budget is spent on the various alternatives. It is similar to (11).

Source: greatly simplified from Dept of Environment, Sport, and Territories and Dept of Finance (1995) *Techniques to Value Environmental Resources: An Introductory Handbook*, Australian Government Publishing Service, Canberra.

3.5 Public financing of heritage preservation and conservation

Direct public sector management

The most obvious public financing of heritage preservation and conservation is, of course, when a public agency manages a site, financing both capital works and day-to-day management and maintenance activities out of its own budget. Examples of public agencies are the NSW Historic Houses Trust and national parks services. In many cases, the finances of such agencies depend largely on the annual government budget. This approach may involve a local municipal council running a historic building or park, or national and regional governments being involved in sites of wider significance. Direct public financing through taxes, rates or other general revenues can be, and often is, augmented by entry fees, sponsorship agreements, or fees raised through the hire of the site. Such mixed financial arrangements have become much more common for ostensibly 'public' sites over the last decade or so, both in Australia and elsewhere.

Plate 3.2

Sign indicating the many levels of government, from the European Union through to more local groups, involved in financing conservation works at the Pont du Gard World Heritage property in the Gard Département of Languedoc-Rouisillon, in the south of France. Work involved extensive rehabilitation of the aqueduct itself (see Plate 11.12) and of the surrounding area as an ecological site.

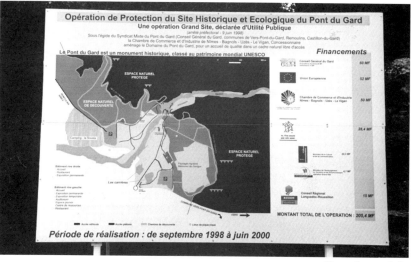

Photo: Graeme Aplin

Grants for preservation and conservation

Governments also operate grants schemes whereby public monies are diverted to private or institutional owners (or to lower levels of government) for heritage-related purposes (Plate 3.2). As well as being applied to the more obvious restoration and maintenance projects, such grants may cover the costs of activities such as identifying and documenting heritage items, archiving documents and photographs, curating museums, and undertaking oral history projects to support heritage work. Competition for heritage grants is usually keen, so considerable work goes into writing applications that allow the grant administrators to choose projects on the basis of significance, sound planning, and 'value for money'. Once grants are made, projects are often officially overseen to ensure that the money is going towards achieving heritage goals and being used in a sound manner, by truly maintaining or increasing heritage value. Both the NSW and Australian federal governments administer grants programs, and one of the major criticisms of new Australian federal legislation is that the federal scheme is likely to be dropped (see Section 9.6).

Tax relief and other incentives

Governments also have less direct ways of diverting public funds into private and community heritage projects. Various forms of tax or local rate relief are available, which involve a loss of government revenue, rather than an up-front payment or grant. Such relief may be for a defined, initial period while work is being carried out, or may be in perpetuity. In the case of taxes, money spent on heritage work may be seen as a legitimate claim to off-set taxable income. Such incentives may be exclusively available to officially listed heritage items, or, less commonly, under more liberal provisions. And, in a related area, private and business donations to non-government heritage bodies may also be available as tax deductions. Finally, heritage properties donated to the state or to voluntary heritage organisations, or left to them in wills, may attract taxation benefits, sometimes of major proportions. Such gifts are not necessarily absolute, and often incorporate agreements for continuing family occupation under specified conditions (see Plate 11.7).

Conditions attached to public assistance

The bodies that administer public financing obviously have an interest in ensuring compliance with the terms of any grant or concession, but they may also attach other conditions. Frequently, there is a condition that at least limited public access to a site be made available where this does not otherwise exist, or is in danger of future withdrawal. In the case of private homes, commercial premises, or semi-private facilities such as places of worship and social clubs, a balance needs to be struck between the needs and rights of the occupiers and those of the public who are, after all, helping to finance the heritage work, and, in a sense, to whom the heritage belongs. Access may be limited to certain 'public' areas of the site, while other private areas remain off-limits. Access may also be limited to just a few occasions, perhaps in the form of annual open days. Such occasions may coincide with the best seasons in the gardens, or with significant anniversaries related to the site, or with local holidays and festivals. Other conditions can relate to the maintenance of the visibility of key elements of a site, especially in relation to a streetscape or landscape. High walls, dense plantings, and the erection of other surrounding buildings may be banned or severely limited to preserve the curtilage (see Section 6.4).

3.6   Commodification and commercialisation

In many cases, heritage has become a commodity to be bought and sold in a market place—it has become commodified (see Plate 3.1). Actually, it is more accurate to say that it is the experience of the heritage site that is the commodity and which is marketed. The actual heritage item is usually managed as a renewable resource, and the experience can be sold over and over again. Of course, all kinds of souvenirs, tasteful or vulgar, reflecting heritage values or otherwise, follow the commodification of the heritage site itself. Tourists around the world either love or hate the commercialisation that follows the recognition of the commodity values of heritage. Local people frequently have similarly polarised views. Some see the more complex side of the decision to commodify and commercialise or not.

Is it possible to commercialise heritage without detracting from the very attributes that attract people in the first place? Perhaps more importantly, is it possible without detracting from the heritage values as perceived by those to whom the heritage primarily belongs, as distinct from short-term visitors from other places? If a definitive answer is required, it is probably 'no', as some compromise is always involved. The mere presence of large numbers of visitors at a place of worship, for example, inevitably detracts from the calm, serene, spiritual atmosphere conducive to worship. Heritage tourism may thus have negative impacts on both the lives of local people and their heritage. Yet another balancing act is required to weigh up the benefits of commercial-isation, which may be the only way of raising funds to preserve the heritage against the intrusions and loss of amenity involved.

If heritage is to be commodified and commercialised, this must be done with as much sensitivity and care as possible. Sensitivity needs to be directed towards both the heritage items themselves, and the people who have an everyday functional and cultural relationship with them. In other words, respect for both the heritage and its primary owners is essential. Images and artefacts that make light of the deeper meanings of the heritage might be fun for tourists to take back home, but might deeply offend local people. Such offence may be based on national pride, religious or cultural grounds, and, while it is often particularly severe when indigenous people are involved (see Sections 7.4 and 7.5), it can arise in almost any set of circumstances. Those commodifying the heritage are also, in a very real sense, interpreting it (see Section 2.2). It is thus crucial that accuracy and sensitivity are applied. Any souvenirs, books, videos, or other items portraying the heritage item or associated features should be without offence to those who primarily own the heritage, and they should be approved or capable of gaining approval, even if there is no formal mechanism for this.

Care of heritage, or concern for local needs and sensitivities, may necessitate limits on the number of visitors to particular sites, to the times of visits, or to the sections of the sites open to visitors. Many aspects of this topic are developed later in this chapter and in Chapters 4 to 7. The common factor is the need to weigh up commercial and heritage priorities.

User-pays principle

Until recently, entry to many heritage sites was free; and still is for many. Increasingly, though, the user-pays principle has been applied to heritage, as it has to so many aspects of life. The argument is that if a person wants to experience, learn from, and enjoy a heritage site, they should pay for the privilege. But is it a privilege or a right? One could argue that membership of the group whose heritage it is should imply free and, where practical, unlimited access to heritage sites. This could range from being a citizen of the global community in the case of World Heritage items, to a member of a local community or of a particular ethnic, religious, or other sub-group. In some cases it is possible to differentiate between 'owners' and 'outsiders' by issuing cheap seasons tickets or permits to the former, or at least charging them lower usage fees. Local councils, for example, often have passes allowing their own ratepayers free or concessional-rate access to heritage properties, museums, or even beachfront car parks under their control, on the basis that ratepayers are already contributing to the upkeep costs. In other cases, and especially when commercial management is involved, everyone pays according to actual usage. It ultimately depends on whether heritage is seen as an essential part of community life or an added extra, yet another contentious political issue.

A more difficult and more general problem arises when comparative social and economic deprivation is considered. If entry and other charges are set at a level that is too high, poorer people and those with large families may be prevented from accessing heritage items. Perceived over-charging may also result in the decline of total visitor numbers, thus adversely affecting the revenue stream that is supposedly being encouraged. On the other hand, if charges are set too low, they will make less than the desired contribution to the financing of heritage management. To some extent, concessional charges can help here, but probably only in the most extreme cases. Perhaps it should be left to the redistributive aspects of the taxation and welfare systems to ensure that all people can enjoy their heritage.

Commercial uses of heritage sites

There are many examples of commercial activity in national parks and other natural heritage reserves (Plate 3.3), and at cultural heritage sites. Most often these are directed at visitors, and include provision of accommodation, food, souvenirs, and local arts and crafts, as well as

Plate 3.3

Commercial marina operation at Akuna Bay, within the Ku-ring-gai Chase National Park, on the Hawkesbury River and its tributaries north of Sydney, NSW.

Photo: Graeme Aplin

offering a wide variety of activities. Activities can range from the educational (for example, guided walks) to the ultra-adventurous (for example, canyoning or bungy-jumping). They may also involve varying degrees of entertainment, as opposed to education (see also Chapter 2). The direct earnings, if these accrue to site management, or the rent, concession, and other charges levied on private operators can bring valuable extra income, which can then be spent on heritage management. There is, however, the very real danger of detracting from the very heritage values that one is attempting to preserve. Appropriateness, the degree of intrusion and erosion of values, and the impact on other visitors must all be considered.

Different issues arise when considering commercial activities that are unrelated to visitors. In some natural heritage areas, it may be possible to continue to carry out commercial activities such as mining, fishing, timber-cutting, and farming in sections of the area, without adversely affecting either the heritage values or visitor satisfaction—unlikely, perhaps, but possible in limited circumstances, and invariably a political 'hot potato'. The resultant income stream will, of course, be valuable. However, it must be remembered that it is much easier to place a monetary value on minerals or timber than on scenery or biodiversity, and the costs and benefits of all terms in the equation need to be taken into account. Similarly, cultural heritage sites may sometimes be able to sustain other uses even when open to the public; the question of adaptive re-use of heritage buildings is discussed in Sections 4.1 and 6.8.

3.7   Tourism, recreation, and heritage

We have already made extensive mention of visitors to heritage sites, and have alluded to the fact that many of these come from outside the local area. Tourism generally has become increasingly important, both internationally and domestically (Table 3.1). People generally, but especially in the higher-income nations of the world, are more able to afford to travel; they have more leisure time and longer retirement periods; and technical advances in transport make wider travel possible, even for the less adventurous. There is also a much greater awareness of other places, other cultures, and other people's heritage through books, television, and electronic media. A lot of effort is put into advertising tourist destinations, often at least in part on the basis of the natural and cultural heritage they have to share with visitors.

It is not only tourism on the national and international scales that impacts on heritage. Local people also visit natural or cultural heritage sites for the purpose of recreation; people can enjoy a short break that combines education and entertainment with, in many cases, a chance to connect with a group ethos through shared heritage. Even with little or no outside tourism, local crowds can place enormous pressure on heritage sites and impose major management problems, especially during holiday and festival periods. When combined with foreign visitors, the pressures can be immense (Plate 3.4).

Table 3.1

Short-term overseas visitor arrivals in Australia for the 1990s and forecasts to 2008[*]

Year	Number of short-term overseas visitor arrivals	Year	Projected number of short-term overseas visitor arrivals
1991	2 370 371	2000	4 700 000
1992	2 603 268	2001	5 100 000
1993	2 996 334	2002	5 400 000
1994	3 361 721	2003	5 700 000
1995	3 725 825	2004	6 200 000
1996	4 164 825	2005	6 600 000
1997	4 317 870	2006	7 100 000
1998	4 167 206	2007	7 700 000
1999	4 459 503	2008	8 400 000

Note: [*] In the year ending July 2000, 56 per cent of arrivals stated that a holiday was their main reason for coming to Australia.

Some other figures:

Export earnings from tourism: A$12.8 billion (1997–98)

Total visitor expenditure: A$18.8 billion (1999, up 5.7 per cent on 1998)

Tourism as proportion of total export earnings: 12.2 per cent

Total nights away for domestic travel: 293 456 (1998, about half for pleasure/holiday)

Sources: Australia Bureau of Statistics and Australian Tourism Commission web sites: http://www.abs.gov.au and http://www.atc.net.au.

Plate 3.4

Tourists in the main courtyard outside the Château de Versailles (also known as the Palace of Versailles), in Yvelines Département, south of Paris, France. The Palace was started in 1678, and added to in the late 18th century. It is now open to the fee-paying public on a regular basis.

Photo: Margaret Dudgeon

Ecotourism, cultural tourism, and heritage tourism

Consideration of these three sub-types of tourism is relevant to our discussion. Increasingly, all types of heritage have been highlighted in tourist advertising material. Cultural tourism, in particular, has a long history, including the grand tours of Europe and beyond made by the English from at least the 17th century. It was only later that an appreciation of wilder, natural landscapes developed, and the mountain landscapes of the Alps featured alongside the historic cities.

Ecotourism is portrayed, with much justification, as an environmentally friendly form of tourism, concentrating on natural landscapes, but often including a cultural element—especially that of indigenous peoples. It is generally low-key, energy efficient (as far as travel can be), ecologically sound, and educationally oriented. As with any form of business or any profession, there are some bad apples in the barrel. So both the industry itself and many governments have set standards and put in place regulatory frameworks and an example is given in Box 3.4. The very best ecotourism ventures give visitors a low-key, relatively authentic experience of natural landscapes and, often, of indigenous peoples and their cultures. They also help develop a knowledge and appreciation of, and a feeling for, particular ecosystems or landscapes, and for the environment, ecology, and other cultures in general. However, ecotourism is not welcomed in every situation, as the benefits do not always outweigh the costs. The introduction of visitors will inevitably have some effect on a heritage site, so such impacts need to be very carefully considered in each case.

Box 3.4　The Code of Environmental Practice of the Australian Tourism Industry Association

Because Australia's unique resources are key assets to the tourism industry, the Australian Tourism Association affirms the following code of environmental practice:

Philosophy

1　To recognise both development and conservation as important and valuable expressions of human utilisation of the environment.
2　To recognise tourism as legitimate and valuable resource utilisation.
3　To work towards an improved understanding of the allocation process of land and other resources and establish uniform environmental policy guidelines for the tourism industry.
4　To support local, regional and national planning concepts and participate in the associated processes.
5　To work towards the highest level of professionalism in the industry.

Assessment

1　To develop an appreciation of the land and an understanding of its capabilities to support alternative uses in order to establish a basis for environmentally sustainable activities.
2　To ensure assessment processes recognise individual and cumulative implications of each activity.
3　To establish and apply methods to enhance beneficial and minimise adverse effects on the environment.
4　To assess actual and potential effects on the environment from individual tourist development and use which may positively or negatively affect aspects of the environment.

Protection

In cooperation with relevant agencies help:

1　To review private sector tourism infrastructure environmental management and modify such management where necessary.
2　To contribute towards protection and management of those irreplaceable segments of the natural and created environment on which the industry relies and to review and modify protection management activities where necessary.
3　To protect and preserve existing habitat, flora and fauna and natural and cultural areas of local, national or international significance directly related to and involved with tourism development and use.

Responsibility

1 To accept responsibility for the enterprise-related environmental impacts of tourism development, operation and use and to undertake responsible corrective and remedial action where necessary.
2 To ensure that natural ecosystems are not used beyond their sustainable capability by the activities of the tourism industry.
3 To take account, where appropriate, of environmental policies and codes of environmental practice in developing tourism proposals, including the incorporation of such policies and codes in contract documents.
4 To cooperate with relevant authorities and communities in order to integrate environmental requirements into tourism management and land use processes.

Information

1 To incorporate environmental policy and codes of environmental practice within tourism training programs.
2 To ensure all involved in tourism, both directly and indirectly, have the opportunity to develop a sound knowledge of the natural resources and environmental principles associated with a sustainable tourism industry.
3 To support the inclusion of conservation principles in education, training and planning for tourism.
4 To enhance visitors' appreciation and understanding of their surroundings within the conservation objectives for the area.

Public interest

1 To consider the value of other legitimate developments and utilisations and respect those values in making decisions for tourism development and utilisation.
2 To participate in and facilitate positive discussions on tourism related land utilisation issues.

Source: Australian Tourism Industry Association, 1990.

Cultural tourism can take many forms, ranging from giving tourists experiences in relatively authentic village settings in cultures and ethnic minority or indigenous groups relatively untouched by modern lifestyles, to 'high-culture' tours of Renaissance palaces and the world's top concert halls. The use of the word 'relatively' twice in the first part of the preceding sentence is quite intentional. As soon as such groups start welcoming tourists, they are inevitably changed. People do seem to be much more interested in other cultures now than in the past. At least some tourists are keen to actually experience them, too, rather than just read about them or see them in television documentaries, even if a fair degree of discomfort and inconvenience is involved. However, any such tourist ventures need to be extremely careful to take into account the cultural sensitivities of the hosts, and should be run and managed by the local people as much as possible (see Sections 7.4 and 7.5).

Heritage tourism is often taken to be somewhat similar to cultural tourism. In many people's minds it is based on cultural heritage, particularly historic buildings and sites of historical events or those associated with the rich and famous. Of course, the heritage of the poor and not so famous is also important, and can be part of a type of tourism that combines cultural and heritage elements; guided tours of the Black township of Soweto, South Africa, are one example. Heritage tourism can also include natural heritage sites; for example, a heritage tour could be built around a nation's natural World Heritage sites (see Chapters 8, 9, 11, and 12).

The 'pros' and 'cons' of tourism

Tourist income can be an important source of funding for heritage management, yet there are dangers arising from tourist and recreational use of heritage. Tourist uses can damage heritage sites in any number of ways and may ultimately lead to what is sometimes known as the 'loving heritage to death' syndrome (Table 3.2). However, it can also bring benefits to particular heritage sites as well as to local and national economies (see Table 3.1). But the fact is that an excess of visitors, even if they are extremely well behaved and exceptionally well managed, can simply constitute too much pressure for a heritage site to bear without irreparable damage or (at an earlier stage) without changing the atmosphere of the site so much that it destroys the ambience that attracted people in the first place. A visit to the Sistine Chapel in Rome, even though it was out of 'high season', was largely spoilt for me by the chapel being literally filled wall-to-wall with tourists, most of whom seemed intent on talking (or oohing and aahing) very loudly. It is difficult to strike the right balance between attracting and catering for visitors, on the one hand, and making sure reasonable capacities are not exceeded, on the other.

Table 3.2

Conflict between conservation and recreation and tourism

	Pressures created by tourism on natural and cultural heritage	
	Negative	*Positive*
Pressures on place	Disruption of ecosystems	Revegetation programs
	Pollution	Protection of wildlife
	Waste disposal problems	Development and implementation of management plans based on zoning
	Graffiti and vandalism	
	Collection of souvenirs	
Pressures on values and meanings	Overcrowding/over-pricing of host community facilities	Sharing and increased understanding of other cultures
	Invasion of privacy	Renewed cultural activity
	Privatisation of public space	Stimulus to art and craft activities
	Loss of access to traditional land	Promotion of the conservation ethic
	Debasement, commodification, and exploitation of culture	Re-invigoration of communities with a knowledge of traditional skills and values
	Rapid changes in traditional lifestyle	

Source: State of the Environment Advisory Council (1996) *Australia: State of the Environment 1996*, CSIRO Publishing, Melbourne, Table 9.15, pp. 9–32.

There also needs to be effective cooperation between those in the tourist industry and those in the heritage field. Greater awareness of the issues at stake at heritage sites on the part of tourist operators, bus drivers, guides, and everyone else involved is essential. Accurate information needs to be conveyed to visitors, too. Tourist operators can play an important role in the interpretation effort (see Chapter 2) by preparing visitors before they reach the site. They can also be an important heritage management tool by requesting visitors in advance to take action to help protect the sites, as well as ensuring the visitors' own safety. If operators are insensitive and unhelpful, they will undo heritage management's best efforts. The accreditation schemes for guides already mentioned are helpful in this context.

Tourism can be sensitive to the local community and to local environments, but it can also, of course, be the exact opposite. Table 3.3 summarises the approaches of what are often termed 'hard' tourism and 'soft' tourism. 'Soft tourism' is much more sensitive, more conservation-minded, and more likely to be sustainable in the medium- to long-term. It is less overtly exploitative of local people, local ecosystems, and heritage. Many groups in the tourism industry are now keenly aware of the need to cooperate with those caring for the environment and heritage, and to ideally become carers themselves. They do, after all, depend to a major extent on the environmental and heritage resources for their continuing business. One example of an attempt to incorporate some of these factors into tourism was given in Box 3.4, the Code of Environmental Practice of the Australian Tourism Industry Association. Heritage can be viewed for present purposes as part of the 'environment' addressed in that document.

Table 3.3

'Hard' and 'soft' tourism development strategies

	Hard strategies	Soft strategies
1	Development without planning	Planning before development
2	Project-thinking	Concept-thinking
3	Each community plans for itself	Centralised planning for larger areas
4	Indiscriminate development	Concentrate development on particular areas
5	Haphazard and scattered building	Conserve land, build in concentration, keep open spaces
6	Exploit especially valuable landscapes particularly intensively	Conserve especially valuable landscapes (reserves)
7	Create new building-stock. Build new bedspaces.	Improve use of existing building-stock. Exploit existing bedspaces.
8	Build for indefinite demand	Fix limits on expansion
9	Develop tourism in all areas	Develop tourism only in suitable areas and where local population available

	Hard strategies	Soft strategies
10	Tourism development left to outside	Opportunity for decision-making concerns and participation by local population
11	Utilise all available labour (also outsiders)	Development planned according to indigenous labour potential
12	Consider only economic advantages	Weigh up all economic, ecological, and social advantages and disadvantages (cost benefits)
13	Regard farming population only as tourist labour	Preserve and encourage agricultural landowners
14	Leave social costs to be paid by society	Leave costs to be paid by perpetrators
15	Favour private transport	Encourage public transport
16	Provide facilities for maximum demand	Provide facilities for average demand
17	Remove natural obstacles	Preserve natural obstacles
18	Urban architecture	Local architecture (building design and materials)
19	General automation of tourist resorts	Selective technical development, encouragement of non-technical tourism forms

Source: after J. Krippendorf (1982) 'Towards new tourism policies: the importance of environmental and sociocultural factors', *Tourism Management* 3, pp. 135–48.

3.8   Marketing heritage

Finally, if heritage is to be commodified and commercialised, this involves marketing it to the public, including both local people and tourists from further afield, perhaps from other countries.

Section 2.4 introduced visitor surveys as a requirement for good, targeted interpretation and presentation. Such surveys are also essential for good, targeted marketing campaigns. They also allow experiences and management strategies to be constructed to suit the market or markets most likely to generate visitors. At the same time, however, it must be borne in mind that some sites of general community importance should really be targeted at all segments of the population. And, finally, any marketing campaign should take into account the conservation and preservation requirements and visitor capacities of sites as well as the financial possibilities.

Further Reading

Allcock, A. *et al.* (1994) *National Ecotourism Strategy*, Australian Government Publishing Service, Canberra.

Australian Heritage Commission (2001) *Successful Tourism at Heritage Places: A Guide for Tourism Operators, Heritage Managers and Communities*, AHC, Canberra.

Ceballos-Lascaurain, H. (1996) *Tourism, Ecotourism and Protected Areas*, IUCN—The World Conservation Union, Gland, Switzerland.

DCITA Department of Communications, Information Technology and the Arts (1999) *Tourism with Integrity: Best Practice Strategies for Cultural and Heritage Organisations in the Tourism Industry*, Canberra.

Driml, S. & Common, M. (1995) 'Economic and financial benefits of tourism in major protected areas', *Australian Journal of Environmental Management* Vol. 2, pp. 19–29.

Freeman, A. M. (1993) *The Measurement of Environmental and Resource Values: Theory and Methods*, Wiley, London.

Gale, F. & Jacobs, J. M. (1987) *Tourists and the National Estate: Procedures to Protect Australia's Heritage*, AHC Special Australian Heritage Publication Series No. 6, Australian Government Publishing Service, Canberra.

Hall, C. M. & McArthur, S. (eds) (1996) *Heritage Management in Australia and New Zealand: The Human Dimension*, Oxford University Press, Melbourne, selected chapters.

Hatch, D. (1998) 'Understanding the Australian nature based tourism market', in Ecotourism Association of Australia *Australia's Ecotourism Industry: A Snapshot in 1998*, EAA, Brisbane.

Johnston, C. (1992) *What is Social Value? A discussion paper*, Australian Government Publishing Service, Canberra.

Lockwood, M. & Tracy, L. (1995) 'A contingent valuation survey and benefit cost analysis of forest preservation in East Gippsland, Australia', *Journal of Environmental Management* 38, pp. 233–43.

Orbasli, A. (2000) *Tourists in Historic Towns: Urban Conservation and Heritage Management*, E. & F. N. Spon, New York.

Read Sturgess & Associates (1999) *Economic Assessment of Recreational Values of Victorian Parks*, Read Sturgess & Assoc., Melbourne.

Wahab, S. & Pigram, J. J. (eds) (1997) *Tourism, Development and Growth: The Challenge of Sustainability*, Routledge, London, especially Part IV.

Young, M. D. *et al.* (1996) *Reimbursing the Future: An Evaluation of Motivational, Voluntary, Price-based, Property Right and Regulatory Incentives for the Conservation of Biodiversity*, Department of the Environment, Sport and Territories, Canberra.

CHAPTER 4

Some General Principles of Conservation and Management

This chapter deals with principles that apply broadly across all types of heritage. Some follow directly from the two preceding chapters, while many are dealt with further in later chapters, especially in Chapters 5 to 7, where more specific applications to particular forms of heritage are discussed.

4.1   Definitions

It is appropriate to firstly discuss definitions of some key terms. While the particular definitions quoted are taken from the *Burra Charter*, Australia's guide to built heritage protection (see below), they can be applied, with adaptation where appropriate, to all forms of heritage. Commentaries on the Burra Charter definitions attempt to provide such a broadening of coverage. All definitions are taken from Article 1 of the Charter. The first three definitions set the scene for the crucial concepts that follow, and are given here as they are basic terms used in later definitions. Further discussion of the Burra Charter is left to Section 6.7, while the *Australian National Heritage Charter* (ANHC) and its slightly different definitions relating to natural heritage sites are dealt with in Section 5.8.

Place

> **place**—site, area, building or other work, group of buildings or other works together with pertinent contents and surroundings.

This definition is simply establishing the generality of the term and, in the process, alluding to the wide variety of 'things' that can fall under the heritage banner. To encompass natural heritage, too, this definition would need to be extended to more obviously include landforms (for example, wetlands or beaches) and ecosystems, which are hidden in the non-specific terms 'site' and 'area' in the definition given above.

It is of general importance to note the inclusion of *contents* and *surroundings* in the definition of 'place'. The heritage values of historic buildings frequently encompass their interiors along with fittings, furnishings, and other items relating to previous occupancy and use (Plate 4.1). Similarly, natural heritage sites encompass the whole complexity of their physical make-up and ecosystems even if their main aim is, for example, to protect one or two endangered species, or a unique geological feature. Furthermore, every site, natural or cultural, exists in a given spatial or environmental context, and that context is often important to the integrity of the site. In the case of cultural heritage, the surrounding area is commonly referred to as the *curtilage* of a building, a concept dealt with at greater length in Section 6.4. With natural heritage sites, the surrounds are often incorporated by making the boundaries of a reserve larger than strictly required in order to encompass the feature of primary concern, be it a water body, rock outcrop, or specific vegetation assemblage. In other cases, zoning within a reserve (see Section 5.6) or cooperation with surrounding landowners may achieve a similar outcome. In most cases the surroundings are important for reasons of aesthetic and visual integrity, as well as for the protection of key heritage items from off-site influences and processes damaging to their heritage values.

Plate 4.1

Room with period furnishings in the Georgian-style Treaty House, Waitangi, Northland, New Zealand (see also Plate 4.2). The house was built as a home for the British Resident, 1832–40; the Treaty of Waitangi was signed there in 1840. The house was in poor repair in 1932 when it was purchased by the Governor-General and presented to the nation. Note the relatively unobtrusive rope barrier in the foreground to gently, but effectively, keep visitors away from the furniture.

Photo: Graeme Aplin

(Cultural) Significance

> **cultural significance**—aesthetic, historic, scientific or social value for past, present or future generations.

This definition can be easily modified to encompass natural significance, chiefly by emphasising the aesthetic (scenic) and scientific components more than the others. Nevertheless, it is important to remember that purely 'natural' sites can also have historic and social significance through associations with people or events, and that the majority of natural heritage sites also encompass at least some cultural heritage. The general process of establishing significance is discussed in Sections 1.5 and 4.2, and cultural heritage applications are specifically discussed in Sections 6.2 and 6.3.

Fabric

> **fabric**—all the physical material of the place.

This definition is largely self-explanatory. In the case of buildings, it includes physical components such as walls and roofs and the specific materials from which they are built and the ways in which those materials have been used (Plate 4.2). In other words, a wall is not simply any old wall, but a very particular wall, the integrity of which must be maintained. In natural heritage areas, all aspects of an environment or ecosystem could be included within the term 'fabric'; hence objects such as rocks and fallen tree branches are an integral part of the site (Plate 4.3), even though they may seem expendable and exploitable to some. The particular assemblage of flora and fauna, their relative spatial placements, and the interactions between them are all crucial to the integrity of the site.

Conservation

> **conservation**—all the processes of looking after a place so as to retain its cultural significance … includes maintenance and may according to circumstance include preservation, restoration, reconstruction and adaptation … commonly a combination of more than one of these.

Conservation is the most inclusive of this group of process terms and may include some or all of the other processes. Conservation is the overall process of caring for the natural and/or cultural significance of a place so as to retain that significance. If heritage sites are not adequately cared for—conserved—they can easily lose their significance as building fabric deteriorates or weeds invade a natural area. One important difference is that natural processes such as the siltation of water bodies or the occurrence of wildfires may seemingly detract from the values of a natural site, but are frequently allowed to run their course because they are natural processes, and hence form part of the natural heritage values (Plate 4.4; see Chapter 5

Plate 4.2

Treaty House, Waitangi, New Zealand, where a section of a rear interior wall was left uncovered after restoration to show the lathe and plaster construction technique (see also Plate 4.1).

Photo: Graeme Aplin

Plate 4.3

Forest-floor debris in a moist section of Bulahdelah State Forest, Mid-North coast, NSW. The fallen vegetation decomposes and the nutrients it contains are recycled. Many species of flora and fauna also live amongst and beneath the litter. The ecology of a forest like this one would be upset if litter, rocks, or logs were removed.

Photo: Graeme Aplin

Plate 4.4

Mirror Lake, Yosemite National Park, California, has been gradually filling in with silt since this photograph was taken in 1981 and has been in the process of becoming a meadow. This process has been allowed to proceed because it is 'natural'. Half Dome can be seen on the right.

Photo: Graeme Aplin

for further discussion and examples). Cultural heritage, on the other hand, is usually protected from the 'natural' ravages of time, and fabric is specifically maintained and, if necessary, even replaced (see Chapter 6). Maintaining significance may also, in some cases, necessitate keeping surrounding areas or curtilages intact, and may require continuing present uses where the significance lies as much, or more, in use and association than in the physical fabric.

Maintenance

> **maintenance**—the continuous protective care of the fabric, contents and setting of a place ... to be distinguished from repair which involves restoration or reconstruction.

As hinted at in the previous paragraph, maintenance or 'protective care' is a necessary, positive process to help maintain significance. It does, crucially, involve maintaining fabric, not repairing, restoring, or replacing it (see subsequent definitions). Examples from historic buildings are fairly obvious, including painting, cleaning out roof guttering, and weeding gardens. In the natural heritage context, many maintenance activities are oriented towards maintaining visitor facilities such as tracks, rather than maintaining the natural environment itself, which is largely self-maintaining and natural processes are allowed to operate as unhindered as possible. Maintenance beyond the human-imposed facilities and structures is likely to be limited to removing or preventing intrusion of a nature that is not natural at that site, such as controlling exotic flora and fauna, or trapping silt entering the site's stream system. Natural siltation, however, would normally be allowed to continue (Plate 4.4).

Preservation

> **preservation**—maintaining the fabric of a place in its existing state and retarding deterioration.

Preservation is very closely allied to maintenance, but may involve more comprehensive works and programs directed at not only maintaining the fabric, but actively mitigating damage to it. In the case of buildings and other cultural sites, it usually involves slowing or even halting processes of deterioration, but not reversing previous deterioration (which would be considered to be restoration, as discussed below). For example, in the realm of moveable heritage, valuable manuscripts or paintings are often kept in glass cases with climate-controlled conditions to preserve them. On the other hand, when they are thoroughly cleaned and, perhaps, new paint is added to paintings, this becomes restoration. Preservation of either cultural or natural sites may include closing them to public access if their fragility demands it, or at least tightly controlling access. There is much controversy in the heritage community as to the amount of active preservation (and, even more controversially, restoration) that should be undertaken. Does, for example, an actively preserved site become unauthentic? It is usually agreed that intervention should be kept to a minimum, but how should 'minimum' be defined?

Restoration

> **restoration**—restoring the EXISTING fabric of a place to a known earlier state by removing accretions or by reassembling existing components without the introduction of new material.

The definition above is an extremely narrow definition of restoration, as a limited amount of new, but appropriate and authentic, material usually needs to be introduced, at least in most cultural heritage restoration projects (Plate 4.5). Commonly 'restoration' has a broader meaning than that given by the Burra Charter and there is a continuum between maintenance, strict restoration as defined above, more broadly defined restoration, and major reconstruction projects. Again, if all the stone required for a ceremonial arch is still on site, but in a collapsed pile, rebuilding of the arch would seem to be restoration rather than reconstruction, even though it would certainly require new cement or mortar. The difference is in the type and quantity of new material; perhaps cement, plaster, nails, and so on are permissible, but not newly quarried stone or newly milled timber. Restoration of natural sites may involve weeding, elimination of feral animals, removal of structures with no heritage or management value, and possibly revegetation of disused tracks or other disturbed areas, provided that seeds and plants from the site itself are used. Or is this last process one of reconstruction?

Plate 4.5

Restoration work on the Pont Neuf, over the River Seine, Paris, France (see also Plate 1.9). Recently restored stonework can be seen on the left, while work is progressing further to the right. New stone is being used to replace that which is too eroded to restore.

Photo: Graeme Aplin

Reconstruction

> **reconstruction**—returning a place as nearly as possible to a known earlier state … distinguished by the introduction of materials (new or old) into the fabric … not to be confused with either re-creation or conjectural reconstruction.

Reconstruction involves partial or, occasionally, complete rebuilding of a heritage building or other structure on the basis of firm evidence of its previous state. Such evidence can be drawn from documents, plans, photographs, other similar extant buildings, and oral histories. There should not be any conjecture or guess-work involved, nor any adaptations to tell a 'better' story or appeal more to visitors. Reconstruction is still firmly within the bounds of heritage practitioners, not theme-park builders. Occasionally, reconstruction on another site may be necessary, but this should be a last resort, only used if there is no way of saving a significant structure on site. Re-creations and conjectural reconstructions are not really part of heritage practice at all, but may serve valid educational and entertainment purposes. If they purport to be educational, they, too, should be based as firmly as possible on sound evidence. The Shakespearean Globe Theatre (Plate 4.6) is an example of a conjectural reconstruction. The original theatre was built in 1599 and it burned down in 1613. It was rebuilt in 1614, then demolished in 1644 after being closed by the Puritans in 1642. It has now been reconstructed close to its original site. As well as the semi-outdoor theatre, the 'Elizabethan' complex includes an indoor theatre for winter use, a pub, and an exhibition hall.

Plate 4.6

Reconstructed replica of the original Shakespearean Globe Theatre on the South Bank of the Thames, London.

Photo: Margaret Dudgeon

Adaptation and compatible uses

adaptation—modifying a place to suit proposed compatible uses.

compatible use—a use which involves no change to the culturally significant fabric, changes which are substantially reversible, or changes which require a minimal impact.

Sometimes the best, or the only, way to preserve a site is to adapt it for another use. The definition of *compatible use* concentrates on the *significant fabric*, requiring that there be no change, changes that are substantially reversible, or changes with minimal impact. Changes that are substantially reversible for a gracious home adapted for a restaurant might include using false ceilings to lower the ceiling height and hide necessary electrical wiring and air-conditioning ducts while retaining and protecting the original decorative ceiling. At times, the only feasible way of saving a building in a financially acceptable manner (see Section 3.6) may be to go beyond the spirit and the letter of this definition. The exterior of a historic building may be saved, or its role in an important streetscape assured, even if the interior is substantially altered to allow a new use. Again, ends may justify less than ideal means. It ultimately depends on a complex combination of factors, not the least of which is the nature and strength of the heritage significance of the site.

It is more difficult to find examples of adaptation and compatible uses for natural sites. Perhaps limited water sports uses may be possible on a water body if such use is needed to justify its retention and help finance its management. Nature reserves may be able to be partially opened for tourist and recreation uses (see Section 5.9), or even leased to private operators in these areas. Even commercial exploitation of certain naturally occurring products might be possible under strictly determined and imposed conditions. Many areas designated as national parks host a wide range of uses, although managing authorities often have trouble accepting prior and continuing uses such as quarrying and military exercises as compatible with their primary aims of nature and landscape protection (see Boxes 11.3 and 11.5).

4.2   Identifying and documenting heritage values

Conservation and the other more specific processes defined above all rely on comprehensive documentation of the heritage sites concerned. Central to any documentation is a statement of significance, which essentially gives the justification and reasons for conserving a site (for some examples see Box 1.5). It should also clearly state the specific heritage values ascribed to the site, which will, in turn, inform decision-making about the site's management. The statement of significance outlines the goals and the outcomes expected from conservation efforts. Section 1.5 introduces the main criteria for heritage value, and later chapters provide more specific examples of both individual listing statements and official requirements.

When researching a site with potential for heritage listing, or when building a knowledge base upon which to develop conservation and management plans, as many sources as possible should be consulted. This is especially true for historic buildings and other cultural heritage items, because different sources may give different information. It is desirable to cross-check sources as much as possible. Scientific studies of natural sites, on the other hand, may not require cross-checking, as long as the studies have been well planned and carried out. Nevertheless, the goal should be to collate the most reliable and comprehensive database possible, allowing for practical limitations and the law of diminishing returns. It is ultimately up to heritage professionals, including those involved in decisions, to list and to approve plans, to judge the adequacy of the information base and whether or not further studies are warranted.

Suggestions for items to be listed can come from individuals or community organisations. They may be one-off, *ad hoc* submissions, or they may be the result of an organised and structured heritage survey of an area, or type of object (for example, a survey of all post offices in a state). Public input does not stop there, however, as new information can arise at any stage, before or after listing. The public should also be involved in commenting on, and having meaningful input to, conservation and management plans (see Section 4.8 for further comment on this issue). Listing proposals often have a difficult passage through many committees and other bodies before receiving approval, so they need to be well prepared, and backed by sound, comprehensive sources. Above all, they need to have statements of significance that are carefully worded and persuasive, but still accurate.

4.3   Published guidelines for managing heritage

A number of commonly accepted sets of guidelines for conserving and managing heritage exist at various levels, from UNESCO World Heritage guidelines (see Section 8.3) to local council policy documents (see Section 10.2 and elsewhere in Chapters 10 to 12). While the details of the types of guidelines available vary between jurisdictions, there are certain common elements. Non-legislative examples in the natural heritage area that are dealt with at some length in later chapters include the ANHC (see Section 5.8 and Figure 5.5) and management guidelines of the NSW National Parks and Wildlife Service (NPWS; see Section 10.2). Examples from the cultural heritage area include the Burra Charter and a set of conservation plan guidelines originating from the National Trust of Australia (NSW) (see Figure 6.2). Internationally agreed guidelines that are widely used have been published by the International Council on Monuments and Sites (ICOMOS) secretariat (as the *International Charter for the Conservation and Restoration of Monuments and Sites* agreed to in Venice in 1966, and also referred to as the Venice Charter or ICOMOS Charter) and, for the natural environment, by the International Union for the Conservation of Nature and Natural Resources (IUCN; see Box 5.3). The full title of the Burra Charter is the *Australian ICOMOS Charter for the Conservation of Places of Cultural Significance*, a local adaptation of the international guidelines. The ANHC is derived from both the Burra Charter and IUCN guidelines. Reference will also be made to relevant legislation from many jurisdictions, especially in Chapters 9 to 12.

Thus, guidelines exist in many guises, all intended to assist heritage managers and owners of heritage sites. In addition to legislation and guidelines from the official government heritage bodies, such as the Heritage Council of NSW (see Section 10.2), and from voluntary bodies such as the National Trust (see Section 10.5), there are many published volumes of guidance for both public and private sector heritage managers, a few of which are included in the 'Further Reading' at the end of this chapter.

4.4   Heritage plans

It is of paramount importance that heritage managers have heritage plans. Frequently these are called either *conservation plans* or *management plans*, but in reality they are often a combination of the two. Conservation plans are most relevant in the early stages of the recognition of a heritage site, and after recognition, when the more active aspects of conservation, such as restoration, reconstruction, and adaptation, are being undertaken. They may also be needed when particular buildings or sub-sections of large natural sites are being conserved. As such, the conservation plan may be a section of a larger management plan, or a separate document referred to in the management plan. Management plans are usually concerned with the maintenance and preservation of heritage values, rather than the restoration, recon-struction, or adaptation. Management plans may also describe budgets, marketing, visitor management, and many aspects of day-to-day management practices and strategies.

4.5   Who manages, and for whom?

Managers of heritage sites are, in a real sense, managing their sites for present and future generations in the relevant community or group. The extent to which a site is managed for a particular group depends on the scale and group-specificity of the site's identification and statement of significance. For example, a site may be managed first and foremost for a local Aboriginal community because it primarily represents a part of the community's group heritage and because it is significant at a local level, but not necessarily at regional, state, national, or international levels. In other cases, a site may be managed for all Australians if the site has been deemed to be of national significance.

In reality, however, most managers are working for themselves as owners or lessees of heritage sites, or for government or non-government heritage bodies, or for commercial operators of commercialised heritage sites. This means that conflicts with the 'pure' heritage aspects of management can easily arise. The resolution of these conflicts may mean that legislation and the kinds of guidelines mentioned earlier play a key role. In other words, while we might like to think that managers are managing heritage sites to protect and preserve the heritage, that might be only one among a number of objectives, and it might even depend more or less on other objectives, such as earning enough income from the site to pay for the heritage protection. It is in this sense that managers often have to weigh up the aims of conservation (which often conflict themselves) with the provision of public access. Public access is important, not only as a potential money-making venture, but as a means of allowing people access to what is, in a sense, their heritage for educational, entertainment, and other reasons. Chapters 2 and 3 deal with various aspects of these dilemmas at some length.

4.6   Visitor management

On all but the most remote sites, heritage site management involves visitor management even if this simply means trying to prevent visitors from gaining access when and where they are prohibited. However most sites encourage visitors, but access may come at the cost of damage to the site from human impact and at the cost of a lessening of enjoyment and the value of visitors' experiences. There is a large literature dealing with visitor management, and a small sample is included in the 'Further Reading' given at the end of this chapter. Only the briefest of introductions is possible here, which is not in any sense to be taken as an indication of the importance I ascribe to this issue.

How can managers control visitors? In particular, how can visitor numbers be limited when necessary? One common method is to zone more extensive sites, especially national parks and similar natural reserves, by restricting all or most visitor activity to certain limited areas, while protecting others. A similar technique across a number of sites might be to 'sacrifice' some sites in order to preserve others. For example, one historic building of a particular type might be opened to the public while other similar buildings are not opened, or only in a more limited and controlled way (Plate 4.7). Perhaps the most common way of controlling visitor access to areas within a site is through a mixture of signs and structures. The signs can direct people along particular routes and direct their attention to particular features, while keeping them away from other areas. Other signs might expressly prohibit access to some areas or along some routes, although these will usually be more successful if some explanation for the prohibition is given, as discussed in Section 2.3. Physical structures, such as fences and moats, can also keep people in some areas and away from others. As well as protecting the site, signs and structures can also address safety and public enjoyment issues (Plate 4.8).

Plate 4.7

Northern side of Charlotte Square, built in the 1790s, in the New Town district of Edinburgh, Scotland. One terrace contains the offices of the National Trust for Scotland and next door a museum house called the Georgian House is operated by the Trust and furnished and repainted in original colours. The other terraces are tenanted.

Photo: Graeme Aplin

Plate 4.8

Signs warning of the crocodile danger and the management practices used to reduce the hazard, Kakadu National Park, Northern Territory.

Photo: Monica Green

As discussed in Chapter 3, there has been an increasing trend over recent years to charge entry fees to heritage sites. While this can also be a means of limiting visitor numbers, it may run counter to the desire and need to raise revenue from visitors. Managers need to balance the increased returns from higher charges with the possibility of losing too many potential customers. Where visitor numbers need to be rather severely restricted, or where visitor pressures are intense, systems of advanced booking and, if necessary, balloting for entry permits may be used. Both of these systems are used in some national parks and at some cultural heritage sites, more commonly overseas than in Australia. Batches of visitors may be admitted at set intervals, or the number of visitors exiting the site may be counted and a replacement number allowed to enter. The various means of limiting numbers may be seasonal in nature, and could even include periods when the site is closed altogether.

4.7   Private owners' rights and obligations

Private owners, lessees, and occupiers are important in two different ways. Firstly, they may have a management role in properties that are in private use or open to the public as heritage properties on a commercial basis. Such people may need assistance, including advice, on managing the heritage values of their properties. It may also be reasonable to pay them a subsidy or allow tax relief on the condition that they respect and manage heritage values and, perhaps, allow limited public access on an agreed basis where this is not otherwise available (see Section 3.5). Heritage bodies may have a role in overseeing a site and, while respecting the rights of the private sector, they must insist that the sector meets its heritage obligations. Similarly, lessees and franchise or licence holders operating in heritage sites have both rights and obligations; good cooperation between them and site management is crucial.

Private owners and occupiers may also be involved as neighbours to heritage sites, with relevant rights and obligations. Agreements are sometimes necessary for joint management of a 'buffer zone' around a heritage site to prevent unsympathetic development that detracts from the site's heritage values (normally administered through local planning regulations). In this case, some form of compensation may be appropriate. On the other hand, activities pursued on the heritage site, especially related to visitors at popular sites, must be managed in a way that respects the rights of neighbouring owners and occupiers to enjoyment of their properties. Factors that need to be taken into account could include risks of fire, pest species of flora and fauna, run-off, noise, traffic, and litter. Again, particular examples arise in later chapters. Cooperation on such matters, particularly if based on high-quality interpretation and public relations (see Chapter 2), helps build community support for heritage conservation generally, and specifically for local sites.

Finally, it needs to be recognised that heritage protection will ultimately only be successful on any reasonable scale if private owners are willing to preserve the heritage values of their own properties. Those involved in natural heritage management now recognise that off-reserve conservation is absolutely essential if biodiversity is to be preserved. The cooperation of private landowners is also necessary in areas such as catchment management and the control of salinity problems, although these topics are beyond the scope of this book. Similarly, cultural heritage items are preserved by private owners more often than by government agencies, especially in the cases of residential and commercial buildings, and when more extensive heritage precincts are delineated (see Section 6.4).

4.8   Management principles

Finally, it is worth listing some fundamental principles that should be applied in any heritage management situation. This is certainly not an all-inclusive list, nor is it a handbook of practice, and each item is only briefly introduced. Many are treated at greater length in the next three chapters in the context of particular types of heritage, and particular examples of management issues.

Information base

Any heritage decision, and certainly any conservation or management plan, must be based on the best possible information, gathered from a range of sources, wide enough to ensure accuracy and adequate coverage. Different sources used together will often help overcome inconsistencies or divergent views. Furthermore, a wide range of views from different groups in the community must be considered, not just the views of a dominant or powerful group. Original research should be carried out if necessary. Most importantly, this information base must include a clear statement of the significance of the heritage under consideration.

Goals and objectives

Goals and objectives need to be clearly stated from the beginning of any planning exercise, and should be related to the statement of significance; they give direction to the entire management process. Particular actions should then be devised to help meet the stated goals and attain the objectives. The goals and objectives also give concrete benchmarks against which to measure progress and assess outcomes.

Outcomes and evaluation

A series of expected outcomes should be listed, preferably in a way that allows for easy evaluation of success, though quantitative measures may not always be appropriate. A means of, and schedule for, evaluation of outcomes should also be included. It is crucial that the evaluation be carried out, and that a report be prepared and acted on. The evaluation and consequent report will be an important part of the database for the next plan, just as previous evaluation reports, if available, should have informed the present plan.

Flexibility and monitoring

As well as the major evaluation mentioned above, there should be ongoing evaluation of success. There should be inbuilt flexibility and adaptability to allow changes to methods and processes that are not working. Major external changes or new information may even warrant a change in one or more of the goals or objectives, although such fundamental changes should be approached with caution and only made after careful consideration. Ongoing monitoring also allows managers to take advantage of new opportunities that arise.

Awareness of societal context

Any heritage plan should be prepared on the basis of a sound awareness of the perceptions, goals, and expectations of the community and society in which the heritage item is situated. To some extent managers can lead public opinion on particular issues, but public support is lost if they run too far ahead. As we have seen in Chapter 1, heritage is society-specific and inherently political, as well as being founded on individual perceptions. Thus heritage management cannot be removed from the cultural and political milieu that communities and citizens share.

Building community support

Heritage plans will be most successful when they have community support. Hence, as well as being aware of the context (see previous paragraph), managers also need to take the public into account in practical ways, some of which have been mentioned earlier in this chapter. Interpretation (see Chapter 2) can be invaluable in engendering community support. Parts of Section 5.6 deal specifically with the need for natural reserve managers to work cooperatively with adjoining landowners.

Doing as little as possible

This may seem strange, but the best heritage plans are usually based on the assumption that managers should do as little as possible when it comes to actual conservation of heritage items. Major restoration, or drastic measures such as moving a building to a new site, are only appropriate when less intrusive methods are inadequate to preserve the key heritage values involved. Thus, simpler forms of conservation are preferred by many practitioners over strict preservation or restoration. Furthermore, much of the heritage value may be overlooked if attempts are made to halt or even reverse change, or if questions of originality loom too large, points discussed further in Chapter 6. However, even in the case of minimal conservation activity, major management efforts on other fronts may well still be required, in areas such as finances and visitor management.

Dealing with change

Change occurs naturally in the biophysical environment and most management plans now allow natural processes to proceed unhindered, even if present values such as scenic attractiveness are markedly altered as a result (see Plate 4.4). It is also important to consider the degree of change that should be expected or allowed to occur in cultural heritage contexts. Should heritage items be frozen in time when they have been subject to ongoing change in the past? Should they be returned to some prior state with subsequent changes and

Plate 4.9

The Piazza dei Miracoli, Pisa, Italy, with the Baptistry (left), Duomo or Cathedral (centre) and Leaning Tower (right). Given the world's long fascination with its lean, should the tower be straightened, if this were possible?

Photo: Graeme Aplin

additions removed or reversed (Plate 4.9)? Similar questions may need to be answered in natural heritage contexts, too, where the contested concepts of authenticity and originality are relevant (Section 6.6).

Balancing competing goals

Managing heritage almost inevitably implies many balancing exercises, weighing up the relative importance of competing goals, and giving priority to some over others, or reaching compromises. Results that fail to achieve any of the goals well are usually inadequate. It may be preferable to achieve some goals well and to leave others until the next planning period. In some cases this may not be possible and compromise is essential. In the dilemma of determining optimal visitor numbers, for example, large numbers might be desirable from the point of view of the budget, but may risk the site being 'loved to death'.

Managing visitor pressure

Like it or not, management is commonly as much about managing visitors as it is about managing heritage, and this is contrary to the instincts of many heritage managers. Visitor management thus needs to be built into the management plan. Chapter 2 treats interpretation and creating awareness of management needs, and Chapter 3 discusses entry fees and other charges. Chapters 5 to 7 deal with structures and some aspects of day-to-day, on-site visitor management as related to different types of heritage sites.

Funding and budgetary issues

Many heritage managers probably wish they did not have to worry about budgets and cash flows, but they do. A key issue in budgeting is to find ways of augmenting income without adversely affecting heritage values so that, ultimately, money is available to enhance those values. Many relevant factors have been discussed in Chapter 3.

4.9   Conclusion

Heritage does not manage itself. Even if the ultimate goal is to preserve an item exactly as it is, with no public access to it, positive management is still needed to protect it from undesirable change or irreversible damage. No heritage site, with the possible exception of one or two very isolated sub-Antarctic islands, exists in isolation from outside influences. In particular, human influences, intended or not, are felt by virtually all heritage sites. Overall management can often be equally, or even more, concerned with management of off-site activities, sometimes indirectly. Heritage management is certainly equally concerned with managing human behaviour as it is with managing a biophysical environment or a built structure. Furthermore, heritage management cannot be isolated from community philosophies and behaviours; these factors must be incorporated, even though this undoubtedly makes the manager's task more complex.

Further Reading

Australian Heritage Commission (1998) *Protecting Local Heritage Places: A Guide for Local Communities*, AHC, Canberra.

Hall, C. M. & McArthur, S. (eds) (1996) *Heritage Management in Australia and New Zealand: The Human Dimension*, Oxford University Press, Melbourne, selected chapters.

Pearson, M. & Sullivan, S. (1995) *Looking After Heritage Places: The Basics of Heritage Planning for Managers, Landowners and Administrators*, Melbourne University Press, Melbourne.

Press, T. *et al.* (eds) (1995) *Kakadu: Natural and Cultural Heritage and Management*, Australian Nature Conservation Agency/North Australia Research Unit, Darwin.

Whitehouse, J. F. (1993) *Managing Multiple Use in the Coastal Zone: A Review of the Great Barrier Reef Marine Park Authority*, Australian Government Publishing Service, Canberra.

Worboys, G. *et al.* (2001) *Protected Area Management: Principles and Practice*, Oxford University Press, Melbourne.

CHAPTER 5

Natural Heritage and Its Management

5.1 Natural heritage—an introduction

General comments

Earlier chapters, especially Chapter 1, have introduced the concept of heritage in a general sense. This chapter is concerned specifically with natural heritage—those parts or aspects of the natural or biophysical environment we consider so significant that they must be maintained for both present and future generations to enjoy. Examples of some of the principles introduced in Chapters 2 to 4 are also applied to natural heritage sites.

Once again the concept of scale is crucial. For example, a small wetland may be considered highly significant to a local community or for waterbirds in a local district, but not considered significant at a state, national or international scale. A small patch of remnant forest may be vital to preserve links with pre-clearing vegetation cover in a local area, but may be too small and isolated to play any practical role in the conservation of biodiversity. On the other hand, endangered species of either flora or fauna may exist only in one or more small, isolated areas of native vegetation, and saving those patches, minute in the wider scheme of things, may be the only way of saving the species from extinction. A small area of natural vegetation may thus have much broader, conceivably even global, significance for its heritage values.

It is crucial to reiterate the impossibility, in most cases, of separating natural heritage from cultural heritage, and certainly the impossibility of separating the very concept of natural heritage from community beliefs and perceptions about the environment. While it is theoretically possible to form objective definitions and make objective rules concerning the conservation of biodiversity, less objective human factors invariably come into play, as we shall see in later discussion. To conserve any heritage item—natural, cultural, or mixed—there must be political will and financial capability. Frequently a mix of natural and cultural values gives a place its heritage importance and leads to community support for its conservation. Even sites that are as entirely natural as possible are perceived as heritage sites on the basis of socially based conceptual constructs, as established in the discussions in Chapter 1.

World Heritage definitions

The full wording of the definitions in the World Heritage Convention and reasons for inscribing natural heritage sites are given in Section 8.3. The following section is a brief summary with added commentary, intended to illustrate the range and diversity of natural heritage sites. I have removed the repeated mention of 'universal values' present in the original, so that the descriptions and comments that follow can be applied at all levels, not just the global one.

Not surprisingly, natural heritage is concerned with 'natural features', which may be primarily physical (for example, geological formations or landforms) or biological (for example, ecosystems or plant communities), possessing aesthetic or scientific value. In other words, they may be considered significant not only because of their scientific value, for example, biodiversity conservation, but they may also be considered significant because they have scenic or other aesthetic values that have nothing to do with biophysical science. (The third point in the 'natural' part of Section 8.3 definitions mentions natural beauty as a form of significance.) Further, natural heritage areas may be significant specifically because they constitute the habitat of threatened species of animals or plants, which makes them important in terms of biodiversity conservation.

The natural properties that give an area its natural heritage status are wide-ranging. First, a natural heritage site may represent and illustrate major stages of the earth's history including the evolution of life; it may be an example of significant ongoing geological processes involved in the development of landforms; or it may contain significant geomorphic or physiographic features. Secondly, a natural heritage site may contain significant examples representing and illustrating ecological and biological processes involved in the evolution and development of particular types of ecosystems and communities. Thirdly, the list quite specifically refers to 'superlative natural phenomena or areas of exceptional natural beauty and aesthetic importance'. Finally, on a more practical note, natural heritage sites may be significant for their value as sites for *in situ* conservation of biological diversity and threatened species (Box 5.1).

Box 5.1   Wollemi pine

Australia has representatives from two genera within the Araucariaceae family. It had long been known that Australia had two species in the *Araucaria* genus: the hoop pine (*Araucaria cunninghamii*), ranging along the east coast from the Bellinger River in northern NSW to Cape York, and the bunya pine (*A. bidwillii*), limited to a small area of the ranges of southern Queensland. The Norfolk Island pine is also in this genus (*A. heterophylla*) and is planted as an ornamental tree in coastal areas, including suburban Sydney. There are also three species in the *Agathis* genus, *Agathis robusta*, known as Queensland kauri, and two other kauris, *A. microstachya* and *A. atropurpurea*. (The well-known New Zealand kauri is also in this genus.)

In 1994, much to the astonishment of both experts and the public, a third Australian genus was discovered by a ranger from the NPWS in a deep, secluded sandstone gorge in the Wollemi National Park, only some 120 km north-west of the centre of Sydney. The Wollemi pine, *Wollemia nobilis*, grows up to 40 m in height, and has bark and foliage quite unlike the other genera mentioned above. At that time, only one stand of about twenty mature trees and about the same number of saplings were thought to exist. Fossil leaves, twigs, and pollen all suggested that this tree was very closely related to ones of the Jurassic period, about 140 million years ago. Not surprisingly, the exact location was kept secret to protect it from unscrupulous collectors, and the tree was quickly protected by law.

Later, a second stand was found, bringing the total number to about 40 mature trees and 200 seedlings, and even more recently a third stand has been located. Helicopter and ground surveys seem to have ruled out any further discoveries of *Wollemia*. Park rangers, at times with the aid of helicopters, have harvested seeds and other material from the trees and a reasonably large number have been propagated by the Royal Botanic Gardens at Mt Annan, where some 500 trees were 'knee-high' by mid-1996, and, more recently, by a contracted Queensland horticultural firm. They will eventually be sold to gardeners in order to help preserve the species and to raise money to be reinvested in the NPWS's activities. Until then, all the trees are kept under lock and key. This 'living fossil' has also been colourfully dubbed a 'dinosaur tree'. The trees are now protected under the *Threatened Species Conservation Act 1995 (NSW)*, and a recovery plan was in preparation by late 1998 and had been approved by the Minister by the end of 1999.

The discovery of *Wollemia* has provided the impetus for further work in the Wollemi National Park and NPWS rangers and other scientists have collected 50 species, about one-third of them probably new to science. In the meantime, US researchers have examined frozen *Wollemia*, and have found two new fungi living within the tissue that produce taxol, a known anti-cancer chemical (previously only found in Northern Hemisphere yew trees). Tests are also underway on four potential new antibiotics derived from the tree.

Source: compiled from a range of media reports and web sites.

Plate 5.1

View over the wilderness areas of the Kanangra-Boyd National Park, NSW (see also Plate 2.4). This area is included in the Greater Blue Mountains World Heritage property, inscribed by the World Heritage Committee in November 2000 (see Box 8.2).

Photo: Graeme Aplin

5.2 Reasons for conserving ecosystems and landscapes

Overview

Many reasons for conserving and preserving ecosystems and landscapes have been alluded to in the previous section. The natural environment provides many services to humans, most of which are difficult to cost in standard economic terms, and hence are frequently omitted from policy analyses. Natural environments also hold many values for people, including non-use, intrinsic, and existence values. Ecosystems and landscapes are preserved for many reasons, ranging from the economic return expected from tourism because of beautiful views (Plate 5.1) or the possibility of experiencing unique Australian flora and fauna at close range, to an ill-defined, but strongly felt, belief that some natural environments should be left as free as possible from human impact because to do so is ethically and morally sound.

Three types of reasons for conserving natural areas are worthy of further consideration: the provision of environmental services; biodiversity conservation; and non-material values. The importance of these factors in relation to tourism will be discussed towards the end of this chapter.

Environmental services

Natural environments provide a range of environmental services that are valuable to human communities, and which are impossible, or extremely difficult and expensive, to replace. Because these services are natural and largely outside our market system, we tend to take them for granted and do not value them appropriately. While normally not considered to be heritage values, environmental services certainly fit the definition of items 'worth handing down to future generations'.

Natural environments play an important role in assimilating and effectively breaking down or neutralising water-borne and airborne pollutants. Wetlands, for example, both absorb pollutants and provide cleaner sources of water. Urban forests and other greenery help clean the air, cut down on dust, and reduce visual and noise pollution. Natural ecosystems can have an important local microclimatic effect, providing shade and shelter from winds. The effect of vegetation change on climate at larger scales is less certain, but there is some evidence that rainfall is reduced by clearing forests and woodlands, and, at the global level, forests—particularly tropical rainforests—play an important and complex role as carbon sinks. It is certainly well known that vegetation cover is a crucial factor in limiting erosion, and in controlling overland flows and reducing the magnitude of peaks and troughs by providing conditions conducive to infiltration. Wetlands are especially important as reservoirs that can absorb flood waters and later gradually release water to streams or ground-water reservoirs.

Biodiversity conservation

One of the most important reasons for preserving areas of natural or near-natural ecosystems is to preserve biodiversity. For a start, diverse ecosystems seem more capable of absorbing the shocks of major perturbations and using feedback loops to readjust to the state of ongoing (but not invariant) dynamic equilibrium.

Biodiversity (or biological diversity) refers to diversity among living things. Biodiversity is seen by many as an important component of our global heritage, and the significance of the concept is reflected in growing concern world-wide over loss of biodiversity. Reducing the rate of that decrease is, in fact, one of the key reasons for conserving natural heritage areas. Diversity can, of course, be measured at many different scales, from the local through the regional to the global, and at genetic, species, and ecosystem levels. It is valid to speak of genetic diversity within a species, as well as diversity among species, while diversity among ecosystems is a crucial element of overall biodiversity.

From an instrumentalist perspective, it is important to preserve biodiversity because we can use many species for food, medicine, industrial raw materials, and sundry other purposes. Part of our lack of knowledge of the biosphere is a lack of knowledge of potentially useful species. Despite recent scientific advances on a number of fronts, once a species is extinct there is not yet any proven, practical way of bringing it back. Furthermore, destroying habitats may well destroy unknown or unstudied species (see Box 5.1).

There are also non-instrumental reasons. Do we, as one species among millions, have the right to destroy other species, or to destroy or dramatically reduce genetic diversity within species? Do we have the right to deny indigenous people's access to traditional biotic resources? How vital is diversity to the healthy functioning of the earth-system? We do not know the answer to the last question, so it would be wise to follow the precautionary principle and preserve as much biodiversity as possible.

There has long been an implicit understanding of the need to preserve endangered species, although the focus has been mainly on large and newsworthy species such as the giant panda, the condor, whales, and the giant sequoia. Locally, small songbirds, butterflies, and even snails have been recognised as endangered species and protected by law and/or through habitat preservation. Despite such examples, humans have been very selective in their attempts to preserve biodiversity, and until recently have tended to conserve individual species, and not biodiversity in a holistic sense. However, there is now a more widespread realisation that all members of a natural community are important to the functioning of that community, not just the pretty or cuddly species. We now aim to preserve entire ecosystems, rather than just particular species in danger of extinction. For example, there are efforts to preserve the whole Great Barrier Reef, rather than individual species of fish, sea anemones, or corals. By preserving substantial, representative areas of major ecosystems we maximise the chances of species surviving.

Non-material values

While landscapes with major human modifications may fulfil many environmental service roles and provide worthwhile recreational and tourist experiences, they fail to provide reference points against which to judge human impact. Many individuals and societies seem to need a link with untrammelled nature. It might be going too far to speak of an inherited biological need, but many, perhaps most, people need to know that nature is still 'there' and hope to experience it from time to time to be refreshed and revitalised (see Plate 5.1). Natural landscapes are also a symbolic part of each nation's image and self-image; all nations include elements of the natural landscape among their places of heritage significance. They obviously also have an important role in more active recreation and in tourism. Finally, for many people natural ecosystems have existence values, a right to exist quite apart from any anthropocentric view of their value.

5.3   Protecting endangered species and ecosystems

Individual species can sometimes be kept alive in zoos and game reserves. For example, Przelski's horses have been bred at the Western Plains Zoo, in Dubbo (NSW), and taken back to their ancestral homelands in Mongolia and released with at least limited success in re-establishing the species there. Plant species can similarly be bred in artificial garden and arboretum surroundings, and gene lines from plants or animals can be preserved through seed and sperm banks. But the most natural and ultimately successful way of preserving species is through preservation of ecosystems.

Habitat destruction or degradation is the greatest single pressure on most endangered species. Habitat destruction does not have to be total to put a species at risk; the habitat may be so degraded that the complex community structure cannot survive and the particular niche occupied by an endangered species is changed irreversibly. Changes in the population sizes of other species, whether increases or decreases, can also seriously affect an endangered species. There can be a real 'domino' effect as the loss of one species results in the loss of another dependent on it. Alternatively, habitat may be reduced in area or diminished in quality so much that the population of a species falls to below its viable long-term survival level due to reduced chances of mating or pollination, or because of loss of genetic vigour in the population. Protecting key representative ecosystems not only preserves those ecosystems, but is the best way of conserving biodiversity and individual endangered species. The full value of an ecosystem goes well beyond its 'star' species, and includes bacteria, worms, fungi, and slime moulds. Quite apart from any other values they might have, these species are ultimately necessary for the preservation of the better-known species in their natural settings.

What should be preserved?

If we accept that it is best to preserve species in their natural habitats, then we need to address fundamental questions of how representative examples of environments and ecosystems can be protected. Biodiversity will not be adequately preserved if some biomes or, at a more localised scale, some ecosystem types, are not protected. A statistic showing the total area in reserves, or the proportion of the land surface in reserves nationally, means little—the composition of the total area in reserves is all-important.

Not all of the virtually infinite variety of ecosystems that exists in Australia, or in any other nation, can be included in a reserve system, but attempts can be made to include examples of all biomes and major ecosystem types. In Australia's case the goal could be to include ecosystem types in proportion to their presence before European settlement.[1] This was the aim of the system of Regional Forests Agreements agreed to in the 1990s for Australian forest ecosystems. The National Reserves System Cooperative Program, set up in 1992, aimed to establish a national database to help achieve a representative reservation system, and the Interim Biogeographic Regionalisation of Australia has since been developed, identifying eighty biogeographical regions. However, this broad-brush approach needs considerable refinement. Within each biome there are many different ecosystems, some of which can be recognised as major variants. The differentiating feature may be species composition, or soil type, or climate, or some combination of these and other factors. A representative sample of these major variants, at the very least, needs to be included in reserves.

Another approach, best used as a complement to the one above, is to look for areas where there is a combination of species under pressure. Together these two approaches may give the most efficient and cost-effective means of conserving a wide range of ecosystem types and of simultaneously preserving as many species as possible. Diversity at both species and community or ecosystem levels is important and the combined result maintains a high degree of biodiversity. This may appear to be sacrificing endangered species that do not fit into a system of reserves based on the principles espoused here. In a sense, it is, but we must remember that some extinctions are inevitable, and minimising that number, rather than eliminating extinctions altogether, is the only practical goal. However more focussed campaigns to save particular species deemed to be of great importance may still be warranted.

Geographical distribution of reserves

Ecosystem variations depend on climate, soils, and topography, each of which is highly spatially variable. If a wide range of ecosystem types is included in a reserves system, inevitably a wide geographical spread of reserves will be

Figure 5.1

Distribution of major vegetation types in NSW prior to European settlement

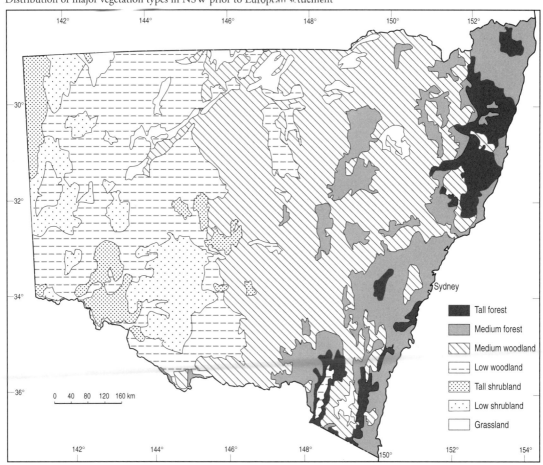

Source: after R.J Harriman & E.S. Clifford (eds), *Atlas of New South Wales*, Central Mapping Authority, Bathurst, 1987, p. 95.

required. This spread has rarely been achieved, and certainly not in Australia. For example, compare Figure 5.1, which maps pre-European-settlement vegetation types in NSW, with Figure 5.2, showing national parks and other major reserves. Here, as elsewhere, some types of ecosystems have been seen as more worthy of attention than others, resulting in a high proportional representation of forests (see Plate 5.1) and arid/semi-arid ecosystems in Australian reserves generally, and a very low level of representation of open woodlands and grasslands (Plate 5.2). Forests are seen as the archetype, primeval wilderness and fairly obviously have a high biomass, but not always a high degree of diversity. Arid and semi-arid areas are also seen as wilderness, though not in the same sense, and, in Australia, are somehow considered to be nationally symbolic, perhaps of human attempts to battle against environmental forces. Arid areas are also of low economic value, narrowly defined, and hence politically easy to place in reserves. Grasslands and woodlands fall between the two other types of ecosystems; not wilderness in either sense, apparently without a high degree of diversity, but economically valuable. Grasslands and woodlands are under-represented largely because they were almost all taken up for grazing or cropping in the early days of settlement, whereas many forested areas now in national parks began as reserves for timber production or protection of water catchments, and were available for conversion to conservation reserves. At the beginning of the new millennium, we are still losing large areas of scrubland and woodland to clearing at a great rate, especially in Queensland and, to a lesser extent, in NSW (Box 5.2).

Plate 5.2

Inland semi-arid scrubland, near King's Canyon, in Watarrka National Park, Northern Territory. The Park contains some 600 plant species.

Photo: Monica Green

Figure 5.2

Distribution of national parks and other major reserves, NSW, 2000

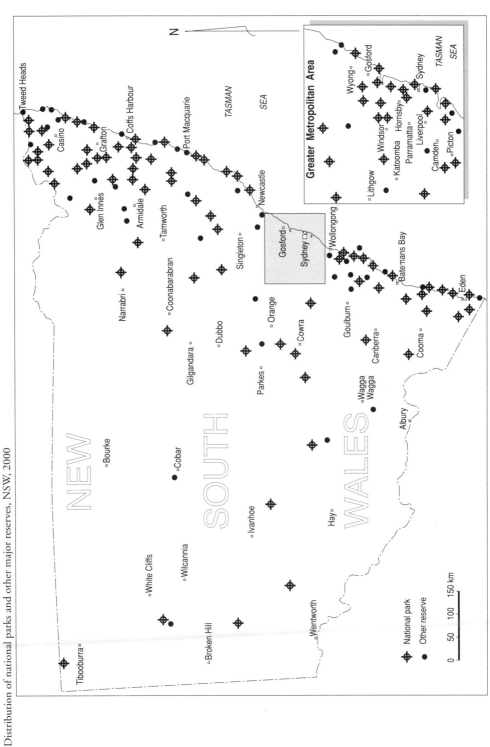

Source: NSW National Parks & Wildlife Service, *Gregory's National Parks of New South Wales* (Fourth edition), Gregory's Publishing Co., Sydney, 2000; and NSW National Parks & Wildlife Service, *Best Bush: Recreation Opportunities in NSW's Public Bushland Areas* (map), NPWS, Sydney, 1999.

Box 5.2   Federal–state politics and land clearing in Queensland

For many years there has been a great deal of controversy over land clearing in Australia, particularly in Queensland and to a lesser extent in NSW. This short exploration concentrates on the period from September 1999 to August 2000.

In mid-1999, the Queensland Government had land protection measures in the pipeline that were stricter than they had been previously. Fearing the new controls, many farmers, especially on the Darling Downs and in neighbouring districts in the south-east of the state, began rapidly clearing large areas 'while they had the chance', in some cases even working overnight under floodlights. Perhaps 300 000 hectares had been cleared by the end of October 1999, most of it legally—permits for 246 000 hectares were issued in the nine months to September. While the new measures were a State Government initiative, they were contingent on Federal Government financial assistance to compensate farmers and the Queensland Government refused to proceed without the requested A$100 million federal assistance.

There were thought to be a number of adverse effects of the clearing. First, it could lead to increased salinity levels in the already greatly stressed Murray–Darling Basin. Secondly, it would inevitably lead to increased greenhouse gas emissions as the cleared vegetation was burnt, while also reducing the sink potential of growing vegetation. Finally, biodiversity was in danger of being lost as woodland and scrub vegetation communities not well represented in reserves were at risk.

Meanwhile, farmers were claiming that they had to clear the land to plant more crops or run more livestock because of low commodity prices, although many scientists and agronomists argue that any increase in production is purely short-term.

An archetypical federal–state stand-off seemed to have developed. The Federal Government has responsibility for greenhouse negotiations, while the state retained responsibility for land management, including the management of clearing. The Federal Government wanted the state to cooperate with them on greenhouse issues, but were not willing to meet the cost of doing so. Given Australia's negative stance at the Kyoto Conference, in which it claimed both the right to increase national emissions and the right to count 'clearing foregone' as part of its countermeasures, this was viewed as a serious matter. In fact, the Federal Government was trying to force the Queensland Government to act, even threatening a reduction in funding if they did not.

Tree-clearing laws were rushed through Parliament in the very last days of 1999, but in a game of brinkmanship the Premier refused to have them proclaimed. The war of words continued into the second half of 2000 and the stalemate over funding continued into July and beyond. Meanwhile, a report in July claimed that an average of 408 000 hectares were being bulldozed each year, up from the annual average of 340 000 hectares in the 1995–97 period. An estimated 80 million trees were felled between 1997 and 1999. The act of passing, but not enacting, the new law only further fuelled farmers' desires to clear before it was too late. To complicate matters further, the National Party arm of the Federal Coalition seemed opposed altogether to restrictions on clearing and argued against federal funding on these very different grounds. They opposed an apparent willingness on behalf of the Prime Minister and federal Minister for the Environment to largely meet the Queensland Premier's request for assistance.

Source: compiled from a range of media reports and web sites.

There are further reasons for ensuring a comprehensive geographical coverage of reserves rather than a spatial concentration in some regions. Most importantly, it spreads the reserved areas so that the impacts of either human or natural forces are more likely to affect only part of the reserve stock of any given ecosystem type. In addition, development pressures might affect one or two reserves, but not all reserves of a given type. In addition, a geographic spread of reserves enables people access to a reserve at a relatively short distance from wherever they live, and this has educational and recreational value, and spreads the load of maintenance among more communities and administrative units. Such a spread of reserves also makes it more likely that local communities will 'adopt' reserves, take pride in them, and perhaps even help with their upkeep on a voluntary basis.

A number of smaller reserves in geographically separated areas may be preferable to one very large reserve because genetically distinct populations can be preserved, which may serve to increase the genetic vitality of a species. It is also possible for a particular species to occupy different niches and to play a different role in different areas. Although subtle, such variations may be well worth taking into account when planning a reserve system. At the same time, it is important not to overstate this point, and to recognise the need for contact between populations.

Size and shape of reserves

The quest for a wide geographical spread runs the risk of over-fragmenting reserves. While it is more obvious, and less politically manageable, if a small reserve is taken over for other uses than if the same area is excised from a large reserve, a system consisting of a large number of small reserves is vulnerable in a number of ways.

Having the same number of animals or plants distributed over many spatially separated reserves is not an adequate substitute for having that population in a single reserve with the same total area if individuals in one

Figure 5.3

Size and shape considerations in planning natural reserves. (A) is a roughly circular reserve, giving a higher area to boundary ratio than, for example, (F). (B) shows the use of a buffer zone around the reserve, while (C) also uses a central, highly protected, core zone. (D) comprises three small reserves approximately equivalent in area to (A) and these are linked by corridors in (E).

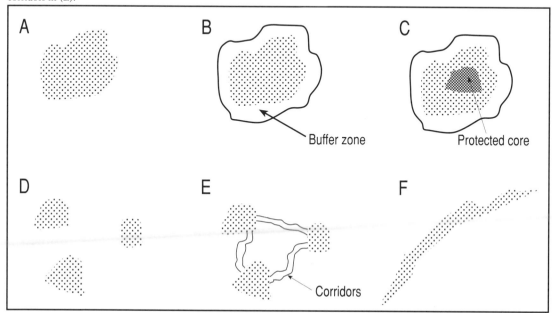

Source: G. Aplin, *Australians and Their Environment: An Introduction to Environmental Studies*, Oxford University Press, Melbourne, 1998, p. 256.

reserve cannot interact with individuals in others (Figure 5.3). In order to survive as viable, genetically healthy populations, all species require areas of a certain size in which the population can interact to reproduce and find sustenance (see Figure 5.3). Larger animals generally require larger areas in which to hunt or gather their food and to sustain a sufficiently large population to maintain genetic variability and vigour. Cross-fertilisation in plants may not be possible in a small reserve because pollen is not blown far enough, or animal and bird carriers do not cross intervening, unreserved, and possibly cleared, land. Animals may not be able to safely cross farmland, roads or other intervening areas to mate. Furthermore, small reserves may not allow for the migrations that are necessary for some species where seasonal resources change in different areas, or as rainfall varies spatially, or as the breeding cycle demands. Corridors of suitable land linking reserves can only partially overcome these problems. Corridors are usually narrow and, like small reserves, they are more vulnerable to adverse external influences. In both cases, it is more difficult to provide a buffer zone to protect a core area from effects such as pests, fire, and wind-blown seeds of exotics, than it is in a large reserve.

The shape of reserves can be important, because of the variance in the ratio of boundary length to area (see Figure 5.3). The shape will also alter the relationship between peripheral buffer zones and protected cores. That is not to say, however, that compact, near-round reserves are always best. In some cases, almost linear reserves may be necessary to follow streams or coastlines, for example, while in many other cases the shape of the reserve will follow the shape of the ecosystem or other feature being protected. If a buffer is advisable, it may need to be a managed zone in which the protected ecosystem type is not present, but within which certain activities are prohibited or controlled, and management procedures implemented.

5.4   Wilderness—a contested concept

Wilderness is one of the most hotly contested concepts in heritage management circles, and the arguments involved can only be briefly touched on here. Issues of definition are introduced in Box 5.3 and Figure 5.4: Box 5.3 sets out the 1994 IUCN management objectives for wilderness areas, while Figure 5.4 indicates the criteria used to define wilderness areas in a recent study covering eastern Victoria. The Victorian definition implies a relative lack of human use, or is often interpreted that way. A more useful and more widely acceptable definition for Australia might involve a lack of current intrusion (such as settlement or transport routes) and a minimal and perhaps non-recent history of intrusion by non-Aboriginal people. This approach is preferable considering objections to the implication of the previous definition that Aboriginal Australians and Torres Strait Islanders are non-human and merely part of the natural ecosystem. Nevertheless, wilderness areas around the world allow for traditional, indigenous uses (see Section 12.4 for a South African definition), as do the IUCN management guidelines (Box 5.3). Wilderness is not a clear-cut concept at all, but rather a question of degree.

Box 5.3   The 1994 IUCN objectives for management of wilderness areas

The objectives for the management of wilderness areas are to:

- maintain the essential natural attributes and qualities of the environment over the long term;
- ensure that future generations have the opportunity to experience understanding and enjoyment of areas that have been largely undisturbed by human activity over a long period of time;
- permit non-motorised public access at levels which will serve best the physical and spiritual well-being of visitors and maintain the wilderness qualities of the area for present and future generations; and
- enable indigenous human communities living at low density and in balance with available resources to maintain their lifestyle.

Source: 19th Session of the General Assembly of the International Union for Conservation of Nature and Natural Resources (IUCN), 1994.

Figure 5.4

Criteria used to define wilderness areas in a recent study covering eastern Victoria

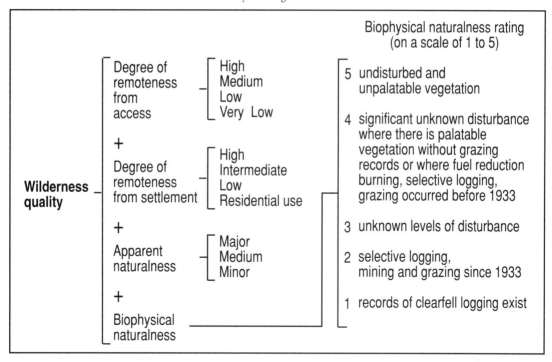

Source: G. Aplin (1998), *Australians and Their Environment: An Introduction to Environmental Studies*, Oxford University Press, Melbourne, p. 264; originally derived from *Wilderness of the Eastern Victorian Forests Report*, Land Conservation Council, Victoria, Melbourne, 1996.

Recent developments in Australia, however, indicate that definitions in that country may now be more in line with those in other countries. The National Wilderness Inventory defines wilderness by using four 'wilderness quality indicators' that represent two essential qualities of wilderness: 'remoteness' and 'naturalness'—similar to the Victorian study, but defined somewhat differently. The National Wilderness Inventory defines wilderness using the following indicators:

- remoteness from settlement: the distance to the nearest house, hamlet or town
- remoteness from access: the distance to the nearest track or road
- apparent naturalness: the distance to the nearest human-built structure of any kind, for example, fence, powerline, transmission towers
- biophysical naturalness: an estimate of the extent to which the area's original plant and animal communities have been disturbed by modern technology

Numeric values are calculated for each of these indicators, and when combined they give an estimation of 'wilderness quality'. Note that the interference with 'naturalness' is now specifically qualified by the phrase 'by modern technology'.

An increasing number of areas in Australia are being declared protected wilderness areas, despite objections from horse-riders and four-wheel-drive enthusiasts who claim to be locked out of their traditional recreation areas, and from the forestry and mining industries claiming valuable resources are being made unreachable. These areas act as 'benchmark' reserves against which to compare change elsewhere and in which to preserve biodiversity. They also allow the enjoyment of relatively pristine areas for visitors on foot and willing to forgo modern comforts. Whether some way should be found to allow others, perhaps older or less mobile, to get some feel for such areas is a moot point, and perhaps not even possible. But if wilderness is not accessible to everyone, should it be preserved at all?

5.5   Preservation outside reserves

Private land is a crucial and often neglected resource for conservation purposes. No nation can hope to include enough land in government-managed natural reserves to adequately preserve biodiversity and protect the other values of natural landscapes. Private owners and occupiers and government agencies need to cooperate, not fight each other. Governments and their instrumentalities are now aware of this and are using a wide range of approaches to achieve better conservation outcomes, from joint projects to a variety of both 'carrots' and 'sticks' (Box 5.2). Financial incentives and recompense for conservation work carried out on behalf of the wider community are discussed in Chapter 3.

There has been a growing willingness and even enthusiasm by landowners in many parts of the world to devote sections of their property to flora and fauna reserves, including areas of native vegetation (Plate 5.3). These initiatives have positive value for processes such as erosion control and moisture management, and also have an extremely beneficial effect on the preservation of biodiversity, through the preservation and even enlargement of areas of native vegetation and through the increased integration of separate patches of it. More comprehensive conservation of ecosystems and particular endangered species on private land is a more controversial issue. It seems to work well in some private game parks in South Africa (see Section 12.4, Box 12.7), and is being tried in Australia by John Walmsley's Earth Sanctuaries. The absence of greater attention in this section should not be taken as an implication that such private efforts are unimportant.

Plate 5.3

Landcare and Land for
Wildlife signs, Grampians
Pioneer Cottages, just
outside Grampians
National Park, Victoria.
Property owners are
increasingly becoming
involved in caring for
various aspects of the
environment and heritage,
including the soil,
vegetation, and wildlife.

Photo: Graeme Aplin

5.6   Managing protected natural areas

Many of the economic and visitor management aspects of natural reserve
management have already been covered in earlier chapters, but there are other
aspects more specific to natural reserves. Park managers are in a perpetual
quandary: how can reserves be made accessible to the public without imposing
undue pressures on the very features that are being conserved, and which
attract visitors in the first place? Managers are often short of funds and need to
raise money from visitor charges, especially in the present era of economic
rationalism with the catch-cry of 'user pays'. For many reserves, user fees are an
important source of income, as well as a management device (see Chapter 3).
However, many reserves, including most (if not all) national parks, simply
cannot draw enough paying customers at a high enough entry charge to meet
all operating costs. Furthermore, if they did succeed in drawing larger
numbers, they would run the risk of being literally 'loved to death'.

Other management issues arise whether or not a park is popular with
visitors. Some issues are endogenous (arising within the park itself), while
others are exogenous (relating to external factors). Reserves generally have very
porous boundaries and external influences may affect the park, while at the
same time, factors arising in the park may affect neighbouring landholders.

Specific environmental problems within reserves

Only a few of the most prominent environmental problems within and
immediately adjacent to reserves can be treated here. Problems arising outside
reserves may be just as important as those arising inside. Park managers need to
maintain good relations with neighbouring landowners to minimise
management problems, and with the wider community to help fight those who
see no value in land unless it is logged, farmed, or mined. The remainder of this
section introduces some of the major environmental problems associated with
reserves, while later sections deal with management practices aimed at
overcoming, or at least mitigating, them.

Erosion

Most natural reserves largely retain their vegetation cover, so erosion is not a problem over most of their area. Erosion becomes a serious problem when human activity is concentrated in particular locations within a park. Most visitors stay only a short time and want to see the most spectacular or best publicised features of a reserve, preferably without walking very far from the car park. There are in fact sound management reasons for restricting the human impact to a few areas, and maintaining the integrity of others. These factors tend to concentrate people, and hence disturbance, in particular areas and on particular tracks. The construction of public facilities can also lead to erosion and sedimentation.

Visitors can cause erosion on walking tracks with natural surfaces purely by reason of their numbers. Erosion may take place even if visitors are careful and considerate, staying on the marked track and obeying any direction or advisory signs (Plate 5.4). Greater problems arise when visitors leave designated tracks, hardened to reduce impact or not, and take short cuts or diversions through more fragile areas. Problems also arise when horse-riding and off-road vehicle use, permitted or not, impinge on a reserve. Those who participate in those activities often demand access or simply take it, despite the fact that it is almost always incompatible with the reserve's management objectives.

Plate 5.4

Old eroded track and new boardwalk near The Balconies, Grampians National Park, Victoria.

Photo: Graeme Aplin

Ecosystem degradation

A number of factors can bring about vegetation degradation, which in turn affects fauna. A major concern for native flora and fauna is the infiltration of exotic species, including pests and diseases. The vulnerability of a reserve depends on its size, shape, and location in relationship to other surrounding land uses (see Figure 5.3). Even if natural animal movement and windborne seeds are not a problem, people and their vehicles can bring seeds and pathogens into reserves. The extent of the problem of privet and lantana is often surprising in seemingly remote parts of Australian reserves where there is public access by road or walking track. Merely disturbing the ground to improve tracks or build other facilities often gives these vigorous exotics a toehold. Exotic animals like rabbits, foxes, and deer can also have severe effects on natural ecosystems in Australia, and reserves often provide very good refuges for these animals, which are usually controlled on surrounding farmland. These invaders can seriously compromise the integrity of ecosystems and plant and animal communities, even endangering the continuing existence of some species. Some of the worst problems involve feral cats and (to a lesser extent) dogs that have escaped from human habitations or have been abandoned or even dumped in the reserves. Small native animals, including birds and reptiles, are particularly vulnerable, as they often have no equivalent native predators.

Pollution of waterways

Stream and lake pollution can occur in a number of ways, and almost always involves the pressure of visitor numbers. Erosion can lead to an increase in local sediment loads, sewage and rubbish can pollute waterways unless carefully managed, and waters used for recreational boating can suffer from sewage, rubbish, and oil pollution. Polluted water can flow into a reserve from unreserved land upstream, adversely affecting reserved ecosystems. For example, streams in reserves downstream from suburban development are particularly vulnerable to weed infestation.

Environmental effects of reserves on surrounding land

Pests and weeds

As discussed previously, reserves can provide havens for plants and animals that are pests in the eyes of surrounding landholders, and this forms one of the main points of contention between farmers and graziers, on the one hand, and conservationists and park managers, on the other. In most cases, everyone would benefit from controlling the problem species, as they are usually exotics that interfere with both natural ecosystems and farming operations. One solution may be for landholders to contribute to the control of pests and weeds in reserves, or at least in buffer zones around their perimeters. Many park managers organise local pest-awareness days and arrange financial assistance for pest control on private land through various incentive schemes. In whatever way possible, the goal of reserve managers is to keep core areas free from exotics, and a cooperative effort in the buffer zone could be one solution. A more difficult situation exists when a native species conserved as one of the key objectives of a reserve is seen as a pest by farmers. Examples in Australia are wedge-tailed eagles, dingos, emus, and various species of kangaroos and wallabies, while in Europe they include wolves and bears, and in India, tigers and elephants.

Fire

Landholders often claim that fires start in reserves and spread to surrounding areas, although the opposite is equally possible and probably occurs equally as frequently. A particular point of contention is that reserve management plans sometimes do not include an adequate fire management component. It is argued that natural fires are suppressed in reserves, and that there is therefore a greater build-up of flammable material. Landholders claim that reserve management practices that preclude controlled burning endanger their properties. However most Australian reserve management plans now include components on fire management and controlled burns. There is also an argument that fire-fighting facilities and human resources within reserves are inadequate.

Management practices to counter visitor pressure

Many approaches to limiting the effects of visitor pressure are discussed in previous chapters. In Chapter 2, interpretation and signage were discussed; in Chapter 3 we looked at financial and related policies. The following sections deal with zoning, and with physical measures such as fences and other structures.

Internal zoning

Internal zoning of reserves is a common management tool and can serve to either differentiate between degrees of public access allowed to different areas, or to enable the employment of different management plans aimed at achieving different objectives in each zone. (Some examples of management plans including zoning are given in Section 5.7, and another in Box 9.2 and Figure 9.4.) Commonly, ready public access, with car parks, toilets, kiosks, and picnic facilities, is provided in spatially limited areas on the fringes of a reserve or close to particularly attractive features. In the latter case there is a danger that those features will rapidly become less attractive through the pressure of numbers and the intrusion of human structures. An alternative means that is frequently used is to have designated walking tracks from the car park and facilities to the feature, which may be complemented by concentrating any signage and other interpretive work along the tracks.

Other areas, which usually include a core where human impacts are minimal, are made less accessible, on the one hand through a combination of regulation and prohibition, and on the other through a lack of facilities and guidance, which reduces the incentive for many people to enter those areas. Restrictions on access, or a lack of encouragement, may also be employed to keep people out of particularly sensitive areas, including areas prone to erosion and those with endangered species of plants or animals. Seasonal closures may be necessary to protect wildlife (such as nesting birds) or for the visitors' own safety, either on a seasonal basis (due to fire danger or snow cover) or more permanently (areas with unstable cliff edges, poisonous plants, or dangerous animals).

Structures

Finding the right balance between providing access and fulfilling experiences for visitors, and protecting ecosystems and flora and fauna is always difficult. The mere presence of sizeable numbers of people will frighten animals and birds from accessible areas, thus reducing the value of the visitor experience. Structures can sometimes help overcome such problems, while education and interpretation can also help heighten the visitor experience, while safeguarding animal populations. Another balance needs to be struck between using structures to assist and manage visitors and ameliorate environmental problems, and the reduction in the value of undisturbed nature that structures inevitably bring. The careful design and siting of structures such as walkways, lookouts, hides, and barriers of various types can control the flow of visitors and provide them with access to particularly advantageous viewpoints, while minimising the impact on plants, animals, and cultural features (Plate 5.5). The key is to provide access without adversely affecting the very things people wish to see.

Plate 5.5

Steel mesh walkway extending between the Crackenback Range and Mt Kosciuszko, Kosciuszko National Park, NSW. The steel mesh was transported in by helicopter in an extremely costly operation in order to protect the fragile alpine vegetation and to prevent erosion along the former track. The open mesh allows rain and light to reach the plants beneath.

Photo: Graeme Aplin

One of the most controversial forms of structure is the walking track (see Plate 5.4). The ideal situation is to retain a natural surface, but heavy use of a natural track can lead to rapid erosion, damage to adjacent vegetation, injuries to visitors because of uneven surfaces or precipitous edges, and the track becoming impassable in wet weather because of poor drainage. Hard or slip-resistant surfaces, steps, drainage, and safety barriers may all help to overcome these problems; with care, they can be made relatively unobtrusive. Some structures are clearly designed to help overcome the dilemma of balancing the desire to promote access while protecting the environment. Elevated tracks or boardwalks are one example because they lessen the impact on fragile vegetation. Examples of these include the Thredbo–Kosciuszko track in Kosciuszko National Park, where an elevated, open-mesh, steel track is used (see Plate 5.5) and the Minnamurra National Park in NSW, where a boardwalk takes visitors to higher levels in the vegetation. The Tree Top Walk in the Valley of the Giants in south-western Western Australia (WA) was constructed by the Department of Conservation and Land Management to achieve two aims: to keep walkers off the extremely sensitive roots of the magnificent but rare tingle tingle (*Eucalyptus* spp.) trees; and to allow visitors the experience of being near the crowns of those trees, forty metres above the ground. Other structures include hides that allow people to view birds without frightening them away, and moats and fences that separate people from larger animals, although unless great care is taken with design, the degree of artificiality is greater than in previous examples.

Re-creations

We are all familiar with 'historic theme parks', although that term is sometimes unfair, given the serious educational goals of places like Sovereign Hill, Ballarat, Victoria, and many others (see Section 6.9). Parallel examples from the natural heritage field are much rarer, as recreating a natural landscape is much more difficult than recreating a building, or even a village. Botanic gardens often attempt to do this on a small scale, with areas of desert or alpine plants in a reasonably natural setting. The Alice Springs Desert Park, operated by the Northern Territory (NT) Parks and Wildlife Commission, is one very successful attempt at bringing landscapes and ecosystems within the experience of visitors, where they are otherwise difficult and potentially hazardous to access, as well as inherently fragile. Situated near the town of Alice Springs, the Desert Park has re-creations of three distinct landscape and ecosystem types over a large area: the first very dry; the second receiving a small amount of moisture; and the third normally dry but subject to occasional flash floods. Interpretation at this Park enhances the experience further.

Public involvement

Related to education and interpretation and to management generally is the issue of public involvement in day-to-day park management. This is distinct from public participation on management committees and the like. In some cases, organisations (often called 'Friends' groups) provide volunteers, raise money, and otherwise help in running the park under the guidance of professional staff or, in the case of smaller, local reserves, without such guidance. Queensland and Victoria (at least) have systems of Volunteer Rangers. Any community involvement gives the local community a sense of ownership of the park and will inevitably have a positive effect on the relationship between park management and local landholders.

5.7   Management plans

Reserves of all types and sizes now tend to have carefully constructed management plans, and those without them need to remedy the deficiency. A comprehensive plan for a large national park must cover a wide range of issues, from weed management through to visitor management. If cultural heritage items are present, or if there is large-scale tourism, their management must also be catered for, which will further broaden the scope of the plan. Reserve management is a complex area that cannot be discussed in detail here, although some principles were dealt with in Chapter 4. Many techniques with a more general application are also part of the reserve management package, such as impact assessment techniques and geographic information systems (GIS). Management plans for large reserves are more complex and require input from a wide range of specialists, such as park staff, consultants, or academic experts. Brief comments on some Australian and overseas examples follow, concentrating on broad goals, objectives, and principles, rather than detail. Another Australian example, Kakadu National Park, is given in Box 9.2, while an example from the United Kingdom is dealt with in Box 11.3 and one from New Zealand in Box 12.1. The following examples illustrate various factors explored earlier in this chapter or in previous chapters, so try to relate these summaries to earlier sections.

Some examples

Cradle Mountain–Lake St Clair National Park

A range of management practices was put in place in the late 1990s to deal with visitor pressures in the Cradle Mountain–Lake St Clair National Park, Tasmania. The main points are as follows.

1 *Cost and safety*—Independent walkers are charged for access to the park's walking trails, and organised group walks are also provided. Independent walkers must carry sufficient food for five days and a tent in case huts are full. They must record departure and arrival dates at each end of the walk and in each hut to aid any search procedures.

2 *Structures*—The main three–five day through-walk (the major attraction for visitors) is clearly signposted; boardwalks and raised platforms are provided where needed over the boggiest sections.

3 *Education*—Information is provided for walkers, pointing out particular types of care needed to preserve ecosystems. Some of this is provided off-park through camping supplies outlets and agencies (some interstate) where visits can be booked.

4 *Fire prevention*—Timber cannot be used for heating or cooking (to prevent scavenging and breaking of vegetation): coal-burning stoves are provided in huts, but gas or spirit stoves must be carried for cooking. Stoves must be lit in huts or adjacent cleared areas to prevent escapes.

5 *Litter management*—All rubbish must be carried out of the park, including items such as tea-bags and cigarette butts, and organic matter such as fruit cores and peel.

6 *Faecal matter*—Huts have self-composting toilets; when away from huts or other toilets, faecal matter must be buried at least 15 centimetres deep and be at least 100 metres from any campsite or watercourse.

7 *Trail marking*—No cairns or other marks for people to follow can be made when hiking across country.

8 *Landscape protection*—Where boardwalks are provided on tracks they must be used. Walkers should avoid cutting corners and walking through the edges of bogs, to prevent breaking track edges, and extending bogs. If walkers leave the main tracks, certain rules must be followed.

9 *Disease prevention*—To prevent the spread of a serious exotic fungal disease, when leaving the designated tracks all cross-country walkers must disinfect their boots and other equipment likely to have soil particles attached.

Solitary Islands Marine Park

An example of the way multiple-use zoning can be structured for a marine park is given in Table 5.1. The Solitary Islands Marine Park, extending north from Coffs Harbour, NSW, and including headlands and estuaries on the mainland coast as well as the islands, has four zones. The most sensitive and protected areas are sanctuary zones. In these areas, activities that involve the removal of natural marine flora and fauna are prohibited, and disturbance to marine ecosystems and communities is minimised. Passive use of the area is permitted, including diving and observing marine life, but strict regulations are imposed for whale watching. Moorings off the islands are provided in areas where dropping anchor is prohibited. Sanctuary zones are used as scientific reference areas against which to compare change elsewhere. Refuge zones allow only very limited use of natural resources and serve as buffer areas around most of the sanctuary zones, or to protect sensitive upper reaches of estuaries and certain headlands and beaches. Recreation zones allow for more recreational uses, but still severely restrict commercial uses, while general use zones allow most uses, except the collection of corals, damage to marine plants, and mining; fishing is allowed within the state licensing conditions and regulations.

Table 5.1

Multiple use zoning in the Solitary Islands Marine Park, NSW

Activity		Sanctuary Zone	Refuge Zone	Recreation Zone	General Use Zone
Recreational	line-fishing	No	Yes	Yes	Yes
	netting	No	No	Yes	Yes
	trapping	No	Limited[2]	Limited[1]	Yes
	spear-fishing	No	Limited[3]	Yes	Yes
	collecting	No	No	Limited[4]	Yes
	diving	Limited[5]	Yes	Yes	Yes
Commercial	line-fishing	No	Licensed	Licensed	Licensed
	trawling	No	No	No	Licensed
	trapping	No	Limited[2]	Limited[1]	Licensed
	netting	No	No	No	Licensed
	collecting	No	No	Limited[4]	Limited[4]
	tourist activity	Permit	Permit	Permit	Permit
Competitions	line- and spear-fishing	No	Club permit	Club permit	Club permit

Activity		Sanctuary Zone	Refuge Zone	Recreation Zone	General Use Zone
Collecting for	aquariums	No	No	Permit	Permit
	group educational excursions	No	Permit	Permit	Permit
	scientific research	Permit	Permit	Permit	Permit

Notes: [1] Rock lobsters, crabs and abalone only.
[2] Rock lobsters in headland Refuge Zones only.
[3] Certain listed species only.
[4] Rock lobsters, crabs, abalone, pipis, beach worms, yabbies, cunjevoi, oysters, green sea lettuce, blackfish weed, sea urchins, prawns and dead objects only.
[5] No pre-certified diver training allowed.

Source: Marine Parks Authority (1991) *Solitary Islands Marine Park—A Special Place: A User Guide and Information Manual*, MPA, Coffs Harbour, p. 38.

Wet Tropics of Queensland World Heritage Area

The draft management plan of the Wet Tropics of Queensland World Heritage Area begins as follows:

The Primary Goal of the Wet Tropics World Heritage Area is to implement Australia's international duty to protect, conserve, present, rehabilitate and transmit to future generations the Wet Tropics World Heritage Area, within the meaning of the World Heritage Convention.

The 'subordinate principles' of the 1995 Draft Plan of Management, in somewhat abbreviated form, were as follows:

1 The integrity of the Area is best conserved by protecting as much of it as possible from disturbance and threatening processes.

2 Achieving the primary goal is dependent on the cooperation of all levels of government and many other groups. It is essential that the management of the Area does not adversely affect adjoining areas and vice versa.

3 Existing systems should be built on, rather than duplicated, and additional regulation used only when necessary.

4 The best possible information should be used, but the precautionary principle should be invoked in cases of uncertainty.

5 Processes for, and decisions about, the conservation, management, and use of the Area should be clear, efficient, equitable, and consistent, and must ensure that the use is ecologically sustainable.

6 Prudent and feasible alternative methods or sites for potentially damaging activities should be used where possible to reduce adverse impact.

7 Australia has a global responsibility to develop a successful model for community involvement in management of the Area, and of tropical rainforests in general.

8 The cultural and natural heritage of the Area should have a part in the life of the community, and the local community should be involved in management of the Area.

9 Management of the Area is the shared responsibility of a wide range of stakeholders, including neighbouring landholders. Economic, social, and cultural benefits from World Heritage listing should be shared equitably.

10 The Authority will develop a collaborative relationship with Aboriginal peoples, whose culture and the rainforest environment are inextricably linked.

11 Trusting relationships should be built through openness, fair dealing, active listening and acknowledgment of protocols.

12 Visitors are welcome to enjoy the Area in ways that maximise their appreciation and inspiration while minimising potential adverse impacts.

Yosemite National Park, USA

The 1980 General Management Plan for Yosemite established five broad goals which also guide the April 2000 Draft Yosemite Valley Plan. These goals are:

1   to reclaim priceless natural beauty

2   to allow natural processes to prevail

3   to promote visitor understanding and enjoyment

4   to markedly reduce traffic congestion

5   to reduce crowding

The detailed criteria that provide further guidance for achieving these five broad goals are listed in Box 5.4. This large and comprehensive draft management plan gives five alternative approaches to future management of the valley, and discusses how well each approach meets the criteria, striking balances between the competing demands of the criteria where necessary.

Box 5.4   Criteria for judging effectiveness of alternatives in 'Draft Yosemite Valley Plan'

Protection of natural and cultural resources
1 Protect highly valued natural and cultural resources.
2 Remove facilities and locate new facilities outside highly valued resource areas where possible.
3 Meet given criteria of the *Draft Merced Wild and Scenic River Comprehensive Management Plan*.
4 Provide the opportunity for continuing traditional use by culturally affiliated Indian people and protect places important to them.
5 Preserve National Historic Landmarks.
6 Preserve and adaptively use historic structures in place, whenever possible, and preserve historic districts.
7 Protect important cultural landscape resources, especially scenic routes and vistas, from development.
8 Protect known human burials.

Visitor experience

 9 Make sure visitors feel welcome and have equitable access for appreciating the Valley's natural beauty.
10 Provide high-quality basic facilities and services, including a variety of camping and lodging experiences.
11 Provide a wide range of opportunities for contact with natural and cultural environments, including areas of solitude and quiet.
12 Make high-quality interpretive and educational facilities and services available.
13 Provide a reliable, cost-effective shuttle bus service.
14 Reduce, consolidate and formalise day-visitor parking.
15 Provide increased opportunities for non-motorised touring.

Park operations

16 Ensure that park operations are cost-effective and sustainable.
17 Locate certain facilities and emergency-support structures outside geologic hazard zones.
18 Remove employee housing from the Valley as far as possible.
19 Ensure that Yosemite Valley is not the base for parkwide operations.
20 Provide for effective and efficient emergency response.

Source: National Park Service (USA) (2000) *Draft Yosemite Valley Plan*, NPS, Yosemite Valley, pp. 1-11–1-12.

Conclusion

The examples presented in this section demonstrate the complexity and broad scope of management plans for areas that are primarily natural heritage areas, but which often also have important cultural values. Recognition of the need to work with local communities and the various stakeholders is shown in all of these examples, and the last two specifically refer to the need to sensitively accommodate the wishes and needs of indigenous peoples. There is an artificial division between natural, cultural, and indigenous heritage in this book, but many heritage sites intimately combine natural and cultural (including indigenous cultural) heritage and a management plan must clearly acknowledge this relationship.

5.8   Australian Natural Heritage Charter

The ANHC was released in 1996 in a joint effort by the Australian Committee for IUCN and the Australian Heritage Commission (AHC) with the aim of producing guidelines parallel to those of the Burra Charter for cultural heritage (see Sections 4.1 and 6.7). The ethos of the charter is encompassed in four principles: intergenerational equity, the principle of existence value, the principle of uncertainty, and the precautionary principle. Figure 5.5 summarises the conservation practice implied in the document, while the following paragraph summarises some key points from it.

Section B of the ANHC, on conservation principles, stresses that the primary aim is to retain the natural significance of a place, respecting natural systems and processes, and to intervene as little as possible. The decision about which conservation techniques to employ should be based on all relevant disciplines, a sound database, and relevant experience. A statement of significance is crucial to the definition of a desired future state and the associated policies required. Elements should not be removed from a place unless this is the sole way of ensuring their survival. Section C deals with the various conservation processes. It stresses that restoration and reinstatement are dependent on sound evidence of an earlier state, and strongly implies that these processes should not be attempted in the absence of such evidence. In all conservation processes, intervention should be kept to the minimum necessary in order to retain the significance of a site. Finally, Section D, on conservation practice, emphasises the need for research, records of evidence and procedures, a written conservation policy and plan, consultation with interested parties, and ongoing monitoring.

Figure 5.5

Conservation practice implied in the *Australian Natural Heritage Charter*

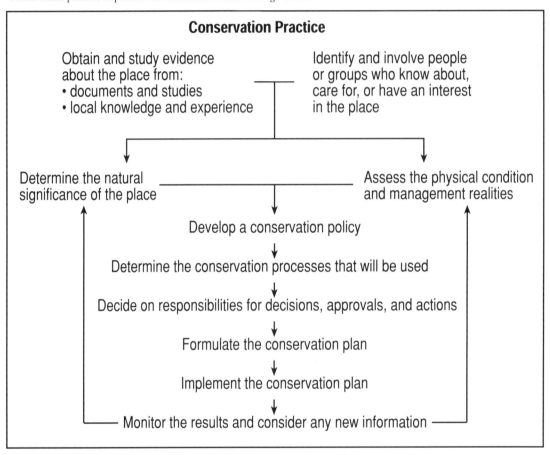

Source: after L. Cairns (1996), *Australian Natural Heritage Charter*, Australian Heritage Commission/Australian Committee for IUCN, Sydney, p. 4.

5.9   Recreation and tourism uses of the natural environment

We need little reminder that in the last quarter of the 20th century tourism became increasingly important to the Australian economy, and to many national, regional, and local economies around the world (see Table 3.1). That trend shows every sign of continuing. Many tourists, both foreign and domestic, are attracted by elements of the natural environment, including flora and fauna and overall landscape assemblages. Increasing numbers, often catered for in an increasingly luxurious and invasive manner, can have serious impacts on the environment, and may ultimately destroy the very features that attract them. Very careful consideration of the impact of tourism in a particular locality is required if the industry is to be sustainable.

Multiple uses including recreation and tourism

Many areas are valuable for tourism alongside other activities, particularly ecological activities as opposed to economic ones. Extractive industries such as forestry and mining are generally incompatible with tourist activity, although some areas within State Forests in NSW and similar reserves elsewhere are suitable for recreational use even though other nearby areas are being logged. Commercial fishing is often carried out in waters used for recreation, while agriculture and grazing may be an integral part of views and landscapes that are scenically attractive to tourists. Specific tourist infrastructure can be, and often is, handled sensitively enough to avoid major conflict with heritage and environmental values.

Many natural areas that are deemed valuable tourist destinations are also sites that fulfil vital environmental functions such as flood mitigation, soil protection, water purification, and the provision of 'nurseries' for marine life. Whether or not these ecological or environmental functions are compromised by tourist activity depends on the scale and management of that activity. If tourists view an area from beyond its boundaries, dangers are minimal, but could include waste-water run-off into reserved areas, or the introduction of weeds and other pests. Once visitors enter an area and undertake activities within the protected ecosystem or environment, the risks become much greater, but need not be overwhelming.

Ecotourism

Ecotourism was introduced in Section 3.7, where it was pointed out that the effects of ecotourism on the environment are not always as positive and non-detrimental as the more vocal supporters of ecotourism claim. Nevertheless, good ecotourism can be environment-friendly and heritage-friendly. For example, the goals of the Ecotourism Association of Australia are to ensure that:
- all tourism in natural and cultural settings is ecologically sustainable
- ecotourism contributes to the conservation of places visited and to the conservation of biodiversity
- ecotourism benefits host communities
- there is a range of ecotourism opportunities available to visitors of different socio-demographic backgrounds

Thus, the goal of the association is to achieve 'soft' tourism, as shown in Table 3.3, and to work with local communities and local environments as much as possible to minimise impact on them. Box 5.5 gives an extensive list of action items from the Association's Code of Environmental Ethics, which elaborates on their main goals. It is worth noting the emphasis placed on interpretation and education, as they relate to specific sites and in a more general sense. There are also many practical ways to minimise impact.

Box 5.5   Code of Practice of the Ecotourism Association of Australia

---

The Association has adopted the following code of Practice for Ecotourism Operators.

A   Strengthen the conservation effort for, and enhance the natural integrity of, the places visited.

B   Respect the sensitivies of other cultures.

C   Be efficient in the use of natural resources, for example, water and energy.

D   Ensure waste disposal has minimal environmental and aesthetic impacts.

E   Develop a recycling program.

F   Support principals (that is, hotels, carriers etc.) who have a conservation ethic.

G   Keep abreast of current political and environmental issues, particularly of the local area.

H   Network with other stakeholders (particularly those in the local area) to keep each other informed of developments and to encourage the use of this Code of Practice.

I   Endeavour to use distribution networks (for example, catalogues) and retail outlets to raise environmental awareness by distributing guidelines to consumers.

J   Support ecotourism education/training for guides and managers.

K   Employ tour guides well versed and respectful of local cultures and environments.

L   Give clients appropriate verbal and written educational material (interpretation) and guidance with respect to the natural and cultural history of the areas visited.

M   Use locally produced goods that benefit the local community, but do not buy goods made from threatened or endangered species.

N   Never intentionally disturb or encourage the disturbance of wildlife or wildlife habitats.

O   Keep vehicles to designated roads and trails.

P   Abide by the rules and regulations applying in natural areas.

Q   Commit to the principle of best practice.

R   Comply with Australian safety standards.

S   Ensure truth in advertising.

T   Maximise the quality of experience for hosts and guests.

Source: Ecotourism Association of Australia brochure.

Whether or not tourist operators are given the seal of approval by the Ecotourism Association, they must avoid major negative impacts on the heritage and environment that they need for their own continued existence. Heavy impact tourism is simply unsustainable, as it destroys the very features visitors come to see and enjoy.

5.10   Conclusion

Natural areas form a key part of our heritage at all geographical scales. While primarily considered to be significant for their natural values, they are rarely devoid of cultural features, whether these relate to indigenous or non-indigenous groups. Indeed, European and Asian reserves, including those designated as national parks, commonly include agricultural land and entire villages or towns. All areas require careful management, although the emphasis will obviously differ according to a number of factors including the type of reserve, its relationship to surrounding land uses, and the number of visitors. Careful management with clear goals and objectives is crucial if natural heritage areas are to be successfully conserved.

Note

1   Establishing benchmarks in this context is very difficult. What benchmark for vegetation coverage would be used in European and other nations that have been settled in a 'modern' fashion for much longer than Australia? Should Australia be looking further back to the pre-Aboriginal period? Or should each nation preserve as much natural or near-natural vegetation as possible? Should some areas be replanted to increase the amount?

Further Reading

Agee, J. K. & Johnson, D. R. (eds) (1988) *Ecosystem Management for Parks and Wilderness,* University of Washington Press, Seattle.

Australian Committee for IUCN (1999) *Natural Heritage Places Handbook: Applying the Australian Natural Heritage Charter to Conserve Places of Natural Significance,* Australian Heritage Commission, Canberra.

Australian Nature Conservation Agency (1996) *Application of IUCN Protected Area Management Categories: Draft Australian Handbook,* ANCA, Canberra.

Barton, W. (ed.) (1994) *Wilderness—the Future: Papers from the Fourth National Wilderness Conference,* 1993, Envirobook/Colong Foundation for Wilderness, Sydney.

Bradstock, R. A. *et al.* (eds) (1995) *Conserving Biodiversity: Threats and Solutions,* Surrey Beatty, Sydney.

Cairnes, L. B. (1996) *Australian Natural Heritage Charter: Standards and Principles for the Conservation of Places of Natural Heritage Significance,* Australian Heritage Commission/Australian Committee for IUCN, Sydney.

Ceballos-Lascaurain, H. (1996) *Tourism, Ecotourism and Protected Areas,* IUCN—The World Conservation Union, Gland, Switzerland.

Furze, B., DeLacy, T. & Birckhead, J. (1996) *Culture, Conservation and Biodiversity: The Social Dimension of Linking Local Development and Conservation through Protected Areas,* Wiley, London.

Lesslie, R. G., Taylor, D. & Maslen, M. (1993) *National Wilderness Inventory: Handbook of Principles, Procedures and Usage,* Australian Government Publishing Service, Canberra.

National Parks & Wildlife Service (NSW) (1999) *Compendium of Case Studies: Protected Area Management Principles and Practice,* NSW NPWS, Queanbeyan.

Pigram, J. J. & Sundell, R. C. (eds) (1997) *National Parks and Protected Areas: Selection, Delimitation and Management,* University of New England, Armidale.

Robertson, M., Vang, K. & Brown, A. J. (1993) *Wilderness in Australia: Issues and Options—A Discussion Paper,* Australian Heritage Commission, Canberra.

Spellerberg, I. F. (1992) *Evaluation and Assessment for Conservation: Ecological Guidelines for Determining Priorities for Nature Conservation,* Chapman Hall, London.

Ward, E. N. (1987) *Heritage Conservation: The Natural Environment,* Heritage Resource Centre, University of Waterloo, Waterloo, Canada.

Worboys, G. *et al.* (2001) *Protected Area Management: Principles and Practice,* Oxford University Press, Melbourne.

Wright, R. G. (ed.) (1996) *National Parks and Protected Areas: Their Role in Environmental Protection,* Blackwell, Cambridge.

Young, M. D. *et al.* (1996) *Reimbursing the Future: An Evaluation of Motivational, Voluntary, Price-based, Property Right and Regulatory Incentives for the Conservation of Biodiversity,* Department of the Environment, Sport and Territories, Canberra.

CHAPTER 6

Cultural Heritage and Its Management

6.1   Definitions and scope

Cultural heritage results from human processes and activities, rather than biophysical ones. It reflects both productive or material activities, and non-material activities and values, which are more difficult to define and can include social, religious, artistic, traditional, and iconic values. Cultural heritage spans *moveable heritage*, *immoveable heritage*, and largely *non-material heritage*. Immoveable heritage can include historic buildings and important sites with culturally based meanings and significance, while non-material heritage encompasses dance, music, craft work, and folk stories, among other things. All forms of cultural heritage are important, and key examples should be preserved.

As we have already seen, the various forms of cultural heritage are often closely linked. In particular, the moveable and non-material forms are frequently linked to particular localities or sites, and should sometimes be preserved *in situ* in order to preserve those associations. Cultural and natural heritage are also, of course, very commonly inter-related, and many important heritage sites combine aspects of all types of heritage.

Museums, art galleries, libraries, and other collections are crucial to the task of preserving, presenting, and interpreting the less obviously place-bound aspects of cultural heritage. Such institutions are often best located on or near a significant site. For example, the best place for a collection of a famous artist's works may be in one of his or her former homes. Likewise, antiquities are often best housed in a museum attached to an archaeological site (Plate 6.1), rather than being removed to a distant national or regional museum. In this way, key contextual relationships are more easily preserved, especially if the art works or artefacts can be related directly to a building or site in the same visit.

Even when limited to immoveable items, which must be preserved on site, cultural heritage encompasses much more than the historic buildings we most commonly associate with the term. Other important cultural heritage items include gardens, cemeteries, archaeological sites, industrial archaeology, and shipwrecks (see Section 6.5). While this chapter concentrates primarily on buildings, groups of buildings, and sites with historic and other significance (such as associational or aesthetic significance), many points also apply to other equally important forms of cultural heritage.

Plate 6.1

Glanum Visitors' Centre,
St-Rémy-de-Provence,
Bouches-du-Rhône,
France. The archaeological
site of Glanum is listed on
the *Caisse Nationale des
Monuments Historiques et
des Sites.* The Roman ruins
were unearthed in 1921
and a small museum and
very good interpretive
centre tell the story of the
site (see also Plate 11.9).

Photo: Graeme Aplin

Despite the arbitrariness of the distinction between indigenous and non-indigenous heritage, sites that are important because of the presence of indigenous cultural heritage are discussed separately in Chapter 7. Even in a nation such as Australia, where relations between the indigenous Aboriginal population and other Australians are less than ideal, it is entirely possible to argue that all forms of Australian cultural heritage belong to all Australians. While I realise that I might be accused by some of taking an indefensibly 'assimilationist' stance, that is not the intent, and I hasten to point out that I am not for a moment suggesting that any type of heritage is superior to any other, or that any group should appropriate or overwhelm the heritage of another group. Some heritage items obviously have more significance for some groups than for others and remain first and foremost the heritage of one particular group. To my mind, however, all Australians should be able to accept all items as part of their shared national heritage, and to respect the significance of each and every item. The same could be said for any nation where heritage relates most specifically to a minority group. Is, for example, Basque heritage part of Spanish national heritage, or Inuit heritage part of Canadian heritage? Hopefully, all nations see the heritage of all their citizens as important. In such an ideal world, all people are equal, respected citizens of the nation, and the heritage of each group combines to constitute the national heritage. The reality of the matter is, of course, that many national heritage lists are dominated by the heritage of the most powerful group, and the heritage of other groups is subsumed or neglected. The definition of cultural heritage can serve to further enhance the power of the dominant group, while further relegating other groups to positions of subservience.

Why, then, treat indigenous (and minority) cultural heritage in a separate chapter? Firstly, for practical reasons, because many governments and heritage agencies treat it separately, in Australia and elsewhere. Secondly, there are particularly important sensitivities required if most of the administrators, tourist operators, and visitors are from groups other than the relevant indigenous or minority group. Nevertheless, there are also many factors common to the identification, preservation, and management of all cultural heritage. Just as there is a great deal of overlap between this chapter and the previous one, there is also overlap between this chapter and the next one.

It is important to stress that this chapter should be read in conjunction with Chapters 2 to 4. Many of the key concepts, definitions, and processes covered in those earlier chapters are crucial in the context of cultural heritage.

6.2   Application of criteria to cultural heritage

As always, the three key general criteria outlined in Section 1.5—scale, importance, and either uniqueness or representativeness—should be applied to cultural heritage. In addition, there are some common but uniquely cultural criteria, including technological innovation, aesthetics, and important associations with people or events. (These may also apply to sites that have both cultural and natural significance.) One example of the wide variety of factors that can contribute to a site's cultural significance is shown in the themes proposed by the NSW Heritage Council, which are contained in Box 6.1. These themes are intended to highlight the broad range of factors that can give significance to cultural heritage items and to assist people proposing sites for listing. In the case of historic buildings, architectural significance and associational significance stand out, and these are treated in greater depth in the paragraphs that follow.

Box 6.1   Proposals for more detailed criteria and state themes for the NSW State Heritage Inventory Program

---

Statement of Significance and Register Criteria

Criterion A: Its importance in the course or pattern of Australia's natural or cultural history.

A1 Importance in the evolution of Australian flora, fauna, landscapes, or climate.

A2 Importance in maintaining existing processes or natural systems at the regional or national scale.

A3 Importance in exhibiting unusual richness or diversity of flora, fauna, landscapes, or cultural features.

A4 Importance for association with events, developments, or cultural phases which have had a significant role in the human occupation and evolution of the nation, state, region, or community.

Criterion B: Its possession of uncommon, rare or endangered aspects of Australia's natural or cultural history.

B1 Importance for rare, endangered, or uncommon flora, fauna, communities, ecosystems, natural landscapes, or phenomena, or as wilderness.

B2 Importance in demonstrating a distinctive way of life, custom, process, land use, function, or design no longer practised, in danger of being lost, or of exceptional interest.

Criterion C: Its importance to yield information that will contribute to an understanding of Australia's natural or cultural history.

C1 Importance for information contributing to a wider understanding of Australian natural history, by virtue of use as a research site, teaching site, type locality, reference, or benchmark site.

C2 Importance for information contributing to a wider understanding of the history of human occupation of Australia.

Criterion D: Its importance in demonstrating the principal characteristics of a class of Australia's natural or cultural places, or of a class of Australia's natural or cultural environments.

D1 Importance in demonstrating the principal characteristics of the range of landscapes, environments, ecosystems, the attributes of which identify it as being characteristic of its class.

D2 Importance in demonstrating the principal characteristics of the range of human activities in the Australian environment (including way of life, philosophy, custom, process, land use, function, design, or technique).

Criterion E: Its importance in exhibiting particular aesthetic characteristics valued by a community or cultural group.

E1 Importance for a community for aesthetic characteristics held in high esteem or otherwise valued by the community.

Criterion F: Its importance in demonstrating a high degree of creative or technical achievement at a particular period.

F1 Importance for its technical, creative, design or artistic excellence, innovation, or achievement.

Criterion G: Its strong or special associations with a particular community or cultural group for social, cultural, or spiritual reasons.

G1 Importance as a place highly valued by a community for reasons of religious, spiritual, cultural, educational, or social associations.

Criterion H: Its special association with the life or works of a person, or group of persons, of importance in Australia's natural or cultural history.

H1 Importance for close associations with individuals whose activities have been significant within the history of the nation, state, or region.

The *degree* to which a place exhibits characteristics covered by these criteria influences significance. Merely meeting a criterion is not enough.

STATE THEMES

1   Aboriginal culture and interaction with settlers
2   Convict settlement in town and country
3   European exploration of the country
4   Surveyors and land tenures; closer settlement
5   Pastoral expansion; interactions with settlement, ecology, and communications; rural industries
6   Pastoral diversification; change and development
7   Agricultural expansion; interactions with settlement, ecology, and communications; rural industries
8   Agricultural diversification; new crops, technologies, sites
9   Changing the environment; Aboriginal and European impacts
10   The gold rushes and less dramatic gold-winning
11   Extraction and processing of (other) minerals
12   The growth and dominance of Sydney
13   The foundation, growth, and changing role of country towns
14   Migration; ethnic communities
15   The transport network
16   Growth of democratic government and bureaucracy: federal, state, and local
17   Cultural and social life, including the arts and education
18   Leisure; tourism
19   Environmental awareness
20   Use and abuse of water resources
21   A place to live, apart or together; town planning
22   Emergence of building styles and types of construction
23   Booms and busts; economic cycles: global, national, state, local
24   Industrialisation and de-industrialisation
25   Rural population changes
26   The life cycle: from hospital to home to cemetery

Architectural significance

Buildings can be architecturally significant for a number of reasons: because they are outstanding examples of a particular form of architecture or a particular style, because they are representative of a major style, or because they are unique. The Sydney Opera House (Plate 6.2) clearly falls into the last category, while the Art Deco hall in Oberon, NSW (Plate 6.3) is both locally unique and also a rare surviving example of the style on a national scale. A building may also be significant because it represents the work of a famous or important architect or builder (see Plate 11.20). Alternatively, it may be significant because it is a supreme example of building and craftsmanship, or because it is the first (or an early) example of an important technological or stylistic development.

Plate 6.2

'No other building on Earth looks like the Sydney Opera House', as one guidebook says. Built over 14 years to 1972, the Opera House is universally recognised as being unique and one of the outstanding architectural feats of the 20th century. A proposal for World Heritage listing for 'The Sydney Opera House in its Harbour Setting' also includes the Sydney Harbour Bridge and Fort Denison.

Photo: Graeme Aplin

Plate 6.3

Malachi Gilmore Hall, a famous Art Deco building dating from 1937 situated in the NSW country town of Oberon. The ground floor now houses the Tourist Information Centre. This unusual and remarkable building has survived largely because of the relative lack of development in the town and because local people have adopted it as a local heritage icon.

Photo: Graeme Aplin

Finally, a building may be significant for aesthetic reasons, or because of its contribution to the value of the wider streetscape or landscape (see Section 6.4). Many of these criteria also apply to gardens and industrial sites, among others.

Where possible, statements of significance should contain references to a specific architectural style. (Where this is not possible, terms such as *eclectic* or *vernacular* are often used.) Therefore, a knowledge of architectural styles and how they relate to a particular nation or region is important. Categorisation of styles can take many forms, and may involve varying degrees of detail. Table 6.1 is a particularly detailed, but well regarded, categorisation of Australian styles; it is used by the NSW Heritage Council, among other groups.

Associational significance

Buildings and sites of all types (including natural sites) are also frequently deemed significant because of their association with particular people, organisations, or events (Plate 6.4). These cultural heritage sites might be thought of as the 'Queen Victoria slept here' type. If the association is significant enough, the building itself can be insignificant in terms of architecture and aesthetics. The National Trust of Australia (NSW), for example, agreed to list one of the single-storey, street-corner pubs with verandahs in the western NSW town of Bourke. It was not outstanding architecturally or in terms of building quality; indeed, it was one of many pubs in Bourke that were very similar. But it was the one in which the famous 19th-century Australian author Henry Lawson chose to stay while he was involved in early union activities and where he wrote some of his well-known works. Associations can also be with particular organisations, industries, or events, as the list of state themes in Box 6.1 clearly implies.

Plate 6.4

Fitzgerald's Hotel, Avoca, Co. Wicklow, Ireland. Busloads of tourists, including many from the United Kingdom, Australia and elsewhere, now descend on the little town because it has become part of their heritage through the extremely popular television series 'Ballykissangel'.

Photo: Graeme Aplin

Table 6.1

List of styles in Australian architecture

A	**Old Colonial period 1788–c.1840**	D2	Inter-war Academic Classical
A1	Old Colonial Georgian	D3	Inter-war Free Classical
A2	Old Colonial Regency	D4	Inter-war Beaux-Arts
A3	Old Colonial Grecian	D5	Inter-war Stripped Classical
A4	Old Colonial Gothick Picturesque	D6	Inter-war Commercial Palazzo
B	**Victorian period c.1840–c.1890**	D7	Inter-war Mediterranean
B1	Victorian Georgian	D8	Inter-war Spanish Mission
B2	Regency	D9	Inter-war Chicagoesque
B3	Victorian Egyptian	D10	Inter-war Functionalist
B4	Victorian Academic Classical	D11	Inter-war Art Deco
B5	Victorian Free Classical	D12	Inter-war Skyscraper Gothic
B6	Victorian Filigree	D13	Inter-war Romanesque
B7	Victorian Mannerist	D14	Inter-war Gothic
B8	Victorian Second Empire	D15	Inter-war Old English
B9	Victorian Italianate	D16	Inter-war California Bungalow
B10	Victorian Romanesque	**E**	**Post-war period c.1940–1960**
B11	Victorian Academic Gothic	E1	Post-war Ecclesiastical
B12	Victorian Free Gothic	E2	Post-war International
B13	Victorian Tudor	E3	Post-war Melbourne Regional
B14	Victorian Rustic Gothic	E4	Post-war Brisbane Regional
B15	Victorian Carpenter Gothic	E5	Post-war American Colonial
C	**Federation period c.1890–c.1915**	**F**	**Late 20th-century period 1960–**
C1	Federation Academic Classical	F1	Late 20th-century Stripped Classical
C2	Federation Free Classical	F2	Late 20th-century Ecclesiastical
C3	Federation Filigree	F3	Late 20th-century International
C4	Federation Anglo-Dutch	F4	Late 20th-century Organic
C5	Federation Romanesque	F5	Late 20th-century Sydney Regional
C6	Federation Gothic	F6	Late 20th-century Perth Regional
C7	Carpenter Gothic	F7	Late 20th-century Adelaide Regional
C8	Federation Warehouse	F8	Late 20th-century Tropical
C9	Federation Queen Anne	F9	Late 20th-century Brutalist
C10	Federation Free Style	F10	Late 20th-century Structuralist
C11	Federation Arts and Crafts	F11	Late 20th-century Late-modern
C12	Federation Bungalow	F12	Late 20th-century Post-modern
D	**Inter-war period c.1915–c.1940**	F13	Late 20th-century Australian Nostalgic
D1	Inter-war Georgian Revival	F14	Late 20th-century Immigrants Nostalgic

Source: R. Apperly, R. Irving & P. Reynolds (1989) *A Pictorial Guide to Identifying Australian Architecture: Styles and Terms from 1788 to the Present*, Angus & Robertson, Sydney.

6.3   Listing cultural heritage items

Data required

Both the proposal to list and the final listing of an item or site of cultural heritage value should contain comprehensive information about it. It is extremely important that sound research be carried out to the extent that this is possible, and that full documentation, including plans and photographs, be provided. This information serves both to assist the relevant committee or individual to determine whether or not the site is to be officially listed, and, once it is listed, to provide documentation of the site for the register. Later, such information can also become the basis for conservation and management plans.

Box 6.2   Guide to assessing buildings

Summary of information required

1   Name/Use
Give the present name (if any) and use of the place. Give former names and uses if known.

2   Address/Location
Give *exact* and *detailed* address or location information. Map coordinates should be given in rural areas.

3   Historical
If known, give the year or approximate year of construction, information on the designer and builder, and the history of ownership and use if this is of interest. Give sources of this information.

4   Description
Give a reasonably detailed point-by-point description of the site, starting with the basics (shape, materials) and proceeding to details.
Describe interiors if they were seen.
Describe all related elements such as outbuildings and garden features.
State which features are of particular significance.
Comment briefly on the present condition and integrity.

5   Boundary
Recommend a boundary to the listing—that is, a buffer zone around the significant elements, within which particular care should be taken in fitting in any new developments.

6   Site Plan
Draw a simple sketch plan showing the site.
Show the boundary and all elements within the boundary.
Indicate by shading or hatching which elements are considered significant.

7   Photography
Enclose several recent colour slides showing *all* significant elements of the site. Ensure that each slide is *fully* labelled.

8   Statement Of Significance
If you think that the place has heritage significance, say *why* you think so. Do this regardless of your recommendation.

9   Recommendation
Say whether you think the site should be listed in the National Trust Register.

10 General
The name(s) of the author(s) and the date of submission should be noted.

Source: prepared by Graeme Aplin in 1991 for the Historic Buildings Committee of the National Trust of Australia (NSW).

An example of data requirements is given in Box 6.2. It shows how much detail is required to fully document a heritage item. Both written descriptions and visual material—maps, plans, sketches, photographs—are important. Both historical background and present state are relevant. Wherever possible, a thorough physical, on-site examination should be made. This may not be possible, for example in the case of interiors, particularly if owners are not supportive of heritage listing. Architectural style or styles should be specified as accurately as possible, as should the materials and building techniques used. This detail is crucial for establishing and clearly stating significance, and also for establishing a basis for conservation or preservation (see Section 6.7). How can you know if unsympathetic alterations or additions have been made if there is no clear record of the present and former states? How can you have regard for authenticity, to the extent that you need to, if you do not have that information?

The listing record is more than just a record of a physical site—whether that be a building, a segment of the natural landscape, or something else—it is also a record of part of our history, part of our overall heritage, which is more than the sum of all the individual buildings and sites. Listing records also contribute to documenting the heritage on a community, state, national, or global scale. Thus, research needs to place the item in its broader historical, geographical, architectural, economic, and social contexts.

Statement of significance

A full, clearly worded statement of significance is a crucial part of any listing proposal or final, accepted listing. (This, of course, applies equally to natural sites.) It must distil the essence of the item and its importance in a short, accessible statement. Some examples of statements of significance for National Trust listings in Newcastle and its suburbs were given in Box 1.5. While not necessarily the best possible examples, these sound statements show the wide variety of factors that can lead to a building or site being accepted as significant. Box 6.2 also stresses the importance of the statement of significance.

6.4 Significance of context and contextual significance

In this section, we begin with some general comments about context. Later, we will move onto a discussion about some of the more obvious cases in which context is relevant—heritage groupings, heritage precincts, historic villages and towns, and significant landscapes. Any cultural heritage item exists in a number of contexts, including temporal (historical), spatial (geographical), and social contexts. If an item were taken out of context, it may not have the same significance. No item exists in isolation, nor should it be considered in isolation. In fact, significance cannot be determined without considering context.

Just as the context can enhance the heritage value of something, so can a heritage item enhance the context in which it exists. Quite apart from the possibility of being part of a listed group or larger heritage area, a historic building (or a modern one, for that matter) is often said to have significant landscape or streetscape value, or to represent an important landmark. Such buildings give a place its distinctive character, and help residents and visitors identify with it. They can become symbols or icons for a community, and possibly for one section of a community at the expense of others. Furthermore, they help people form 'mental maps' of an area, get their bearings, and feel at home. Heritage buildings and sites can make a key contribution to giving a location its distinctiveness, its *sense of place*. They can also help promote a *sense of time*; Kevin Lynch[1] asked the pertinent and very interesting question 'What time is this place?', and this question is particularly important in relation to heritage precincts and historic towns, discussed later in this section. Another part of the issue of context is the way in which heritage items can add to a streetscape or landscape aesthetically. What balance should be struck between variety and uniformity? This is not an easy question to answer, and it depends on the situation, but it is a crucial question for planners to consider, and a question with clear heritage relevance. Finally, heritage items also frequently have important social or community meaning, even if they are not particularly outstanding on architectural or historical grounds. A local community hall might, for example, have an important role to play in a town's self-image, even though it is unassuming and has not been the site of specifically important events.

Curtilages

The immediate area around a historic building may contribute to its heritage value in a very important way. The *curtilage* can be considered as an envelope around the main item, the preservation of which is important (see Plate 4.9). In the case of houses, the boundary of the curtilage is usually taken to be the fence line, especially when fences and gardens are in keeping with the building. In many cases, outbuildings are important to the heritage value of a house, and this is more likely to be the case in rural areas. Sometimes, however, the grounds may be so large that the parts that are some distance from the heritage buildings may be able to be used for other purposes, perhaps subdivided, with part of the profit used to restore the heritage building. (See Box 3.2 for a discussion of a particular, controversial case relevant to this point.) For other types of buildings and sites, the curtilage and its boundaries may be much more difficult to determine. Is the heritage value of an old water-powered mill diminished if the stream that powered it is diverted, concreted, put underground in pipes, or allowed to become overgrown or silted up? How much of a significant farm needs to be included in the curtilage around the homestead?

It is also important to consider development outside the immediate curtilage, and whether views of the heritage item are likely to be compromised. Some items are valued for their appearance from a distance, or their contribution to a broader landscape. Alternatively, it may be the views from the heritage site that are crucial.[2] Any modern or out-of-scale development nearby (or in some cases even some distance away) could be detrimental. Here, we are venturing out of the field of heritage planning as such and into the area of more general planning issues, with associated complex and political questions of development rights. The key question is whether or not protection of the area within the proposed curtilage or more extensive surrounding area is required in order to retain the overall significance of the site.

Grouped heritage items

A heritage group comprises a relatively small number of related and spatially adjacent, or at least closely proximate, items, all of which are individually of heritage value and/or which add significantly to the overall heritage value of the group. While some items may not have heritage significance except as part of the group, all components may need to be present to give the group its significance.

We have already mentioned the example of a rural homestead and associated farm buildings, which may also include the garden around the farmhouse, an avenue of trees leading from the road, and perhaps an historic wool-scouring site. This is essentially a group, although in the case of a rural property, it would most likely be treated as a single listing with a large curtilage around the main homestead building. A more common example of a group is a church, the church hall, the rectory/manse/presbytery/parsonage, and perhaps an old burial ground attached to the church. Another fairly common group is a 'civic' or 'main street' group, often including such buildings as the post office, the court house, municipal buildings, banks and the like, which are frequently found around an important intersection. The US National Trust for Historic Preservation, in fact, runs a large and very successful initiative called the Main Street Program to help small communities preserve assemblages of historic buildings (see Box 12.4). The term *precinct* is sometimes used to describe a group, such as the Wallsend Civic Precinct (Figure 6.1). The reasons for listing this group are informative:

> As commercial development of the old town has destroyed many of its valuable 19th-century monuments [meaning buildings etc.] it is most important to protect what remains. Preservation of the public square containing the band rotunda and the Fletcher Memorial, together with the surrounding public buildings … , would enlarge public respect for the standards of public building achieved in early Wallsend and encourage moves to recover the dignity of its 19th-century origins. This civic group of buildings and open space occupies a prominent place in the history and surviving 19th-century townscape of Wallsend, and its curtilage is important to the preservation of its civic character.[3]

'Precinct' is also used to describe a more extensive heritage area (see later paragraph on heritage precincts). Most heritage registers list and describe each significant component, and its significance is stated separately; statements of significance almost invariably include some mention of the way each item contributes to the significance of the group. There is also usually a listing for the group, and this may include other items that would not be considered significant if not part of the group.

Heritage precincts and urban conservation areas

The two concepts of *heritage precincts* and *urban conservation areas* (UCAs) often overlap and the terms may be applied to one and the same area, although precincts are frequently less extensive. Both tend to apply to larger areas than are covered by group listings. To take an example, the Newcastle UCA of the National Trust includes a large area of the central business district (CBD) of that city and the area to the east towards the coast. Reasons for listing are given as follows:

> To encourage the conservation of a visually interesting townscape and complementary landscape. The close-packed streets of buildings in Newcastle Hill juxtaposed and contrasted with a variety of grassed and sparsely vegetated coastline parks provide many pleasing visual experiences. The sea and sky are ever present and form a backdrop for views of many fine late 19th-century and early 20th-century buildings lining streets within the Conservation Area.

> To encourage the redevelopment of vacant sites of Newcastle East in an urban manner which is in keeping with the low-scale remaining buildings.

A large area of Carlton, in Melbourne, including sections of Drummond Street (Plate 6.5), constitutes another urban example, while the main street of Canowindra, in the Central West of NSW (Plate 6.6) is an example of a rural town UCA. The Rocks UCA is covered in some detail in Box 3.1.

Figure 6.1

Wallsend Civic Precinct, in the centre of a formerly separate coal-mining town swallowed up by the suburban expansion of Newcastle, NSW

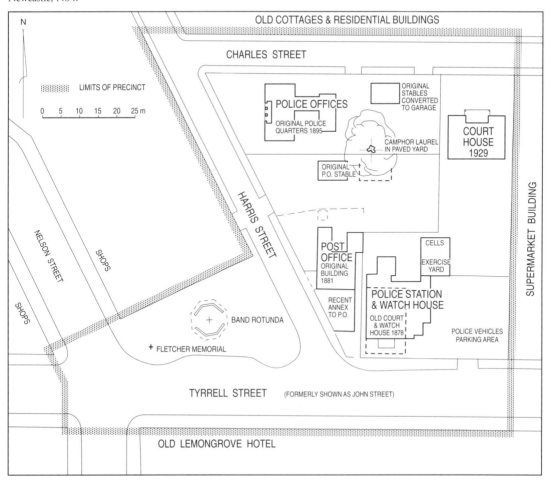

Plate 6.5

Drummond Street,
Carlton, Melbourne,
Victoria; a 19th-century
streetscape with a spacious
median strip and an elegant
row of terraces.

Photo: Graeme Aplin

Plate 6.6

Gaskill Street, the heart of
the Canowindra Urban
Conservation Area,
Canowindra, central-
western NSW. The number
of preserved verandahs and
the curve of the street,
which follows the route of
an old bullock track, make
this streetscape unusual. It
retains a late 19th-century
atmosphere.

Photo: Graeme Aplin

The main aims of a UCA are to try to maintain the overall nature of the area, to retain its heritage value, and to prevent unsympathetic or intrusive developments. Local councils often mandate certain limits to development by imposing covenants on development and redevelopment. The scale and general height and shape of buildings must generally be maintained, so upward extensions, among other changes, may be prohibited. Sometimes details such as colour schemes, exterior finishes, roofing materials, and fence types are restricted to a range deemed suitable. Street set-backs may also be mandated. Are these unreasonable limitations on individual freedom? Does this mean that a home is not a person's castle? Sections of Chapter 3 deal with such questions as these.

Historic towns and villages

In some cases, entire villages and small towns, or substantial parts of them, may be listed as heritage sites. The Hill End–Tambaroora Goldfields Conservation Area, in the central-west of NSW, conceptually lies part-way between a UCA and a landscape conservation area (LCA; see next section), and includes elements of both. Comprising an area of approximately twenty-four square kilometres, the boundaries include the town of Hill End, the remains of the village of Tambaroora, important components of the landscape, and important industrial archaeological sites. A similar example is Maldon in Victoria (Plate 6.7), also a former gold-mining town, which has been listed in its entirety as a historic town (Section 10.3).

Landscape conservation areas

LCAs fall within the ill-defined boundary area between cultural and natural heritage. For example, the Hill End–Tambaroora LCA referred to previously obviously involves cultural (including urban) features, and natural (biophysical) landscape features. The other LCAs on the National Trust (NSW) list are predominantly rural or coastal landscapes, but in reality almost all landscapes in NSW, apart from wilderness areas and some national parks, contain obvious cultural elements. In many cases, it is the combination of cultural and natural elements that gives a landscape its beauty and significance, and its recreational and tourist value. In fact in the United Kingdom and in many other European nations even national parks incorporate major cultural elements, including currently operating farms and villages and towns (see Chapter 11). The Hunter River Estuary LCA of the National Trust provides a good example of an LCA incorporating major cultural elements, as do the Illawarra Escarpment LCA and the Sydney Harbour Entrance LCA.

Plate 6.7

Street scene in the historic town of Maldon, Victoria, a largely intact gold-mining town of the 1850s. Maldon was declared Australia's first 'Notable Town' by the National Trust of Australia (Victoria) in 1966.

Photo: Graeme Aplin

Plate 6.8

Formal gardens, Powerscourt, Ireland, showing Triton Lake, and The Perron (Italianate stairs) that were added in 1874. The gardens are possibly the finest in Ireland; the original 1730s scheme was revived in 1840 after years of neglect. The Palladian mansion of Powerscourt was built in 1731, but appears roofless as it was severely damaged by fire in 1974. In 1999 restoration work was well underway after many years of uncertainty.

Photo: Graeme Aplin

6.5   Cultural heritage sites other than historic buildings

When we consider immoveable cultural heritage we tend to think of buildings and sites with historic or social significance. But many other types of immovable heritage are also considered in the creation of heritage lists by both government agencies and non-government organisations. Gardens, cemeteries, archaeological sites, industrial archaeology items, and shipwrecks all fall into this group; while this list is not exhaustive, it does illustrate the breadth of coverage that is desirable.

Gardens and parks

Gardens often form an important part of an historic building that is listed as a heritage site, as a key contextual element that adds to the significance of the building. Curtilages frequently extend to include surrounding gardens, ranging from the old-fashioned cottage gardens of some small residential sites to the grand 'English' gardens of stately homes such as Powerscourt in Ireland (Plate 6.8) or the more formal French and Italian gardens of continental villas and palaces. In other cases it can be the garden itself, rather than the home or other building, that has heritage significance. A group of classical Chinese gardens in Suzhou, for example, has World Heritage status (see Plate 12.18), while public parks and botanic gardens are quite frequently granted heritage status. Gardens may also be listed because of associations with well-regarded garden designers or because of other associations. Gardens and parks also often have aesthetic values in their own right or as elements in broader precincts and conservation areas.

Cemeteries

Cemeteries have obvious associational values and are usually important to their communities. They can contain a wealth of historical information that documents the history of a community, region, or nation. Some major cemeteries are the resting place for numbers of famous people and draw visitors for that reason; the Cimetière du Père Lachaise in Paris, for example, is the site of the graves of Honoré de Balzac, Frédéric Chopin, Jim Morrison, Simone Signoret, and Yves Montand.

Archaeological sites

Archaeological sites are frequently of heritage significance at one scale or another, even in the absence of significant built remains. The significance often lies in the information that has been gained from the site, or may potentially be gained in the future. It is often possible to provide good interpretation for visitors even when archaeological work is still in progress, and on-site museums (see Plates 6.1 and 11.9) mean that the artefacts are much closer to their original context than they would be if removed to a distant museum. With good interpretation, the artefacts can be integrated into the context in which they were found. In many cases, archaeological sites preserve our pre-history to add to the story told by the historic buildings of later periods.

Industrial archaeology

The realisation of the great significance of early modern industrial sites is only recent, and they are rapidly being replaced, redeveloped, or falling into serious decay. The early phases of our industrial development and older technologies are an important part of our history, often at a local level, sometimes nationally, and even globally—Ironbridge in the United Kingdom is a World Heritage

Plate 6.9

Smelters at abandoned copper mines, Chillagoe, Queensland.

Photo: Don Johnston

area because of its key role in the early Industrial Revolution and because it is the site of significant surviving industrial buildings. Industrial archaeology sites include mines and manufacturing plants. Some agricultural sites and transport sites, such as ports and railway yards, may have similar heritage value. At the end of 2000 there were moves to list the former BHP steel works in Newcastle as a heritage site, while a number of former mining sites are already listed, including the copper mining site at Chillagoe in Queensland (Plate 6.9).

Shipwrecks

Significant shipwrecks require protection to prevent less ethical divers from pillaging them for artefacts that are part of the heritage of a nation or a community. There is some controversy over whether such artefacts should be left on site or removed and placed in museums, especially as it is very difficult and costly to adequately preserve them once removed from the water.

6.6   Dealing with change: alterations and additions

Guides to managing natural heritage, including the ANHC (see Section 5.8), generally recommend allowing processes of change to progress unhindered, even if scenic or iconic values are diminished. How, then, should change in cultural heritage properties be viewed?

How should alterations and/or additions to a heritage building, garden, park, or other site be treated? Such changes certainly do not automatically disqualify an item from being listed. After all, many buildings have grown 'organically', with alterations, additions, adaptations, and even fundamental changes of use over time. In fact, if these changes had not occurred, the building may have been demolished and replaced long ago (see Plate 11.10). Change is part of history and, as long as it is not overly out of character, it need not detract from a site's heritage value, and may even add to significance. In some cases, even sudden and dramatic change may, in itself, be of heritage value. Significant association with an eccentric person of note might give heritage value to almost anything! The detail of the very lively debate on the level of originality required in the condition of a heritage property (assuming that originality can even be identified) cannot be dealt with here, but the discussion is taken a little further in this section.

It may, however, be desirable to remove or reverse additions and alterations that are out of character, or that somehow detract from the core heritage values of a building or site. In many cases, the key building, associated outbuildings, fences, and other features of the same period or with important associations may be listed, but other alterations such as a new carport or a Japanese pebble garden near a Colonial-style house may be omitted from the listing. Alternatively, these additions may be specifically noted as out of character and non-significant. Occasionally it is better to intentionally use distinctively modern additions (Plate 6.10), than it is to attempt to replicate the historic fabric, which could potentially result in an unsuccessful attempt to achieve authenticity. (Note that authenticity is another contentious term.)

Plate 6.10

Musée du Louvre, Paris, with modern entrance pyramid designed by I. M. Pei in 1989. The earlier buildings were constructed over a long period from 1515 to 1870. The entrance was built in glass and steel to allow the earlier buildings to be seen through the structure, and no pretence was made of fitting into the earlier architectural styles.

Photo: Katie Barnett

How original is original? How authentic is authentic?

The questions of originality and authenticity are vexed, frequently difficult to resolve, and perhaps the most divisive issues faced by the heritage community. The resolution of these questions is made even more difficult by the subjectivity of taste and aesthetics, and the way in which one style merges into another, and one period into the next. Exactly what is authentic for a time and place and type of building? What were the authentic materials and techniques at that time? Can we insist that a building be as authentic as possible? Does it always matter? To what extent should buildings be listed according to their potential for restoration to an 'original' or 'authentic' state, rather than on their present condition, which may be very poor and unauthentic? These and related issues are discussed further when we consider conservation and restoration.

Organic change and realistic expectations

Looking forward, we need to ask to what extent future change should be prevented. Is the primary aim of the conservation and management of cultural heritage to freeze things as they are now, or as they were at some previous time? In many cases, change is significant in itself. Perhaps it is desirable to allow a certain amount of ongoing evolution of a building and its uses. A church, or a shopping precinct, may lose significance for the community if it becomes a museum piece instead of a living place of worship or commerce. Should residential tenants or commercial owners of heritage properties be denied modern amenities and the benefits of technology if these can be provided without detracting from heritage values in a major way? Many commentators argue that in all but a few highly significant cases, the 'museum' approach to heritage conservation loses public support and empathy, and that it is possible to preserve key heritage values without preventing the sympathetic development and evolution of most properties.

6.7   Management of cultural heritage

Who manages, and for whom?

Much has already been said about the issue of management, particularly in Chapter 3. In many cases, private or corporate owners manage heritage sites for a combination of their own ends and community heritage outcomes. In many cases, there will be potential conflict between conservation and preservation on the one hand, and access by the public on the other. As we saw in the case of natural heritage sites (Chapter 5), this may be true even when the site is entirely operated and managed by heritage agencies. The 'loving heritage to death' danger is just as great for cultural heritage as it is for natural heritage. If it is the heritage of the public at large, should they have unlimited, unrestricted access? What if public access damages the very heritage values that give the site its significance? Much of the discussion in Chapters 2, 3, and 4 is also relevant here.

The Burra Charter

The Burra Charter was introduced in Chapter 4. Its full title is the *Australian ICOMOS Charter for the Conservation of Places of Cultural Significance*. A secretariat body, also called ICOMOS, meets regularly to discuss relevant issues and to promote the conservation of cultural heritage. The Burra Charter provides a set of guidelines for practitioners in the field of cultural heritage conservation, and is analogous to, and a forerunner of, the ANHC discussed in Chapter 5. The basic definitions of the Burra Charter were introduced in Section 4.1, so the following discussion will focus on the remainder of the short document.

The first section of the Charter that follows the definitions deals with *conservation principles*, starting from the premise that 'the aim of conservation is to retain or recover the cultural significance of a place and must include provision for its security, its maintenance, and its future'. Conservation must be based on sound knowledge, sufficient resources, and a respect for the existing fabric. It should involve the least possible physical intervention, and thus may not be expensive. Techniques employed should be traditional, or soundly based modern ones used for well-justified reasons. The importance of maintaining an appropriate visual setting is stressed. Heritage items should be retained in their historical locations unless moving them is the sole means of ensuring their survival, and contents and fittings should similarly be kept *in situ* if at all possible.

The following section of the Charter deals with *conservation processes*. *Preservation* is appropriate where the existing state of the fabric itself constitutes evidence of specific cultural significance, or where insufficient evidence is available to allow other conservation processes to be carried out. It is limited to the protection, maintenance, and, where necessary, stabilisation of the existing fabric. *Restoration* is appropriate only if there is sufficient evidence of an earlier state, and only if returning the fabric to that state recovers the cultural significance of the place (see for example Plate 4.5). It must be based on respect for all the physical, documentary, and other evidence available, and stops at the point where conjecture begins. *Reconstruction* is appropriate where a site is incomplete through damage or alteration, and where it is necessary for the site's survival, or where it recovers the cultural significance of the place as a whole, but should be limited to situations where the form is known from sound evidence. *Adaptation* is acceptable where the conservation of the site cannot otherwise be achieved, and where the adaptation does not substantially detract from the site's cultural significance; this process is further discussed in Section 6.8.

The third major section of the Charter is concerned with *conservation practice*. It stresses the need for professional approaches at all stages, from background studies to physical work on the fabric (see Plate 10.10). A well-prepared conservation policy and plan are seen as essential, and detailed records are to be kept throughout the conservation processes.

The conservation plan

Figure 6.2 sets out the basic elements and sequence of steps involved in a conservation plan. The top half of the diagram emphasises the importance of establishing cultural significance before proceeding to any attempt at devising a conservation or management plan. Good planning must necessarily be based on full and reliable evidence, gleaned from a wide variety of sources. That evidence must then be analysed, and the significance of the item under consideration assessed, before a formal statement of the significance is made, if indeed it is considered to be sufficiently significant to warrant listing and/or conservation work.

The lower section of the diagram then outlines the stages in preparing a typical conservation policy and plan. While conservation policies set broad directions, conservation plans deal with specific processes and actions. A conservation policy must use the statement of significance as a key element of the necessary baseline data, but it also needs to incorporate other factors, as shown in the diagram.

The physical condition of the building or site will offer both opportunities and constraints for conservation professionals, but in either case a clear understanding of the fabric and its condition is vital. A clear understanding of any relevant laws, regulations, or funding possibilities is necessary, and it is important to be aware of the political and social context, as the good will of the public and politicians is often the key to successful acceptance of a proposal and its implementation. It is always preferable if a community, at the relevant scale or scales, feels it has ownership of a conservation undertaking. Finally, a client's requirements need to be known and taken into account. In every situation there is a client, although often the client is a state or a local council, rather than an individual. Feasible uses, whether or not they require adaptation of the heritage item, also need to be considered.

Once all this information is assembled and analysed, a conservation policy is prepared and presented, and opportunities may be allowed for public comment in addition to feedback from the client. A broad strategy for implementation is then prepared. A detailed conservation plan that outlines appropriate actions, processes, and desired outcomes will be drawn up by professionals, possibly by specialised heritage architects and builders. They may need to involve highly specialised craftspeople (stonemasons, carpenters, etc.) who restore heritage buildings or re-create fixtures and detailing. There will normally be a close relationship between the conservation plan and an ongoing management plan for the site, and often these plans will seamlessly merge.

Figure 6.2

The basic elements and the sequence of steps in a conservation plan

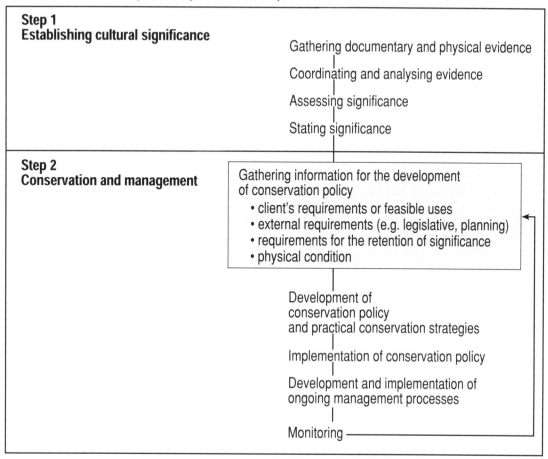

Source: adapted from J. S. Kerr (1985), *The Conservation Plan: A Guide to the Preparation of Conservation Plans for Places of European Cultural Significance*, second edition, National Trust of Australia (NSW), Sydney, p. 2.

Eventual management needs and potential problems must be also be addressed in the conservation plan.

Technical issues that need to be addressed may include:

- choosing between using original materials, where available, and compatible new materials that may well have structural, safety, and durability advantages
- choosing between using original, and possibly now rare, building and finishing techniques, or modern equivalents that are probably faster, cheaper, and easier to obtain
- safety and security requirements, including smoke detectors, fire-fighting systems, railings, burglar alarms, and movement detectors
- parking and other visitor facilities, including toilets, shops, and interpretive signs and displays
- furniture and fittings, especially if these need to be brought from other locations

Practical management issues

The factors raised in general terms in Chapter 4, and those arising from consideration of interpretation (Chapter 2) and economics (Chapter 3), apply equally to cultural as to natural heritage sites. Some of the more specific management issues raised in Chapter 5, which deals with natural heritage, also apply to cultural heritage sites, possibly in a modified form. Of particular relevance is the triangular interplay between raising funds, catering for visitors, and conservation and preservation, and the many resulting conflicts. Physical barriers and other structures, and even forms of 'hardening' to make sites more 'visitor-proof', may be necessary to allow access to large numbers of visitors while protecting the heritage. For example, fragile rooms or sections of rooms may be behind glass or perspex screens, or more commonly beyond ropes or railings (see Plate 4.1). Exceptionally valuable or fragile items or sections of buildings may need to be placed off limits completely, perhaps presented to the public in the form of physical replicas or, increasingly commonly, as 'virtual' replicas.

In addition to the conservation plan for the site, which would include provision for the maintenance of the fabric, cultural heritage managers need to take into consideration budgets, staff, marketing (in most cases), visitor safety and satisfaction (where relevant), and the maintenance of cooperative relationships with neighbours and other stakeholders. They must specifically allow for the many pressures on heritage items. Finally they must work within the broad legislative and regulatory frameworks outlined in some detail for Australia in Chapters 9 and 10, and more briefly for some other nations in Chapters 11 and 12.

6.8   Adaptive re-use

As we saw in Section 4.1, *adaptation* means 'modifying a place to suit proposed compatible uses', a process often referred as adaptive re-use. It is important to consider the definition of *compatible use*—one involving no change to the culturally significant fabric; substantially reversible changes; or minimal-impact changes. Sound adaptive re-use falls within one of those areas, preferably within the first one. Obviously, the re-use of many heritage sites and buildings involves considerably greater change. There is, in fact, a continuum from preservation in an unchanged state all the way through to demolition of a building or major redevelopment of a site. Is saving a heritage site at the expense of major change that impacts on its significance worthwhile? Yet another 'balancing act' is involved in this situation. (They are very common in heritage management.) Is the significance great enough, and can enough of it be retained? Is there no viable alternative? More change may be tolerated if it is the only way a building can be saved, but there is always a very real risk of losing the significance that people are trying to save, thus negating any gains.

One of the most contentious forms of re-use involves preserving the façade of a building (often referred to as *façadism*) and completely renewing the fabric of the remainder. Occasionally, this approach might be justified when the only significance of the building is in the form of its contribution to a streetscape and where there are buildings immediately adjacent to it. Other somewhat less extreme examples might involve preserving all of the exterior but making major changes to the interior, or retaining some portions of the building (exterior and interior) and rebuilding other sections. In some cases, the entire historic or heritage building, or parts of it, might be incorporated into a much larger modern building (Plate 6.11). Again, the ability to justify such actions depends on the exact significance of the various components, including the detailed finishes and furnishings of the interior, and the significance of the curtilage or context.

Plate 6.11

Kircaldie and Staines Building, Wellington, New Zealand, showing new high-rise construction with partial retention of historic department store façade (left), although another façade has been modernised. This is not a successful attempt to preserve heritage as the old is overwhelmed by the new and the result smacks of façadism.

Photo: Graeme Aplin

Many heritage buildings have been successfully re-used in ways that give them new life and finance their retention and restoration. Table 6.2 gives just a few of the large number of examples of successful re-use of (mainly) heritage buildings in Australia. The Jam Factory, in South Yarra, Melbourne, however, holds an important lesson. Its first re-use was commendable; not only was the handsome brick factory exterior retained, but the interior was remodelled as a shopping complex in such a way that important elements of the factory were kept as reminders of the building's history, including the bases of chimney stacks, selected machinery, and even some of the overhead conveyor lines for the cans. A second remodelling in the 1990s removed all of these industrial reminders except the chimneys (presumably too difficult and expensive to get rid of), and these have been 'camouflaged' with brightly coloured plastic 'wrapping' around their bases. The whole interior is now open and garish and the exterior brickwork is the only real reminder of the past. Presumably it was decided that the first remodelling had lessened the building's heritage value to such an extent that the further losses did not matter—loss of heritage value in stages, or by attrition. In contrast, a noteworthy example of a very successful adaptive re-use from France is the Musée d'Orsay, shown in Plate 6.12. Formerly a mainline railway station, the building has been brilliantly transformed into a museum of Impressionist and other late 19th- and early 20th-century art.

Table 6.2

Re-use of old buildings: some Australian examples

State	Original use	New use
NSW	New South Wales Club, Bligh St, Sydney	Head Office, IPEC-Tjuringa Securities
	Garage service centre, Rushcutters Bay	Squash courts
	Tyre factory, Birkenhead Point, Drummoyne	Shopping complex
	Bird seed sorting factory, Balmain	Residence and artist's studio
Victoria	Faraday Street Public School, Carlton	Women's Medical Education Centre
	Church of Christ, Abbotsford	Branch library
	The Jam Factory, South Yarra	Shopping complex
	Factory, Clifton Hill	House
	Malmesbury Mill, Malmesbury	Restaurant
Western Australia	Swan River Colony Asylum, Fremantle	Fremantle Museum and Arts Centre
	Lilly's Building (warehouse), Fremantle	Three residences, two offices, dental surgery
Tasmania	Warehouses, Salamanca Place, Hobart	Trade Union offices, community arts centre, puppet theatre, post office, museum, arts and craft outlets, restaurants
Queensland	Mining company offices, Rockhampton	Australian Broadcasting Corporation studios
	South Brisbane City Hall	Queensland Conservatorium of Music

Source: many of these examples are from A. Latreille, P. Latreille & P. Lovell (1982) *New Uses for Old Buildings in Australia*, Oxford University Press, Melbourne.

Plate 6.12

Musée d'Orsay, Paris, France, formerly a major railway station, which narrowly avoided demolition in the 1970s, and was successfully converted to a museum of paintings and fine arts of the period from 1848 to 1914. It was reopened in 1986 with much of the magnificent turn-of-the-century architecture intact.

Photo: Graeme Aplin

Plate 6.13

Reconstructed village street, Beamish, The North of England Open Air Museum, Co. Durham, England. The Museum has a farm, a coal mine, a village, and a manor house. The village street is complete with houses, a dentist's surgery, a motor dealer (garage), and shops (see also Plate 13.6). An electric tram runs around the site. School children are obvious in this photograph, but older visitors on a 'nostalgia trip' were equally well represented on the day it was taken.

Photo: Graeme Aplin

6.9 Outdoor museums or heritage theme parks?

The Burra Charter emphasises that buildings and other items should be retained on their original sites unless there is absolutely no other way of saving them. After all, most heritage buildings gain some, perhaps most, of their significance from their context, whether that be for physical or aesthetic reasons, or for reasons of more abstract associations. Occasionally, however, a heritage building can be successfully moved to another site if the new site is suitable and can incorporate the building sympathetically. Sometimes, a number of representative buildings are grouped together in a 'heritage theme park', such as the 'village' at Beamish, Yorkshire (Plate 6.13) or the collection of Irish farm buildings at the Bunratty Folk Park (see Plate 1.3). Collections such as these have a valid educational role, often heavily leavened with entertainment, but their value in conserving heritage is frequently doubtful, to say the least. Similarly, re-creations like Old Sydney Town or Sovereign Hill, Ballarat, are one step further removed from authentic originals. Again, they do have valuable educational, recreational, and tourist roles.

6.10   Commodification and commercialisation

Heritage needs to be presented to the public for many reasons, including financial reasons, but also very important educational and social reasons. Section 3.6 discussed the commodification and commercialisation of heritage sites. Many heritage town centres and suburban precincts are kept alive by tourist-oriented uses and more locally oriented equivalents, such as craft markets and Devonshire teas. These uses can be valuable because they allow heritage buildings to be used in ways that require minimum adaptation. Unless a building is so important that conservation can be financed entirely from the public purse, it must be used in some other way, or else it can easily fall into neglect and disrepair. Simply opening a site to the public demands a certain amount of adaptation and necessarily involves commodification and commercialisation because its heritage significance is being marketed as a commodity. These processes become much more problematic, however, when gimmicks and kitsch elements are introduced, which detract from a site's significance.

Notes

[1]   Lynch, K. (1972) *What Time Is This Place?*, MIT Press, Cambridge, MA.
[2]   One objective of the Ku-ring-gai Chase National Park *Plan of Management* is to challenge planning applications for surrounding areas (some of which are part of suburban Sydney) that would allow development of buildings that would be visible from within the park and hence intrude on its air of naturalness and the ability of visitors to escape from urban features.
[3]   Adapted from National Trust of Australia (NSW) listing card.

Further Reading

Alfrey, J. & Putnam, T. (1992) *The Industrial Heritage: Managing Resources and Uses*, Routledge, London.
Apperly, R. Irving, R. & Reynolds. P. (1989) *A Pictorial Guide to Identifying Australian Architecture: Styles and Terms from 1788 to the Present*, Angus & Robertson, Sydney.
Birmingham, J., Jack, I. & Jeans, D. (1979) *Australian Pioneer Technology: Sites and Relics—Towards an Industrial Archaeology of Australia*, Heinemann, Melbourne.
Cantacuzino, S. (1989) *Re/Architecture: Old Buildings/New Uses*, Thames & Hudson, London.

Davison, G. & McConville, C. (eds) (1991) *A Heritage Handbook,* Allen & Unwin, Sydney, Parts 2 & 3.

Jeans, D. N. & Spearritt, P. (1980) *The Open Air Museum: The Cultural Landscape of New South Wales,* Allen & Unwin, Sydney.

Johnson, R. W. & Schene, M. G. (eds) (1987) *Cultural Resources Management,* Kreiger Publishing Co., Malabar, FL.

Kerr, J. S. (1982) *The Conservation Plan: A Guide to the Preparation of Conservation Plans for Places of European Cultural Significance,* National Trust of Australia (NSW), Sydney.

Larkham, P. J. (1996) *Conservation and the City,* Routledge, London.

Latreille, A., Latreille, P. & Lovell, P. (1982) *New Uses for Old Buildings in Australia,* Oxford University Press, Melbourne.

McDougall & Vines (consultants) (2000) *Heritage Advisory Services Handbook: Guidelines for Government, Advisers and the Community,* available through the Environment Australia website at http://www.heritage.gov.au/heritageadvisors/her_advisory.htm

Orbasli, A. (2000) *Tourists in Historic Towns: Urban Conservation and Heritage Management,* E. & F. N. Spon, New York.

Pearson, M. & Sullivan, S. (1995) *Looking After Heritage Places: The Basics of Heritage Planning for Managers, Landowners, and Administrators,* Melbourne University Press, Melbourne.

Sagazio, C. (ed.) (1992) *The National Trust Research Manual: Investigating Buildings, Gardens and Cultural Landscapes,* Allen & Unwin, Sydney.

Sullivan, S. (ed.) (1995) *Cultural Conservation—Towards a National Approach,* Special Heritage Publication Series No. 9, Australian Heritage Commission/Australian Government Publishing Service, Canberra.

CHAPTER 7

Indigenous and Minority Heritage and Its Management

7.1 Introduction

As discussed in previous chapters, the separation of indigenous heritage from other forms of cultural heritage is not ideal. However the inclusion of a separate chapter on indigenous and minority heritage allows certain questions of sensitivity to be raised. While heritage of all groups should be sensitively dealt with, indigenous heritage is often the form that is most removed from dominant groups and governments, and also most under threat. This chapter concentrates on the heritage of indigenous groups in nations settled and now dominated by predominantly European colonists and immigrants. Much of the discussion also applies to local communities or minorities defined in quite different ways. In reality, the heritage of any local or minority community runs the risk of being either ignored or appropriated by the dominant group in society, or by higher levels of government and bureaucracy. Every group would ultimately like to retain *ownership*, in the broadest sense, of what it considers to be its heritage, even though it may be quite happy to see it recognised also as part of regional, national, and even global heritage. The key to ownership is involvement at much more than merely a tokenistic level: in research, the development of listing proposals, the preparation of conservation and management plans, interpretation, and sharing financial rewards where they occur. For these reasons, this chapter is by its very nature likely to be the most controversial and overtly political one in the book.

7.2 National and minority heritage

In many nations one group holds power at the expense of others, whether the groups are defined on the basis of race, ethnicity, religion, or something else. As we have seen, one way of reinforcing the power of the hegemonic group, and the inferior position of others, is through definitions of *national heritage*. These definitions, and the perceptions behind them, have powerful positive and negative effects on different sections of the population, and on outsiders. Emphasising the heritage of one group at the expense of other groups reinforces the feelings of superiority of the dominant group, and those of inferiority of the other groups. Yet heritage can be a powerful uniting force within a non-hegemonic group, helping to maintain the group's identity and the will to keep fighting for its human rights and greater recognition within the nation. In some cases, minority groups do not wish to be a part of their host nation, and are therefore unlikely to want their heritage to be included within the national heritage. Their heritage can then be a rallying factor, giving renewed vigour to their battle for self-determination or independence.

It is therefore true to say that a nation's definition of its national heritage is a major part of its self-definition and self-image, and a highly political topic. It can also be used to project a chosen image in the rest of the world. If a nation is inclusive of its various ethnic, religious, and social groups—in practice as well as in philosophical and legislative terms—examples of heritage items from those groups will be included on officially recognised national lists and registers. If a nation is democratic, its national heritage will reflect this; if not, the official heritage will be biased towards the group in the position of power. The heritage of minority groups (who are referred to in this chapter as the *primary owners*) should be given the same recognition and protection as the heritage of the hegemonic group, and not simply appropriated for purposes of commercialisation and commodification. For example, using indigenous heritage as a tourist drawcard without granting it due respect is usually worse than ignoring it altogether. Inclusion on a national heritage list must be sensitive and made with the approval and full involvement of the primary owners. If approval is not forthcoming, the decision should be respected, even though the outcome may be unfortunate.

The minority group whose heritage is excluded, poorly represented, or appropriated by the dominant group is often an indigenous people, or a series of different indigenous groups. In part this is simply due to the fact that the greater the cultural differences, the harder it seems to be for the majority group to include the heritage of a minority group within the national heritage. However frequently there are also more sinister overtones, and the exclusion of the minority heritage is another way of keeping that group 'in its place', in subjugation. Yet an indigenous group's heritage is a crucial element of its group identity and of its members' individual identities, part of their sense of belonging to the group and of their individual and collective sense of purpose. A group fighting for due recognition will often draw strength from a renewed identification with its heritage, by rejuvenating, even resurrecting, key elements of it. Dignity can flow from heritage, particularly if the majority also recognises the value and importance of the minority's heritage.

At the beginning of 2001, Australia was still stumbling towards reconciliation between its indigenous and non-indigenous citizens. Most Australians now recognise the key role of Aboriginal heritage in establishing Aboriginal identity and dignity, and this was reinforced by the prominent and sensitive incorporation of elements of Aboriginal culture in the opening ceremony of the Sydney 2000 Olympic Games. In general, Australians appreciate that, in a very real sense, Aboriginal people and Torres Strait Islanders have a greater feeling for their heritage than most non-Aboriginal Australians have for theirs. Perhaps this is because non-Aboriginal Australians are still establishing their Australian identity, as distinct from an inherited or imported identity from the United Kingdom or elsewhere. In other words, people are still coming to grips with the Australian part of their heritage. Part of Australia's 'new' national heritage must surely be Aboriginal heritage, but indigenous Australians must be comfortable with both the processes and outcomes of inclusion in the national heritage. In heritage terms, as well as in other senses, reconciliation must be a two-way process, one agreed to and actively participated in by the Aboriginal and Torres Strait Islander people, not one foisted upon them. Above all there must be a great deal of care, understanding, and sensitivity. More will be said about these issues in later parts of this chapter.

Perhaps minority heritage is difficult for majority groups to accept and incorporate into national heritage not only because it is different, but also because it is vital and dynamic. In this way it may be seen as a competing or even threatening heritage. This might explain why it is easier to accept that prehistoric heritage in Europe or Asia is part of our heritage, than it is to accept indigenous heritage as part of the heritage of Australia or the USA. Furthermore, members of the majority groups in Australia, the USA, and many similar nations are not descendants of the indigenous people, while European and Asian communities can accept the notion of direct descent from their prehistoric forebears. Overcoming these prejudices is crucial for the maintenance of national unity and basic human rights.

7.3   Context and significance

The heritage of indigenous and minority peoples is part of living culture. Indigenous groups include the Australian Aboriginal and Torres Strait Islander people, Amazonian Indians, Canadian Inuit, Southern African Ju/'hoansi (Bushmen or San), while examples of minority groups are the Basques in Spain, the Cornish in England, and the Kurds in several nations. In many cases, the minority culture itself, as an entity, is a part of heritage that needs to be preserved for the future; the world would be impoverished if we were to diminish the current rich spread of cultures.

One of the key impacts of globalisation is likely to be the loss of many minority cultures, including their languages, music, dancing, costumes, rituals, religions, crafts, art of all kinds, architecture, and ways of living. Should the world be dominated by a few increasingly similar cultures? Can we afford to lose alternative, traditional approaches to any aspect of life? Can we assume that modern, 'western' culture contains all the answers, the only possible answers, or even the most useful and appropriate answers to the various problems facing the world? Preserving minority culture and heritage (the two are closely intertwined) is justified by a list of reasons similar to those justifying preservation of biodiversity, ranging from existence values through to materialistic or use values (see Section 5.2). All groups have a basic right to preserve their culture and heritage, and there are sound ethical and moral reasons for supporting this statement. They might also be custodians of important knowledge.

Minority and indigenous heritage is even less appropriately preserved in museums and theme parks than majority heritage. Much minority heritage gains its significance from being part of a living culture and way of life. Minority heritage also gains significance from being maintained in its traditional biophysical and environmental setting, an issue that is increasingly recognised by the World Heritage Committee's (WHCom) emphasis on 'cultural landscapes' (see Section 8.3). While prehistoric and early historic heritage may be consigned to museums or preserved on sites that are essentially outdoors museums, living minority cultures and their heritage cannot. The latter need their cultural and environmental contexts to retain their integrity and meaning.

7.4   Ownership and involvement

It is important for any group to retain ownership of its heritage, in the emotional and intellectual senses, as well as in the legal sense. Involvement in how sites and artefacts are interpreted is also desirable, to ensure that the group's meanings are placed on those items. This is true for minority groups anywhere—for small-town or rural communities and for migrant groups—but it is particularly true for indigenous people and persecuted ethnic or religious groups. Even when the majority government is keen to officially recognise minority heritage as part of the national heritage, this can only be successfully achieved with the full cooperation of the primary owners of that heritage. Without the cooperation of primary owners, the government would simply be appropriating the heritage of others. Primary owners need to feel a sense of ownership of their heritage, and must feel part of the decision to make their heritage a part of national heritage. A sense of ownership relies on respect above all else, and the sensitivities of the primary owners must be respected at all stages. When the Glen Canyon Dam in the USA was completed in 1963 to create Lake Powell, the Navajo Nation was granted, in partial recompense, the former Monument Valley National Park, and they now manage and control this area through the Navajo Parks and Recreation Department as the Monument Valley Tribal Park (Plate 7.1). They gain pride and a feeling of independence from doing so.

Research, listing, and planning

Like all forms of heritage, indigenous and minority heritage needs to be thoroughly researched to add to basic knowledge, to provide a sound basis for interpretation, and for conservation and management planning. Research is essential in the preparation of statements of significance, proposals for listing or for conservation, and, ultimately, in the documentation of listed and protected items. Primary owners must be fully involved in research and aware of its implications. If the research is being carried out by government agencies or academics alone, primary owners will be revealing traditions, knowledge, beliefs, and sometimes secrets to outsiders. The primary owners must agree to the knowledge being collected and documented, whether or not this is done by qualified experts (such as archaeologists, anthropologists, and ethnologists) and especially if it is to appear in the public domain in any form. Requests for certain things to be kept off the record, or to be available only to certain groups (perhaps only to heritage professionals in the course of their duties), must be respected. This can make the listing and conservation processes quite tortuous at times, as shown by the example of Hindmarsh Island in South Australia. In that case, local Aboriginal women claimed the proposed bridge to the island from Goolwa would desecrate a sacred site, but the full reasons could never be

Plate 7.1

Monument Valley Tribal
Park, Navajo Nation, USA,
which preserves the culture
of the Navajo people and a
semi-arid landscape of
sandstone buttes, mesas
and spires.

Photo: Richard Aplin

revealed to men (immediately excluding the vast majority of politicians and
bureaucrats judging the case) as it was 'women's business'. The case was
eventually heard by a female commissioner, but even then there was not a free
flow of information for cultural reasons. The case was lost and the bridge
opened in March 2001.

Some sites may be so sacred that the primary owners do not want the exact
location, or even the existence of the site, to be revealed to outsiders. The only
feasible way to deal with such cases seems to be to train members of the
indigenous group in heritage matters, and then trust them to make the
appropriate decisions; a major leap of faith for many non-indigenous people.
Managers require sound information, and if indigenous managers pass this down
by word of mouth, as is often the tradition, valuable knowledge runs the risk of
being lost, as cultures are weakened over time due to outside influences.
Databases are needed, but might need to be carefully protected to restrict access
to those approved by the indigenous people, possibly only to their own people,
and quite possibly to an even smaller group within their people. It is possible that
some things are never able to be committed to paper or electronic databases.

Special committees of primary owners may be required for the assessment
of listing proposals, as well as for the generation and approval of documents
such as environmental impact statements, and conservation and management
plans. The difficulty is that often items are sacred and secret to a particular tribe
or group, and other indigenous people are no more privy to those secrets than
are non-indigenous people. These practical problems can only be overcome
with trust and respect.

Interpretation and presentation

Primary owners should be heavily involved in interpretation, and in the way
items are presented to visitors. Respect for minority cultures and any hope for
authenticity demand that primary owners are instrumental in the
interpretation of heritage, with help from scholars and professionals if
appropriate. Outside interpretation should never be forced or unwelcome.

However, help may be needed with the technical aspects of interpretation and presentation, and with processes such as visitor management and market research. Ideally, primary owners would be trained in as many aspects of the heritage process as possible. Australia, in particular, has a wonderful legacy to draw on, as the travel writer Bill Bryson points out:

> It is a fact little noted that the Aborigines have the oldest continuously maintained culture on earth, and their art goes back to the very roots of it. Imagine if there were some people in France who could take you to the caves at Lascaux and explain in detail the significance of the paintings—why this bison is bolting from the herd, what these three wavy lines mean—because it is as fresh and sensible to them as if it were done yesterday. Well, Aborigines can do that. It is an unparalleled human achievement, scarcely appreciated … [1]

Plate 7.2

Uluṟu (Ayers Rock) in the Uluṟu–Kata Tjuṯa National Park, Northern Territory, a World Heritage property. Uluṟu is probably the most instantly recognisable symbol of Australia, but this more unusual detailed photograph reveals the intricate weathering patterns on the monolith.

Photo: Monica Green

Respecting the wishes of primary owners may mean that certain activities are forbidden or discouraged, or that certain standards of dress and behaviour are required; we are probably all familiar with the need for modest dress in places of worship, and the need to remove shoes at many sites. Often photography and loud talking are forbidden or firmly discouraged, because such activities are viewed as inappropriate by the guardians of the heritage. In certain cases, items and sites may not be made available to visitors, or restrictions may be placed on visitors on the grounds of age or gender. However, restricting entry to sites by some groups of visitors and not others needs careful explanation in a society such as modern Australia that values equality of opportunity. Blanket bans (or discouragement) are easier to put in place. For example, visitors are strongly discouraged from climbing Uluṟu (Ayers Rock; Plate 7.2) because of its sacred significance to the local Aboriginal traditional owners, and many people take heed. Whether a total ban, with the associated potential loss of visitors and revenue, should be enforced remains a controversial issue that must be decided by the site's managers, a group that includes many traditional owners. In early 2001, Uluṟu's traditional owners also expressed serious reservations about the way commercial concerns used images of the site in films, television, and advertising material, and sought greater control over such uses. In May 2001 the right to climb Uluru was withdrawn during a period of mourning following the death of a respected traditional owner. Interestingly, the majority of affected visitors accepted the decision with little or no complaint.

Should primary owners have the right to see and approve all material that interprets their heritage? Many people from outside the group of immediate owners may be responsible for material that interprets indigenous or minority heritage, from bus drivers who give commentaries, to government tourism bodies that produce brochures. This material may contain anything from innocent errors, through misinformation, to racial slurs and quite deliberate misrepresentations that damage reputations. The best way to avoid such errors is probably to increase the education of all those involved, including exposure to the cultures and groups concerned. Policing all bus commentaries is impossible, but a system of education and accreditation for guides is not.

Planning and managing heritage

The management of heritage should involve local communities, indigenous peoples, minority groups, and any other primary owners of heritage, including involvement in drawing up and carrying out conservation and management plans (Plate 7.3). Much has already been said about the importance of local or group knowledge, and of the need to take into account the sensitivities of the primary owners. In most cases there will be a need for input from outside professionals in fields ranging from economics and law to the biophysical sciences. On the other hand, local people, particularly traditional owners, will often have detailed knowledge that is not available to even the best-resourced park management team from outside the area. We thus need a constructive partnership between the two broad groups, something that has certainly been achieved in Kakadu National Park (see Box 9.2). In many cases, especially if sacred sites or traditional lands are involved, it may be reasonable for the owners to have a right of veto, or a majority on any committee or working group. (Kakadu is again an example of practical application.)

Plate 7.3

Sign at Basin Aboriginal Engraving Site, Ku-ring-gai Chase National Park, north of Sydney, NSW. The sign highlights the involvement of the Metropolitan Local Aboriginal Land Council in managing the site and sets out penalties for damaging Aboriginal sites in NSW.

Photo: Graeme Aplin

Appropriation

One of the main fears of indigenous peoples is that their culture and heritage will be appropriated—'stolen' is not too strong a word in many cases—by others. This fear is well justified based on past experience. Indigenous heritage can legitimately be seen to be part of national heritage and, as argued previously, this is the ideal situation. But it is still primarily the heritage of the indigenous group. There have been many cases in Australia of specific art works being used commercially as designs on fabrics, cards, and even Australian banknotes, without the artist's permission, or that of his/her tribal group, and without any financial return to the artist or group. There are also more subtle forms of appropriation of images and ideas, which often give false impressions about Aboriginal culture.

Advantages and disadvantages of heritage exploitation

Active involvement in managing heritage sites and opening them to visitors brings both advantages and disadvantages to indigenous and minority peoples. Economic returns can be gained directly through a share in entry fees and other income, and indirectly through employment opportunities at the sites and in related tourist enterprises. By showing their arts and crafts and demonstrating their culture to others, a group may develop a renewed interest and pride in these traditions, which otherwise may have been neglected and have lost vigour. For example, traditional crafts, songs, and dances may be taught to younger members of the group, enhancing group morale. On the other hand, greater exposure to outside influences through visitors and the tourist industry can have the opposite effect, diluting and corrupting group culture. Adverse effects such as disease, drugs, and alcohol can also be introduced. Furthermore, the spiritual and cultural significance of the heritage may be diluted in order to present it to outsiders, and may eventually be lost completely. There is a fine line between exposing visitors to confronting aspects of other cultures, and making them too uncomfortable; between 'telling it like it is', and misrepresenting facts that are too strange or distasteful. Privacy and the chance for a normal community life may also be lost through the presence of visitors. It is up to a cooperative effort by group leaders and appropriate individuals and agencies from beyond the group to maximise the positive impacts and minimise the negative ones.

Active conservation and maintenance

Many indigenous sites are prone to fairly rapid deterioration. Rock engraving sites (Plate 7.4) are gradually eroded by wind and water until the grooves are too shallow to show up clearly. The pigments used for cave paintings (Plate 7.5) are rarely long-lasting, even at the best of times, and they can quickly fade when exposed to algal, fungal, and bacterial attack; the weather; the abrasive activities of animals; and interference from human visitors. Some of these destructive forces can be slowed or even halted. Silicon drip-lines can keep water away from cave paintings, and fencing can keep larger animals out of fragile sites. Various barriers can also keep visitors out, but they are frequently intrusive, detracting from the atmosphere of the site and sometimes interfering with views of the protected artefacts. Barriers are, nonetheless, sometimes necessary, especially in publicised but non-patrolled sites (Plate 7.6). In other cases, a mixture of interpretive and exhortative signs and simpler, less intrusive barriers may be all that is needed (Plate 7.7). Protecting the site shown in Plate 7.4 from natural wind abrasion is, however, an unsolved problem, even though protection from visitor impact could easily be improved.

Given that engravings inevitably will be worn down and paintings will fade, who, if anyone, should re-engrave or repaint them? In most indigenous cultures, it must be a member of the group or tribe that originally created them, and usually only quite specific members of the group. In many cases, these people are no longer available, or the sequence of people that would have passed on the tradition has been broken. (Box 7.1 discusses one such case.) Frequently, then, indigenous art sites, whether paintings or engravings, cannot and will not be renewed. In some circumstances, reproductions may be created off site, or in on-site museums (Plate 7.8A and B). The originals should, at very least, be fully documented, if that is feasible and allowed by the culture concerned. (In some cases photography, for example, may not be welcomed.)

Plate 7.4

A large engraving of an emu, Elvina Aboriginal Engraving Site, Ku-ring-gai Chase National Park, north of Sydney, NSW. This site is poorly signed, almost completely unprotected from visitors, and is in a very exposed position which makes it prone to natural sand-blasting by strong winds. Visitors often walk on the engravings before realising they are doing so.

Photo: Graeme Aplin

Plate 7.5

Bunjil's Cave, in the Black Range east of the Grampians National Park, Victoria (see also Plate 2.6). Bunjil is common in the Aboriginal mythology of south-eastern Australia, and is seen as a God-like figure. Two dingoes are pictured to the right of Bunjil.

Photo: Graeme Aplin

Plate 7.6

Protective fencing to prevent visitor damage at Red Hands Cave (Manja Shelter) in the western section of the Grampians National Park, Victoria.

Photo: Graeme Aplin

Plate 7.7

Basin Aboriginal Engraving Site, Ku-ring-gai Chase National Park, north of Sydney, NSW, showing the low log barrier used to delimit visitor space without impeding the view of the carvings. One of the explanatory signs can just be made out.

Photo: Graeme Aplin

Plate 7.8 (A)

Rock engraving of male and female human figures, Basin Site, Ku-ring-gai Chase National Park, NSW.

Photo: Graeme Aplin

Plate 7.8 (B)

Reproduction of these
figures outside the Kalkarri
Visitors' Centre, Ku-ring-
gai Chase National Park,
NSW.

Photo: Graeme Aplin

Box 7.1   Ku-ring-gai National Park rock engravings

What, if anything, should be done to restore Aboriginal rock paintings and engravings to their original, newly executed, state? Should they merely be conserved in an attempt to prevent further deterioration? Is this even possible when engravings, in particular, are fully exposed to weathering processes, and when cave paintings are open to defacement by graffiti and other types of vandalism? We can all accept, I think, that further damage should be prevented as much as possible, so let us turn to restoration.

Personnel from the NSW NPWS and representatives of the Metropolitan Local Aboriginal Land Council have worked together to remove moss and lichens and clean graffiti from engravings in the West Head area of Ku-ring-gai Chase National Park (Plates 2.1, 7.4, 7.7 and 7.8A), using clean water and soft nylon brushes to avoid further damage. The local Aboriginal spokesperson said that the Aboriginal community would have to consider whether or not the figures should be re-engraved:

> The problem is coming up with who is going to do it and how they are going to do it in the traditional way. We are still talking about it. It will be up to the elders.[1]

For the time being, however, cleaning is limited to once every 18–24 months because of a lack of certainty regarding the long-term effect of cleaning on the engravings. One positive benefit of cleaning is seen to be that visitors can see the engravings more easily and therefore are less tempted to cross barriers or walk very close to the engravings for a better view or to attempt to 'enhance' the engravings for photographs by scratching around the outlines or using chalk or other similar materials.

A similar dilemma faces the State Forest's Aboriginal Liaison Officer in relation to a cave in the Hunter Valley that has over 800 hand stencils dating from 2000 to 3000 years ago. The effects of weathering, water, insects, lichen, and humans are all taking their toll. The officer says they should be 'touched up', or restored, for future generations. In his view, even though the events of European settlement have broken the direct line of descent linking the original artists to present Aboriginal residents of the Hunter, 'all Aboriginals have a responsibility to manage and protect indigenous heritage'.[2] In his view, indigenous sites, including art sites, give modern Aboriginal Australians a sense of belonging to the land, even if they come from a different tribal area, and such sites are in most cases the only remaining physical evidence of pre-settlement Aboriginal occupation. He sees reworking as the only way of retaining many sites.

An archaeologist, however, is quoted as expressing grave misgivings about the proposal: 'unless the restorers can come up with exactly the same chemical composition of materials, and unless they are skilful and tribally connected to the sites, they risk defacing the true record of rock art'.[3] She quotes earlier attempts to 'restore' Aboriginal art sites in the Kimberley that were less than totally successful and caused major upset in the local indigenous community.

Notes: [1]   *The Manly Daily*, 17 August 2000.
     [2,3]   *The Sydney Morning Herald*, 9 March 1998.

7.5 Indigenous tourism and Australian Aboriginal cultures

The focus of tourism is as much on indigenous and minority heritage as on any other form of heritage. Much of this short section, along with Box 7.2, is based on material in a brochure entitled *Indigenous Tourism: Product Development Principles* published by Tourism New South Wales in 1997. While the discussion relates specifically to Australia, it contains valuable principles with much wider application. It makes a number of relevant general points, some related closely to ones made earlier in the chapter, before addressing specifics.

Aboriginal culture is living and dynamic, as reflected in the quote from Bill Bryson given earlier, and is an important source of identity and self-esteem for the indigenous population. A strong resurgence of Aboriginal culture is underway, along with clear growth in local and international interest in, and respect for, Aboriginal culture in all its forms. Aboriginal arts and cultures give a unique character to many Australian tourist experiences, and potentially could provide a distinctive component to the Australian identity, provided that Aboriginal and non-Aboriginal Australian communities allow this partial merging of cultures. These factors add to Australia's appeal in the international tourist market.

At the same time, tourism offers significant potential for indigenous Australians, provided that there is a good working relationship between the tourism industry and Aboriginal people. Tourism can provide employment and other economic benefits, help foster self-determination and self-sufficiency, increase understanding and appreciation of Aboriginal culture by non-Aborigines, and assist in the reconciliation process. It can more specifically assist local communities to promote and strengthen their culture and heritage through the process of recording, conserving, and interpreting Aboriginal culture and, with careful management, protect Aboriginal heritage sites. A major challenge is to find the appropriate balance between cultural integrity and responsiveness to market demands and expectations.

Box 7.2 outlines the key principles and sensitive issues in the area of indigenous tourism, many of which have already been discussed in this chapter. Most of the points raised also apply to issues of indigenous heritage that do not involve tourism, while some are more general and apply to attitudes to heritage that are present across the Australian community. Many of the sensitive issues listed in Part B of the Box relate to appropriation in one way or another. Above all, heritage professionals and others involved in heritage need to be acutely aware of the diversity and dynamic nature of Aboriginal culture. It was particularly pleasing at the opening ceremony of the Sydney 2000 Olympic Games to see a number of very different styles of song and dance being performed by distinct indigenous groups from various parts of Australia, not just one stereotyped version of indigenous culture. People also need to be sensitive to the fact that Aboriginal outlooks on many aspects of life often differ markedly from non-Aboriginal ones.

Box 7.2   Key indigenous tourism principles and sensitive issues

A   Principles
1   Aboriginal people are best positioned to determine the content and interpretation of the product.
2   Aboriginal culture is living and dynamic—both contemporary and traditional values and customs need to be acknowledged and presented.
3   Development should occur in a way which Aboriginal communities feel is appropriate.
4   Aboriginal participation should ensure that integrity, authenticity, and accurate representation are maintained.
5   Non-Aboriginal partners should undertake cross-cultural awareness training.
6   Quality-of-life benefits should be delivered to the communities concerned.
7   Aboriginal community protocols should be adhered to, including: giving consideration to traditional 'tribal' lands and boundaries; seeking permission to view heritage sites from those with the appropriate cultural authority; consulting and negotiating with tribal elders on matters of significance; using Aboriginal decision-making processes where appropriate; taking into account distinctions between men's and women's business and sites; and generally being sensitive towards Aboriginal law, customs, beliefs, and culture.

B   Sensitive issues
A   Copyright and intellectual property rights, including publication, use and sale of Aboriginal designs, images etc.
B   Interpretation of Aboriginal culture by non-indigenous guides.
C   Performances and presentations of Aboriginal music, song, and dance by non-indigenous performers.
D   Reproduction and sale of Aboriginal artefacts, crafts, and artworks.
E   Photographing and/or exposing sacred sites etc., without prior permission.
F   The need to foster an awareness of spiritual and emotional aspects of Aboriginal culture.
G   Insensitive reinforcement of stereotypical images, even when based on market expectations.
H   Need for respect for Aboriginal law, customs, beliefs, and culture.
I   Protection of sacred and heritage sites.
J   Recognition of cultural diversity, rather than view of Aboriginal people as homogenous.
K   Need to consider Aboriginal perspectives on life.
L   Patronising attitudes towards Aborigines.
M   Need for sensitivity to impacts on the land and on communities—not merely response to markets.
N   Placing traditions, beliefs, and ways of life in jeopardy.

Source: Tourism NSW (1997), *Indigenous Tourism: Product Development Principles*, Tourism New South Wales, Sydney.

7.6   An integrated view of heritage

It is important to realise that the dichotomy between cultural heritage and natural heritage, difficult to sustain in many circumstances, becomes meaningless when indigenous people are involved. As for most indigenous peoples, the Aboriginal relationship with the land is intimate and cooperative, not dominating. Culture is *country*, and *vice versa*. It is precisely for this reason that four of Australia's World Heritage properties are inscribed under both cultural and natural criteria and viewed as *cultural landscapes* (see Sections 8.3 and 9.4; Table 9.1).

Note

[1]   Bryson, B. (2000) *Down Under*, Doubleday, London, p. 102.

Further Reading

Baker, R. (ed.) (2001) *Working on Country: Contemporary Indigenous Management of Australia's Lands and Coastal Regions*, Oxford University Press, Melbourne.

Birckhead, J., De Lacy, T. & Smith, L. (eds) (1992) *Aboriginal Involvement in Parks and Protected Areas*, Aboriginal Studies Press, Canberra.

Flood, J. (1993) *The Riches of Ancient Australia: An Indispensable Guide for Exploring Prehistoric Australia* (revised edn), University of Queensland Press, Brisbane.

Jacobs, J. M. & Gale, F. (1994) *Tourism—And the Protection of Aboriginal Cultural Sites*, Australian Government Publishing Service, Canberra.

Jonas, W. (1991) *Consultation with Aboriginal People About Aboriginal Heritage*, Australian Government Publishing Service, Canberra.

Kauffman, P. (2000) *Travelling Aboriginal Australia: Discovery and Reconciliation*, Hyland House, Melbourne.

Rose, D. B. (1996) *Nourishing Terrains: Australian Aboriginal Views of Landscape and Wilderness*, Australian Heritage Commission, Canberra.

Smyth, D. (2001) 'Joint management of national parks', in Baker, R. *Working on Country: Contemporary Indigenous Management of Australia's Lands and Coastal Regions*, Oxford University Press, Melbourne, pp. 75–91.

Stevens, S. (ed.) (1997) *Conservation through Cultural Survival: Indigenous Peoples and Protected Areas*, Island Press, Washington DC.

Woenne-Green, S. *et al.* (1994) *Competing Interests: Aboriginal Participation in National Parks and Conservation Reserves in Australia—A Review*, Department of Education, Employment & Training, Canberra.

Zeppel, H. (1999) *Aboriginal Tourism in Australia: A Research Bibliography*, CRC for Sustainable Tourism, Griffith University, Gold Coast.

CHAPTER 8

Global Heritage: The World Heritage Convention and Other Treaties

8.1 The concept of World Heritage

We have seen that heritage, cultural or natural, can be perceived as significant at many different scales. One of these is the global scale; at this level items have significance for the whole human population. This does not, of course, mean that each and every individual sees each item as globally significant, or even significant at all; we are all different and have our own backgrounds, beliefs, perceptions, and priorities. But the WHCom and its advisers in the fields of cultural and natural heritage deem that World Heritage items are significant at the global scale for one or more reasons from an accepted list. (These will be discussed in Section 8.3.) The administrative structure for the recognition and conservation of items at this level of significance is established under the *Convention Concerning the Protection of the World Cultural and Natural Heritage*, usually referred to as the World Heritage Convention (WHC).

8.2 The World Heritage Convention

The (WHC), administered through the UNESCO was adopted in Paris in November 1972, and came into force in December 1975. By the end of January 2001 there were 162 parties to the convention, all of which had ratified, accepted, or acceded to it. (Such cooperating nations are known as *State Parties*.) The number of parties grew steadily throughout the period from 1974 to 2000, apart from a sudden influx of the newly independent eastern European states in the mid-1990s (Figure 8.1). Table 8.1 gives the dates at which nations became State Parties to the WHC.

In the period from December 1996 to December 2000, the number of World Heritage sites, or *properties* (as they are usually known), grew from 506 in 107 countries to 690 in 122 countries (Table 8.1 and Figure 8.2). As outlined below, a site needs to be nominated and supported by the national government of the country in which it is located. It is not a case of a world body imposing its wishes on reluctant participants. In early 2001, 529 of the 690 sites were cultural sites, 139 were natural sites, and 22 were mixed sites, deemed significant for both cultural and natural reasons (Figure 8.2 and Table 8.1).

Figure 8.1

Numbers of State Parties to the World Heritage Convention and number of State Parties with World Heritage properties inscribed, 1975–2000

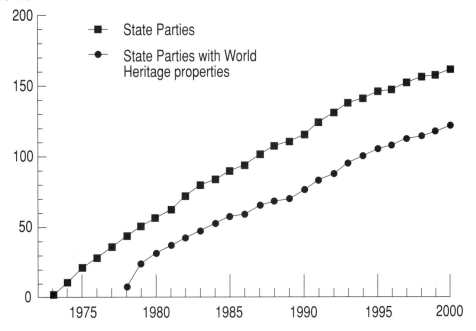

Table 8.1

Status of World Heritage State Parties and type and number of sites as at March 2001

State Party	Status[1]	Date of deposit	Number of sites			Initial inscription		
			Cultural	*Natural*	*Mixed*	*To 1989[2]*	*1990–2000[2]*	*Total*
Afghanistan	R	1979	-	-	-	-	-	-
Albania	R	1989	1	-	-	-	1	1
Algeria	R	1974	6	-	1	6	1	7
Andorra	Ac	1997	-	-	-	-	-	-
Angola	R	1991	-	-	-	-	-	-
Antigua and Barbuda	Ac	1983	-	-	-	-	-	-
Argentina[3]	Ac	1978	2	4	-	2	4	6
Argentina and Brazil		n.a.	1	-	-	1	-	1
Armenia	S	1993	1	2	-	-	3	3
Australia	R	1974	-	10	4	8	6	14
Austria	R	1992	6	-	-	-	6	6
Azerbaijan	R	1993	-	1	-	-	1	1
Bahrain	R	1991	-	-	-	-	-	-
Bangladesh	Ac	1983	2	1	-	2	1	3

State Party	Status[1]	Date of deposit	Number of sites			Initial inscription		
			Cultural	Natural	Mixed	To 1989[2]	1990–2000[2]	Total
Belarus[4]	R	1988	1	-	-	-	1	1
Belarus and Poland		n.a.	-	1	-	1	-	1
Belgium	R	1996	8	-	-	-	8	8
Belize	R	1990	-	1	-	-	1	1
Benin	R	1982	1	-	-	1	-	1
Bolivia	R	1976	5	1	-	1	5	6
Bosnia and Herzegovina	S	1993	-	-	-	-	-	-
Botswana	Ac	1998	-	-	-	-	-	-
Brazil[3]	Ac	1977	8	5	-	6	7	13
Bulgaria	Ac	1974	7	2	-	9	-	9
Burkina Faso	R	1987	-	-	-	-	-	-
Burundi	R	1982	-	-	-	-	-	-
Cambodia	Ac	1991	1	-	-	-	1	1
Cameroon	R	1982	-	1	-	1	-	1
Canada[5]	Ac	1976	5	6	-	9	2	11
Canada and the USA		n.a.	-	2	-	1	1	2
Cape Verde	Ac	1988	-	-	-	-	-	-
Central African Republic	R	1980	-	1	-	1	-	1
Chad	R	1999	-	-	-	-	-	-
Chile	R	1980	2	-	-	-	2	2
China	R	1985	20	3	4	6	21	27
Colombia	Ac	1983	4	1	-	1	4	5
Comoros	R	2000	-	-	-	-	-	-
Congo	R	1987	-	-	-	-	-	-
Congo, Dem. Rep. of the	R	1974	-	5	-	4	1	5
Costa Rica[6]	R	1977	-	2	-	-	2	2
Costa Rica and Panama		n.a.	-	1	-	1	-	1
Côte d'Ivoire[7]	R	1981	-	2	-	2	-	2
Croatia	S	1992	5	1	-	3	3	6
Cuba	R	1981	5	1	-	2	4	6

State Party	Status[1]	Date of deposit	Number of sites			Initial inscription		
			Cultural	Natural	Mixed	To 1989[2]	1990–2000[2]	Total
Cyprus	Ac	1975	3	-	-	2	1	3
Czech Republic	S	1993	10	-	-	-	10	10
Denmark	R	1979	3	-	-	-	3	3
Dominica	R	1995	-	1	-	-	1	1
Dominican Republic	R	1985	1	-	-	-	1	1
Ecuador	Ac	1975	2	2	-	3	1	4
Egypt	R	1974	5	-	-	5	-	5
El Salvador	Ac	1991	1	-	-	-	1	1
Estonia	R	1995	1	-	-	-	1	1
Ethiopia	R	1977	6	1	-	7	-	7
Fiji	R	1990	-	-	-	-	-	-
Finland	R	1987	5	-	-	-	5	5
France[8]	Ac	1975	25	1	-	17	9	26
France and Spain		n.a.	-	-	1	-	1	1
Gabon	R	1986	-	-	-	-	-	-
Gambia	R	1987	-	-	-	-	-	-
Georgia	S	1992	3	-	-	-	3	3
Germany	R	1976	23	1	-	8	16	24
Ghana	R	1975	2	-	-	2	-	2
Greece	R	1981	14	-	2	10	6	16
Grenada	Ac	1998	-	-	-	-	-	-
Guatemala	R	1979	2	-	1	3	-	3
Guinea[7]	R	1979	-	-	-	-	-	-
Guinea and Côte d'Ivoire		n.a.	-	1	-	1	-	1
Guyana	Ac	1977	-	-	-	-	-	-
Haiti	R	1980	1	-	-	1	-	1
Holy See[9]	A	1982	1	-	-	1	-	1
Honduras	R	1979	1	1	-	2	-	2
Hungary[10]	Ac	1985	5	-	-	2	3	5
Hungary and Slovakia		n.a.	-	1	-	-	1	1
Iceland	R	1995	-	-	-	-	-	-

State Party	Status[1]	Date of deposit	Number of sites			Initial inscription		
			Cultural	Natural	Mixed	To 1989[2]	1990–2000[2]	Total
India	R	1977	17	5	-	19	3	22
Indonesia	Ac	1989	3	3	-	-	6	6
Iran, Islamic Republic of	Ac	1975	3	-	-	3	-	3
Iraq	Ac	1974	1	-	-	1	-	1
Ireland	R	1991	2	-	-	-	2	2
Israel[11]	Ac	1999	-	-	-	-	-	-
Italy[9]	R	1978	32	1	-	5	28	33
Italy and the Holy See		n.a.	1	-	-	1	-	1
Jamaica	Ac	1983	-	-	-	-	-	-
Japan	Ac	1992	9	2	-	-	11	11
Jerusalem (proposed by Jordan)[11]		n.a.	1	-	-	1	-	1
Jordan[11]	R	1975	2	-	-	2	-	2
Kazakhstan	Ac	1994	-	-	-	-	-	-
Kenya	Ac	1991	-	2	-	-	2	2
Kiribati	Ac	2000	-	-	-	-	-	-
Korea, Dem. People's Rep.	Ac	1998	-	-	-	-	-	-
Korea, Republic of	Ac	1988	7	-	-	-	7	7
Kyrgystan	Ac	1995	-	-	-	-	-	-
Lao People's Dem. Rep.	R	1987	1	-	-	-	1	1
Latvia	Ac	1995	1	-	-	-	1	1
Lebanon	R	1983	5	-	-	4	1	5
Libyan Arab Jamahiriya	R	1978	5	-	-	5	-	5
Lithuania[12]	Ac	1992	1	-	-	-	1	1
Lithuania and Russian Fedn		n.a.	1	-	-	-	1	1
Luxembourg	R	1983	1	-	-	-	1	1
Macedonia, former Yugoslav Republic of	S	1997	-	-	1	1	-	1
Madagascar	R	1983	-	1	-	-	1	1

State Party	Status[1]	Date of deposit	Number of sites			Initial inscription		
			Cultural	Natural	Mixed	To 1989[2]	1990–2000[2]	Total
Malawi	R	1982	-	1	-	1	-	1
Malaysia	R	1988	-	2	-	-	2	2
Maldives	Ac	1986	-	-	-	-	-	-
Mali	Ac	1977	2	1	-	3	-	3
Malta	Ac	1978	3	-	-	3	-	3
Mauritania	R	1981	1	1	-	1	1	2
Mauritius	R	1995	-	-	-	-	-	-
Mexico	Ac	1984	19	2	-	8	13	21
Monaco	R	1978	-	-	-	-	-	-
Mongolia	Ac	1990	-	-	-	-	-	-
Morocco	R	1975	6	-	-	3	3	6
Mozambique	R	1982	1	-	-	-	1	1
Myanmar	Ac	1994	-	-	-	-	-	-
Namibia	Ac	2000	-	-	-	-	-	-
Nepal	Ac	1978	2	2	-	3	1	4
Netherlands	Ac	1992	7	-	-	-	7	7
New Zealand	R	1984	-	2	1	-	3	3
Nicaragua	Ac	1979	1	-	-	-	1	1
Niger	Ac	1974	-	2	-	-	2	2
Nigeria	R	1974	1	-	-	-	1	1
Niue	Ac	2001	-	-	-	-	-	-
Norway	R	1977	4	-	-	4	-	4
Oman	Ac	1981	3	1	-	2	2	4
Pakistan	R	1976	6	-	-	5	1	6
Panama[6]	R	1978	2	1	-	2	1	3
Papua New Guinea	Ac	1997	-	-	-	-	-	-
Paraguay	R	1988	1	-	-	-	1	1
Peru	R	1982	6	2	2	7	3	10
Philippines	R	1985	3	2	-	-	5	5
Poland[4]	R	1976	8	-	-	4	4	8
Portugal	R	1980	9	1	-	6	4	10
Qatar	Ac	1984	-	-	-	-	-	-
Romania	Ac	1990	6	1	-	-	7	7

State Party	Status[1]	Date of deposit	Number of sites			Initial inscription		
			Cultural	Natural	Mixed	To 1989[2]	1990–2000[2]	Total
Russian Federation[12]	R	1988[13]	10	5	-	-	15	15
Saint Christopher and Nevis	Ac	1986	1	-	-	-	1	1
Saint Lucia	R	1991	-	-	-	-	-	-
San Marino	R	1991	-	-	-	-	-	-
Saudi Arabia	Ac	1978	-	-	-	-	-	-
Senegal	R	1976	2	2	-	3	1	4
Seychelles	Ac	1980	-	2	-	2	-	2
Slovakia[10]	S	1993	4	-	-	-	4	4
Slovenia	S	1992	-	1	-	1	-	1
Solomon Islands	A	1992	-	1	-	-	1	1
South Africa	R	1997	2	1	1	-	4	4
Spain[8]	Ac	1982	32	2	1	16	19	35
Sri Lanka	Ac	1980	6	1	-	6	1	7
Sudan	R	1974	-	-	-	-	-	-
Suriname	Ac	1997	-	1	-	-	1	1
Sweden	R	1985	9	1	1	-	11	11
Switzerland	R	1975	4	-	-	3	1	4
Syrian Arab Republic	Ac	1975	4	-	-	4	-	4
Tajikistan	S	1992	-	-	-	-	-	-
Tanzania, United Republic of	R	1977	2	4	-	5	1	6
Thailand	Ac	1987	3	1	-	-	4	4
Togo	Ac	1998	-	-	-	-	-	-
Tunisia	R	1975	7	1	-	7	1	8
Turkey	R	1983	7	-	2	7	2	9
Turkmenistan	S	1994	1	-	-	-	1	1
Uganda	Ac	1987	-	2	-	-	2	2
Ukraine	R	1988	2	-	-	-	2	2
United Kingdom	R	1984	16	4	-	14	6	20
United States of America[5]	R	1973	8	10	-	16	2	18
Uruguay	Ac	1989	1	-	-	-	1	1

State Party	Status[1]	Date of deposit	Number of sites			Initial inscription		
			Cultural	*Natural*	*Mixed*	*To 1989*[2]	*1990–2000*[2]	*Total*
Uzbekistan	S	1993	3	-	-	-	3	3
Venezuela	Ac	1990	2	1	-	-	3	3
Viet Nam	Ac	1987	3	1	-	-	4	4
Yemen	R	1980	3	-	-	2	1	3
Yugoslavia	R	1975	3	1	-	4	-	4
Zambia[13]	R	1984	-	-	-	-	-	-
Zambia and Zimbabwe		n.a.	-	1	-	1	-	1
Zimbabwe[13]	R	1982	2	1	-	3	-	3
			529	139	22	320	370	690

Notes:
[1] R   Ratified
Ac Accepted
A   Acceded
S   Succession notified; these nations have seceded from the former Czechoslovakia, USSR, and Yugoslavia which accepted in 1990, ratified in 1988, and ratified in 1975 respectively.
[2] Many sites have been extended since their original inscription, but only the original date of inscription is included in this table.
[3] See also joint listing for Argentina and Brazil.
[4] See also joint listing for Belarus and Poland.
[5] See also joint listing for Canada and the USA.
[6] See also joint listing for Costa Rica and Panama.
[7] See also joint listing for Guinea and Côte d'Ivoire.
[8] See also joint listing for France and Spain.
[9] See also joint listing for Italy and the Holy See.
[10] See also joint listing for Hungary and Slovakia.
[11] In a unique departure from normal practice, the Old City of Jerusalem was inscribed as the result of a proposal by Jordan which was clearly not the sovereign state in which it is located. Israel was not a State Party at the time.
[12] See also joint listing for Lithuania and Russian Federation.
[13] See also joint listing for Zambia and Zimbabwe.

Source: various World Heritage Committee printed and web site materials.

The UNESCO Constitution, in part, 'provides that it will maintain, increase, and diffuse knowledge by assuring the conservation and protection of the world's heritage' (as stated in the WHC Preamble). The single stated objective of the WHC itself is:

> To establish an effective system of collective protection of the cultural and natural heritage of outstanding universal value, organized on a permanent basis and in accordance with modern scientific methods.

A more detailed 'Summary of Provisions' is given in Box 8.1. Three phrases in the main objective are of particular importance: *collective protection, universal value* and *modern scientific methods*. Each of these is worthy of brief discussion.

Collective protection is referred to in a number of ways in the Summary of Provisions (Box 8.1). Provision is made for assistance on financial or technical grounds through the World Heritage Fund (WHF), or through agreements between nations, or between a non-government organisation (NGO) and a national government. Parties are expected to improve heritage protection by, among other things, developing and using modern scientific methods. Specific provision is made to assist less wealthy nations in this regard.

Figure 8.2

Number of World Heritage properties inscribed each year from 1978 to 2000, showing number of cultural, natural, and mixed inscriptions

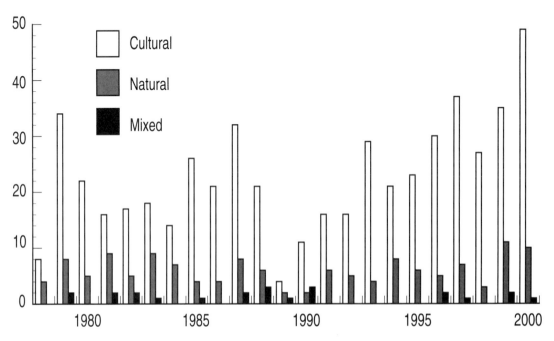

Source: various World Heritage Committee printed and web site materials.

Box 8.1   'Summary of Provisions' of the World Heritage Convention

The main provisions of the Convention are as follows:

1   Each State Party to the Convention recognises that it has the primary duty to identify, protect, conserve, and transmit to future generations its own cultural and natural heritage.
2   State Parties are to integrate their heritage protection into comprehensive planning programs, set up protection services, undertake relevant studies, and take necessary legal, scientific, administrative, and financial steps to protect their heritage.
3   State Parties undertake to assist each other in heritage protection.
4   A WHCom is established and each State Party is to submit to it an inventory of its own national heritage.
5   The WHCom will publish a 'World Heritage List' and a 'List of World Heritage in Danger'.
6   A WHF is established and financed by the State Parties and other interested bodies.
7   Any State Party may request assistance in protecting its heritage, and this may be granted in the form of studies, experts, training, equipment, loans, or subsidies.
8   All States which are members of UNESCO, and other States on invitation, may ratify or accept the WHC and thus become Parties to it.

The primary responsibilities for identifying and protecting heritage, even when deemed to be of universal value (that is, World Heritage) remains with the sovereign state in which it is located. (The Old City of Jerusalem is the single exception to this rule.) The provisions in Box 8.1 are designed to be applied by State Parties to their own individual heritage lists, and the WHC only holds any practical sway over World Heritage properties. The WHCom, UNESCO, and associated NGOs can, however, encourage, and to some extent assist, wider heritage protection programs. The WHCom, for example, funds a number of general projects, such as studies into particular thematic types of heritage, surveys of geographic regions, and research on methods of conservation, and it sponsors large numbers of conferences, workshops, and other gatherings. These programs fit well within the intent of the UNESCO Constitution, the relevant section of which was quoted earlier. However, once a property is listed as World Heritage (or, put more officially, *inscribed* on the WHL) the WHCom has much greater power to influence the 'host' government. This type of influence is discussed further later.

The ongoing administrative functions of the WHC are carried out by the World Heritage Bureau (WHB), which has a small staff housed at the UNESCO World Heritage Centre in Paris. A General Assembly of State Parties meets every two years and elects the twenty-one members of the WHCom (representatives from twenty-one State Parties that are chosen to represent the major regions and cultures of the world).The WHCom now meets twice a year.

8.3 Identifying, assessing, and managing World Heritage

Defining World Heritage

In Article 1 of the WHC, cultural heritage is defined in the following way:
- monuments: architectural works, works of monumental sculpture and painting, elements or structures of an archaeological nature, inscriptions, cave dwellings and combinations of features, which are of outstanding universal value from the point of view of history, art, or science (for example, Plate 8.1)
- groups of buildings: groups of separate or connected buildings which, because of their architecture, their homogeneity, or their place in the landscape, are of outstanding universal value from the point of view of history, art, or science (for example, Plate 8.2)
- sites: works of man or the combined works of nature and man, and areas including archaeological sites which are of outstanding universal value from the historical, aesthetic, ethnological, or anthropological point of view (for example Plate 8.3)

Article 2 defines natural heritage as:
- natural features consisting of physical and biological formations or groups of such formations, which are of outstanding universal value from the aesthetic or scientific point of view (for example see Plate 7.2)

Plate 8.1

East entrance of the Annexe to the Nunnery, a late-Classical Mayan building at Chichén Itzá. The walls illustrate the intricate stone carving typical of the period. Chichén Itzá, in Yucatán, Mexico is one of a group of Mayan sites that constitute a World Heritage property.

Photo: Richard Aplin

Plate 8.2

Goslar World Heritage town, Germany, which has 168 buildings dating from before 1550 and retains the structure and atmosphere of a medieval town. Founded in 922, the town, together with nearby Rammelsberg Mines, was inscribed on the World Heritage List in 1992. This view of the Marktplatz (Market Place) shows the 'Kaiserworth' Hotel (left) and Rathaus (Town Hall; far right).

Photo: Richard Aplin

Plate 8.3

Stonehenge, England, in 1977 when visitors were much freer to wander around the site as they wished, compared to the more ordered and protective approach of the 1990s. Built in several stages from approximately 3000 BC, Stonehenge is Europe's best known prehistoric site.

Photo: Graeme Aplin

- geological and physiographical formations and precisely delineated areas which constitute the habitat of threatened species of animals and plants of outstanding universal value from the point of view of science or conservation
- natural sites or precisely delineated natural areas of outstanding universal value from the point of view of science, conservation or natural beauty.

As one would expect from such a convention, these definitions are very broadly worded. The WHCom, however, has approved Operational Guidelines, which include selection criteria for the assessment and evaluation of sites. Cultural properties should meet one or more of the following criteria:

Ci represent a masterpiece of human creative genius

Cii exhibit an important interchange of human values, over a span of time or within a cultural area of the world, on developments in architecture or technology, monumental arts, town planning, or landscape design

Ciii bear a unique or at least exceptional testimony to a cultural tradition or to a civilisation which is living or which has disappeared

Civ be an outstanding example of a type of building or architectural or technological ensemble or landscape which illustrates a significant stage or significant stages in human history

Cv be an outstanding example of a traditional human settlement or land use which is representative of a culture or cultures, especially when it has become vulnerable under the impact of irreversible change

Cvi be directly or tangibly associated with events or living traditions, with ideas, with beliefs, or with artistic and literary works of outstanding universal significance (a criterion used only in exceptional circumstances, or together with other criteria)

Natural properties should meet one or more of these criteria:

Ni be outstanding examples representing major stages of the earth's history, including the record of life, significant ongoing geological processes in the development of landforms, or significant geomorphic or physiographic features

Nii be outstanding examples representing significant ongoing ecological and biological processes in the evolution and development of terrestrial, fresh water, coastal and marine ecosystems and communities of plants and animals

Niii contain superlative natural phenomena or areas of exceptional natural beauty and aesthetic importance

Niv contain the most important and significant natural habitats for *in situ* conservation of biological diversity, including those containing threatened species of outstanding value from the point of view of science or conservation

Some additional requirements are also set out. Natural heritage properties must fulfil certain conditions relating to the integrity of the sites. For example, a site in which a waterfall is a key element should also include the catchment feeding that waterfall, and a site inscribed under

(Niv) should include the complete range of flora and fauna typical of that region, and should be large enough to ensure the continuation of all species in a viable state. Cultural sites, on the other hand, have to satisfy a test of authenticity (see Section 6.6) and reconstructions are only acceptable in exceptional circumstances. All sites, whether natural or cultural, must have adequate legal or institutional protection (which may be 'traditional' rather than 'modern') and plans of management. In other words, they must not only possess integrity, but there must be the potential for the integrity to be maintained.

Identifying and assessing World Heritage

The WHCom recognises the international importance of certain properties through their inscription on the WHL. State Parties to the WHC can nominate properties within their territory on the basis that they meet one or more of the criteria above—natural, cultural, or a combination of the two. Properties can also be nominated in stages; for example, Australia's Kakadu National Park was inscribed in three stages over the course of eleven years (see Section 9.4 and Table 9.1). Five properties from various countries were extended in area in December 1999, and another four in November 2000, when the Château de Chambord was incorporated into a new, extended area (Plate 8.4 and see Section 11.3, Table 11.2).

Plate 8.4

Château de Chambord, Loire Valley, France, a French Renaissance château, 1519–1685, comprising 440 rooms. It was inscribed on the World Heritage List in 1981, and incorporated into a much more extensive property covering a large area of the Loire Valley in 2000 (see Section 11.3).

Photo: Graeme Aplin

The rest of this Section describe the processes for assessing heritage that were in place in early 2001, but at that time, the Operational Guidelines were in the process of being revised.[1] While details, including the timing and frequency of various events, are likely to change, the broad framework will remain intact.

The WHB assesses each nomination based on an evaluation by one of three relevant international non-governmental bodies recognised by the convention. Evaluation of cultural heritage sites is undertaken by either

ICOMOS or the International Centre for the Study of the Preservation and Restoration of Cultural Property (ICCROM), while evaluation of natural heritage sites is undertaken by the IUCN. After evaluation and assessment, the WHB makes recommendations regarding inscription to the WHCom, which hears submissions and votes on each proposal at its second meeting every year. Box 8.2 summarises the stages of this process in the case of the Greater Blue Mountains property (see Plate 5.1), inscribed in November 2000.

Box 8.2   Greater Blue Mountains World Heritage nomination

The Greater Blue Mountains Area was inscribed on the WHL at the end of November 2000 as the result of a unanimous vote by the twenty-one members of the WHCom. There had been hopes of an earlier inscription, dating back fourteen years, in fact, but limited funds for the preparation of the application, concerns over proposed airport and highway developments (see below), and 'islands' of private land within the area prevented success, despite support from the State Government, the Federal Government, the local council, conservationists, and the tourism industry. The nominated area contained eight protected areas west of Sydney: Wollemi (see Box 5.1); Yengo; Gardens of Stone; Blue Mountains, Kanangra–Boyd (see Plates 2.4 and 5.1), Nattai, and Thirlmere Lakes National Parks; and the Jenolan Caves Karst Conservation Reserve (see Plates 10.1 and 10.11). The official World Heritage short description is given in Table 9.1.

   According to the Australian Conservation Foundation web site, prepared before the listing was accepted and closely reflecting the official nomination documents, the 1 million hectare property will:
- provide an exceptional living example of the evolution of the modern Australian flora to its present distinctive character in the classic Australian circumstances of low-fertility soils, an increasingly dry climate, and geographical isolation—one of the great stories of the evolution of the earth's plant cover
- grant international recognition to Australia's eucalypt forests and other sclerophyll vegetation

The basis of the case for nomination consisted of the following claimed universal values:
- The area is the largest, most intact, and best protected sclerophyll forest wilderness.
- The ecological and biological processes involved in the evolution of Australia's eucalypt-dominated ecosystems are represented.
- It contributes to the representation of the taxonomic, physiognomic, and ecological diversity developed by eucalypts.
- Species of outstanding universal significance from the point of view of science and conservation are represented (including *Wollemia*—see Box 5.1).
- The area is one of outstanding natural beauty.

   Initially, some members of the WHCom and other experts believed that a number of different eucalypt communities from different parts of Australia should be included in a consolidated property, and that the Greater Blue Mountains nomination should not proceed. A number of possible threats worrying experts and placing the nomination in jeopardy seemed to have been averted, at least in the short term: Badgerys Creek airport was not likely to proceed for a decade or more (if ever); the proposed 'superhighway' over the Blue Mountains had been rejected; and catchment land was soon to be transferred to the NSW NPWS, thus further consolidating land holdings.

Sources: Australian Conservation Foundation web site (see list of web sites in the back of this book); various press stories in the *Sydney Morning Herald* and *Sun-Herald*.

The Bureau also deals with administration of the WHF, and with organisation and sponsorship of workshops and conferences, both regionally and globally. Furthermore, it prepares material for the WHCom to consider in relation to any proposals to place properties on the List of World Heritage in Danger (LWHD) (see Section 8.4).

Role of non-government organisations

The three key NGOs—the IUCN, ICOMOS, and ICCROM—provide assessment of properties proposed for inclusion on the WHL and of proposals to include properties on the LWHD. More generally, the IUCN provides technical and scientific advice relating to the natural environment, and monitors and measures the condition and conservation status of natural properties, and hence the degree of compliance by parties with their WHC obligations. UNESCO itself, in consultation with ICOMOS and ICCROM, provides corresponding services in relation to cultural sites. As much as possible, all of these bodies act in conjunction with the State Parties concerned, but they may sometimes present reports that are unfavourable to the parties, and occasionally even against the wishes and judgment of the national governments concerned.

National responsibilities

After inscription, World Heritage properties do not pass into the control of the WHCom or WHB, as ownership and government control essentially do not change. This means that an extensive World Heritage property may fall under a complex variety of land tenures. For example, in the case of the banks of the Seine in Paris (see Section 11.3, Table 11.2 and Plate 1.9), neither the WHCom nor the French Government are totally owners or primary administrators of the site. The French national government is, however, responsible for ensuring that the property as a whole is administered in such a way that its World Heritage values and integrity are maintained. This may be done by setting up new management structures, or by using existing ones, perhaps within a city or provincial government, or within a relevant department of a national or state government (see Section 11.3 for the French case). In Australia's case, some World Heritage properties have joint federal–state management groups in place (see Section 9.4).

National governments must pass legislation that gives effect to their ratification of the WHC. Such legislation will normally involve setting out specific requirements for managing World Heritage properties in a way that fulfils the obligations of the WHC. In the case of Australia, and possibly also of some other federations, complementary state legislation is also required (see Sections 9.1 and 9.4). The particular legislative and structural frameworks are thus adapted to suit the political structure and climate of each State Party.

There are other general, non-site-specific obligations on the part of each party to the WHC. Under the WHC, each nation specifically agrees to:

1 adopt a general policy which aims to give the cultural and natural heritage a function in the life of the community and to integrate the protection of that heritage into comprehensive planning programs

2 take the appropriate legal, scientific, technical, administrative, and financial measures necessary for the identification, protection, conservation, presentation, and rehabilitation of this heritage

3 refrain from any deliberate measures which might damage, directly or indirectly, the cultural and natural heritage of other parties

4   help other parties in the identification and protection of their properties

The first of these obligations relates specifically, though not uniquely, to complex sites such as the Banks of the Seine. It implies that World Heritage and other heritage properties are not merely 'open-air museums', but living sites, used for tourist and educational purposes and, where appropriate, ones which function as sites of commercial and other day-to-day activity in both indigenous and modern communities. The second obligation relates to the need to devote adequate resources to manage and protect existing heritage properties at various scales, and so that potential sites can be identified and nominated. Finally, the WHC also carries an ideal of promoting cooperation towards establishing a world-wide, comprehensive network of properties that represent the global heritage of the world's people. All nations are encouraged to be represented so that instead of an incomplete assemblage of national heritages, there is a unified body of global heritage.

Global coverage and representativeness

There are different emphases in the types of World Heritage properties in different parts of the world. In Europe, most World Heritage properties are inscribed for cultural reasons; in Australia and other 'new world' nations (including the USA and Canada), most properties are at least partly inscribed for natural reasons; while inscriptions for Asian and African nations are more mixed (see Table 8.1). This division between cultural and natural sites has caused debate within the World Heritage fraternity. In recent times, it has been recognised that *mixed sites*, which have both outstanding natural and cultural values, are particularly important, and should be more prominent on the WHL. Since 1992, sites where there are significant interactions between people and the natural environment have been increasingly recognised as World Heritage Cultural Landscapes. Mixed sites were actually inscribed in a fairly constant, but very small, stream throughout the period of operation of the WHC, with the notable exception of a period in the early 1990s. Five of the twenty-one mixed sites have been added since the beginning of 1996, and the first to be inscribed under the new cultural landscapes criteria (in 1993) was New Zealand's Tongariro National Park (see Section 12.2 and Table 12.1). For reasons that are unclear, however, only one of the sixty-one sites inscribed in November 2000 was a mixed site.

Table 8.1 and Figures 8.2 and 8.3 illustrate the temporal and geographical dimensions of World Heritage. Slightly less than half the inscriptions occurred before the end of 1989, the remainder having been made since then, with somewhat increased numbers since 1996, culminating in the large group of sixty-one inscriptions in November 2000 (see Figure 8.2). State Parties must ratify or accede to the convention before sites from their territories can be inscribed, so the date of ratification or other sign of compliance obviously affects the dates of inscriptions (see Table 8.1). It is for this reason that some north-western European nations have no sites inscribed in the earlier period. For example, Austria and Ireland only ratified or acceded to the WHC in 1991; the Netherlands in 1992; and Belgium in 1996. Other nations had key sites inscribed much earlier, and no others have been added recently, in many cases because there are no other sites of equal significance that would meet the WHC criteria. In some cases, changing political circumstances have led to little or no involvement over particular periods: all of the Russian Federation's inscriptions, for example, have occurred since 1990, while Yugoslavia's were all prior to that date.

It is difficult to judge the geographical representativeness of the WHL without knowing a great deal more about unlisted but potential sites, which is why the WHCom has repeatedly requested State Parties and the key NGOs to submit tentative lists of potential sites. Table 8.1 and Figure 8.3 indicate a reasonably sound coverage of the world's major regions, at least at a superficial level. One recent World Heritage press release does, however, specifically mention a lack of both State Parties and listings in the South Pacific, which is perhaps understandable given the small size and economic difficulties of many island states. On the other hand, some of the earliest nations to become State Parties were poorer African nations, which presumably recognised the opportunity to access foreign funds and technical assistance to help care for their heritage. There also may well have been a desire to boost national pride and identity (see Section 1.4) in relatively newly independent states. Many of the State Parties that have not had sites listed are small and sometimes less-developed nations, but some, including perhaps Afghanistan, Iceland, Saudi Arabia, and Sudan, might be expected to have sites suitable for listing.[2] Israel, a nation that obviously has properties worthy of listing, only acceded to the WHC in 1999, and may well propose sites in the near future, provided that lasting peace can be brought to the region. In fact, Jerusalem is the only site on the WHL not clearly proposed by the sovereign nation in which it is located; it was proposed by Jordan. The Old City of Jerusalem is also inscribed on the LWHD because, in part, of the uncertain political situation there. It seems particularly likely that its heritage values were being seriously compromised in late 2000 and early 2001.[3]

Global Strategy

In 1994 the WHCom approved a Global Strategy aimed at improving the representative nature of cultural heritage sites on the WHL. In particular, it aimed to redress a perceived bias towards European, Christian, and 'monumental architectural' sites, and to encourage the nomination of properties illustrating archaeological, industrial, and technical heritage, particularly from non-European cultures. It also aimed to find sites representing traditional societies and their interactions with natural environments. That was not to say that these categories were previously unrepresented: in Australia, for example, Kakadu National Park and Uluṟu–Kata Tjuṯa were inscribed for both (traditional) cultural and natural reasons, and each of these properties is clearly significant for the cultural–natural interactions it contains (see Section 9.4 and Table 9.1). Ironbridge Gorge, in the United Kingdom, was listed in 1986 as a prime example of industrial heritage, albeit European industrial heritage (see Table 11.1), and was joined in the 1990s by a French canal system (Canal du Midi—Table 11.2), German ironworks (Völklingen) and mines (Rammelsberg, near Goslar), a Finnish timber mill (Verla), and in 2000 by the Welsh coal-mining site of Blaenavon. It remains true, however, that non-

Figure 8.3

World map of World Heritage property distribution by nation

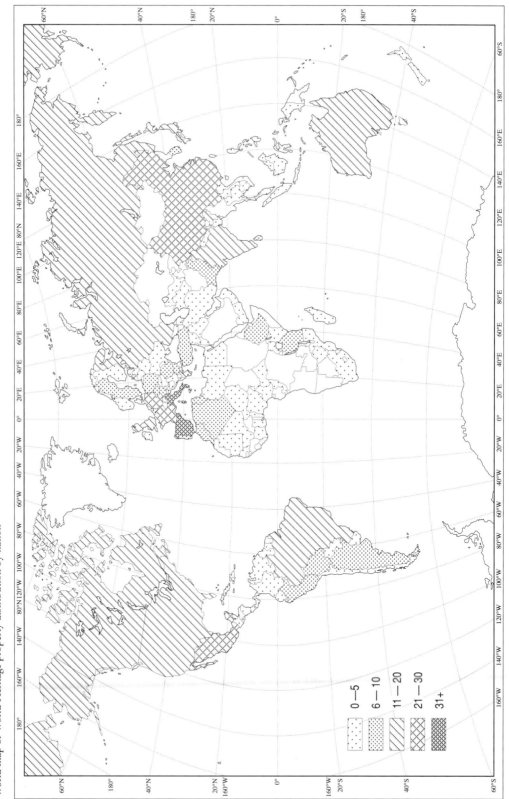

Source: various World Heritage Committee printed and web site materials.

0 — 5
6 — 10
11 — 20
21 — 30
31+

European examples of industrial heritage are very rare. There is a similar situation with archaeological sites: there are many from Europe, and relatively few elsewhere, although there are some magnificent examples in Latin America and other regions, but usually of the 'monumental architecture' type (Plate 8.1). Regional Global Strategy meetings, such as those in Africa in 1997 and Central Asia in May 2000, have worked on preparing lists of possible future WHL inscriptions, while at least two working groups were in the process of re-examining the strategy in 2000–01.[4]

8.4   List of World Heritage in Danger

The WHCom also maintains a LWHD, sometimes on the basis of requests from the State Parties concerned, other times as a result of representations and submissions from NGOs, particularly the most immediately concerned international NGOs: IUCN, ICOMOS, and ICCROM. In late 2000, the LWHD contained thirty properties (three were added in November 2000), fourteen of which were in Africa. Table 8.2 lists these properties, and gives brief summary statements as to why the properties were listed. The reasons for listing a site on the LWHD fall into four main categories:

1   environmental threats, such as tornado or earthquake damage

2   human threats relating to development, including roads into natural areas, changes to hydrological conditions, poaching of wildlife, timber cutting, and pressures from visitors

3   war and civil unrest, particularly in Africa

4   lack of adequate management and conservation plans, and/or adequate legislative and bureaucratic support

Inclusion on the list has often led to financial or technical support from outside the host State Party.

Some properties previously listed on the LWHD have been removed, and many of the properties currently on it are now some way towards being removed, as conditions have often improved with WHF assistance. One example, the Plitvice Lakes National Park in Croatia, was placed on the LWHD in 1992 because of the threat of armed conflict. While the 1990–95 war caused less damage than feared, it left the park without adequate staff or infrastructure. In 1996 the Croatian Government was considering new administrative arrangements and park plans; these projects, supported by the WHF, allowed the property to be removed from the LWHD in 1997. The Old City of Dubrovnik, also in Croatia, Wieliczka Salt Mine in Poland, and the Virunga National Park in Zaire were also removed from the LWHD between January 1995 and December 1999. Dubrovnik was seriously damaged during fighting in late 1991 and immediately listed as 'in danger'; the fighting ceased and restoration of damaged buildings was undertaken, enabling removal from the LWHD in 1998. At Wieliczka, excessive humidity was destroying the unique salt carvings in an underground salt mine, but dehumidifying equipment has stopped this deleterious process and the site was taken off the list in 1998.

Table 8.2

List of World Heritage in Danger, March 2001

Nation	World Heritage property	Date of original inscription on World Heritage List	Date of inscription on List of World Heritage in Danger	Reasons for inscription
Albania	Butrint	1992	1997	Civil disturbances; looting; lack of adequate protection, management, and conservation; lack of fencing.
Benin	Royal Palaces of Abomey	1985	1985	Tornado damage.
Brazil	Iguacu National Park	1986	1999	Illegal road built through park.
Bulgaria	Srebarna Nature Reserve	1983	1992	Destruction of freshwater habitat of bird populations through dams and neighbouring land uses.
Cambodia	Angkor	1992	1992	Long-term civil disturbances; looting; weak national protection agency.
Central African Rep.	Manovo-Gounda St Floris National Park	1988	1997	Illegal grazing and poaching; deteriorating security for staff and tourists.
Côte d'Ivoire/Guinea	Mount Nimba Nature Reserve	1981	1992	Proposed iron-ore mining concession; arrival of large number of refugees.
Dem. Rep. Of Congo	Virunga National Park	1979	1994	War in neighbouring Rwanda and massive influx of refugees, leading to deforestation and poaching.
Dem. Rep. Of Congo	Garamba National Park	1980	1996	Listed on two separate occasions. From 1984 to 1992, due to serious decline in white rhinoceros population. More recently, due to civil unrest and attacks on infrastructure of park.
Dem. Rep. Of Congo	Kahuzi-Biega National Park	1980	1997	Deforestation, hunting, war, and civil strife; influx of refugees.
Dem. Rep. Of Congo	Okapi Wildlife Reserve	1996	1997	Armed conflict; looting of facilities; killing of elephants; gold mining.

Nation	World Heritage property	Date of original inscription on World Heritage List	Date of inscription on List of World Heritage in Danger	Reasons for inscription
Dem. Rep. Of Congo	Salonga National Park	1984	1999	Poaching; housing construction; civil unrest.
Ecuador	Sangay National Park	1983	1992	Heavy poaching of wildlife; illegal grazing; encroachment on perimeter; unplanned road construction.
Ethiopia	Simen National Park	1978	1996	Deterioration of population of the Walia ibex; road construction and human population increase.
Honduras	Rio Platano Biosphere Reserve	1982	1996	Commercial and agricultural intrusions; timber extraction and commercial wildlife hunting; introduction of exotic species; absence of management plan and adequate staff.
India	Manas Wildlife Sanctuary	1985	1992	Political instability; invasion and destruction by tribal militants.
India	Group of Monuments at Hampi	1986	1999	Construction of two suspension bridges which dominate the site; road-building and associated relocation of an historic monument.
Jerusalem (site proposed by Jordan)	Old City of Jerusalem and its Walls	1981	1982	Political uncertainties over sovereignty; impacts of urban development, tourism, and lack of maintenance.
Mali	Timbuktu	1988	1990	Encroachment by desert sands; lack of conservation plan.
Niger	Air & Ténéré Natural Reserves	1991	1992	Military conflict and civil disturbance; poaching.
Oman	Bahla Fort	1987	1988	Degradation of structures and of the oasis; lack of management plan.
Pakistan	Fort and Shalamar Gardens, Lahore	1981	2000	Destruction of water supply to fountains due to road widening, deterioration of perimeter walls.

Peru	Chan Chan Archaeological Zone	1986	1986	Deterioration; lack of conservation, restoration, and management plans; inappropriate excavations.
Senegal	Djoudj National Bird Sanctuary	1981	2000	Threat of invasion by the water plant *Salvinia molesta*.
Tunisia	Ichkeul National Park	1980	1996	Significant deterioration of values; three dams cutting off freshwater flows to lake which is leading to increased salinity.
Uganda	Rwenzori Mountains National Park	1994	1999	Rebel occupation and security concerns.
USA	Everglades National Park	1979	1993	Nearby urban growth; pollution; poisoning of fish and wildlife; reduction in water levels.
USA	Yellowstone	1978	1995	Likely impact of nearby mining; sewage and waste contamination; animal disease; introduction of exotic fish; road construction; visitor pressures.
Yemen	Historic Town of Zabid	1993	2000	City decline, very poor state of conservation, 40 per cent of houses replaced by concrete buildings
Yugoslavia	Natural and Culturo-Historical Region of Kotor	1979	1979	Major earthquake damage.

A long and controversial series of submissions and meetings saw Australia's Kakadu National Park barely escape inclusion on the LWHD in 1999–2000. The WHCom is maintaining a watching brief on Kakadu to monitor the likely or actual impact of uranium mining on both the cultural and natural values of the site (see Section 9.4 for further discussion). As a consequence, in the lead-up to the Cairns WHCom meeting in November 2000 the Australian federal Minister for the Environment, Senator Robert Hill, sought to clarify that only the national government of the country in which a property was situated could ask for it to be inscribed on the LWHD (which was the case for all three properties added in November 2000).[5] It seems quite possible, however, that a national government, for a variety of reasons, might not want a property listed even if it were clearly in danger, or that on rare occasions the national government might even be the source of that danger. After all, a LWHD listing is one of only a few ways in which the WHCom can act to show its displeasure at a government not fulfilling its responsibilities under the WHC. The Australian request for clarification followed a number of disagreements between the Howard Government and the United Nations over human rights and environmental issues, and seems to be part of a campaign to emphasise Australia's sovreignty and self-determination for both philosophical and domestic political reasons.

8.5   Other international initiatives

A number of other international treaties, conventions, and similar initiatives are also relevant to heritage conservation, although they do not necessarily make specific reference to heritage terms. Most of these initiatives apply mainly to natural heritage, and three of the most important ones will be very briefly introduced here. In addition, many other instruments focus on particular regions, or on particular species, or groups of species. Some organisations and agreements also deal with types of cultural heritage items, for example, archaeological, industrial, and urban.

Biosphere Reserves

The concept of *Biosphere Reserves* pre-dates the WHC by a few years. In 1968 UNESCO convened the Biosphere Conference, which established the Man and the Biosphere Programme (MAB), and the idea of a World Network of Biosphere Reserves grew from the MAB. Biosphere Reserves and the World Heritage program are complementary, and many sites are included on both lists. In May 1999, there were 357 Biosphere Reserves, fifty-three of which were wholly or partially included within World Heritage properties, and some of these are also Ramsar sites (see next part of this Section). Biosphere Reserves also pre-date the Convention on Biological Diversity (see final part of this Section), and yet they now act as a practical expression of this convention. A particular site may initially be listed either as a Biosphere Reserve or a World Heritage site. In December 1999, for example, six Biosphere Reserves became wholly or partly World Heritage properties, while two World Heritage properties were listed for the first time as Biosphere Reserves.

The predominant aim of Biosphere Reserves is to protect key areas that are deemed to be crucial in conserving biodiversity in general, with a secondary aim to protect individual endangered species in particular. The idea of Biosphere Reserves was conceived in order to reconcile conservation and sustainable development. The reserves are recognised representative environments that form a global network, and the aim is to ultimately cover all major ecosystem types. Each reserve fulfils three functions:

- biodiversity conservation—conserving a representative sample of major ecosystems
- development—humans in the biosphere, with an emphasis on an integrative role for local, especially traditional, communities
- logistics—combining research, education, training, and monitoring

Each reserve must be effectively managed to minimise damage to the ecosystem contained within the area. This usually involves the use of core, buffer, and transition zones with different management intensities (see Section 5.6). The transition zone, in particular, allows for managed human use while minimising impacts on the buffer zone, which in turn protects the core zone.

Ramsar sites

The Ramsar Convention is the short name for the Convention on Wetlands of International Importance Especially as Waterfowl Habitat, which first came into force in 1971. Sites listed under the Ramsar Convention are known as *wetlands of international importance*. It is a much more tightly focussed agreement than either the WHL or the Network of Biosphere Reserves.

The Convention's preamble refers to 'the fundamental ecological functions of wetlands as regulators of water regimes and as habitats supporting a characteristic flora and fauna, especially waterfowl' and the fact that 'wetlands constitute a resource of great economic, cultural, scientific, and recreational value, the loss of which would be irreparable'. Wetlands thus need to be conserved to slow or even stop the loss of wetlands through development, and to ensure that migratory waterfowl can make use of wetlands regardless of national borders. Such conservation of wetlands can be ensured, according to the Preamble, by combining national policies with coordinated international action.

Nations that are parties to the Convention are known as 'Contracting Parties', and each of these parties agrees to fulfil the following obligations:

- to designate suitable wetlands that are situated within its territory for inclusion in a List of Wetlands of International Importance
- to fulfil its international responsibilities for the conservation, management, and wise use of migratory stocks of waterfowl
- to formulate and implement planning so as to promote the conservation of wetlands included in the list, and the wise use of wetlands in their territory more generally

Furthermore, Contracting Parties must encourage research and the exchange of data and publications regarding wetlands and their flora and fauna and promote the training of personnel in appropriate fields. It is implied that wealthier nations will assist others in these ways.

Convention on Biological Diversity

The Convention on Biological Diversity, sponsored by the United Nations Environment Programme (UNEP), was deliberated for nearly four years before being finalised in late May 1992. It was finally signed by 153 states and the European Community (EC; but not by the USA) by the end of the United Nations Conference on the Environment and Development (UNCED), also known as the Earth Summit, held in Rio de Janeiro. Much emphasis is placed on the role of natural reserves as the prime means of preserving biodiversity, and on the rights of indigenous peoples and rural communities to continue patterns of sustainable use which have existed over centuries. Indeed, such groups are also seen as vitally important in preserving biodiversity, especially of crop and livestock species. The treaty came into effect in December 1993 after being ratified by the requisite number of nations, including Australia, by the previous October. However it is merely the first step in a long process, but one that is closely related to both the Biosphere Reserve program and to the concept of natural and mixed World Heritage properties.

Although the Convention on Biological Diversity covers more than *in situ* conservation of biodiversity in reserves, some of the 'key provisions' relate specifically to natural heritage. The State Parties have the following duties:
- to conserve biological diversity within their jurisdiction
- to formulate and implement strategies, plans, and programs for the conservation and sustainable use of biological diversity
- to monitor the elements of biological diversity, determining the nature of the urgency required in the protection of each category and the risks to which they are exposed
- to provide for research, training, general education, and the fostering of awareness in relation to measures for the identification, conservation, and sustainable use of biological diversity

The Convention thus offers potential for powerful synergistic interactions between national and local efforts to conserve natural heritage sites.

8.6   Conclusion

The concept of World Heritage emerged from the 1972 United Nations Conference on the Human Environment, held in Stockholm. The idea that some sites are so important as to belong to all humankind in the form of a global heritage probably long pre-dates this conference, at least for people who are relatively well educated and well travelled. The coining of the phrase 'the seven wonders of the world' indicates some acceptance of this concept in ancient times. More recently, efforts have been made to widen definitions beyond the Eurocentric, Christian-based view of global heritage that was promoted by the world's economically and politically dominant nations, primarily from Europe and North America. The WHCom and WHB are now actively promoting a more inclusive approach through their Global Strategy, and that seems to be bearing fruit. Virtually every nation—162 in early 2001—has agreed to the philosophy underlying the WHC and the obligations it places on them. Furthermore, 122 of the parties have at least one property listed as World Heritage. Even so, the actual management, the legislative backing, and the will to actively conserve these properties still lie with the nations concerned and performances have been mixed.

The next four chapters look in more detail at the heritage lists in a number of nations and how these are administered. Chapters 9 and 10 deal with Australia, most specifically with the role of the Commonwealth (Chapter 9) and with the model in NSW (Section 10.2), but also more briefly with the other states and territories (Section 10.3). Chapter 11 discusses a number of European nations: the United Kingdom, Ireland, France, Spain, and Italy. Examples from other parts of the world—New Zealand, the USA, South Africa, Thailand, and China—are dealt with in Chapter 12. The role of local government and non-governmental organisations (NGOs) is also touched on where appropriate.

Notes

[1] A Report of the International Expert Meeting on the Revision of the *Operational Guidelines for the Implementation of the World Heritage Convention* was presented at the meeting of the WHCom in November 2000. Its recommendations were generally accepted and detailed changes will be introduced in phases over a number of years. Separately, changes relating to the timing of nominations and meetings were adopted.

[2] Afghanistan did submit a number of nominations for inscription, but these were not accepted due to inadequate documentation or concerns about management structures.

[3] Not surprisingly, given the parlous state of peace talks and the renewed violence of late 2000, there were heated exchanges at the Cairns meeting of the WHCom, at least in written submissions, between the Israeli delegation and Palestinian observer over the status of heritage properties in the disputed territories.

[4] These were the group referred to in Note 1 and the Working Group on the Representativity of the WHL. Many recommendations from the latter group were accepted at the November 2000 meeting and will be implemented. Particular attention was paid to the question of capacity-building for under-represented regions.

[5] The group referred to in Note 1 has sought legal advice on whether or not properties can be inscribed on the LWHD against the wishes of the host State Party. As far as the author can ascertain from the Report of the Cairns WHCom meeting, the Australian delegate did not press this point, and constructive steps toward resolving issues concerning Kakadu National Park seem to be in progress, involving the IUCN, the Australian Government, the traditional owners, and other parties.

Further Reading

Updated information on changes to legislation and bureaucratic structures is available at the web site associated with this book, at http://www.es.mq. edu.au/courses/REM/heritage.htm.

International Union for the Conservation of Nature and Natural Resources (1994) *Paradise on Earth: The Natural World Heritage List*, JIDD Publishers/Harper-MacRae, Patonga/Columbus, OH.

International Union for the Conservation of Nature and Natural Resources (1980) *World Conservation Strategy: Living Resource Conservation and Sustainable Development*, IUCN, Morges.

International Union for the Conservation of Nature and Natural Resources (1994) *Guidelines for Protected Area Management Categories*, IUCN, Gland.

International Union for the Conservation of Nature and Natural Resources (1994) *Masterworks of Man and Nature*, Harper-MacRae, Patonga.

Lane, M. & McDonald, G. (1997) 'Not all world heritage areas are created equal: world heritage area management in Australia', in Pigram, J. J. & Sundell, R. C. (eds) *National Parks and Protected Areas: Selection, Delimitation and Management*, University of New England, Armidale, pp. 369–86.

McDowell, D. (1995) *IUCN and the World Heritage: A Review of Policies and Procedures*, IUCN, Gland.

Oulion, M-H, & Maurin, X. (1995) *World Heritage Cities* (CD-ROM), Cyberion/UNESCO, Paris.

von Droste, B., Plachter, H & Rössler. M. (eds) (1995) *Value: Components of a Global Strategy*, Gustav Fisher Verlag, Jena, Germany.

WHNews—a regular email newsletter service for anyone who registers through the World Heritage Commission web site (see Appendix 2 for URL).

World Heritage Review, published since 1996, and now on a bi-monthly basis, by UNESCO and Ediciones San Marcos, Madrid. This is a beautifully illustrated and highly informative magazine on all matters concerning World Heritage.

CHAPTER 9

Regulatory Frameworks and Approaches to Heritage: Commonwealth of Australia

This is the first of a series of four chapters that discusses approaches to heritage conservation and administration in selected nations. The choice of countries is primarily based on the availability of information and the author's familiarity with the nations. Sources include published material, agency web sites, and visits to all but one of the nations covered, though by no means to all of the sites mentioned.

This chapter focuses on the heritage and the approaches to managing heritage in Australia. In the first instance it is essential to reflect on the system of government involved. The bureaucratic and legislative arrangements for heritage cannot be understood without an appreciation of this background.

9.1   Australia: a federation

Australia, as a federation, has a three-tier system of government. In general terms, local or municipal government is less important than in many other nations and it certainly does not perform the range of activities ascribed to local government in either the United Kingdom or the USA, for example. However Australian local government has jurisdiction over the majority of planning decisions, and it is in this area that local government plays a vital role in relation to heritage. Unfortunately, it is difficult to make generalisations, as the details vary considerably between states (discussed more fully in Chapter 10).

At the next level of government, the six Australian states and two major internal territories are more important and more powerful than in many other federations. The states certainly assert their independence rhetorically and, at times, in practical and legal ways. Much heated debate has occurred throughout the years over demarcations between state and federal jurisdictions, as much in heritage matters as in others. The political uncertainty and actual and potential overlap also have implications for bureaucracies and the administration of heritage regulations.

The bulk of practical, day-to-day heritage responsibilities beyond the local level rests with the state and territory governments. All state governments have established departments or agencies, or sections within departments, to deal with heritage matters, including the listing and consequent protection of heritage sites. The names and functions of these departments differ from state to state (see Chapter 10), as does the degree of independence they have from overtly political interference. (Section 10.2 deals in some detail with the structure in NSW, while Section 10.3 more briefly outlines arrangements in the other states and the territories.) In all cases, the state governments and their ministers retain the right to overrule their departments and agencies if major projects are rejected, or major constraints are placed on developments and activities, which are deemed to be in the state or public interest (see also Section 9.2). In practice this frequently means that economic forces hold a power of veto over heritage matters, but this is undoubtedly common in many other nations. The Federal Government is thus left with a residual role in the heritage area, the details of which will be discussed in the following pages.

9.2   Historical and cultural influences

Before looking at the details of the various jurisdictions some common background material needs to be introduced. This can be given under three broad yet interconnected headings: history and perceptions of heritage; developmentalism; and the administrative categorisation of heritage.

Australian history and perceptions of heritage

Australia has a very long history of human occupation; the Aboriginal and Torres Strait Islander people arrived on the continent at least 60 000 years ago, possibly considerably earlier. However, as far as we know, the first Europeans arrived less than 400 years ago, and permanent non-indigenous settlement began only a little over 210 years ago, in 1788. Until fairly recently the perception of most non-Aboriginal Australians was that the indigenous people were largely nomadic, and left few permanent or lasting signs of their occupation of the land. More recently, however, there has been increasing recognition of the great variety among indigenous lifestyles and cultures, and of the fact that the 'desert Aborigine' is a stereotype that does not apply to many groups across the continent. Sites such as elaborate stone fish traps and groups of huts with stone foundations have now been discovered by non-indigenous people (although the huts are almost certainly post-1788).

For those people who equate cultural heritage with built heritage in the European sense, or even in the sense of the cultural heritage present in Asia, Africa or the USA, then Australia has little or nothing pre-dating the foundation of Sydney in January 1788. Much of the continent was only settled by Europeans much later than that date, usually by pastoralists and prospectors (themselves at least semi-nomadic), and only in a second wave by permanent settlers, with the associated towns, homesteads, and other infrastructure that now typifies rural and regional Australia. Thus, for people with a strongly ingrained European view of cultural heritage—sadly, possibly still the majority of the Australian population—Australia has little to offer. This is especially true when linked to a perception that something has to be old to have heritage value. Compared to just about any other nation, Australia simply does not have much non-indigenous heritage that is older than 100–150 years.

The general perception of heritage on behalf of many Australians changed in the second half of the 20th century in two important ways. First, Australians began to appreciate that even if European-Australian heritage is not very old, it is nevertheless very important. At the same time, it became recognised that there are important non-Anglo-Celtic and even non-European aspects to our non-indigenous heritage that have arisen from the increasingly multicultural and migrant-based nature of Australia's population (Box 1.2). Secondly, Australians began to give much greater recognition to indigenous cultural heritage. This trend was partly based on an increased knowledge and appreciation of that heritage, perhaps reflecting increased exposure to other cultures more generally, with the realisation that there is a complex and fascinating indigenous culture here in Australia, in addition to those found in Asia, Africa, and the Americas. There has also been an increased willingness to admit that our dominant, European-derived culture and religion do not have a monopoly on truth and wisdom, and that we actually have a lot to learn from indigenous cultures. Acceptance of the importance of indigenous culture is a crucial part of the slow but perceptible path to reconciliation in Australia. Perhaps the majority of Australians now clearly see the need for that process of reconciliation to reach its culmination as quickly as possible, even if elements within the Federal Government and some state governments cling to aspects of a more racist past.

Developmentalism

In the time-scale used by its European settlers, Australia is a young country that has developed very rapidly. The major focus has been on growth and change, not on the preservation of either natural landscapes or cultural heritage. The dominant philosophies throughout European-Australian history have been *developmentalism* and *economic rationalism*. The focus of developmentalism is almost exclusively on development, although the present form of developmentalism in Australia is a little less raw and unrestrained than at some times and some places in the past. Even now, however, developmentalism tends to be more extreme and more dominant in the 'newer economies' of the NT, Queensland, and WA than it is elsewhere. Economic rationalism or neo-classical economics, however, holds sway throughout most segments of Australian life and the Australian population, and any gains in the environmental or heritage fields have been hard won. Like people all over the world, Australians have problems giving economic value to intangible concepts such as heritage significance in order for them to be incorporated on equal terms into processes such as benefit–cost analyses or environmental impact assessments. This issue is discussed in more general and theoretical terms in Section 3.4.

Administrative categorisation of heritage

The aspects of Australian history that were discussed in the previous paragraphs have led to a fragmentation of responsibilities for heritage. The earliest heritage-related activities were related to conservation of natural areas, and were essentially more concerned with resource management than with heritage management. (Forests are one key example.) Cultural heritage only became a political issue in the second half of the 20th century when

Australians collectively realised that they did have significant non-indigenous cultural heritage items despite the relatively recent settlement by non-indigenous people. A general community awareness of indigenous cultural heritage came even later, despite earlier work of anthropologists and ethnologists, as non-indigenous Australians gradually began to see Aboriginal cultures as more than textbook curiosities. A re-awakening of community identity and spirit within indigenous communities contributed to a general acceptance that indigenous cultures were living cultures, not merely museum pieces. Australians have still to accomplish the ultimate step, to reach a point where indigenous heritage is seen as one aspect of Australia's national heritage. This step is closely connected with reconciliation between indigenous and non-indigenous Australians, and when it occurs, it need not diminish the importance of indigenous heritage to indigenous peoples, the primary owners of that heritage, but it will need to be handled with great care and sensitivity.

Although administrative structures vary between jurisdictions in Australia, as shown in the discussion in the remainder of this chapter and the next, some general comments can be made. Across the states, natural heritage is commonly treated as separate from cultural heritage, especially non-indigenous cultural heritage. Early moves to conserve natural heritage barely involved the concept of heritage used in this book; they revolved around natural resource management, and the conservation of endangered plants and animals and occasionally of ecosystems and scenic attractions. Administratively, natural heritage conservation and natural resource exploitation generally have been part of the same department or under the same minister. One of the most recent examples of a merge of departments that were once separate occurred in Victoria, with the creation of the Department of Natural Resources and Environment (DNRE) in 1996. Even when the functions are not combined in the one department, proponents of conservation and exploitation have forcefully opposed each other in political discussions, including those at cabinet level. When agencies to administer national parks were established, their remit was normally restricted to administering natural heritage areas, although they have generally successfully and professionally managed non-indigenous and indigenous cultural heritage items that happen to fall within park boundaries. However, as discussed in Chapter 1, the Australian definition of *national park* is very much based on the idea of natural heritage and biodiversity conservation, and park boundaries are usually delineated to exclude most evidence of human occupancy (unlike the situation in European national parks—see Chapter 11).

The recent growing realisation that non-indigenous cultural heritage was also important and worthy of conservation resulted in the establishment of separate agencies, commonly in different departments and under different ministers from those with jurisdiction over natural heritage. The fact that this is not the case at the federal level, as shown by the inclusiveness of the RNE (see Section 9.3), is at least in part a reflection of the fact that the Federal Government became involved in heritage matters even more recently than the states. At the state and territory levels, management of built heritage has most commonly been closely connected with urban and rural planning, and much of the responsibility has commonly been devolved to local or municipal government. It must be said, however, that this separation of responsibilities for natural and cultural heritage outside major national and regional parks is also common in Europe (Chapter 11) and elsewhere (Chapter 12).

For complex historical and philosophical reasons, the administrative 'home' for indigenous heritage varies between jurisdictions and over time. In NSW (see Section 10.2), the primary responsibility lies with the NPWS, thus aligning indigenous cultural heritage more closely with natural heritage than with non-indigenous cultural heritage. Elsewhere, indigenous heritage is administered by a Department of Aboriginal Affairs or similar, while in some cases it is more obviously integrated with other types of heritage.

9.3   The Federal Government and its agencies

The role of the Federal Government

The involvement of the Federal Government in heritage is limited to matters involving its external or foreign affairs responsibilities, its own property (including external territories) and activities, and matters delegated to it by the states. In recent years it has also attempted to play the role of coordinator, by introducing national standards and uniform procedures, but it can only succeed with the good will, cooperation, and, ultimately, agreement of all states and territories. This degree of consensus in heritage, as in the broader field of the environment, has almost always been difficult to achieve, as the nine governments involved are rarely, if ever, all of the same political persuasion, or have the same perceptions and philosophies. Furthermore, all states jealously guard their own functions and responsibilities, and the concept of state rights more generally. However since 1998 a key process of change has been underway, more clearly delineating federal roles on the one hand, and those of the states and territories on the other. This is likely to reach its culmination in the second half of 2001. This process is discussed in Section 9.6.

Apart from the coordinating role of the Commonwealth Government, which will be discussed further in later sections, federal activities in heritage matters have been in two main areas. First, the national government has necessarily been the body that negotiates, agrees to, signs, and ratifies international agreements in general and, more specifically, the WHC (see Section 8.2). Once a convention has been ratified, the Federal Government must legislate to ensure that the conditions of the agreements are met in Australia (see Sections 8.2 and 8.3). First, however, as we have seen, for all practical purposes most heritage matters are in the hands of the states, so state legislation and other arrangements are often also required, which at times may lead to major difficulties. Secondly, the Federal Government is responsible for its own heritage standards in relation to federal land and buildings, including those in the ownership of federal instrumentalities such as Australia Post (Plate 9.1), and those in its external territories.

Environment Australia

Environment Australia is the corporate name for the relevant section of the Department of the Environment and Heritage, and includes the Australian Heritage Commission (AHC) and Parks Australia (PA, formerly the

Plate 9.1

Post office, Bendigo, Victoria. Australia Post is a federal agency, and therefore all major post offices fall within federal heritage legislation. The impressive size and architecture of this post office reflect Bendigo's role as a major gold producing centre in the second half of the 19th century.

Photo: Graeme Aplin

Figure 9.1

Organisational diagram of the relevant sections of Environment Australia

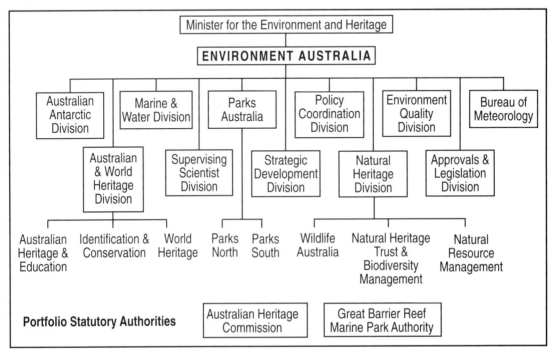

Source: Environment Australia web site: http://www.environment.gov.au/, updated August 2000, accessed January 2001.

Australian Nature Conservation Agency (ANCA)) The structure of Environment Australia is shown in Figure 9.1. Environment Australia deals specifically with the management of Australian World Heritage properties and with other international treaty obligations, especially those concerning the Ramsar and Biological Diversity conventions (see Sections 8.5 and 9.5). In recent years environmental matters, including issues of heritage, have had a relatively settled 'home', after they had been shunted around from one department to another over previous decades, often forming part of a large 'Department of Miscellaneous Affairs', which reflected the relatively low priority previously given to these matters by Australian politicians and voters. [1]

Australian Heritage Commission

The AHC is a Commonwealth statutory body formed under the *Australian Heritage Commission Act 1975* (Cth) (AHCA) to 'identify, conserve and promote Australia's National Estate—those parts of the natural and cultural environment that have special value for current and future generations'.[2] In 1976, following the Hope Inquiry into the National Estate, the AHC was established after rare bipartisan support in the federal parliament resulted in the AHCA. Section 7 of the Act sets out the major functions of the Commission as follows:

  (a) to give advice to the Minister on:

  (i) issues about the National Estate including the identification, conservation, improvement and presentation of the National Estate;

  (ii) Commonwealth expenditure on the identification, conservation, improvement and presentation of the National Estate;

  (iii) grants or other assistance by the Commonwealth for the identification, conservation, improvement or presentation of the National Estate;

  (b) to encourage public interest in, and understanding of issues relevant to the National Estate;

  (c) to identify places included in the National Estate and to prepare a register of those places in accordance with Part IV [which outlines the process for listing places on the RNE];

  (d) to provide advice and reports in accordance with Part V [which defines the responsibilities of Commonwealth ministers as they relate to the National Estate];

  (e) to administer the National Estates Grants Program [added through 1991 amendments];

  (f) to promote training and education in fields related to the conservation, improvement and presentation of the National Estate;

  (g) to make arrangements for the administration and control of places included in the National Estate that are given or bequeathed to the Commission;

(h) to organise and engage in research and investigation necessary for the performance of its other functions.

The National Estate Grants Program is outlined in Part VA of the 1991 amendments to the Act. It has the important function of channelling federal money to heritage research programs and, in certain circumstances, to specific restoration and conservation programs.

Register of the National Estate

Section 7(c) of the AHCA requires the AHC to prepare a RNE in accordance with Part IV of the Act. According to the Australian Heritage Commission's *Annual Report 1996–97*, the Register is:

> an inventory of all those parts of Australia's natural, historic, Aboriginal and Torres Strait Islander heritage which have special value for present and future generations … [a]ny place within Australia, its territories, its territorial sea or its continental shelf may be entered in the Register.[3]

As a result of the Hope Inquiry and the AHCA, the concept of the *National Estate* took root in Australia at a federal level, and this reinforced the variable, and often piecemeal or even virtually non-existent, approaches to heritage at the state level, especially cultural heritage. So, what is the National Estate? The National Estate is defined in the AHCA as:

> those places, being components of the natural environment of Australia, or the cultural environment of Australia, that have aesthetic, historic, scientific or social significance or other special value for future generations, as well as for the present community.

Australia's National Estate is thus a wide ranging concept which covers a variety of places. According to an AHC brochure, the types of places include:

1   The natural environment:

   a   national parks, nature reserves and other places for the protection of native fauna and flora;

   b   the coastline and islands;

   c   inland water expanses, rivers, lakes and other wetlands;

   d   special landforms, geological features, caves, forests, woodlands, grasslands;

   e   areas of scientific interest.

2   The man-made [*sic*] or cultural environment:

   a   historic buildings and structures, either individual or in groups;

   b   historic towns and precincts;

   c   urban parks and gardens.

3   Aboriginal sites

4   Areas of archaeological interest (both Aboriginal and European).

It can thus be seen that natural, indigenous cultural and non-indigenous cultural heritage are all included. The actual criteria for inclusion on the RNE, the official listing of heritage deemed to be of national significance, are given in Box 1.4.

The effects of a site being listed on the RNE are as follows:

- Planners and decision-makers at all levels of government and in the private sector are provided with objective information about the National Estate value of sites, so that this can be considered when decisions are being made.
- The Commonwealth Government is obliged to avoid damaging National Estate places (unless there are no feasible and prudent alternatives) and to consult with the Commission before taking any action which could harm or affect the registered place.
- All Australians are alerted to the presence of National Estate sites and to their natural and cultural heritage values.
- Researchers and scientists are provided with information about Australia's National Estate.
- Owners of heritage buildings and properties become eligible for tax rebates for conservation works on their properties.
- Places become eligible for grants for identification, conservation, or promotion under the National Estates Grants Program.[4]

On the other hand, listing a place on the register does not:

- give the AHC or the Commonwealth the right to acquire, manage or enter properties
- restrict the activities of any entity other than the Commonwealth Government on properties

Listing is thus largely advisory, giving moral rather than legal protection, except in very limited circumstances stemming directly from the Commonwealth's powers. The process for listing a property on the RNE as it stood in mid-2001 is outlined in Box 9.1, while a sample of listings (for part of south-western Victoria) were given in Box 1.3 to demonstrate the breadth of coverage. You can search the RNE through the general AHC web site at the address given in Appendix 2. The future of the Register is a little unclear at the time of writing, and this will be discussed further in Section 9.6.

Box 9.1   Process for listing places on the Register of the National Estate

1   Assessment

Places are assessed by independent experts and/or AHC staff. 'The Commission assesses places proposed for entry in the Register against detailed technical criteria outlining national estate values ... which include evolutionary significance, contribution to research, rarity, and historic, aesthetic, technical, creative or social values ... economic values are not considered.'[*]

2   Consideration

Commissioners meet four to six times a year to consider register entries. Commissioners can enter a place on the 'Interim List'.

3   Notification and advertisement

Private owners of properties on the interim list are notified of the proposed listing, and places on the interim list are advertised in the *Commonwealth of Australia Gazette* and the AHC informs state, territory, and local governments.

4 Objections
Any person can object or comment on interim listings within three months of advertisement.

5 Final entry
After considering objections the AHC makes a final decision on listing on the RNE.

Note: * Australian Heritage Commission (1997) *Annual Report 1996–97,* AHC, Canberra, p. 19.

Natural Heritage Trust

A Coalition election promise in the 1996 federal election led to the setting up of the Natural Heritage Trust (NHT), with funding of A$1.5 billion over a number of years. It focuses on five key environmental themes: land, vegetation, rivers, coasts and marine, and biodiversity. According to the Trust's web site: '[t]he programs of the Natural Heritage Trust will play a major role in developing sustainable agriculture and natural resource management, as well as protecting our unique biodiversity through improved management and delivery of resources'. It is thus only partly relevant in the present context as it also has major resource management and land rehabilitation functions. It does, though, provide funding for activities at a community level and encourages coordination of community involvement, as well as also funding state- and national-level projects. Despite serious questions raised in early 2001 concerning the Trust's management and procedures, it may yet play an important role in helping to preserve natural heritage sites.

9.4   Australian World Heritage properties

Table 9.1 lists Australia's fourteen World Heritage properties, together with their date of inscription (and any later enlargements), the criteria under which they were judged significant (see Appendix 1 for an explanation of the codes), and a brief statement of the reasons for inscription, which is akin to the statement of significance introduced in earlier chapters. These properties are mapped in Figure 9.2. It is worth noting that four Australian properties have been inscribed for both natural and cultural heritage reasons—Kakadu National Park (Plates 9.2 and 9.3), Uluṟu–Kata Tjuṯa (Plates 7.2 and 9.4), south-western Tasmania (Plate 9.5) and Willandra Lakes. This dual inscription on both natural and cultural criteria is quite rare on a world scale (Section 8.3) and reflects the intimate connection that exists between Australia's indigenous peoples and their environments. No sites in Australia relate to non-indigenous cultural heritage, either alone or in conjunction with natural heritage, which means that natural heritage sites are much more dominant than they are in many other countries (see also Section 1.6, Table 8.1, and Chapters 11 and 12). The latest Australian World Heritage property, the Greater Blue Mountains Area, was inscribed in November 2000. (Box 8.2 briefly summarised the process involved.)

Table 9.1

Australian World Heritage properties

Property	Criteria (see Appendix 1 for key)	Date of inscription (and of enlargements)	Brief description and reasons for inscription (from World Heritage List)
1 Kakadu National Park	N ii, iii, iv; C i, vi	1981, 1987, 1992	A unique archaeological and ethnological reserve, located in the Northern Territory, the region has been inhabited continuously for more than 40 000 years. The cave paintings, rock carvings, and archaeological sites present a record of the skills and lifeways of the region's inhabitants, from the hunters and gatherers of prehistoric times to the Aboriginal people still living there. It is a unique example of a complex of ecosystems, including tidal flats, floodplains, lowlands, and plateau, that provide habitat for a wide range of rare or endemic species of plants and animals.
2 Great Barrier Reef	N i, ii, iii, iv	1981	A site of remarkable variety and beauty on the north-eastern coast of Australia, the Great Barrier Reef contains the world's largest collection of coral reefs, with 400 types of coral, 1500 species of fish, and 4000 types of mollusc. It also holds great scientific interest as the habitat of species, such as the dugong and the large green turtle, which are threatened with extinction.
3 Willandra Lakes Region	N i; C iii	1981	Fossil remains of a series of lakes and sand formations that date from the Pleistocene can be found in this region, together with archaeological evidence of human occupation dating from 40 000 years ago. It is a unique landmark in the study of human evolution on the Australian continent. Several well-preserved fossils of giant marsupials have also been found here.
4 Tasmanian Wilderness	N i, ii, iii, iv; C iii, iv, vi	1982, 1989	In a region that has been subjected to severe glaciation, these parks and reserves, with their steep gorges, covering an area of over 1 000 000 hectares, constitute one of the last expanses of temperate rainforest in the world. Remains found in limestone caves attest to the occupation of the area for more than 20 000 years.
5 Lord Howe Island Group	N iii, iv	1982	A remarkable example of isolated oceanic islands, born of volcanic activity more than 2000 metres under the sea, these islands boast a spectacular topography and protect numerous endemic species, especially birds. A number of rare and threatened rainforest species are of international significance for science and conservation.
6 Central Eastern Australian Rainforest Reserves	N i, ii, iv	1986, 1994	This site, comprising several protected areas, is located predominantly along the Great Escarpment on Australia's east coast. The outstanding

Property	Criteria (see Appendix 1 for key)	Date of inscription (and of enlargements)	Brief description and reasons for inscription (from World Heritage List)
7 Uluṟu–Kata Tjuṯa National Park	N ii, iii; C v, vi	1987, 1994	This park, formerly called Uluṟu (Ayers Rock–Mount Olga) National Park, features spectacular geological formations that dominate the vast red sandy plain of central Australia. Uluṟu, an immense monolith, and Kata Tjuṯa, the rock domes located west of Uluṟu, form part of the traditional belief system of one of the oldest human societies in the world. The traditional owners of Uluṟu–Kata Tjuṯa are the Aṉangu Aboriginal people. geological features displayed around shield volcanic craters and the high number of rare and threatened rainforest species are of international significance for science and conservation.
8 Wet Tropics of Queensland	N i, ii, iii, iv	1988	This area, located in the far north-east of Australia, is made up largely of tropical humid forests. This biotope offers a particularly extensive and varied array of plants, as well as marsupials and singing birds, along with other rare and endangered animals and plant species.
9 Shark Bay, Western Australia	N i, ii, iii, iv	1991	On the far west coast of Western Australia, Shark Bay, with its islands and the land surrounding it, has three exceptional natural features—its vast marine herbariums, which are the largest (4800 square kilometres) and richest in the world, its dugong ('sea cow') population, and its stromatolites (colonies of algae which grow up alongside the mounds are among the oldest forms of life on earth). Shark Bay also shelters five species of endangered mammals.
10 Fraser Island	N ii, iii	1992	Along the eastern coast of Australia lies Fraser Island. At 122 kilometres long, it is the largest sand island in the world. Majestic remnants of tall rainforest growing on sand and half the world's perched freshwater dune lakes are found inland from the beach. The combination of shifting sand dunes, tropic, humid forests and lakes make it an exceptional site.
11 Australian Fossil Mammal Sites (Riversleigh/Naracoorte)	N i, ii	1994	Riversleigh and Naracoorte, in the north and south respectively of eastern Australia, are among the world's ten greatest fossil sites. They superbly illustrate the stages of evolution of Australia's unique fauna.
12 Heard and McDonald Islands	N i, ii	1997	Heard Island and McDonald Island are located in the Southern Ocean, approximately 1700 kilometres from the Antarctic continent and 4100 kilometres south-west of Perth. As the only volcanically active subantarctic islands they 'open a window into the earth', thus providing opportunities to observe ongoing geomorphic processes and glacial

13 Macquarie Island	N i, iii	1997	dynamics. The distinctive conservation value of Heard and McDonald, one of the rare pristine island ecosystems on our globe, lies in the complete absence of alien plants and animals, as well as of human impact. Macquarie Island, is a 34 kilometres long by 5 kilometres wide oceanic island in the Southern Ocean, 1500 kilometres south-east of Tasmania and approximately half way between Australia and the Antarctic continent. The island is the exposed crest of the undersea Macquarie Ridge, raised to its present position where the Indo-Australian tectonic plate meets the Pacific plate. It is a site of major geoconservation significance, as the only place on earth where rocks from the earth's mantle (six kilometres below the ocean floor) are being actively exposed above sea level. These unique exposures include excellent examples of pillow basalts and other extrusive rocks.
14 The Greater Blue Mountains Area	N ii, iv	2000	The Greater Blue Mountains Area consists of 1.03 million hectares of mostly forested landscape on a deeply-incised sandstone plateau 60–180 kilometres inland from central Sydney. The site comprises eight protected areas in two blocks separated by a transportation and urban development corridor. The site is particularly noted for its wide and balanced representation of *Eucalyptus* habitats including wet and dry sclerophyll, mallee heathlands, as well as localised swamps, wetlands, and grassland. Ninety *Eucalyptus* taxa (13 per cent of the world's total) occur in the Greater Blue Mountains. The site hosts several evolutionary relic species (including the Wollemi pine) which have persisted in highly-restricted microsites.

Figure 9.2

Map showing Australian World Heritage properties, Ramsar Wetlands of International Importance, and Biosphere Reserves

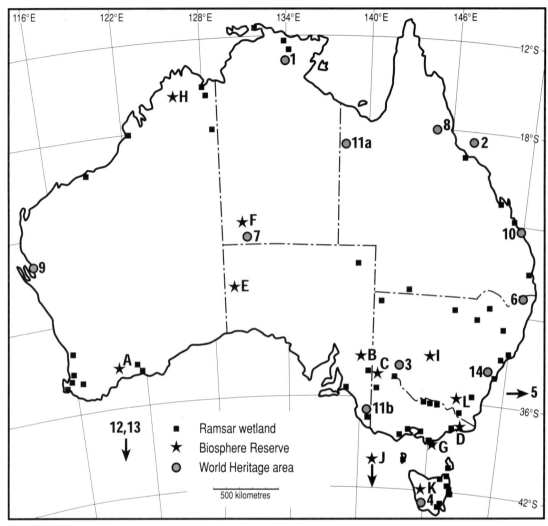

Source: various Environment Australia printed and web site materials.

Key: World Heritage areas
1–14: see Table 9.1.
Biosphere Reserves
A Fitzgerald River National Park
B Bookmark Biosphere Reserve
C Hattah-Kulkyne National Park and Murray-Kulkyne Park
D Croajingalong National Park (Vic) and Nadgee Nature Reserve (NSW)
E unnamed Conservation Park
F Uluṟu–Kata Tjuṯa National Park
G Wilsons Promontory National Park
H Prince Regent Nature Reserve
I Yathong Nature Reserve
J Macquarie Island Nature Reserve
K Southwest National Park
L Kosciuszko National Park

Plate 9.2

Aboriginal paintings at Ubirr (Obiri Rock), Kakadu National Park, Northern Territory, a World Heritage property. Ubirr alone has six major Aboriginal rock art galleries, some of them with paintings more than 20 000 years old.

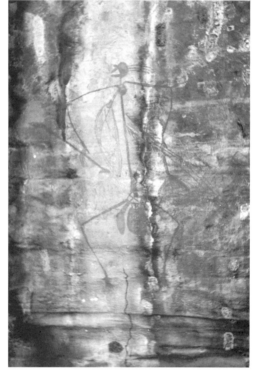

Photo: Don Johnston

Plate 9.3

Barramundie Gorge, in the southern section of Kakadu National Park, Northern Territory.

Photo: Monica Green

Plate 9.4

Kata Tjuṯa (The Olgas),
Uluṟu–Kata Tjuṯa National
Park, Northern Territory,
comprising thirty-six rock
domes, separated by gorges
and chasms.

Photo: Monica Green

Plate 9.5

Lush temperate rainforest
and limestone outcrops on
the banks of the Gordon
River, in the
Franklin–Gordon Wild
Rivers National Park,
which is included in the
Tasmanian Wilderness
World Heritage property,
south-western Tasmania. A
large section of the river
was in danger of being
drowned by a hydroelectric
scheme in the early 1980s.

Photo: Graeme Aplin

There has been much political controversy over World Heritage sites in
Australia, which has at times overshadowed the values of the sites as
important components of the heritage of Australia and the world, and the
benefits of having them inscribed on the WHL. Much of the controversy has
involved disagreement between the Federal Government and some state
governments over the properties proposed for inscription. As discussed in
Chapter 8, the national government must propose properties, and some
states have claimed that they were inadequately consulted or overruled.
Following extensive and sometimes heated discussions, the
Intergovernmental Agreement on the Environment of 1992 now requires
the Commonwealth to consult the states on World Heritage proposals, a
requirement backed by the new *Environment Protection and Biodiversity
Conservation Act 1999* (Cth) (EPBCA; see Section 9.6). A second bone of

contention has been the limitations on land use which are potentially required in order for Australia to meet its obligations under the WHC. Furthermore, there are conflicts of interest arising from the fact that World Heritage listing does not change ownership of land within properties, and because much of the day-to-day management of World Heritage sites is necessarily carried out under state or territory laws, and by state or territory agencies. Earlier discussion (especially in Chapter 3) of the rights and responsibilities of owners is also relevant here. Two particularly controversial, but quite different, cases are briefly summarised in the following paragraphs.

South-western Tasmania

The creation of the South-west Tasmania Wilderness World Heritage Area (Figure 9.3 and Plate 9.5) arose from a heated conflict over the Gordon-below-Franklin Dam proposal. The Tasmanian version of developmentalism (Section 9.2) was based on hydroindustrialisation—attracting industry through very cheap hydroelectric power. This policy was pushed extremely vigorously by the state's Hydro-Electric Commission (HEC). The earlier development of hydroelectric resources in Tasmania included flooding Lake Pedder in 1973 under the 'Gordon Stage One' scheme. Conservationists who were opposed to this scheme turned to the Federal Government which:

> lacked clear constitutional powers to protect Lake Pedder from the waters which were by this stage inundating it, and it did no more than establish an inquiry and subsequently offer full financial compensation to Tasmania to save the lake. Indeed, it probably could have done little more under constitutional law at the time. The Tasmanian Government refused the compensation, continued with the dam and was resentful of the attempt to meddle in state affairs.[5]

In 1979 an HEC report recommended that the Gordon-below-Franklin Dam proceed, and conservationists were determined not to lose on this issue. In December 1982 the Western Tasmanian Wilderness National Parks were inscribed on the WHL; ironically, this inscription was actually the end result of the Tasmanian Government recommending nomination of the property to the Commonwealth following creation of the Franklin–Lower Gordon Wild Rivers National Park and extension of the Southwest National Park in May 1981. The World Heritage status of the property gave the Commonwealth power (under the external affairs provision of the Constitution) to protect the World Heritage values of the property. Soon after being elected in March 1983, the Hawke Federal Labor Government passed the *World Heritage Properties Act 1983* (Cth), which was challenged as constitutionally invalid in the High Court by the Tasmanian Government. On 1 July 1983, the High Court upheld (by a four-to-three majority) the constitutional validity of the Act, effectively halting development of the Gordon-below-Franklin dam.

Kakadu National Park

Kakadu is an unusual form of World Heritage site, because it has enclaves within it which are subject to mining leases. The result is that areas of actual or potential uranium mining, whilst not technically or legally part of the park, are

Figure 9.3

A and B—Two alternative proposals for the Gordon-below-Franklin hydroelectricity scheme; and C—the ultimate Franklin–Gordon Wild Rivers National Park, now incorporated in the South-west Tasmania Wilderness World Heritage Area.

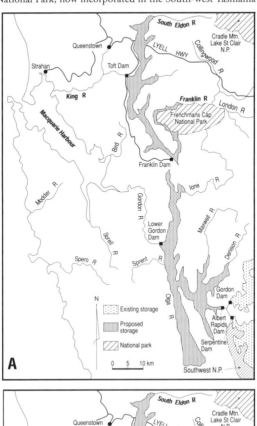

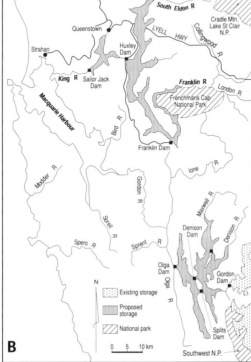

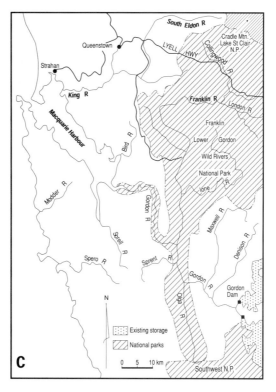

Source: G. Aplin (1998), *Australians and Their Environment: An Introduction to Environmental Studies*, Oxford University Press, Melbourne, pp. 160–1.

surrounded by it (Figure 9.4). Box 9.2 highlights features of the park's management plan, which is especially notable for the attention it pays to the involvement and aspirations of the traditional Aboriginal owners of the land, and is an extremely good example of the use of internal zoning as a park management tool.

In the late 1990s, proposals were accepted by the developmentalist and economic-rationalist Howard Coalition Government to allow a new mine to operate over a period of several years. Both conservation groups and the traditional owners of Kakadu made moves to have the area inscribed on the LWHD (see Section 8.4), on the grounds that there was potential for both environmental and cultural impacts and a significant risk of serious downgrading of the property's World Heritage values. The WHCom ultimately did not place Kakadu on the LWHD, but, from many accounts, it came extremely close to doing so in 1999, and expressed major concerns about the way the Australian Government handled the issue. Prior to its consideration of the issue, the WHCom sent a mission to Kakadu to examine the case and released the *Report on the Mission to Kakadu...*, which included the recommendations listed in Box 9.3. The Australian Government responded vigorously through the media, and by sending an unusually large delegation, including many people in prominent positions, to lobby WHCom members. The Aboriginal traditional owners and conservation groups also sent representatives and lobbied hard, although they could not match the Australian Government in terms of finances or infrastructure.

Figure 9.4

Zoning in Kakadu National Park

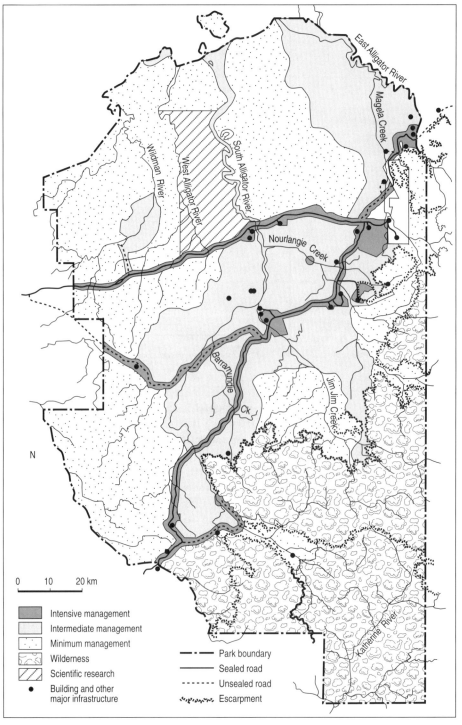

Source: simplified from P. Wellings (1995), 'Management considerations', in T. Press *et al.* (eds), *Kakadu: Natural and Cultural Heritage and Management*, Australian Nature Conservation Agency and North Australia Research Unit, Australian National University, Darwin, p. 265.

Box 9.2   Key features of Plan of Management, Kakadu National Park, 1991

Overriding principles of the Kakadu Plan of Management

1   Aboriginal rights—including the right to hunt and forage
2   Natural and cultural heritage—conservation of key features and areas
3   Tourism—encouraging public appreciation and enjoyment of the park, but not at the expense of, or taking priority over, principles 1 and 2
4   Communication of park values

Key management objectives

A   to establish a plan of management in which Aboriginal people associated with the park may play a key role
B   to give special protection to Aboriginal art sites, sacred sites and other sites of significance to Aboriginal people
C   to institute an innovative park management regime conforming to the highest international standards
D   to protect park resources from the undesirable consequences of fire, erosion, environmental change, pollution, and other activities of humans
E   to rehabilitate areas damaged by feral and introduced animals and plants, and recent human impacts
F   to cooperate with neighbours in complementary management programs that help to protect park resources
G   to develop an inventory of all relevant resources in the park
H   to stimulate interest in nature conservation and Aboriginal culture by the development and implementation of an imaginative communication program
I   to provide information and guidance to visitors about potential hazards in the park and ensure their safety as far as possible

Zoning

The zones referred to on Figure 9.4 permit the following activities and uses:

A   Intensive management zones provide for maximum recreation and infrastructure development. They include all main roads and the principle accommodation areas and administrative facilities.
B   Intermediate management zones allow for infrastructure development (but not hotel/motel developments) as long as they do not intrude significantly into the landscape. Aboriginal outstations may be included.
C   Minimum management zones are generally remote, extensive areas where priority is given to conservation. Access is allowed on established 4WD tracks. Park management is generally limited to erosion control, feral animal control, fencing of sensitive or damaged areas, approved research, and limited signposting. Bushwalking and bush camping are allowed under a permit system, but limits are sometimes placed on the number of visitors in one place at one time.
D   Wilderness zones are reserved and designed to protect examples of land system types in the park and to provide for long-term research and conservation. No permanent facilities are to be established except for access for research and rehabilitation purposes. Appropriate uses are bushwalking and non-manipulative scientific research.
E   Scientific research zone, including the Kapalga Research Station, is used for the development and maintenance of approved scientific research or educational programs related to wildlife management.

Source: adapted from P. Wellings (1995), 'Management considerations', in Press, T. *et al.* (eds), *Kakadu: Natural and Cultural Heritage and Management*, Australian Nature Conservation Agency/North Australia Research Unit, Australian National University, Darwin, pp. 238–70.

Box 9.3 Summaries of the recommendations of the UNESCO Mission to Kakadu National Park and the Australian Government's response

A UNESCO Mission recommendations

1 Mining and milling of uranium at Jabiluka should not proceed due to severe ascertained and potential threats to the natural and cultural values of the Park.

2 The precautionary principle should be applied due to unacceptably high degrees of scientific uncertainty, and that mining operations at Jabiluka should thus cease.

3 Further visual encroachment on the Park's integrity through mining and urban expansion at Jabiru should be prevented.

4 The Jabiluka Cultural Heritage Management Plan should be as thorough as possible and prepared according to international best practice, and with strong participation by the traditional owners. An accurate inventory of cultural sites should be compiled.

5 An utmost priority should be given to an exhaustive cultural mapping of the mineral leases as these areas are an integral part of the Kakadu cultural landscape.

6 The Australian Government should take a decisive role in implementing the Kakadu Regional Social Impact Study (KRSIS) recommendations to ameliorate the negative regional socio-cultural impacts of development on Aboriginal people and the Park's cultural values.

7 The Australian Government should recognise the special relationship of the Mirrar to their land, and their rights to participate in decisions affecting them. The 1982 agreement with Energy Resources Australia and the 1991 transfer of ownership should be reconsidered.

8 The full extent of the outstanding cultural landscape of Kakadu should be recognised and protected, and that the State Party should propose to the WHCom that cultural criterion (iii) and the World Heritage cultural landscape categories also be applied to Kakadu. The living traditions of the traditional owners and their spiritual ties to the land form the basis of the integrity of the cultural landscape.

9 The Australian Government should examine the feasibility of extending the boundaries of the National Park and World Heritage property to protect more of the East Alligator River catchment.

10 The Aboriginal two-thirds majority on the Board of Management should be maintained, and proposed changes to the status of the Director of National Parks should be reconsidered.

11 It is imperative that the evident breakdown in trust and communication be repaired. Proper consultation with traditional owners must continue to be a requirement when considering any issues relating to the management of their lands. All indigenous and non-indigenous stakeholders should engage in a dialogue to ensure conservation of the outstanding heritage of Kakadu for future generations.

12 The Environmental Research Institute of the Supervising Scientist (ERISS) in Jabiru should be maintained and membership of the Advisory Committee should be reconsidered.

13 The Australian Government should discuss rescinding the 1981 *Koongarra Project Area Act* with the traditional owners and seek their consent to include the Koongarra Mineral Lease in the Park and thus preclude mining.

14 Urban and infrastructure development at Jabiru should be strictly controlled, with Parks Australia North and the Board of Management playing a greater role in management and future planning of the town.

15 Adequate additional funds should be guaranteed for control of *Mimosa nigra* and *Salvinia molesta*.

16 Additional necessary funds should be provided to research the threat of cane toads to the Park, and to develop countermeasures.

B Response from the Australian Government

The Australian Government has:

A reviewed all the perceived threats to World Heritage and instituted necessary protective measures (Recommendations 1 & 2)

B undertaken an exhaustive independent review and further risk analysis of all claims of scientific uncertainty relating to the project (2)

C ascertained that any expansion of urban and infrastructure development in Jabiru as a result of the mine will be minimal, with the utilisation of existing housing stock to cater for workers (3)

D   ensured that the Interim Cultural Heritage Management Plan is subjected to independent peer review and invited further consultation with traditional owners to protect all sites in the lease area (4)

E   instituted dust and vibration studies to ensure the protection of rock art sites (4)

F   ensured that existing extensive records of cultural values are complemented by a cultural mapping exercise along the lines recommended (5)

G   accelerated the implementation of the KRSIS at Commonwealth, Territory and local levels with practical projects designed to address local issues of social and economic disadvantage (6)

H   sought the views of traditional owners, the NT Government, and the Northern Land Council* (NLC) on renomination of the Park on cultural criterion (iii) and cultural landscape criteria, and on extending the Park's boundaries (8 & 9)

I   engaged in high-level discussions on outstanding issues relating to joint management of the Park (10)

J   taken positive steps to confirm Government commitment to consultation and cross-cultural dialogue (11)

K   confirmed an ongoing presence of ERISS at Jabiru (12)

L   sought the views of the NLC*, traditional owners, and the mining company on potential options for the Koongarra Mineral Lease, pending the outcome of negotiations with traditional owners on the lease (13)

M   ensured that mechanisms in place will effectively limit the expansion of Jabiru to prevent any threat to the World Heritage property (14)

N   ensured that the impact of introduced species on the wetlands of Kakadu continue to be managed using best-practice approaches (15 & 16)

Note: *   It has been argued that the Northern Land Council does not represent the views or wishes of the traditional owners, the Mirrar people.

Source: various web sites accessible from the Environment Australia home page: http://www.environment.gov.au/.

A summary of the Government's response to the mission's recommendations is also given in Box 9.3. Particular concern (and obvious displeasure) is expressed in relation to recommendations 1, 2, 3, and 7 from the mission. The Government argues that the mission does not give Australia enough credit for measures that have been taken; does not provide objective assessment of threats; and does not adequately defer to the role of the State Party in relation to management decisions. It then argues that there is much less scientific uncertainty than the mission's report implies. In regard to recommendation 3, the Government argues that the mine cannot be seen from the ground from within the park; that the area disturbed by infrastructure amounts to only 0.007 per cent of the park; and that future expansion of Jabiru will still leave it with a lower population than at its past peak. Recommendation 7 is the only one not addressed at all in the list of responses in Box 9.3. The Government argues that the traditional Mirrar owners were consulted as required by law and that they consented to the 1982 and 1991 agreements, and that this recommendation goes beyond the ambit of the WHCom. Many groups, however, are still dissatisfied and are continuing their calls for an 'in danger' listing and a ban on further mining expansion. Inscription on the 'in danger' list was again avoided at the Cairns meeting of the WHCom in November 2000, but the issue may not yet be finalised, even though low uranium prices in 2001 made the expansion of mining less likely in the short term.

Management of World Heritage properties

The following list summarises the management objectives set by the Federal Government to meet its obligations in relation to World Heritage properties:

• to protect, conserve, and present the World Heritage values of the property

- to integrate the protection of the area into a comprehensive management program
- to give the property a function in the life of the Australian community
- to strengthen appreciation and respect of the property's World Heritage values, particularly through educational and information programs
- to keep the community broadly informed about the condition of the World Heritage values of the property
- to take appropriate scientific, technical, legal, administrative, and financial measures necessary for the achieving of the foregoing objectives

The legislative backing for these objectives, until 1999, was the *World Heritage Properties Act 1983* (Cth) (see Section 9.6 for the 1999 changes and the present situation). Most World Heritage properties are managed by state management agencies, but others—the Tasmanian Wilderness, the Great Barrier Reef, and the Wet Tropics of Queensland—are the subject of joint management arrangements under which day-to-day management is carried out by state agencies, but federal input, advice, and financial assistance are provided. In such cases, there are dual property-specific Acts of parliament, one Commonwealth and one state. The partial autonomy of the NT Government means that the Uluṟu–Kata Tjuṯa National Park and Kakadu National Park are managed by PA North. Both properties are now owned by the local Aboriginal communities and leased back to PA, and the traditional owners are well represented on both boards of management.

As we have seen, it has often been difficult for the Federal Government and all states and territories to agree on environmental matters. Sometimes, when foreign affairs powers could be invoked, the Federal Government has overridden a state government. Such action was taken in south-western Tasmania by invoking World Heritage provisions, and in relation to Fraser Island when an export licence for beach-sand minerals was refused. At other times, legislation or specific action was delayed for long periods or even abandoned because it was 'too hard'.

9.5   Other Commonwealth legislation and related reserves

Australia signed the Convention on Biological Diversity in June 1992 and ratified it a year later. However compliance with the obligations of the convention has remained less than whole-hearted. While the convention does not directly call for reserves to be set up in the way that the WHC inscribes properties, it is nonetheless an important supporting framework for the whole natural heritage reserve system (Section 8.5). Australia actually got in first, so to speak, and established a public advisory committee in 1991 to develop a national biodiversity strategy. By September 1992, this strategy was developed as the National Strategy for the Conservation of Australia's Biodiversity (NSCAB), although in March 1995 the Minister for the Environment was still referring to it as the 'draft' strategy for reasons discussed later in this section. An initial meeting on the Convention on Biological Diversity was held in Geneva in October 1993, and it had national strategies as one of its main priorities. One would have hoped that this would give all Australian governments the impetus to implement the NSCAB nationally, but it took some time for that to occur.

The NSCAB went to all state, territory, and federal environment ministers at the end of 1992, but only emerged in 1996 as a document on which there was consensus. Federal Cabinet endorsed the document in November 1993, but NSW and WA refused to do likewise. The older National Threatened Species Strategy had suffered a similar fate. In early 1995, the NSW Government had agreed to sign both documents in the run-up to what turned out to be a cliff-hanger state election, but WA continued to hold out, as it has on so many environmental matters. The Council of Australian Governments representing all states and territories endorsed the document in 1996. During the period leading up to the endorsement of the Convention on Biological Diversity, a number of related developments took place. The federal Minister for the Environment established a Biodiversity Advisory Council in 1991, and expressed interest in the suggestion from the Australian Committee for the IUCN that national biodiversity legislation was needed. At the end of 1992, the Federal Parliament passed the Endangered Species Protection Act, legislation that became watered down due to concerns by a number of members of Cabinet, who gave priority to economic concerns over conservation. In June 1993, the ANCA (now PA) was created to take over the responsibilities of the Australian NPWS, but also to administer the *Endangered Species Protection Act 1992* (Cth) and Australia's responsibilities under the Convention on International Trade in Endangered Species (CITES) and other international agreements and conventions. It has played a major coordinating role in implementing and administering the NSCAB.

Australia is also a party to many other regional and bilateral treaties that are involved in the conservation of natural heritage, in the broader meaning of the word. The various responsibilities and relevant legislation mentioned in these paragraphs have recently been consolidated under a new piece of legislation, which will be discussion further in Section 9.6. This legislation also deals with Biosphere Reserves and Ramsar wetlands (see Section 8.5).

9.6   New and proposed legislation, 1998–2001

At the end of the 20th century, federal environment and heritage legislation has been in something of a state of flux. The Coalition Government has pushed to rationalise the existing legislation and to give as much responsibility as possible to the states and territories, in line with their generally decentralised, state-rights view of the federation (see Section 9.1).

Indigenous heritage

The Aboriginal and Torres Strait Islander Heritage Protection Bill 1998 (Cth) was introduced to Federal Parliament in April 1998 to replace an earlier 1984 Act with the same title. This was an attempt to reduce duplication between jurisdictions, and the key mechanism for doing this is accreditation of state legislation. The passage of the Bill has been held up for various reasons and is now awaiting debate in the Senate. The Federal Government was given considerable powers in the field of indigenous affairs in a referendum many decades ago, and thus has more scope to act with regard to indigenous heritage than it has with other types of heritage. The

Commonwealth Act and Bill allow for intervention where protection of objects and places is in the national interest. In the meantime, in December 1998, matters relating to Aboriginal heritage were transferred from the Department of Aboriginal and Torres Strait Islander Affairs to the Department of the Environment and Heritage.

World Heritage and natural heritage

The EPBCA replaced a number of earlier Acts in the general environmental field, and included some sections related to heritage. The sections of key relevance here are:

1   Chapter 2, Part 3, Division 1—Requirements relating to matters of national environmental significance: World Heritage; wetlands of international importance; listed threatened species and communities; listed migratory species; and the marine environment.

2   Chapter 5, Part 12—Identifying and monitoring biodiversity and making bioregional plans.

3   Chapter 5, Part 13—Species and communities: listing threatened species and ecological communities; migratory species; whales and other cetaceans; listed marine species; and plans (including recovery plans, threat abatement plans and wildlife conservation plans).

4   Chapter 5, Part 15—Protected areas: managing World Heritage properties; managing wetlands of international importance; managing Biosphere Reserves; Commonwealth reserves; and conservation zones.

5   Chapter 6, Part 16—Application of the precautionary principle in decision-making.

6   Chapter 6, Part 17—Enforcement: including environmental audits and conservation orders.

7   Chapter 6, Part 19—Organisations: including the Threatened Species Scientific Committee; the Biological Diversity Advisory Committee; the Indigenous Advisory Committee; and the Director of National Parks.

There have been a number of statements and academic papers critical of the EPBCA, most focussing on the return of greater responsibilities to the states and territories, and the increased reliance on the varying degrees of commitments shown by those jurisdictions. Critics generally want the Commonwealth to take a stronger lead than that which is allowed by the current political reality and perhaps constitutional law. It should also be noted that the greatest criticism is aimed at sections of the Act that are not directly relevant to heritage conservation as covered in this book.

National heritage and cultural heritage

In mid-2000, it was announced that a Bill dealing specifically with other heritage issues would be introduced into Parliament in the latter part of 2000 or early 2001. It would be debated in the ensuing months, and would perhaps come into force in 2001. Three discussion papers were issued in

1996–97, and a National Heritage Convention was held in August 1998. Following the convention, the Federal Government issued a Consultation Paper in April 1999 with calls for public responses by May 1999. The Purpose and Principles outlined in the document entitled *A National Strategy for Australia's Heritage Places: A Commonwealth Discussion Paper* are listed in Box 9.4.

The Purpose and Principles of the Consultation Paper neglect to make any statement regarding indigenous heritage, which may reflect the Coalition Federal Government's inability or unwillingness to come to grips with reconciliation and the meaningful incorporation of indigenous people in the Australian community. In contrast, the Preamble and Vision on the National Heritage Convention web site made quite specific reference to issues of indigenous heritage, accurately reflecting the feeling at the convention itself. The Preamble states:

> Australia's heritage, shaped by nature and history, is an inheritance passed from one generation to the next. It encompasses many things, the way we live, the traditions we hold dear, our histories, stories, myths, values and places. The diversity of our natural and cultural places helps us to understand the past and our relationship with the Australian landscape. Heritage recognises the indivisible association of culture, nature, country, place, religion for Aboriginal and Torres Strait Islander peoples.

The Vision is given as follows:

> Recognising the diversity of country and cultures in Australia and the unique relationship of Aboriginal and Torres Strait Islander peoples with country, Australia should act as a community that respects, sustains and celebrates its diverse heritage, which connects us with past, present and country for all generations.

Box 9.4   Purpose and Principles of the National Heritage Strategy, April 1999

A   Purpose

The National Heritage Strategy will commit governments (federal, state, territory and local) to:

I   clearly delineate roles and responsibilities of each level of government which minimise duplication between heritage systems and increase certainty for the community and decision makers

II   improved identification and conservation of heritage places by implementing agreed national standards

III   improved protection of all heritage places at the national, state and local levels … through increased compliance with relevant heritage and planning laws.

B   Principles

1   Recognising our responsibilities to past and future generations, the Australian community will conserve its heritage through cooperation and respect between all communities and governments.

2   All levels of government and government agencies must demonstrate leadership in protecting, conserving, promoting and managing heritage values.

3   Recognising the indigenous people are custodians of their heritage and have consequent obligations, the heritage of all Australians should be managed in accordance with evolving traditions, customs and laws.

4   Communities should be actively involved in all processes of identification, protection and use of heritage places, other than where this would be inconsistent with the conservation of heritage values.

5   There should be a comprehensive inventory of heritage places accessible to the general public, subject to confidentiality where this is required to protect, for example, endangered species, fossil sites or indigenous heritage values or customary rights.

6 Identification and assessment should be based on the full range and diversity of heritage values.

7 Determination of significance should be based solely on heritage values and be separate from management decisions.

8 The fundamental aim of conservation is to sustain heritage value with the least possible intervention. Where the use of a place involves a risk of significant irreversible damage to heritage values, lack of scientific certainty should not be used as a reason for allowing that use.

9 The uses of heritage places should, as far as practicable, be limited to those which are compatible with the heritage values of the place. Where there is a conflict between heritage and other values, prudent and feasible management options must be sought and considered.

10 The effective identification and conservation of heritage places is dependent upon relevant research, education and presentation which respects the heritage values of the place and the sensitivities of communities.

11 Conservation of heritage should be adequately resourced, recognising the rights, responsibilities and capabilities of governments, owners, custodians, communities and interested parties, and respecting cultural and gender requirements.

12 Planning processes and decisions must include conservation management planning for heritage.

Source: Minister for the Environment and Heritage (1999) *A National Strategy for Australia's Heritage Places: A Commonwealth Discussion Paper*, MEH, Canberra, pp. 8–9.

What, then, is the likely outcome of the legislative process set in train by the Convention and the Discussion Paper? On 30 June 2000, the federal Minister for the Environment and Heritage announced that the Government would reform its heritage protection structures 'to achieve more effective protection of places of truly national importance'. Legislation was introduced to parliament on 7 December 2000, and it includes provision for:

• a National Heritage List (NHL)

• a Commonwealth Heritage List (CHL)

• an independent expert advisory body, the Australian Heritage Council (AH Council—as distinct from the present Australian Heritage Commission.[6]

The NHL is to replace the RNE and concentrate on places of 'outstanding national heritage significance', while the CHL will be concerned specifically with places owned or managed by the Commonwealth and its agencies. Some Australian heritage professionals and activists fear that the new NHL will be considerably leaner and meaner than the existing RNE, and that many places currently listed on the RNE must henceforth rely on protection under state and territory provisions, which vary considerably in quality and reliability (Chapter 10). The June 2000 briefing seems to imply that the present RNE will be retained and all places listed will come under the protection of the EPBCA (see previous section), even if no additional sites will be listed on the RNE. There is some ambiguity, however, as a concurrent ministerial press release clearly suggests that places on the RNE, but not on the NHL, will be transferred to state and territory lists and jurisdictions after a transitional period.

The AH Council will advise on the eligibility of places for listing and provide statements of significance, and the final decision about listing will be made by the minister. The minister can also provisionally list a place if urgent protection is needed. The AH Council only has the right to directly draw up management plans when sites are owned by the Commonwealth, which is not very different from the present situation. The AH Council will also seek to influence state, territory, and local governments to actively fulfil their obligations, as implied in the principles given in Box 9.4, and will seek bilateral agreements where appropriate. If a place on the NHL is entirely within a state or territory, the federal minister will be required to 'use best endeavours to ensure a management plan is prepared or implemented in cooperation with the State or Territory.' In addition, places on the NHL will be included as an additional 'matter of environmental significance' under the new EPBCA, generally meaning that the minister must approve any activities that will significantly impact on the heritage values of such places. Neither of these provisions, of course, will apply to places currently listed on the RNE that will not be listed on the NHL.

It is proposed that for places on the NHL the AH Council will be able to provide technical and financial assistance for the preparation of management plans; for their protection or conservation; and for their promotion, identification, and presentation. Voluntary conservation agreements similar to those in the EPBCA will enlist the help and cooperation of private owners in the conservation of heritage places. In addition, the Council will perform a monitoring and reporting role, and the minister will formally report to Parliament every two years. It appears that the Council will also coordinate a national database containing information on all heritage properties listed on the NHL, the CHL, and the various state, territory, and local lists.

In summary, there is potential for the new legislation to strengthen heritage protection in Australia, but only if the states and territories are prepared to play a genuine complementary role under their own provisions, which in some cases will need strengthening if desirable outcomes are to be achieved. Chapter 10 introduces the relevant state and territory provisions.

Notes

1   The structure of government departments is fluid at the best of times, and the comments in this and the next three chapters reflect the situation in early 2001.

2   Australian Heritage Commission (1997) *Annual Report 1996–97,* AHC, Canberra, p. 4. As a result of legislative change in 2001, the AHCom is likely to be replaced by an Australian Heritage Council with more restricted responsibilities (see Section 9.6).

3   ibid., pp. 16–18. See Section 9.6 for discussion for likely changes to the role of the RNE.

4   ibid., p. 18.

5   Doyle, T. & Kellow, A. (1995) *Environmental Politics and Policy Making in Australia*, Macmillan, Melbourne, p. 206.

6   For the latest available update on this structure and progress of the Bill, see the web site of Environment Australia:

http://www.environment.gov.au/heritage/infores/publications/newheritage.html

Further Reading

Updated information on changes to legislation and bureaucratic structures is available at the web site associated with this book, at http://www.es.mq.edu.au/ courses/REM/heritage.htm.

Australian Heritage Commission (1981) *The Heritage of Australia: The Illustrated Register of the National Estate*, Macmillan, Melbourne.

Australian Heritage Commission (1994) *Conserving the National Estate: A Bibliography of National Estate Studies* (3rd edn), Australian Government Publishing Service, Canberra.

Australian Heritage Commission (1998) *Protecting Local Heritage Places: A Guide for Local Communities*, AHC, Canberra.

Australian Heritage Commission (1999) *Australia's National Heritage: Options for Identifying Heritage Places of National Significance*, AHC, Canberra.

Bates, G. (1995) *Environmental Law in Australia* (4th edn), Butterworths, Sydney, especially Chapter 9.

Bonyhady, T. (1993) *Places Worth Keeping: Conservationists, Politics and the Law*, Allen & Unwin, Sydney.

Committee of Inquiry Into the National Estate (1974) *Report of the National Estate*, Australian Government Publishing Service, Canberra.

Department of the Environment, Sport & Territories (1996) *The National Strategy for the Conservation of Australia's Biodiversity*, Australian Government Publishing Service, Canberra.

Gale, F. & Jacobs, J. M. (1987) *Tourists and the National Estate: Procedures to Protect Australia's Heritage*, Australian Heritage Commission Special Australian Heritage Publication Series No. 6, Australian Government Publishing Service, Canberra.

Hall, C. M. (1992) *Wasteland to World Heritage: Preserving Australia's Wilderness*, Melbourne University Press, Melbourne.

Hamilton-Smith, E. (ed.) (1998) *Celebrating the Parks: Proceedings of the First Australian Symposium on Parks History*, Rethink Consulting, Melbourne.

Jeans, D. N. (ed.) (1984) *Australian Historical Landscapes*, Allen & Unwin, Sydney.

Lane, M. & McDonald, G. (1997) 'Not all world heritage areas are created equal: world heritage area management in Australia', in Pigram, J. J. & Sundell, R. C. (eds) *National Parks and Protected Areas: Selection, Delimitation and Management*, University of New England, Armidale, pp. 369–86.

Lawrence, D. (2000) *Kakadu: The Making of a National Park*, Melbourne University Press, Melbourne.

Lennon, J. (1992) *Our Heritage: Historic Places on Public Land in Victoria*, Department of Conservation & Environment, Melbourne.

Lloyd, C. (1977) *The National Estate: Australia's Heritage*, Cassell, Sydney.

Molesworth, S. R. (1999) '"Barbarians at the gates of the Garden of Eden—revisited": Heritage Protection Foundation for the New Millennium', in Leadbeter, P., Gunningham, N. & Boer, B. (eds) *Environmental Outlook No.3: Outlook and Policy*, Federation Press, Sydney, pp. 222–47.

Parker, P. (1993) *Biosphere Reserves in Australia: A Strategy for the Future*, Australian Government Publishing Service, Canberra.

Pocock, D. (1997) 'Some reflections on world heritage', *Area*, Vol. 29, No. 3, pp. 260–8.

Robertson, M., Vang, K. & Brown, A. J. (1993) *Wilderness in Australia: Issues and Options—A Discussion Paper*, Australian Heritage Commission, Canberra.

Sullivan, S. (ed.) (1995) *Cultural Conservation—Towards a National Approach*, Special Heritage Publication Series No. 9, Australian Heritage Commission/Australian Government Publishing Service, Canberra.

World Heritage Branch (1999) *Australia's World Heritage*, Environment Australia, Canberra.

CHAPTER 10

Regulatory Frameworks and Voluntary Organisations: Australian States and Territories

10.1 Introduction

Due to the federal structure of Australia and the division of powers under the Constitution, the Commonwealth only has limited powers when it comes to heritage (Chapter 9). Most of the day-to-day management of heritage lies with state and territory governments and with local, municipal government through its planning powers. This chapter deals at some length with the situation in NSW (Section 10.2), and more briefly with the other states and territories (Section 10.3). The final section makes the point that voluntary organisations, particularly the various branches of the National Trust, also play a key role in heritage recognition and conservation in Australia.

10.2 New South Wales

Administrative and legislative framework

Heritage administration in NSW is split between local government and two major state departments. For natural heritage and Aboriginal cultural heritage, the major body is the NPWS. Built heritage—the immoveable component of non-indigenous cultural heritage—is administered through the Department of Urban Affairs and Planning (DUAP), and more specifically through its agency, the Heritage Council of NSW and its administrative arm, the Heritage Office. As we will see in later paragraphs, local government plays a key role through its planning responsibilities, overseen by the Heritage Council and DUAP, and to some extent by the Department of Local Government. Current statutory documents, funding arrangements, and available expertise mean that the three different categories of heritage items—Aboriginal, non-indigenous cultural, and natural—are usually identified and protected by separate processes and legislation.

The *Heritage Office* administers the NSW Heritage Database and the State Heritage Register (SHR). The SHR, by definition, is concerned with heritage at a state level, while national-scale heritage is covered by the RNE (see Section

9.3), and local-scale heritage by the Local Environmental Plans (LEPs) discussed later in this Section. Protection is afforded at the appropriate political level by the RNE, SHR or LEP. The Database, on the other hand, was developed as a catalogue of all sites in NSW included on any of these lists. A document issued prior to a major overhaul of the Heritage Database in the early 1990s discussed criteria under two headings, 'nature' and 'degree' (see Section 1.5). According to this document, significance can be derived from one of the following:

- the historical context (historic significance)
- some creative or technical accomplishment (which incorporates aesthetic significance)
- community regard or esteem (social significance)
- research potential, including for archaeology (scientific significance)
- other special values
- an item's rarity (the uncommon or exceptional)
- its representativeness (the typical or characteristic)
- its associations (links and connections with events, famous people, or organisations)

Of these last three dimensions, the first two correspond to two of the elements shown in Figure 1.2. The last is included to emphasise associations at the state level. More detailed criteria and a number of 'State Themes' are listed in Box 6.1. The NSW Heritage Database can be searched from the web site of the NSW Heritage Office. (See list of web sites in Appendix 2.) The Heritage Council was formed under the *Heritage Act 1977* (NSW) and is responsible to the Minister for Urban Affairs and Planning. The Heritage Council is the main agency dealing with built heritage in the state. In addition, a small number of buildings owned by the government are managed and presented to the public by the Historic Houses Trust.

The Heritage Council has the following functions under section 21 of the Act (as amended):

1   The functions of the Heritage Council are:

    a   to make recommendations to the Minister for or with respect to the exercise by him [*sic*] of any functions conferred or imposed on him [*sic*] by or under this Act or the regulations;

    b   to make recommendations to the Minister relating to the taking of measures for or with respect to:

        i   the conservation of;
        ii   the exhibition or display of;
        iii   the provision of access to; and
        iv   the publication of information concerning,

    items of the environmental heritage.

    c   to carry out investigations, research and inquiries relating to the matters referred to in paragraph (b);

    d   to arrange and co-ordinate consultations, discussions, seminars and conferences relating to the matters referred to in paragraph (b); and

    e to exercise such other functions as are conferred or imposed on it by or under this or any other Act or the regulations.

  2 Without limiting subsection (1), the Heritage Council may:

    a make submissions to persons or bodies in respect of:

      i environmental studies;

      ii draft environmental planning instruments; and

      iii environmental impact statements, prepared under the *Environmental Planning and Assessment Act 1979* in so far as they relate to the environmental heritage;

  and

    b provide opinions, statements or other information relating to the environmental heritage to persons or bodies if the Heritage Council considers it appropriate to do so.

The NSW Heritage Management System, operated by the Heritage Office, is charged with investigating, assessing, and managing heritage significance. A typology for heritage items has been set up under this system. Items can have one of more of the following types of significance: historic, scientific, cultural, social, archaeological, architectural, aesthetic, natural, and Aboriginal. Ostensibly, the system covers all types of heritage, but the emphasis appears to be firmly on non-indigenous cultural heritage. This is probably because the NPWS focus on natural and Aboriginal heritage is complementary to (but nevertheless outside) the major concerns of the Heritage Office.

Built heritage: complementary roles of state and local government

The NSW built heritage management system involves three steps—investigation, assessment, and management of significance. At the local scale, an important part of the investigation and assessment of significance of heritage items is the local heritage study. The management of significance can occur through the protection of items under a LEP, as discussed below. This section emphasises the key role played by local government in heritage management in NSW.

Identifying and assessing significance[1]

Both the Heritage Office and the DUAP define a *heritage study* as 'an analysis of a geographical area, an historical theme or an organisation' which 'investigates historical context and identifies, assesses and lists items of heritage significance associated with that context'. Further, a heritage study 'explains why items are significant and recommends ways to manage and conserve that significance'. It is stressed that, to be successful, a heritage study must involve substantial consultation with the community, particularly at a local level, although broader studies at larger scales are also an essential component of the overall process. As mentioned earlier, heritage studies primarily focus on non-indigenous cultural heritage items, which presents potential problems because the approach to heritage can become unduly fragmented if different groups take responsibility for different types of heritage.

The report that results from a heritage study usually comprises:

- a historical analysis of the area, theme, or organisation
- investigative research and field work
- an analysis of significance and a survey of the condition of items or areas identified during the study
- inventory sheets of significant items
- recommendations relating to management and promotion

Local heritage studies

Local heritage studies provide a systematic way for local government to identify and assess the significance of heritage items. They are managed by local councils via a steering committee which may consist of representatives from the following groups:

- councillors
- council departments such as planning, building, and community services
- the local historical society and/or the local branch of the National Trust
- prominent community groups and organisations such as progress associations, Chambers of Commerce, and Aboriginal Land Councils
- the regional office of the NSW Department of Public Works and Services

Successful local heritage studies provide information to support and develop:

- a community's sense of identity
- cultural resource plans, strategies, and management
- education programs that help increase a community's knowledge, understanding, and appreciation of heritage assets
- heritage tourism strategies
- a community's sense of ownership of its heritage assets

There are many stakeholders in a local heritage study. Councils initiate the local heritage study process, engage consultants to carry out the study, and make decisions about the implementation of the study's recommendations. The consultants establish the scope of the study and undertake it, and provide expert advice to the council on current and potential heritage policies and practices. Business and special interest groups and the community may gather information, generate interest in the process in the wider community, identify the significance of items (especially the social significance), and give the study more credibility and local people a greater sense of ownership. The Heritage Office and Heritage Council provide advice about the heritage management system to councils and help fund studies, but rarely undertake local studies themselves. They do, however, review completed studies. Finally, other state government agencies provide documentation on items they own that may be of heritage significance, and, hopefully, take the results into account when planning their own activities. The key steps in a local heritage study are outlined in Box 10.1.

Box 10.1 The ten stages of a local heritage study

1 Preparation

Necessary background work includes outlining the scope of the study; preparing the consultant brief; allocating funding and resources; appointing a steering committee; and engaging a consultant team.

2 Return brief and program for completion

Upon the return of the brief from the consultant team with its suggestions as to scope and study program, a timetable needs to be prepared and agreed on, and the roles of the steering committee, the consultants, and each council staff member clearly defined.

3 Community liaison program

Community liaison is seen to be vital, and the heritage study community liaison program should start well before the beginning of the formal study and continue through its duration and beyond. The community is defined as those who can contribute to an understanding of items and provide comment on the management of items that may be identified by an historic context report (see Stage 4). Community liaison can include representation of community groups on the study steering committee; consultative meetings; community workshops; media releases; newsletters and fliers; exhibitions and other events; and letters to potentially affected property owners.

4 Historical context report

This report is the beginning of the formal heritage study, and it identifies and analyses the history and historical geography of the study area. It identifies 'themes' (see Box 6.1) which provide the primary context to comparatively assess and evaluate items.

5 Planning the fieldwork and survey

This stage involves development of a study budget, and of a fieldwork plan based on the area's themes and the budget; and a review of registers of previously identified heritage items (including the National Trust Register, as discussed in Section 10.5), and of items newly nominated by the community.

6 Carrying out the fieldwork and survey

A reconnaissance phase will be needed to familiarise the study team with the area, especially if outside consultants are employed; this is crucial as any local heritage study must be carried out within the specific local physical and social contexts. Once this has been finished, a thematically based survey should be carried out to identify items which potentially represent the established themes. Further community input should be sought to gain additional information on items of potential significance, as the local community will almost invariably have a pool of knowledge, opinions, and perceptions not available in documentary evidence, and not easily ascertained during a field survey. A preliminary inventory should then be prepared, summarising all available information on the items, including their history, condition, curtilage, and the esteem in which they are held by the community. The heritage study team can then assess, evaluate, and record the significance of potential items. Again, the importance of community consultation is stressed at this stage:

> For the team to perform its function effectively, it needs to be given support and assistance from the local council and the community. This is more likely to be forthcoming if consultation, involvement and a sense of ownership has been encouraged from the beginning of the heritage study. (*Heritage Studies*, p. 10)

7 Summary and statement of significance

This stage involves the analysis of the collated documentary and fieldwork data to produce a statement of significance for each item. This is perhaps the most important part of the study process, although its effectiveness depends entirely on the quality of work at previous stages. The whole study team, the client council, and the community need to be involved.

8   Recommendations for conservation and management

This stage will usually involve examination of existing provisions that may affect the management of heritage items, and outline the aims and objectives of the proposed heritage management process, together with the policies and statutory and non-statutory strategies available to conserve items identified in the study. It should also suggest a process for dealing with any items that have been 'missed' by the study.

9   Review and decision-making

The completed study is reviewed by the Heritage Office, which may ask for further information or suggest further work before accepting it. The local council will then make decisions about implementing the recommendations, perhaps with advice, and sometimes directives, from the Heritage Office.

10   Heritage databases

A practical outcome of this process, and one that can occur after the actual study is implemented, is the production of a computer database to assist with the ongoing management of each item. This database should be compatible with the NSW Heritage Database (see Section 10.2).

Source: adapted from publications of the NSW Heritage Office and the NSW DUAP, including Heritage Office & DUAP (1996) *Heritage Studies* (looseleaf insert in *NSW Heritage Manual*), HO/DUAP, Sydney, pp. 9–12.

Managing significance: heritage provisions in local planning

The role of managing significance in NSW is essentially undertaken by local government, mainly through the preparation of LEPs based on heritage studies. Through their planning and development control responsibilities councils can decide to protect heritage items identified in heritage studies. The identified items and areas are mapped, and standard heritage clauses apply devised by the DUAP and adapted for local circumstances. These clauses provide comprehensive management tools including:

- aims and objectives expressly related to heritage conservation
- the types of activities (involving heritage items, areas, and relics) that require consent
- ways to notify the community
- opportunities to consult with the Heritage Council and NPWS
- the type of supporting information that is required
- consideration of development proposals and adjoining land
- flexible use, car parking, and floor-space-ratio incentives
- conservation of building interiors

Under the requirements of the *Environmental Planning and Assessment Act 1979* (NSW) (EPAA), the preparation of an LEP requires further community consultation when the draft LEP is exhibited.

Councils may also protect heritage items by preparing a Local Approvals Policy under the *Local Government Act 1993* (NSW) to be used when processing Development Applications (DAs) and Building Applications (BAs). For development proposals on items of high heritage significance councils may also require a BA or DA to include a *Statement of Heritage Impact*. Alternatively, councils may protect heritage items through Development Control Plans and Design Guidelines, designed to prevent intrusive or out-of-character development in heritage precincts. Breaches of locally administered statutory provisions can result in proceedings in the Land and Environment Court.

The role of forward planning for heritage management has increasingly been devolved to local government by integrating heritage protection into the local planning functions spelt out in the EPAA. This change was recognised by the NSW Government, which stated through the DUAP: 'The [Heritage] Act is now more commonly used in emergency situations where urgent protection from demolition or mismanagement is required'. In 1985 a Ministerial directive—*Conservation of Environmental Heritage and Ecologically Significant Items and Areas*—was issued under the EPAA, to provide an appropriate and workable mechanism to deal with heritage through the local environmental planning process. The ultimate goal seems to be to delegate the function of heritage protection in NSW to local government through their local environmental planning and development control powers under the EPAA and the Local Government Act.

Preventative action

The Heritage Council can protect items under immediate threat of development by making either *permanent conservation orders* (PCOs) or *interim conservation orders* (ICOs), which are valid for up to one year. These orders prohibit a range of activities including demolition, defacement, damage, and alteration of heritage items, as well as any development, unless the Heritage Council's approval is first obtained. Emergency orders are also available. Breaches of the Heritage Act may be subject to proceedings in the Land and Environment Court, which can fine or imprison offenders.

Assistance and encouragement

The Heritage Council administers a grant and loan program that allows state government financial assistance to flow through the *Heritage Assistance Program* to projects that directly conserve or restore heritage buildings and sites, or to research into heritage and its significance. In the latter case, the grant can cover projects ranging from investigation state-wide of a particular type of item (for example, a thematic study of cinemas) to research into specific building-conservation techniques. The Heritage Office also publishes a wide range of thematic and regional inventory material, as well as technical bulletins to help owners of heritage items manage and conserve their properties.

Recent revisions

The *Heritage Amendment Act 1998* (NSW) came into effect in 1999, and was the result of a substantial review of the NSW heritage system, which began in 1992. The main effect of the revision is that it gives local government greater powers over, and responsibilities for, heritage places of local significance. The Heritage Council retains its role when it comes to items of state significance, including its consent powers over alterations to, or demolition of, items of state significance.

Natural and indigenous heritage

Primary responsibility for both natural and indigenous heritage lies with the NPWS. National parks and wildlife are clearly involved in any system of natural heritage identification and management, but it is much more difficult to see the logic of including indigenous heritage under the umbrella of the

NPWS. This situation seems to have arisen because the vast majority of surviving indigenous heritage items are located on undeveloped Crown land, frequently in national parks or other reserves administered by NPWS (see Plates 2.1, 7.3, 7.4, 7.7 and 7.8). However, the jurisdiction of the NPWS extends beyond such reserves to include all indigenous heritage in the state. This means that any 'discoveries' of indigenous sites, regardless of their degree of significance, must be reported to NPWS for recording and, in many cases, investigation by their archaeologists. The NPWS also requires that major developments must be preceded by thorough archaeological surveys, which commonly become a component of an environmental impact statement; works such as roads and power lines are covered by this provision. This does not, of course, preclude indigenous heritage sites from inclusion on the NSW Heritage Database or SHR, but the indigenous heritage sites that are included on these lists form a small subset of those recorded by the NPWS.

Natural heritage places are also included on the SHR, but are administered by the NPWS or, in some cases, by other agencies such as State Forests of NSW or the Jenolan Caves Trust (see Plate 10.1). State Forests of NSW should be particularly involved in places mentioned in the *Regional Forests Agreements*, which resulted from negotiations between the Federal Government and state governments during the 1990s in an effort to reconcile the needs of biodiversity and natural heritage conservation, on one hand, and those of commercial forestry on the other.

The NPWS is responsible for almost a hundred National Parks, as well as Wilderness Areas (more often than not part of National Parks), Nature Reserves, and other areas such as State Recreation Areas and Historic Sites.

Plate 10.1

Unique cave formations, Jenolan Caves, NSW. The caves were first discovered in 1838 and nine 'show caves' are open to the public with additional 'wild caves' accessible by special arrangement. The caves are managed by the Jenolan Caves Reserve Trust, an independent body, and are not within the national parks system. The Jenolan Caves Karst Conservation Reserve is included as a component in the November 2000 inscription of the Greater Blue Mountains World Heritage property.

Photo: Jane Chandler

Areas under the management of the NPWS range from isolated wilderness areas with only low-impact human use, to intensively used near-urban, or even intra-urban, reserves with relatively few natural features remaining. The NPWS also has an active section that manages cultural heritage in national parks and other reserves under its control, but not elsewhere. In addition, the NPWS can gazette historic sites, and has done so in a number of cases, usually when they have existed within national parks or other non-urban settings (Plate 10.2).

The following definitions are adapted from the *National Parks and Wildlife Act 1974* (NSW):

- *National parks* are 'spacious areas containing unique or outstanding scenery or natural phenomena' dedicated primarily to public enjoyment and education, yet with strong biodiversity and natural heritage conservation functions.
- *Nature reserves* are 'areas of special scientific interest containing wildlife or natural environments or natural phenomena'. They are more predominantly dedicated to the conservation of ecosystems, biodiversity, and endangered species than the more multi-purpose national parks.
- *Wilderness areas* may be declared in respect of areas within national parks or nature reserves, provided this is compatible with the management of the park or reserve. The declaration and management of wilderness areas may also fall within the provisions of the *Wilderness Act 1987* (NSW).
- *State recreation areas* are sites of regional significance providing recreational opportunities in natural settings without undue detriment to natural or cultural heritage values.
- *Historic sites* are preserved as sites of buildings, events, monuments, landscapes, or objects of national significance, and may be areas in which Aboriginal relics or places of special significance are situated.

Additional possible, but less common, categories allowed for by the Act are *protected archaeological areas* and various types of wildlife reserves. Streams within areas reserved under the Act may be declared *wild and scenic rivers*. In addition, areas of land for which a conservation agreement has been made with a private landowner are termed *conservation areas*.

Plate 10.2

Captain Cook's Landing Place, Kurnell, Sydney, NSW. This rather undistinguished section of shoreline is given special conservation significance as the place where Captain James Cook and his crew came ashore in 1770 while carrying out the first definitely known European exploration of Australia's east coast. It is part of Botany Bay National Park, but the immediate area is managed specifically for its historical importance.

Photo: Graeme Aplin

The Act requires that a plan of management be prepared by the NPWS staff for each national park, and such plans are also often prepared for other types of reserve. For the purposes of preparing plans of management, the NPWS has adopted the IUCN *Guidelines for Protected Area Management Categories*, which defines a national park as:

a natural area of land and/or sea, designated to

a   protect the ecological integrity of one or more ecosystems for present and future generations,

b   exclude exploitation or occupation inimical to the purpose of designation of the area, and

c   provide a foundation for spiritual, scientific, educational, recreational and visitor opportunities, all of which must be environmentally and culturally compatible.[2]

This definition is noticeably narrower than that used in European national parks (see Chapter 11) and this has important implications for management practices.

As we saw in Chapter 5, drawing up a plan of management for a natural area involves many balancing acts. In NSW, the basic framework for this process is contained in the general objectives for park management throughout the NPWS system. These relate to:
- the protection and preservation of scenic and natural features
- the conservation of wildlife
- the maintenance of natural processes as far as is possible
- the preservation of Aboriginal sites
- the conservation of historic features
- the encouragement of scientific and educational enquiry into environmental features and processes, and Aboriginal and historic features
- the provision of appropriate recreation opportunities

The same list, with the omission of the last point, applies to NSW nature reserves, too.

Summary and conclusion

The NSW heritage management framework has advantages and disadvantages. The main disadvantage has been the separation of cultural and natural heritage in different services, although this has allowed specialisation and the development of skills appropriate to each type. The placement of the responsibility for Aboriginal heritage with NPWS is both controversial and of questionable success. The Heritage Office, however, does unite all types of heritage in its Register and Database, and local government also notes all types of heritage in its heritage studies and LEPs. In recent years, the State Government has delegated more and more responsibility to local councils, just as the Federal Government is about to delegate greater responsibility to the states and territories (see Section 9.6). There is merit in such devolution as it involves and empowers local communities and makes it easier to tap into local knowledge. Local-scale heritage should logically be assessed and managed locally. There is a fear, however, that necessary resources will not flow to the lower levels of government along with the responsibilities. In the case of NSW, the Heritage Office and DUAP do provide oversight and considerable practical support for local councils.

10.3 Other Australian states and territories

Each of the other states and the two mainland territories—the Australian Capital Territory (ACT) and the NT—has its own heritage system. However, as a result of the quasi-autonomy of the territories, the major national parks in the NT (Kakadu and Ulu<u>r</u>u–Kata Tju<u>t</u>a) and the Jervis Bay National Park in the ACT are administered by PA. PA is also responsible for the Christmas Island National Park and the Norfolk Island National Park in off-shore Australian territories. Natural heritage conservation reserves exist under a wide variety of titles, some of which will be referred to in the following sections and in Box 10.2. In total, there are about 2800 land conservation areas and 160 marine conservation areas that are administered by federal, state, and territory agencies, which give protection of natural and cultural heritage in some 90 million hectares. A few types of areas, including wildlife and forest reserves, are mentioned briefly in the following sections.

Box 10.2 Forms of reserves in South Australia, Tasmania, and Western Australia

A   South Australia
- *National Parks*—areas considered to be of national significance by reason of the wildlife or natural features of those lands.
- *Conservation Parks*—areas which ought to be protected for the purpose of conserving wildlife or the natural or historic features of those lands.
- *Regional Reserves*—areas reserved for the purpose of the protection of natural features, but where the utilisation of natural resources is permitted.
- *Recreation Parks*—areas to be reserved and managed for public recreation and enjoyment and which may include sporting facilities and picnic areas.

B   Tasmania
- *Conservation Areas*—large, multiple-use reserves, parts of which may be managed as *State Reserves*, *Game Reserves*, or *Wildlife Sanctuaries*.
- *State Reserves*—may be variously proclaimed as *National Parks*, *Nature Reserves*, *Historic Sites* or *Aboriginal Sites*.

C   Western Australia
- *Nature Reserves*—predominantly for the protection of flora and fauna.
- *National Parks*—areas of more general recreational benefit.
- *Conservation Parks*

In addition all types of reserve in WA are classified 'A', 'B' or 'C' to designate increasing ease of revocation:
- 'A' lands can only be revoked by an Act of Parliament
- 'B' lands can be revoked by the Governor
- 'C' lands can be revoked by the Minister

Land may be further classified as wilderness, prohibited, limited access, temporary control or recreation areas.

Source: adapted from G.M. Bates, *Environmental Law in Australia* (4th edn), Butterworths, Sydney, 1995, pp. 262–6.

In terms of the structure of heritage protection, all states and territories have agencies and legislation relating to both built (or European-cultural) heritage and natural heritage. On the other hand, the treatment of indigenous heritage varies considerably. However, as the dates of legislation mentioned in the following sections show, most of the state and territory heritage systems have been developed only quite recently, especially in relation to cultural or built heritage. The following sections can provide only the briefest of introductions to these systems, and do not even mention other legislation that is more indirectly relevant, such as some general planning legislation and specific wildlife and biodiversity conservation legislation and regulations.

Australian Capital Territory

The *Land (Planning and Environment) Act 1991* (ACT) and the *Heritage Objects Act 1991* (ACT) operate jointly to provide protection for the historic heritage of the ACT, the latter being concerned specifically with Aboriginal heritage items and sites. The Land Act provides for the protection of sites on a Heritage Places Register which includes Aboriginal, non-indigenous cultural, and natural heritage sites, and sections of the Act relate specifically to Aboriginal heritage places. A Heritage Council is also established under the Act to deal with objections to a proposed listing, before an intention to register a heritage place is submitted to the ACT Planning Authority. The Minister may impose stop-work orders on certain activities, and prior approval is required to undertake these activities on a registered heritage place. Public land is reserved for a number of purposes, including national parks and nature reserves and in both cases the objectives are to conserve the natural environment and to provide for public recreation, education, and research. Although the objectives are the same, presumably the balance between conservation and recreation differs, as it does in NSW (see Section 10.2). Wilderness areas have the additional objectives of minimal disturbance and provision for solitude.

Northern Territory

The *Heritage Conservation Act 1991* (NT) encompasses natural, Aboriginal, and non-indigenous cultural heritage. It appears that it was weakened in 1998, when amendments gave the responsible minister greater powers to revoke a heritage order, or to authorise works, alteration, or demolition of declared places regardless of management plans in force. This seems to make heritage orders in the NT very exposed to the exercise of political whim, and represents a triumph of the developmentalism ethic that dominates local politics. (For discussion of developmentalism in Australia see Section 9.2.) Under the Act, the relevant minister declares heritage places on the recommendation of the Heritage Council, which keeps a register of declared sites. ICOs can be made by the Minister, and are in force for ninety days or until formal declaration. Works affecting declared places must be in accordance with a conservation management plan prepared by the Heritage Council and approved by the Legislative Assembly. The requirement of parliamentary approval appears to be too cumbersome for larger jurisdictions with many more heritage items to consider, and also allows overt political interference with heritage administration.

The Parks and Wildlife Commission (formerly Conservation Commission) administers parks—other than those administered by Parks Australia North (see Section 9.3)—reserves, protected areas, and historical reserves in line with the *Territory Parks and Wildlife Conservation Act 1976* (NT) (Plate 10.3). The commission also has responsibility for management plans. Areas within parks and reserves may be further classified as wilderness zones. Agreements may be entered into with private owners to help achieve conservation objectives, and financial assistance may be offered to them.

Plate 10.3

King's Canyon, Watarrka National Park, Northern Territory. This park is administered by the NT Parks and Wildlife Commission and is a popular tourist destination as well as a conservation reserve.

Photo: Monica Green

The *Aboriginal Land Rights (Northern Territory) Act 1976* (Cth) protects sites that are 'sacred to Aboriginals or otherwise of significance according to Aboriginal tradition'. It is an offence for people other than traditional owners to enter, remain on, or carry out work on such a site without approval. Other legislation also impinges on the power of the Heritage Council and the Parks and Wildlife Commission to manage heritage in the NT, particularly to manage Aboriginal heritage—in particular, the *Aboriginal Sacred Sites Act 1989* (NT) charges the Aboriginal Areas Protection Authority with maintaining a Register of Sacred Sites. Aboriginal custodians may apply for registration, but landowners have objection rights. The Administrator may acquire sites and non-Aboriginal people are denied entry to sites unless a permit has been issued by the Authority.

Queensland

In Queensland, the *Heritage Act 1992* (Qld) replaced the interim *Heritage Buildings Protection Act 1990* (Qld). Its application is limited to the historical (primarily non-indigenous cultural) environment. It covers places and objects forming part of Queensland's heritage defined in much the same way as the cultural sections of the criteria in the AHCA (see Box 1.4). The Act creates a Heritage Council, supported administratively from the Cultural Heritage Section of the Environmental Planning Division of the Department of the Environment Protection Agency (DEPA). The Council is required to maintain a Heritage Register, which includes all properties registered on the RNE or by the National Trust (see Section 10.5). A place cannot be registered, however, if there is 'no prospect' of the cultural heritage significance of the place being conserved. This provides fertile ground for legal battles and circular arguments, and goes against the more common approach of assessing significance prior to, and separately from, consideration of management issues. Many other jurisdictions world-wide assume that if significance is great enough, a place should be registered and then ways of conserving it found. The Act sets up a long registration and objection process, and, ultimately, the Planning and Environment Court may be called on to make the final judgment as to significance. Giving a court the final decision on significance is a structure that is peculiar to Queensland among the Australian jurisdictions. The Heritage Council must approve any proposal to develop a registered place, although this approval can be delegated to local government authorities which work with the guidance of the *Local Government (Planning and Environment) Act 1990* (Qld) (LGPEA). Urgent stop-work orders can be made by the council. Compensation for owners adversely affected by planning provisions is available under the LGPEA, but the Council cannot provide financial assistance to owners of heritage properties to help them preserve heritage values. Areas or features of 'anthropological, cultural, historic, prehistoric or societal significance' can be protected under the *Cultural Record (Landscapes Queensland and Queensland Estate) Act 1987* (Qld), on the advice and recommendation of various committees. This Act also provides for a Register of the Queensland Estate.

Protected areas are defined by reference to their management objectives. National parks are required to permanently preserve an area's natural condition and its cultural and natural values, and any use must be nature-based and ecologically sustainable. In addition to 'generalist' national parks, individual parks may also be more specifically declared as 'scientific', 'Aboriginal land', or 'Torres Strait Islander land'. Conservation parks differ from national parks in that commercial uses such as fishing and grazing are allowed under certain conditions. Other forms of reserve include nature refuges, wilderness areas, and co-ordinated conservation areas. The last of these forms is interesting because it involves conservation of natural and cultural values through the coordination of management between government agencies and private landholders, while also taking into account landholders' economic interests and commercial, recreational, and educational values and activities. Administration and management is performed by the Queensland Parks and Wildlife Service, which falls within the DEPA.

The primary legislation in regard to Aboriginal heritage is the *Cultural Record (Landscapes Queensland and Queensland Estate) Act 1987* (Qld), but this is an unsatisfactory means of protecting sites and is likely to be superseded in the near future. Under the Act, the Governor-in-Council can declare a Designated Landscape Area (DLA), and may recognise indigenous ownership or access to particular areas. It appears, however, that mining is given precedence, as the minister with jurisdiction over mining must be informed and a report on mineral-bearing potential made before a DLA is declared.

South Australia

The *Heritage Act 1993* (SA) superseded the earlier *Heritage Act 1978* (SA), which was seen as operating in conjunction with the *Planning and Development Act 1966* (SA). The 1993 Act aims at the preservation, protection, and enhancement of the physical, social, and cultural heritage of the state. The State Heritage Authority (supported administratively by Heritage SA) was established to investigate places that had potential heritage value and to make provisional entries on the State Heritage Register if criteria were met. It also negotiates heritage agreements with owners; advises the Minister on financial assistance required for conservation purposes, and on development that might affect heritage values; and provides advice to local authorities, owners, and others. The register can include land, buildings, structures, and shipwrecks. Items are entered on an interim list for twelve months before transfer to the Register, provided public comment and objections have not had an adverse effect on the process. Larger areas, such as historic towns, streetscapes, and natural areas, can be designated State Heritage Areas. Work on heritage properties requires approval from either the local authority or the State Heritage Authority, depending on the scale at which the item is significant and after a recommendation by the Minister (for places of state significance) or heritage advisers to local authorities. Under the 1993 Act the former Heritage Committee was replaced with the more powerful State Heritage Authority, and it introduced an extensive objection process which allows appeals to the courts.

Plate 10.4

Wilpena Pound, Flinders Ranges National Park, South Australia. Wilpena Pound is a natural basin covering about ninety square kilometres, with outer walls 500 metres high.

Photo: Monica Green

Box 10.2 lists the main types of reserves in SA, declared under the *National Parks and Wildlife Act 1972* (SA). (An example of a national park is shown in Plate 10.4.) In addition, wilderness areas may be declared on public or, with permission, private land, and parts of such areas can be declared prohibited areas to protect human life or wildlife. Administration of the *Wilderness Protection Act 1992* (SA) is undertaken by the Wilderness Advisory Committee, which also identifies land that meets the wilderness criteria. Under the Heritage Act heritage agreements can be made in relation to natural and cultural places, and financial assistance can be provided to landowners.

Aboriginal heritage in SA is protected under the *Aboriginal Heritage Act 1988* (SA), which is administered by the Division of State Aboriginal Affairs within the Department of Transport, Urban Planning and the Arts. The minister is advised by an advisory committee comprising Aboriginal Australians from around the state. Blanket protection is provided for all Aboriginal sites and objects that are 'significant according to Aboriginal tradition', and in addition there is a register of specific sites. Traditional owners can be granted certain powers under the Act, and the Branch can restrict or prohibit access to sites, or acquire them for conservation purposes. As in NSW, anyone who discovers an Aboriginal site must notify the authorities and must obtain permission for any work that has the potential to disturb the site.

Tasmania

Historic places are protected by the *Historic Cultural Heritage Act 1995* (Tas), which established the Heritage Council and the Tasmanian Heritage Register. (Prior to 1995, the *National Parks and Wildlife Act 1970* (Tas) enabled reserves to be set up to protect important historic and Aboriginal sites.) In addition, the *Local Government Act 1962* (Tas) allows local authorities to identify and protect or acquire historic places. The latter also allows for compensation if preservation orders have adverse consequences for owners. Cultural heritage is administered by the Historic Heritage Section of the Cultural Heritage Branch (CHB) of the Tasmania Parks and Wildlife Service (TPWS).

Box 10.2 lists the main types of reserves for the protection of natural heritage in Tasmania, which may be set aside for conservation purposes under the *National Parks and Wildlife Act 1970* (Tas). The Act is administered by the TPWS, within the Department of Primary Industries, Water and Environment, with advice from the National Parks and Wildlife Council and other specialised advisory committees.

Aboriginal sites are protected under the *Aboriginal Relics Act 1975* (Tas), administered by the Aboriginal Heritage Section of the CHB, which can declare land containing a 'relic' to be a Protected Site, which the Department must then manage. 'Relics' are defined to include engravings, paintings, middens, and sites bearing evidence of Aboriginal occupation, providing they were created before 1876, when the last full-blood Tasmanian Aborigine is believed to have died. Again, the discovery of any relic must be reported, regardless of the ownership of the land on which it was discovered, and it is illegal to disturb, deface, destroy, or remove a relic. Any work that might disturb a relic requires a permit from the Minister. In addition, action to protect an Aboriginal site may be taken under the National Parks and Wildlife Act.

Victoria

Legislative protection for heritage sites is provided by the *Heritage Act 1995* (Vic). In addition, local authorities have been increasingly active in recent years in the use of their planning powers to protect heritage. Prior to 1995, the *Historic Buildings Act 1981* (Vic) provided for the protection and preservation of buildings and other works and objects of architectural or historic significance. The Historic Buildings Council (HBC) set up under the Act advised the minister regarding listing proposals for inclusion on either the Historic Buildings Register or the Register of Government Buildings. (Plate 10.5 is an example of a site listed on the Historic Buildings Register.) More recently, the HBC has been replaced by the Heritage Council Victoria. The two registers were merged to become the Victorian Heritage Register (VHR), listing the most significant sites, and a more comprehensive Heritage Inventory. The owner of a place proposed for listing on the VHR has the right to object, and a public hearing may sometimes take place. Once a building is registered, it is an offence to remove, demolish, or otherwise damage it, or to carry out other work on it or the land on which it is situated, unless a permit is granted. A process involving public advertisement and a period in which objections may be made is in place. It is also an offence to allow a registered building to fall into disrepair ('demolition by neglect'), and 14-day Interim Preservation Orders can be applied where a threatened building is under investigation for inclusion on the register. The *Planning Environment Act 1987* (Vic) made it obligatory for planning schemes to be administered by local government so as to protect registered places. Although the Historic Buildings Act applied only to buildings, and not to precincts or conservation areas or parks, the Victorian Government had developed a conservation-architect advisory service for each of twelve historic towns designated in the state (see Plate 6.7). Cultural heritage resources on public lands are managed by the DNRE.

The *National Parks Act 1975* (Vic) allows for the gazettal of national parks, state parks, coastal parks, historic parks and wilderness parks (Plate 10.6). In

Plate 10.5

Sign outside the Old Melbourne Gaol, Melbourne, Victoria. Victoria's first extensive gaol complex (1845), this site is now operated by the National Trust, which opens it to visitors, runs 'night performances' and maintains a penal museum. Ned Kelly was executed here and his death mask is a popular exhibit.

Photo: Graeme Aplin

addition to wilderness parks, wilderness zones may be declared within national parks, while other sections of them can be declared Remote and Natural Areas. Unlike in NSW and most other states and territories, Victorian parks are created by legislative rather than executive or administrative action. The Act is administered by the Director of National Parks, located in the same ministry as the DNRE. The objects of the Act include research and the identification of additional areas for reservation, the latter process assisted by the Land and Conservation Council which oversees the use of Crown land generally. The National Parks Advisory Council and special advisory committees or committees of management for particular parks help administer the Victorian park system. Key features of the Grampians National Park (Plate 1.5) and its Plan of Management are summarised in Box 10.3.

Plate 10.6

Distant view from Mount Hotham, Victoria, of alpine country, much of which is protected within the 6460-square kilometre Alpine National Park, proclaimed in 1989. The landscape shown here is just above (left foreground) and just below (right foreground) the tree line.

Photo: Graeme Aplin

Box 10.3 Grampians National Park—background and park management

Background

The Grampians National Park in western Victoria is the state's fourth largest national park and the second most popular in terms of visitor numbers, attracting more than 800 000 visitors annually. The total area of the park is now 167 200 hectares, representing 5 per cent of the total protected area in Victoria. It contains some 80 per cent of known Victorian Aboriginal art sites (see Plate 7.6) and the local Aboriginal community maintains a continuing involvement in the area, and runs the Brambuk Living Cultural Centre adjacent to the Visitor Centre.

The park was proclaimed on 1 July 1984 under the *National Parks (Amendment) Act 1984* (Vic). Small additions were made in 1986 and 1995, and small excisions in 1995 and 1997. It is managed primarily for ecosystem conservation and appropriate recreation according to the IUCN Category II (National Parks). The park is also listed on the RNE. Under the Victorian Act, the Director of Parks Victoria is required to 'preserve and protect the natural condition of the park and its natural and other features and, subject to this, to provide for the use of the park by the public for enjoyment, recreation and education'. In 1992 three Remote and Natural Areas within the park were proclaimed: the Victoria Range, the Serra Range, and the Major Mitchell Plateau (see Plate 1.5). These areas are managed under Land and Conservation Council recommendations which aim to 'protect the areas' remote and natural condition and to preclude new and incremental developments'.

Park management

The major park management aims are:

1 Preserve and protect the natural resource.
2 Allow natural environmental processes to continue with the minimum of interference.
3 Maintain biodiversity.
4 Conserve features of archaeological, historical and cultural significance.
5 Protect water catchments and streams.
6 Protect human life, the park, and adjacent lands from injury by fire.
7 Eradicate, or otherwise control, introduced plants, animals and diseases.
8 Provide opportunities for appropriate recreation and tourism.
9 Promote and encourage an appreciation, understanding and enjoyment of the park's natural and cultural values, and its recreational opportunities.
10 Encourage appropriate park use and visitor behaviour, and foster a conservation ethic in visitors.
11 Take every reasonable step to ensure visitor safety.
12 Provide for and encourage scientific research, surveys and monitoring that will contribute to a better understanding and management of the park.
13 Cooperate with local, state and interstate government authorities, the community and other interested organisations to assist in the management of the park.

More specific sets of aims are given under the following wide range of headings:

- geological and landform features
- vegetation
- landscape
- fire management
- soil conservation
- orientation and advisory information
- Visitor Centre precinct
- scenic viewing and picnicking
- bushwalking
- horse riding
- hang gliding and paragliding (prohibited)
- fishing
- public safety
- friends and volunteers
- schools education
- military training
- public utilities

- aircraft overflying
- rivers and streams
- fauna cultural heritage
- pest plants and animals, and diseases
- marketing
- interpretation
- scenic driving
- camping
- cycling
- rock climbing and abseiling
- orienteering and rogaining
- commercial tourism operations
- advisory committee
- community awareness and park neighbours
- apiculture
- occupancies
- boundaries and adjacent uses

The park has been divided into five management zones:

1 *Reference area zone*, representing 1 per cent of the total area, comprising relatively undisturbed representative land types and associated vegetation, with access for approved scientific research only.
2 *Conservation zone*, representing 39 per cent of the total area, comprising broad areas with sensitive environments, minimal impact recreational activities, and simple visitor facilities, with limited vehicular access.
3 *Conservation and recreation zone*, representing 59 per cent of the total area, which includes areas with important natural values and scope for recreational opportunities, sustainable dispersed recreation activities and small-scale recreation facilities. Public access is generally available.
4 *Recreational development zone*, representing less than 1 per cent, comprising the Visitor Centre and Brambuk Living Cultural Centre, to be developed as an exciting tourist destination.
5 *Education zone*, representing less than 1 per cent, provided primarily for environmental education in a relatively undisturbed area.

Park vision

- A future visitor to Grampians National Park finds a world-class park renowned for its spectacular natural scenery and wildflowers, diversity of flora and fauna, range of highly significant Aboriginal and European cultural sites, and opportunities to enjoy these features in a variety of settings.

- The park is being managed with a deep and increasing understanding of its ecological processes and significant plants and animals. It is well protected; increased visitor use is sensitively and sustainably managed, and disturbance to natural communities is minimal. More remote areas are protected from further development.
- High quality visitor services and facilities, appropriately located throughout the park, cater for the essential needs of a range of visitors with diverse backgrounds and interests, who are able to undertake appropriate activities and enjoy and understand the many aspects of the park.
- The park is an integral component of Victoria's tourism infrastructure acting as a key focus for local, interstate, and international visitors.

Source: Parks Victoria (May 1998) *Grampians National Park Draft Management Plan*, Parks Victoria, Melbourne.

As discussed in Section 9.3, the Federal Government has more powers in relation to Aboriginal heritage than for any other type of heritage. This explains, in part, how the major legislation affecting conservation of Aboriginal heritage in Victoria is the *Aboriginal and Torres Strait Islander Heritage Protection Amendment Act 1987* (Cth), administered in the state by the Victoria Archaeology Survey, which falls within the state's Ministry for Aboriginal Affairs. This arrangement provides comprehensive protection for Aboriginal cultural heritage (see Plates 7.5 and 7.6). Under the Act, temporary or permanent declarations of preservation may be applied to Aboriginal places and objects, and a register of all such declarations is maintained. Aboriginal people are actively involved in many aspects of the Act.

Western Australia

The *Heritage of Western Australia Act 1990* (WA) establishes the Heritage Council of WA and defines criteria for establishing and adding to a Register of Heritage Places, and considers other protective mechanisms available. While Heritage Agreements are available in a number of Australian states, they play a more important role in WA as there is a greater reliance on private-owner participation. The Heritage Council considers public submissions and makes recommendations to the Minister concerned, who must approve any addition to the register. Interim protection is available once the Minister accepts initial advice to list a place, and a conservation order may be issued, whether or not the site is registered, and, in an emergency situation, forty-two-day stop-work orders can be issued. Proposals for development affecting a registered place must be referred to the Heritage Council for advice, but the final decision lies with the consent authority, usually a local council, or the Minister. Compensation may sometimes be available to affected owners.

The *Lands Act 1933* (WA) allows for the reservation of three classes of Crown land (see Box 10.2), including one for historic places or precincts. National parks and nature reserves are now vested in the National Parks and Nature Conservation Authority, set up under the *Conservation and Land Management Act 1984* (WA). (Plate 10.7 shows an example of a national park set up under this Act.) The functions of the authority are to develop policies for the preservation of the natural environment, promote public appreciation of the natural environment and of flora and fauna, promote recreational opportunities, and provide relevant facilities. While the

Plate 10.7

The Bungle Bungles, protected in the 208 000-hectare Purnululu National Park, Western Australia, are made of prominent layers of sandstone, and were only discovered by tourists in the 1980s. There are suggestions in 2000–2001 that this site should be nominated for World Heritage inscription.

Photo: Don Johnston

authority has the responsibility to prepare plans of management, management of the reserves is carried out by the Department of Conservation and Land Management.

The Aboriginal Cultural Material Committee of the Department of Aboriginal Affairs administers the *Aboriginal Heritage Act 1972* (WA), which applies to all known and unknown Aboriginal and archaeological sites to become the property of the state. The Museum Trustees are responsible for the care and protection of such sites, and it is an offence to excavate, destroy, damage, conceal, alter, or deal with any site in a way that is contrary to Aboriginal custom, unless specific consent has been given. The Registrar of Aboriginal Sites maintains a comprehensive register, specifically including any protected areas proclaimed, but also all other Aboriginal sites and cultural material. Aboriginal people are actively involved in these various processes.

10.4 Local government authorities

Throughout the states and territories of Australia, local government has a vital role to play in the conservation and protection of heritage, particularly (but not exclusively) in relation to built or cultural heritage. The exact mechanisms and processes vary from place to place, but heritage protection is frequently an integral part of local planning activities. Unfortunately, there is not room here to give the details for each jurisdiction, but the outline of many is given in the preceding sections. The role of Australian local government was discussed in general terms in Section 9.1. A more detailed discussion of the NSW case is contained in Section 10.2, while reference to some of the other Australian jurisdictions is given in Section 10.3. The role of local government in heritage management should not be under-estimated, although it often is. Examples of local government involvement in jurisdictions outside Australia will be given in Chapters 11 and 12.

10.5   Voluntary and community organisations

The National Trust

The National Trust of Australia is the premier voluntary organisation concerned with cultural heritage and the built environment, and it also plays an important role in natural heritage issues. There are branches of the Trust in each state and territory. The first state branch was established in NSW in the mid-1940s, and others followed shortly after. (Plate 10.8 shows the National Trust of Australia (NSW) headquarters.) This means that the National Trust pre-dates government heritage bodies by up to thirty years. These days, members of the state Trust branches are usually also representatives on the government bodies. All of the state branches, with the exception of SA, maintain registers of their own; Box 1.5 gives some examples of statements of significance from the Register of the NSW branch. All branches lobby hard for heritage items in general to be conserved and, where appropriate, presented to the public, and particularly for those under threat. (Box 10.4 gives one example of a campaign by the National Trust.) Branches have also acquired a small number of properties (Plate 10.9 shows one example), and have helped restore others (Plate 10.10). Not all National Trust properties are open to the public on a regular basis, as the organisation needs to gain income through leases or to otherwise work in conjunction with owners or occupiers.

Box 10.4 The National Trust and the redevelopment of the Sydney Conservatorium of Music

---

Background

Of the surviving buildings from Sydney's first renowned architect, Francis Greenway, this is his and his master's [Governor Macquarie's] greatest whimsy. The design for the Governor's stables is said to be based on Inveraray Castle (1745) [Scotland], which would have appealed to the Governor and Mrs Macquarie.* Regarded as an excessive structure in its day, it only housed an exercise yard, stable rooms on three sides, and sleeping quarters for servants on the other. It was, however, conceived as a minor element in a much grander scheme for remodelling the landscape and building a new Gothic Government House. Such plans were severely criticised by the Crown as 'a state of magnificence far exceeding the wants or allowance of any Governor'.

In 1910, a sensational election promise by the McGowan government to abolish the role of Governor came to nought, except that it did release the stables to become the Sydney Conservatorium of Music. In the conversion, Well's austere central auditorium design [filling in the courtyard] was economical, but uninspired.

G. Jahn (1997), *Sydney Architecture*, Watermark Press, Sydney, p. 22.

In 1995, proposals were made to relocate the Conservatorium of Music to the former Kirkbride Centre at suburban Rozelle, but staff and students objected to moving away from the city centre and its performance spaces. In May 1998, after a change of government, it was announced that the existing site would be redeveloped. This time protests were from heritage conservation groups and the Friends of the Royal Botanic Gardens. The proposed development was directly adjacent to the gardens and the Friends of the Royal Botanic Gardens felt that there would be visual and physical encroachment on the gardens. The remainder of this box will focus on concerns over historical conservation.

The controversy, 1998–2000

Work on the conservatorium extensions began in mid-1998. Excavations were permitted, provided that the Heritage Office was informed of any archaeological finds, and that any significant finds were conserved *in situ*. It was known, for example, that a mill and other buildings from early colonial times had been located in the vicinity.

At some point in the early work on the site, excavations revealed Macquarie Road with drainage works and brick gutters. The Heritage Office was informed, and began the process of consideration over whether or not work should proceed.

The Director of the National Trust stated that the road was 'of immense historical importance'. The Trust called for time for a full archaeological survey of the entire site, along with an opportunity for public comment. One archaeologist, however, claimed that the road might not be the original one (of 1816), but a slightly later one built at the same time as the stables (1819–21). A member of the Engineering Heritage Committee of the Institution of Engineers disagreed with this archaeologist: if the road and drains proved to be significant, then conservation *in situ* would be a major problem as they would be in mid-air in the music workshop. The National Trust held a rally, and a rival rally was organised on the same day by conservatorium students, complete with a brass band.

The State Government responded by offering to eliminate two practice rooms, allowing 'most' of the road section to be preserved *in situ*, a proposal rejected by the National Trust. The Director of the Trust called on the premier to require a full heritage impact assessment of the site, and to preserve the Greenway building and its landscape setting 'as part of open space created for public purposes'. The call for a full heritage assessment was supported by the Chairman of the Australian Heritage Commission.

About two weeks after the first discovery of the road, a second section and additional drains were found. This prompted the Trust to repeat a call for the entire project to be abandoned because it was too large for the site, would encroach on the gardens, and would destroy significant heritage items. The Minister of Public Works declared that work would proceed, and that the new find would be preserved in the new main foyer, adding value to the building. An archaeological management plan was to be prepared and sent to the Heritage Council.

The National Trust commissioned an independent archaeological report, which was released in October. The consultant found that preservation of the discovered remains was, by that stage, 'a lost cause'. He was scathing about the lack of a full study prior to work commencing, and of the current plans to remove and reconstruct the remains. This, he said, was not conservation. He would have preferred to see the remains kept and imaginatively interpreted to the public, for example exhibited through glass in the pavement, if appropriate, or their outline reproduced on the ground.

In November 1999, the union movement placed green bans on the site in response to a National Trust request for assistance. The main union involved stated that the ban was to allow time for dialogue. A few days before Christmas, the green ban was lifted, provoking a letter to all Trust members urging that they maintain their opposition to the project (assuming, of course, that they did oppose it to begin with). The letter was accompanied by a four-page brochure outlining the Trust's case with a mixture of facts and emotive language.

Despite the efforts of the Trust, the redevelopment has continued, but its cost has escalated significantly due to attempts to incorporate heritage considerations into the project. The most recent available report (*Sydney Morning Herald*, 21 March 2001), states that the final cost will be A$134 million. Staff and students are due to occupy the building in July 2001. According to a Public Works Department spokesperson, preservation of historical heritage added A$44 million to the cost.

Note: * There is some difference of opinion over the inspiration of the design of the building. Apperly *et al.* state that it 'recalls the medieval Thornbury Castle, Gloucester, for which Greenway prepared proposals before his conviction' (R. Apperly, R. Irving & P. Reynolds (1989), *A Pictorial Guide to Identifying Australian Architecture: Styles and Terms from 1788 to the Present*, Angus & Robertson, Sydney, p. 36.)

Plate 10.8

National Trust of Australia (NSW) headquarters, Observatory Hill, Sydney, NSW. The eastern wing shown in this photograph was originally built in 1815 as a military hospital, designed by Lieutenant John Watts, Governor Macquarie's aide-de-camp. The original keystone to the arch remains inside the porch, which was added at a later date. The building was altered in 1849 for use by the Model School. Fort Street Girls' High School occupied the site from 1911 to 1974.

Photo: Graeme Aplin

Plate 10.9

Rippon Lea, Elsternwick, Melbourne, Victoria is now owned and managed by the National Trust of Australia (Victoria) and is open to the public. This large and elegant mansion, built in 1868, is constructed of brick and stone which create intricate patterns. The house is set in expansive gardens which are a key component of the property and add to its heritage value.

Photo: Graeme Aplin

Plate 10.10

Interior of the Castlemaine Market Hall, built in 1862 in the goldfields town of Castlemaine, Victoria. The restoration and conversion to a Tourist Information Centre was carried out by the National Trust of Australia (Victoria).

Photo: Graeme Aplin

Branches also typically have a committee system to investigate heritage issues. In the case of NSW, these have now been collapsed into a single Conservation Committee, but they once included:

- Historic Buildings Committee, dealing with individual buildings or small groups
- Urban Conservation Committee, dealing with larger precincts and conservation areas
- Cemeteries Committee
- Parks and Gardens Committee
- Industrial Archaeology Committee
- Railways Heritage Committee
- Landscape Assessment Committee, dealing with rural areas with high landscape value

The role of each of these committees was to assess nominations to the National Trust Register. Nominated properties could come from submissions from the general public, including property owners in some cases; from regional committees of the Trust; or as a result of tours of inspection carried out by members of the committee itself. Any recommendations for listing are considered by the Board of the National Trust (NSW).

Trust listing has no legal force, but does carry strong morally persuasive powers and normally listing will be taken into account in any DA or other planning application. (Again there are differences between states.) The Trust also becomes very vocal in the public arena and in the media when important heritage properties come under threat, for example over the redevelopment of the Walsh Bay wharves for residential and hotel use and the Conservatorium of Music (Box 10.4) in the late 1990s, and the Museum of Contemporary Art in 2001. The NSW branch also has representatives on the NSW Heritage Council and on more specialised bodies such as the heritage committee of the State Rail Authority. At the national level, the Australian Council of National Trusts is represented on federal bodies, and lobbies strongly on federal issues—for example it was a key player in deliberations leading up to the drafting of new Commonwealth heritage legislation (see Section 9.6). One way or another, a large number of dedicated volunteers give time and effort to help achieve the Trust's objectives.

Other local and voluntary involvement

Many other voluntary bodies play a key role in heritage conservation by providing research, notification, lobbying, and persuasive pressure. They include:

- the Royal Australian Institute of Architects (RAIA; which, in NSW at least, has an influential list of important 20th-century buildings, often neglected by both the government bodies and the National Trust—see Box 10.5 for a recent press statement)
- the Institution of Engineers (industrial and engineering heritage—see Plate 10.11)
- National Parks Association (concerned with natural areas, and, in NSW, supports NPWS activities)
- Wilderness Society
- local historical associations

- local progress associations and citizens' committees (but some are very pro-development)
- ethnic community organisations (recently enlisted by the NSW Heritage Office to 'de-Anglicise' the state's listings—see Box 1.2)
- Aboriginal Lands Councils and similar bodies representing indigenous peoples
- specialist groups interested in, for example, railways, theatres and theatre organs, and gardens
- religious organisations and local congregations

Some examples of non-government bodies and their involvement in other countries arise in the next two chapters.

Box 10.5 Royal Australian Institute of Architects (NSW) Heritage Committee nominations, October 2000

In October 2000, the Heritage Committee of the RAIA NSW nominated another six important 20th-century buildings for inclusion on the State Heritage Register. The first RAIA NSW list pre-dated the Register of the National Trust and was long before the State Heritage Register began. The National Trust listing became stronger and larger, but until recently concentrated very much on 19th-century buildings, so, since 1968, new RAIA NSW nominations have all been of 20th-century buildings, a field rightly felt to be relatively neglected by other bodies. By the end of 2000, about fifty 20th-century buildings had been submitted to the Heritage Office for consideration for listing on the Register.

The latest group comprised:
- the Strickland Building in Chippendale, the first purpose-built public housing in NSW
- the former Qantas House in Chifley Square (City)
- Temple Emanuel, Woollahra
- Concord Hospital
- Red Cross House in Clarence Street (City)
- Gloucester House, part of Royal Prince Alfred Hospital, Camperdown

The work of the Committee in researching 20th-century buildings has been aided by Australian Heritage Commission and NSW Heritage Office grants.

Source: G. O'Brien 'Ornaments to a century nominated for heritage listing', *Sydney Morning Herald*, 23 October 2000.

Plate 10.11

Historic Engineering Marker, Jenolan Caves, NSW, installed by the Institution of Engineers, Australia, and the Jenolan Caves Reserve Trust (see also Plate 10.1).

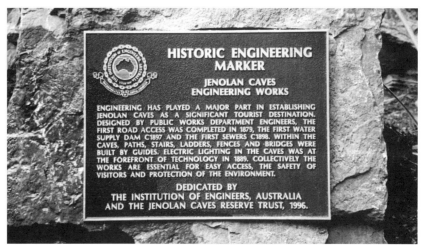

Photo: Jane Chandler

10.6   Conclusion

We have come full circle, in a sense—we obviously all have our own views on what is heritage. Many of us are also prepared to devote time, energy, and money to fight for the conservation of those things dear to us. But while individual actions and those of NGOS are very important, we do rely on governments and their agencies to provide the legal and bureaucratic framework for heritage conservation.

The states and territories in Australia tackle the matter in various ways. They have different legislation and different departmental and agency structures. In particular, the three broad areas of heritage activity—natural, indigenous, and non-indigenous cultural—are combined in different groupings or, in some cases, treated separately. In most cases, however, all types of heritage are combined on one state or territory register. Two common factors are worthy of emphasis. First, all jurisdictions now treat heritage seriously and have genuine structures and agencies in place to protect it. Having said that, however, it must also be stated that some jurisdictions leave the process more open to political pressure and the 'veto of development' than do others. Secondly, local government plays a key role in all cases. The detail differs, but it is generally true to say that a great deal of heritage protection occurs through local planning processes, and that there has been a clear tendency over the last decade to devolve more responsibility to local government and local communities. There remains a fear, however, that devolution leaves heritage vulnerable in the states, territories, and local council areas that have the weakest commitment to its preservation.

Notes

[1]   Much of the following material is drawn from various documents published by the DUAP and its Heritage Office.

[2]   IUCN–The World Conservation Union (1994) *Guidelines for Protected Area Management Categories*, IUCN, Gland, Switzerland.

Further Reading

Updated information on changes to legislation and bureaucratic structures is available at the web site associated with this book, at http://www.es.mq.edu.au/courses/REM/heritage.htm.

Bates, G. (1995) *Environmental Law in Australia* (4th edn), Butterworths, Sydney, especially Chapter 9.

Carment, D. (1991) *History and Landscape in Central Australia: A Study of the Material Evidence of European Culture and Settlement*, North Australia Research Unit, Australian National University, Darwin.

Carment, D. (1996) *Looking at Darwin's Past: Material Evidence of European Settlement in Tropical Australia*, North Australia Research Unit, Australian National University, Darwin.

Department of Planning (NSW) (1990) *Heritage Assessment Guidelines*, Department of Planning, Sydney.

Farrier, D. (1993) *The Environmental Law Handbook: Planning and Land Use in NSW*, Redfern Legal Centre Publishing, Sydney.

Heritage Office & Department of Urban Affairs and Planning (1996) *NSW Heritage Manual*, HO/DUAP, Sydney. (Updated with loose-leaf inserts.)

Kellow, A. (1989) 'The dispute over the Franklin River and South West Wilderness Area in Tasmania, Australia', *Natural Resources Journal*, Vol. 29, pp. 129–46.

Robin, L. (1998) *Defending the Little Desert: The Rise of Ecological Consciousness in Australia*, Melbourne University Press, Melbourne.

Stevens, J. (1995) *Victoria's Great Outdoors: Where to Go and What to Do*, David Syme & Co. Ltd and the Department of Conservation & Natural Resources, Melbourne.

CHAPTER 11

Regulatory Frameworks and Approaches to Heritage: Some European Countries

11.1   Introduction

This chapter discusses the heritage of a small number of European nations, the perception of heritage in those nations, and the administrative and practical arrangements for its conservation and management. It represents only a brief introduction to these issues.[1] The coverage cannot be claimed to be comprehensive or in any sense definitive, but purely indicative of some major themes. It provides a useful comparison to the situation in Australia. Both printed material and the web sites of the key organisations were used, together with material published by the World Heritage Bureau. The 'Further Reading' section at the end of this chapter and the list of web sites in Appendix 2 provide some starting places for further information. This chapter and the next also provide material illustrating the themes listed in the Introduction and developed in Chapters 1 to 8. Material here should be related back to those chapters and themes; in particular, the sections and tables relating to World Heritage properties provide many pertinent examples that illustrate the issues discussed in Chapter 8.

Not surprisingly, *cultural heritage* is generally more prominent in Europe than in Australia, and this is not limited to the countries discussed in this chapter. Most European World Heritage properties meet one or more of the cultural criteria, and the natural criteria rate a mention in only a small minority of cases. Europe has a long history of non-nomadic human settlement with well-established urban centres, and with organisations such as the church and royal households that had the wealth to build on a lavish scale. But it certainly is not only the lavish 'stand-alone' buildings that are prominent in European cultural heritage lists; historic towns such as Goslar, a German World Heritage site (Plate 8.2), and French Provençale hill villages (Plate 11.1) also feature prominently, as do city centres such as that in Bern, Switzerland (Plate 11.2). In contrast to Australia, cultural development has an unbroken lineage joining past and present within the frame of reference used by the presently dominant group, so there seems to be a longer and richer cultural heritage to draw on. This perception is particularly recurrent because non-indigenous Australians still find it difficult to meaningfully incorporate indigenous heritage into the national heritage. As pointed out in Section 9.2, Australians tend to carry this

Plate 11.1

The historic hill town of
Gordes, Vaucluse
Département, Provence,
France, crowned by the
16th-century Château.

Photo: Graeme Aplin

Plate 11.2

Arcaded footpaths, cobbled
roadway and city gate,
Bern, Switzerland.

Photo: Margaret Dudgeon

European heritage 'baggage' with them, and sometimes see little cultural heritage in their country simply because so little is anywhere near as old as most of the heritage in Europe.

Many historic buildings, precincts, and entire towns and city centres in Europe have been continually evolving over many centuries, and adaptive re-use has become the norm, rather than the exception. Much of Europe's cultural heritage has been preserved simply because it has continued to be used, and a preference has been shown for using existing infrastructure rather than demolishing it and building anew. Even individual shopfronts have frequently survived for many decades, rather than being replaced with modern versions as ruthlessly as they have in Australia and the USA. More often than not, this seems to have happened without any conscious planning—in fact, conscious planning has often been the very thing that has destroyed historic areas and resulted in the introduction of high-rise buildings to historic city centres. In Europe, there are some grounds for arguing 'the less intervention the better', although the modern heritage agencies do have a key role to play in conserving heritage, and often play it extremely well.

On the other hand, Europe has virtually no land that does not clearly bear the imprint of many centuries, if not many millennia, of human occupancy. That is also, of course, true of Australia, but the imprint in Europe tends to be more deeply impressed, to be more all-pervasive, and to consist of more permanent and obviously 'modern' artefacts or landscape changes. By Australian definitions, Europe has essentially no wilderness areas and few, if any, 'natural' national parks or other reserves. (For discussion of the concept of wilderness see Section 5.4). In fact, the vast majority of European national, regional, and other parks are at least as much cultural as natural heritage sites, regardless of the fact that a 'natural' government agency administers them. They also often contain large human populations and a considerable amount of privately owned land (see Plate 1.4; Boxes 11.3 and 11.5).

Finally, it is worth repeating the warning given in a note in Chapter 9: the structure and responsibilities of government bureaucracies change rapidly and the following outlines reflect as accurately as possible the situation in early- to mid-2001.

11.2   United Kingdom

Introduction

An immediate difficulty for the management of heritage lies in the governmental and administrative structure of the United Kingdom. In administrative terms, Scotland has long been quite separate from England. Some of the organisational structures in Wales fall under English ones, but it also has some bodies of its own. Administration in Northern Ireland, on the other hand, is largely subsumed under the English model. The full implications of successful 1997 referenda for greater autonomy in both Scotland and Wales and the devolution of the legislative function remain somewhat uncertain. The English model of heritage administration is discussed in the rest of this section, while Scotland and Wales will be referred to more briefly where their systems differ from the English model.

Cultural heritage

Since 1984 a government body called *English Heritage* (more formally known as the Department of National Heritage), which is located within the Ministry for Media, Culture and Sport, has been responsible for the conservation and presentation of cultural heritage in England. Formerly, this role was split between sections of the Ministry of Public Buildings and Works, for ancient monuments, and of the Department of the Environment (DoE) for less-ancient monuments, before both of these were consolidated in the DoE in the early 1970s.

English Heritage offers two degrees of protection to sites of cultural significance. By *scheduling* items it can give legal protection to nationally important buildings and sites where other measures, such as local planning regulations, offer insufficient protection. Alternatively, *listing* (under various 'grades') is a less-restrictive form of recognition of the heritage values of an item, with less legal protection, but which still alerts local authorities, government departments, owners, and occupiers of the value of that item. In the late 1990s, over 500 000 buildings were listed, while the Schedule contains approximately 17 000 entries covering some 30 000 sites. There were also approximately 9000 conservation areas, which are more extensive than individual sites, and which can include many individual heritage sites or buildings (Plate 11.3). English Heritage also provides grants and advice for the conservation, preservation, and maintenance of the most important buildings and sites. It also undertakes research and field surveys to assess the significance of items. In addition, local authorities, in the 1960s to 1980s, all compiled their own *Sites and Monuments Records* (SMRs), which provide the local-scale equivalent to the National Monument Record (discussed under 'The Royal Commissions'). Local authorities were encouraged and assisted in this endeavour by English Heritage.

Plate 11.3

The Royal Bank of Scotland (corner) and adjacent half-timbered buildings, Chester, England. Much of central Chester, including this area, is within a conservation area recognised by English Heritage.

Photo: Graeme Aplin

Although English Heritage is a government body, individuals can become members and by doing so they can take advantage of seasons tickets which admit them to all sites open to the public. English Heritage is responsible for approximately 400 historic properties, ranging from prehistoric sites such as Stonehenge (Plate 8.3) to a 1930s house in London (see Box 11.1), and possibly even more modern buildings. Gardens and contents, including furnishings and fixtures, are often preserved as an integral part of the heritage value of the site. English Heritage publishes a complete list of sites open to the public (see the 'Further Reading' section at the end of this chapter), along with free regional brochures, and the complete lists of scheduled and listed sites are available electronically (see list of web sites in Appendix 2).

Box 11.1 Courtauld House, London

Located in the south-eastern suburbs of London, the Courtauld House site has remains of a relatively little known medieval royal palace called Eltham Palace. However, it is the house completed in 1937 and managed by English Heritage that is the main attraction. Commissioned by the Courtaulds, it is a spectacular example of what was the most up-to-date contemporary design in the 1930s. According to *The English Heritage Visitors' Handbook 1999–2000* (pp. 30–1), 'the house stands as a testament to the couple's choice of interior design and reflects their leisure-filled lifestyle'. Various architects and designers created contemporary interiors influenced by the French Art Deco style and by the Cunard ocean liner style, both modern influences that were in vogue at the time. Modern technology was also a feature of the house, with electric wiring throughout, a central vacuum cleaner, built-in loudspeakers to broadcast records to many rooms on the ground floor, and an internal telephone system. The Courtaulds left the house to avoid the bombing in London during the Second World War and took most of their works of art and furniture with them. Replica 1930s furniture has, however, been carefully reinstated in two show-rooms. Missing wood veneer has been replaced, rooms repainted according to original colour schemes, and appropriate soft furnishings put in place. Restoration of the garden has begun. The house is open to the public for an adult entry fee of £5.50, and is 'available for exclusive corporate and private events'.

Source: *The English Heritage Visitors' Handbook 1999–2000* (pp. 30–1).

Plate 11.4

Conwy Castle, Conwy, northern Wales was constructed between 1283 and 1289 for Edward I as one of a ring of castles to contain the Welsh. Much of the castle's defensive strength springs from the rock on which it is built, rather than from military architecture. It is managed by Cadw Welsh Historic Monuments.

Photo: Graeme Aplin

Other parts of the United Kingdom have similar structures for cultural heritage. In Scotland, the administrative body is called *Historic Scotland*, and it manages over 300 sites; in Wales, the relevant organisation is called *Cadw Welsh Historic Monuments* (Plate 11.4); and in Northern Ireland, it is the *Environment and Heritage Service*, which is an agency within the United Kingdom DOE.

The Royal Commissions

Much of the work of maintaining the lists and compiling and maintaining comprehensive archival material and documentation has been carried out by the three Royal Commissions, which began just under 100 years ago. The first, the *Royal Commission on the Ancient and Historical Monuments of Scotland* (RCAHMS) (Box 11.2), began in 1908, and the *Royal Commission on the Historical Monuments of England* (RCHME) and the *Royal Commission on the Ancient and Historical Monuments of Wales* (RCAHMW) followed soon afterwards. As well as collecting documentary evidence, such as architectural drawings and plans, the three commissions undertake extensive fieldwork, in which they survey, measure, sketch, and photograph sites. Both thematic and regional surveys are undertaken, as well as site-specific surveys when necessary (often when a threat is evident). Failing all else, a sound archival record is achieved when the building or site is lost through development or neglect. Members of the public can consult these huge and incredibly valuable resources in reading rooms that are made available at the commission offices or via the Internet (see list of web sites in Appendix 2). The resource is frequently used in relation to development applications, environmental impact statements, and the like. In the late 1990s the RCHME was incorporated into English Heritage as the *National Monument Record*, the equivalent at the level of England to the local authority SMRs (see previous paragraphs).

Box 11.2 The Royal Commission on the Ancient and Historical Monuments of Scotland

The Royal Commission on the Ancient and Historical Monuments of Scotland (RCAHMS) is an independent non-departmental government body which was financed by the Parliament of the United Kingdom through the Scottish Office and, since 1999, directly through the new Scottish Parliament. It is directed by Commissioners, and has a permanent staff of about sixty based in Edinburgh.

The aims of RCAHMS are to:

1 survey and record the man-made [*sic*] environment of Scotland
2 compile and maintain in the National Monuments Record of Scotland a record of the archaeological and historical environment
3 promote the understanding of this information by all appropriate means

The RCAHMS was established in 1908 to make an inventory of the surviving cultural heritage of Scotland from earliest times to 1707, though it is now also concerned with much more recent buildings. (The Scottish National Buildings Record, founded in 1941, and listing more modern buildings was transferred to the RCAHMS in 1966.) The organisation carries out field surveys and compiles records of built heritage and makes this information available to the professions (for example, architects and planners), to government departments, to business, and to the general public through the National Monuments Record of Scotland and the national archive. A computerised data base known as CANMORE (Computer Application for National

Monuments Record Enquiries) is also now available, and RCAHMS is also a partner in the Scottish Cultural Resources Access Network, which provides public access to a wide range of cultural resources. Data from these sources is frequently used in applying for planning and development permission, in objecting to such applications, in making planning decisions, and in related court actions.

Some of the major functions of RCAHMS are to:

- undertake various surveys, including the Architecture Survey, the Archaeology Survey, the Industrial Survey, and landscape and aerial surveys (mainly to help identify archaeological sites) to add to the knowledge base of Scottish built heritage
- carry out detailed surveys of individual sites or buildings
- through the Threatened Buildings Survey (described in more detail below), survey and record buildings and architectural features threatened with destruction, alteration or serious decay
- undertake thematic surveys of particular types of structures or sites, and geographically based surveys of particular areas
- maintain a reading room and collections of photographs, plans and drawings, documents, and even architectural models, all available for public perusal under certain conditions or via the Internet
- publish relevant material

The Threatened Buildings Survey is a particularly valuable section of the RCAHMS. Under the *Town and Country Planning (Scotland) Act 1997*, RCAHMS is given the opportunity to survey and record any building listed by Historic Scotland as being of special architectural or historic interest, for which permission to totally or partially demolish has been given. A survey is also considered if the site is already derelict, vandalised, or endangered through redundancy. According to the RCAHMS web site, 'almost every sort of building or structure including farms, gravestones, telephone boxes, castles, tower blocks and even public conveniences is considered worthy of recording'.

Source: RCAHMS web site http://www.rcahms.gov.uk/ and leaflets.

Natural heritage

In broad terms, the activities of the two organisations that carry out activities in relation to natural heritage—English Nature and Scottish Natural Heritage—broadly parallel those of English Heritage and Historic Scotland in the cultural field. Many types of reserve exist, and the most common of these is the National Nature Reserve. There are almost 200 National Nature Reserves in England, some owned by English Nature, some leased from the National Trust or private owners, and others jointly managed with other organisations or individuals. Each reserve is nationally important for its flora and fauna conservation values. Other areas that have particular implications in relation to potential development are Sites of Special Scientific Interest and Areas of Outstanding Natural Beauty. These areas can be entirely in private ownership and occupation, but have legal controls on use and change, including clearing.

National parks

Under the *Environment Act 1995*, each of the eleven national parks in England and Wales is administered by its own, largely autonomous Park Authority. All but one of the parks were declared in the 1950s. Together they cover ten per cent of England and Wales (Figure 11.1). A twelfth park, the New Forest, was awaiting declaration in early 1999, but progress seems to have been stalled since then, as discussion continues as to whether or not standard national park authority legislation is adequate, or whether special legislation is needed for this rather different case. In early 2001, the Council for National Parks (CNP) was also promoting the South Downs for national park status.

English and Welsh national parks are far from wilderness areas: the Lake District National Park, for example, is home to at least 168 000 people and is visited by millions each year. The YDNP is described in Box 11.3, which shows how the park is a dynamic, lived-in cultural landscape as well as a natural one (see also Plate 1.4). All the English national parks contain farms and villages, and sometimes even quite sizeable towns. The Northumberland National Park also contains much of the Hadrian's Wall World Heritage property (Plate 11.5 and Box 11.4). Farming and other established uses continue in the parks, but there are definite constraints on development, and even on changes to farming practices.

Box 11.3 Yorkshire Dales National Park Authority and its planning documents

The Yorkshire Dales National Park (YDNP) was designated a National Park in 1954 to protect 1769 square kilometres of the central Pennine uplands. It contains outstanding scenery, a diversity of habitats, flora and fauna, and a rich cultural heritage. Within the park there are many peaceful areas, and it is a favourite district for long-distance walkers. It attracted around 8.3 million visitors in 1994, but also was home to about 18 000 permanent residents.

The *Environment Act 1995* established the YDNP Authority with the following responsibilities:
* conserving and enhancing the natural beauty, wildlife, and cultural heritage of the area
* promoting opportunities for the understanding and enjoyment of the special qualities of the area by the public.

Under the Act, each National Park Authority is required to produce a National Park Plan which includes policies for various aspects of the authority's management of the park. Policies for the YDNP Plan cover the following aspects (some of which an Australian reader will not immediately associate with a national park management plan):

• agriculture	• nature conservation
• forestry, woodland, and trees	• built environment
• archaeology	• mineral extraction
• recreation and access	• transportation
• visitor management	• public relations

Particular pressures on the park are seen as arising from changes in upland farming; tourism development; wear and tear from visitors; mineral extraction; road building and upgrading; and building development. The authority owns little land itself and has to work with farmers, landowners, and many other stakeholders.

The authority is also legally required to draw up a Local Plan to control development (just as a local authority would elsewhere). Policy areas covered in the Local Plan include:

• housing development	• conservation of landscape, nature and
• conservation of the built environment	archaeology
• agricultural development	• facilities for visitors
• traffic and transport	• protection of the water environment
• local employment and community services	

In effect the YDNP Authority acts much as would a municipal council in Australia. Specifically, the authority operates a Farm and Countryside Service to provide comprehensive conservation advice to farmers and landowners—most of the land is farmland and 'very much a working landscape'. It also seeks to foster social well-being and a viable local economy. It is working to promote policies for planning consents for new buildings, which must blend with traditional building styles. It is also working to ensure that quarrying is as environmentally acceptable as possible.

Source: Yorkshire Dales National Park Authority (1997) *Education Resources*, YDNP Authority, Grassington.

Plate 11.5

Excavated remains of granaries at Housesteads Roman Fort, the best-preserved site on the Hadrian's Wall World Heritage property, Northumberland, England. The floor was raised on the short columns visible to allow air to circulate in a way that helped preserve food of many types, including grain. Housesteads is a National Trust property, but is administered cooperatively with English Heritage and the Northumberland National Park Authority, which both also have responsibility for other sections of Hadrian's Wall.

Photo: Graeme Aplin

Box 11.4 Management of the Hadrian's Wall World Heritage property

Although Hadrian's Wall is inscribed as a single World Heritage property (see Table 11.1), its ownership and management is quite complex, as the following details partially explain.

- Measuring 117 kilometres in total, 74 kilometres of the wall are within Northumberland National Park.
- The majority of sites along the length of the Wall are managed by English Heritage, but not necessarily owned by them.
- Banks East Turret, Harrow's Scar Milecastle, Leahill Turret, Pike Hill Signal Tower, and Piper Sike Turret are managed by Cumbria County Council.
- Birdoswald Fort is managed by Cumbria County Council on behalf of English Heritage.
- South Fields Fort and Museum are in the care of Tyne and Wear Museums.
- Wallsend Fort and its Heritage Centre are operated by North Tyneside District Council and Tyne and Wear Museums.
- Chesters Roman Fort is managed independently.
- Housesteads Fort site (Plate 11.5) is owned by the National Trust, but maintained and managed by English Heritage, while the fee-paying car park is run by Northumberland National Park Authority. The National Trust also owns about 8 kilometres of the wall adjacent to Housesteads, and over 1000 hectares of farmland through which this length of wall runs.
- Vindolanda Fort is owned and managed by the Vindolanda Trust, although some features are in the care of English Heritage.
- Willowford Wall, Turrets, and Bridge have access to the bridge controlled by Willowford Farm and a small charge is levied.
- Carrawburgh Fort is in private ownership, but English Heritage cares for an area around it which includes the Temple to Mithras.

Sources: *The English Heritage Visitors' Handbook 1999–2000*, English Heritage, London, 1999, pp. 200–5; *Hadrian's Wall: A Souvenir Guide to the Roman Wall* (third edition), English Heritage, London, 1996; *The National Trust Handbook for Members and Visitors 1999*, The National Trust, Bromley, 1999, p. 279.

Figure 11.1

United Kingdom national parks and World Heritage properties

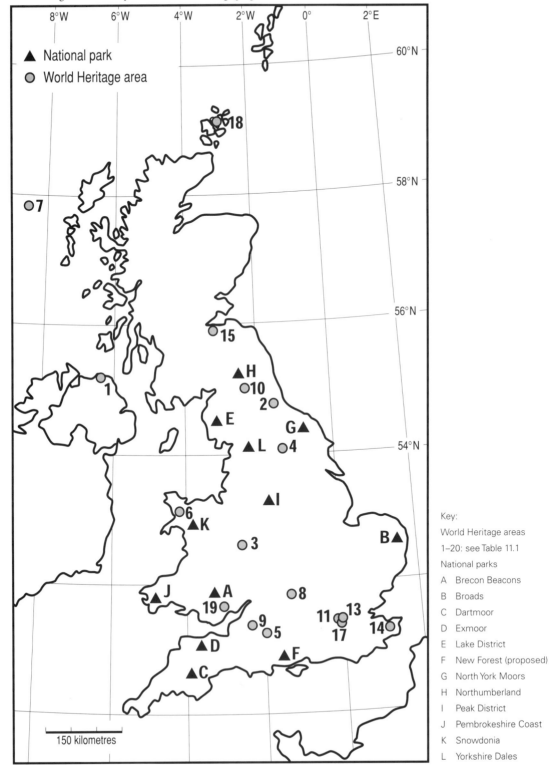

Key:

World Heritage areas

1–20: see Table 11.1

National parks

A   Brecon Beacons
B   Broads
C   Dartmoor
D   Exmoor
E   Lake District
F   New Forest (proposed)
G   North York Moors
H   Northumberland
I   Peak District
J   Pembrokeshire Coast
K   Snowdonia
L   Yorkshire Dales

Each Park Authority is required to produce its own National Park Plan (see for example Box 11.3), which must include management policies covering, amongst other things, agriculture; nature conservation; forestry, woodland, and trees; built environment; archaeology; mineral extraction; recreation and access; transportation; visitor management; and public relations. All Park Authorities try to involve the people living within the park boundaries and nearby, both in discussions over planning and day-to-day management, and as volunteers. Nationally, the CNP is an organisation similar to the National Parks Association in NSW (Section 10.5), and operates the Friends of National Parks. These organisations lobby government on relevant issues, raise funds, and generally promote public interest in the national parks. They also provide voluntary workers for national parks; for example in visitor centres and park shops.

Scotland, on the other hand, has no national parks, although some will be declared in the near future. Scottish Natural Heritage (SNH) conducted wide-ranging public discussions and reported to the Scottish Executive (the new regional parliament) in February 1999, and recommended setting up Scottish national parks. The National Parks (Scotland) Bill was approved by the Scottish Parliament on 5 July 2000. Secondary legislation will be needed to set up each individual park: the first will cover parts of Loch Lomond and the Trossachs (by April 2002); the second, in the Cairngorms, will follow shortly afterwards. In mid-2001 the most extensive basically natural areas within reserves were owned and managed by the National Trust for Scotland (see for example Plate 11.6). However, as in the rest of the United Kingdom, the National Trust and the government agencies cooperate to the extent of sometimes managing each other's properties (see Box 11.4).

Plate 11.6

Valley on the western side of the main valley of Glen Coe, Scotland, much of which is the property of the National Trust for Scotland (NTS). The NTS runs a ranger service and provides guided walks and other services normally associated with national parks personnel. Glencoe is an important geological and botanical site, and also has historical significance as the site of a 1692 massacre of the MacDonalds by the Campbells.

Photo: Graeme Aplin

National Trusts

The National Trust covers England, Wales, and Northern Ireland, while the National Trust for Scotland (NTS) plays a parallel role north of the border. The National Trust was founded in 1895 and by late 2000 it cared for over 240 000 hectares of countryside, 925 kilometres of coastline, and more than 200 buildings and gardens. Most sites are open to the public under varying conditions. The range of properties include cottages and stately homes (Plate 11.7), a Belfast pub, the McCartney family home in a Liverpool suburb (early home of Paul McCartney of the Beatles), and some industrial and farm buildings thrown in for good measure. The NTS was established in 1931 and cares for over 100 properties and 77 000 hectares of land, including such historic sites as Culloden Field and large stretches of wild highland country (Plate 11.6), as well as typical Scottish castle dwellings (Plate 11.8). The highland areas essentially fulfil the role that national parks play elsewhere. Unlike the Australian National Trusts, neither of the Trusts in the United Kingdom lists sites, leaving that to the government bodies. Nevertheless, both do a great deal of lobbying, public relations, and environmental advocacy work, and education is a key concern.

World Heritage properties in the United Kingdom

Table 11.1 contains brief summaries of the United Kingdom World Heritage properties, mapped in Figure 11.1. The descriptions are the 'official' short descriptions taken directly from the WHB web site or other publications.

Only four of the twenty sites are inscribed because they meet natural criteria, and two of these are small, uninhabited island possessions in the South Atlantic and South Pacific, while a third is an island off northern Scotland. The remaining site is the remarkable geologic feature of the Giant's Causeway in Northern Ireland. The bias towards cultural sites is not surprising, given the densely settled nature of most of the British Isles and the length of time they have been occupied by humans. The fourteen cultural sites range from prehistoric sites to 19th-century constructions: from Neolithic sites on Orkney and the remarkable prehistoric monuments of Avebury and Stonehenge (Plate 8.3), to the early industrial site of Ironbridge (18th century) and the later 19th-century iron and coal site of Blaenavon, in Wales. Many sites are associated with either royalty or the established church, including obvious candidates such as the Tower of London, Westminster Abbey, and Canterbury Cathedral. Hadrian's Wall in the north of England (Plate 11.5) is a remarkable reminder of the north-western frontier of the Roman Empire, and is also an example of a cultural property lying largely within a multi-purpose national park, in this case the Northumberland National Park (see Box 11.4). Other World Heritage sites include the centre of Edinburgh (Plate 4.7), the major castles of Wales (Plate 11.4), and Blenheim Palace.

Table 11.1

United Kingdom World Heritage properties

Property	Criteria (see Appendix 1 for key)	Date of inscription (and of enlargements)	Brief description and reasons for inscription (from World Heritage List)
1 Giant's Causeway and Causeway Coast	N i, iii	1986	At the foot of the basaltic cliffs along the sea coast at the edge of the Antrim Plateau in Northern Ireland, the Giant's Causeway is made up of some 40 000 massive black columns sticking out of the sea. The dramatic sight has inspired legends of giants striding over the sea to Scotland. The study of these formations by geologists over a period of 300 years has greatly contributed to the development of the earth sciences, and has led to the conclusion that this striking landscape was caused by volcanic activities during the Tertiary Period some 50–60 million years ago.
2 Durham Castle and Cathedral	C ii, iv, vi	1986	Built in the late 11th and early 12th centuries to house the relics of St Cuthbert (the evangelist of Northumbria) and the Venerable Bede, the cathedral attests to the importance of the early Benedictine monastic community and is the largest and best example of Norman-style architecture in England. The innovative audacity of its vaulting foreshadowed Gothic architecture. Behind the cathedral is the castle, an ancient Norman fortress which was the residence of the prince-bishops of Durham.
3 Ironbridge Gorge	C i, ii, iv, vi	1986	In Ironbridge, known worldwide as the symbol of the Industrial Revolution, all the elements of progress that developed in an 18th century industrial region can be found, from the mines themselves to the railway lines. Nearby, the blast furnace of Coalbrookdale, built in 1708, is a reminder of the discovery of coke, which, together with the bridge at Ironbridge, the first metallic bridge in the world, had considerable influence on the evolution of technology and architecture.
4 Studley Royal Park including the Fountains Abbey	C i, iv	1986	A striking landscape was created around the ruins of the Cistercian abbey of Fountains and Fountains Hall Castle, in Yorkshire. The landscaping, the gardens, and the canal, dating from the 18th century, the plantations and vistas from the 19th century and the neo-Gothic castle of Studley Royal Park make this a site of exceptional value.

Property	Criteria (see Appendix 1 for key)	Date of inscription (and of enlargements)	Brief description and reasons for inscription (from World Heritage List)
5 Stonehenge, Avebury and Associated Sites	C i, ii, iii	1986	Stonehenge and Avebury, in Wiltshire, are among the most famous groups of megaliths in the world. These two sanctuaries are formed of circles of menhirs arranged in a pattern whose astronomical significance is still unexplained. These holy places and the various nearby neolithic sites offer an incomparable testimony to prehistoric times.
6 Castles and Town Walls of King Edward in Gwynedd	C i, iii, iv	1986	In the former principality of Gwynedd, in northern Wales, the castles of Beaumaris and Harlech—thanks largely to the greatest military engineer of the time, James of Saint George—and the fortified complexes of Caernarvon and Conwy, all extremely well-preserved, bear witness to the works of colonisation and defence carried out throughout the reign of Edward I, king of England (1272–1307), and to the military architecture of the time.
7 St Kilda	N iii, iv	1986	This volcanic archipelago—comprising the islands of Hirta, Dun, Soay, and Boreray, with its spectacular landscapes along the coast of the Hebrides—includes some of the highest cliffs in Europe, which provide a refuge for impressive colonies of rare and endangered species of birds, especially puffins and gannets.
8 Blenheim Palace	C ii, iv	1987	Situated near Oxford, in a romantic park created by the well-known landscape gardener 'Capability' Brown, is Blenheim Palace, given by the English nation to John Churchill, first Duke of Marlborough, in recognition of his victory in 1704 over French and Bavarian troops. Built between 1705 and 1722, characterised by eclectic inspiration and a return to national roots, it is a perfect example of an 18th-century princely home.
9 City of Bath	C i, ii, iv	1987	Founded by the Romans as a thermal spa, Bath became an important centre of the wool industry in the Middle Ages. In the 18th century, under George III, it developed into an elegant town with neo-classical buildings inspired by Palladio, which blended harmoniously with the Roman thermal complex.
10 Hadrian's Wall	C ii, iii, iv	1987	Built under the orders of Emperor Hadrian in about 122 AD on the border between England and Scotland, the 118-kilometre wall is a

No.	Site	Year	Criteria	Description
11	Westminster Palace, Westminster Abbey and Saint Margaret's Church	1987	C i, ii, iv	striking example of the organisation of a military zone, which illustrates the techniques and strategic and geopolitical views of the Romans. Rebuilt from 1840 onwards, around striking medieval remains, Westminster Palace is an eminent example, coherent and complete, of the neo-Gothic style. With the small medieval church of Saint Margaret, built in a perpendicular Gothic style, and the prestigious Westminster Abbey, where all the sovereigns since the 11th century have been crowned, the historic and symbolic significance of this site is unmistakable.
12	Henderson Island	1988	N iii, iv	In the eastern South Pacific, Henderson Island is one of the few atolls in the world with ecology that is practically unaltered by man. Its isolated location permits the study of the dynamics of insular evolution and natural selection. It is particularly notable for ten plant species and four species of land bird, endemic to the island.
13	Tower of London	1988	C ii, iv	The massive White Tower, typical of Norman military architecture whose influence was felt throughout the Kingdom, was built by William the Conqueror along the Thames to protect London and to assert his power there. The Tower of London, an imposing fortress rich with history that has become one of the symbols of royalty, was built around the White Tower.
14	Canterbury Cathedral, Saint Augustine's Abbey, and Saint Martin's Church	1988	C i, ii, vi	For three hundred years the seat of the spiritual leader of the Church of England, the town of Canterbury, in Kent, houses the modest church of Saint Martin (the oldest in England), the ruins of the abbey of Saint Augustine (a reminder of the evangelising role of the saint in the Heptarchie from 597), and the superb Christ Church Cathedral, a breathtaking mixture of Romanesque and Gothic perpendicular styles, where the Archbishop Thomas Becket was assassinated in 1170.
15	Old and New Towns of Edinburgh	1995	C ii, iv	Edinburgh, capital of Scotland since the 15th century, presents the dual face of an old city dominated by a medieval fortress and a new neoclassic city whose development from the 18th century onwards exerted a far-reaching influence on European urban planning. The harmonious juxtaposition of these two highly contrasting historic areas, each containing many buildings of great significance, is what gives Edinburgh its unique character.

Property	Criteria (see Appendix 1 for key)	Date of inscription (and of enlargements)	Brief description and reasons for inscription (from World Heritage List)
16 Gough Island Wildlife Reserve	N iii, iv	1995	Gough Island, in the South Atlantic, is one of the least disrupted island and marine ecosystems in the cool temperate zone. One of the largest colonies of sea birds in the world lives there, amidst spectacular scenery of cliffs towering above the ocean. The island is also home to two endemic species of land birds, the gallinule and the Gough rowettie, as well as to twelve endemic species of plants.
17 Maritime Greenwich	C i, ii, iv, vi	1997	The ensemble of buildings at Greenwich, near London, and the park in which they are set, are distinguished symbols of English artistic and scientific endeavour in the 17th and 18th centuries. The Queen's House of Inigo Jones was the first Palladian building in the British Isles, whilst the complex that was until recently the Royal Naval College was designed by Christopher Wren. The park, laid out on the basis of an original design by André Le Nôtre, contains the original Royal Observatory, the work of Wren and the scientist Robert Hooke.
18 Heart of Neolithic Orkney	C i, ii, iii, iv	1999	The group of Neolithic monuments on Orkney consists of a large chambered tomb (Maes Howe), two ceremonial stone circles (the Stones of Stenness and the Ring of Brodgar), and a settlement (Skara Brae), together with a number of unexcavated burial, ceremonial, and living sites. The group constitutes a major relict cultural landscape graphically depicting life in this remote archipelago north of the coast of Scotland 5000 years ago.
19 Blaenavon Industrial Landscape	C iii, iv	2000	The area around Blaenavon is evidence of the pre-eminence of South Wales as the world's major producer of iron and coal in the 19th century. All the necessary elements can still be seen—coal and ore mines, quarries, a primitive railway system, furnaces, workers' homes, and the social infrastructure of their community.
20 The Historic Town of St George Related Fortifications, Bermuda	C iv	2000	The Town of St George is an outstanding example of the earliest and English urban settlement in the New World. Its associated fortifications graphically illustrate the development of English military engineering from the 17th to the 20th century, which were adapted to take account of the development of artillery over this period.

Plate 11.7

Formal garden and garden front of Waddesdon Manor, a French Renaissance-style château 'transplanted' to Buckinghamshire, England, by Baron de Rothschild in the 1870s. The Manor is a National Trust property open to visitors, but still, in part, a residence for a branch of the Rothschild family. It is set in very extensive grounds, most of which are much less formal than the section adjacent to the house.

Photo: Graeme Aplin

Plate 11.8

Drum Castle, Aberdeenshire, Scotland, with its 13th-century keep (left) and the Jacobean mansion house which began construction in 1619 (right). The keep is one of the three oldest surviving tower houses in Scotland. The property is managed by the National Trust for Scotland and is open to the public.

Photo: Graeme Aplin

11.3 France

Introduction

Much of the responsibility for cultural heritage below the rank of 'national importance' rests with the regions, departments, municipalities, and communes, as does much of the responsibility for natural heritage areas other than national parks. In this sense France is more like Australia, where this responsibility is taken on by states and territories, than the United Kingdom. In France, there is, however, considerable assistance and cooperation from the national bodies to support more local agencies. It is important to note that particular conservation works can often involve financial and other input from many levels of government, from the European Union (EU), the national government and from more local bodies. In some cases private sponsorship may also be involved (see Plate 3.2).

Cultural heritage

Cultural heritage matters fall within the jurisdiction of the Directorate of Architecture and Heritage (*La direction de l'architecture et du patrimoine*), part of the Ministry of Culture. This directorate was created in September 1998 through the amalgamation of previously separate groups, and combines an interesting set of functions, illustrated by its mission aims (the first of these in particular is quite unusual):

* to encourage architectural creativity and to promote architectural quality in built or managed spaces, especially in places protected by reason of their historical, aesthetic, or cultural interest
* to catalogue, study, protect, conserve, and make known the archaeological, architectural, urban, ethnological, photographic, and artistic heritage of France
* to follow the activities of architects and to oversee the application of legislation applicable to them
* to observe the standards of heritage professionals and to maintain their know-how
* to participate in the organisation of staffing, funding, and research concerning architecture and heritage

The directorate administers the Register of the National Fund for Historic Monuments and Sites (*Caisse Nationale des Monuments Historiques et des Sites* or CNMHS) and oversees the allocation of public money to cultural works. (As mentioned previously, this may come from several sources.) Once listed, properties are managed and promoted in a coordinated fashion (see Plate 2.2). Several sub-divisions of the directorate have different responsibilities. One sub-division is responsible for documentation and maintaining an inventory. An archival operation similar to that carried out by the three Royal Commissions in the United Kingdom (see Section 11.2) involves well over two million photographs with a further 100 000 added each year, and many other forms of documentation. A second sub-division concerned with historic monuments undertakes classification and, where justified, inscription of monuments (in various classes); organisation and control of work on historical monuments; the definition of the rules for the use of grants for work undertaken and for restoration, re-use, and value adding; and research into technological innovation in conservation. Yet another sub-division focussing on archaeology has a similar list of undertakings in the archaeological heritage area (see Plates 6.1 and 11.9), while an office of national monuments and sites is charged with presenting such items to the public by encouraging visitors and disseminating knowledge.

It is also important to realise that much of the cultural or built heritage of France and other European nations is not reserved in any obvious way, and forms part of everyday life in towns and villages. Much has survived because it has been used and re-used over the centuries. In a sense, adaptive re-use comes naturally in such settings. Likewise, incremental growth and change occur in individual buildings, such as the marvellous St-Etienne-sur-Mont in Paris (Plate 11.10) which incorporates aspects from a range of architectural periods. In Australia, it seems that we might be tempted to try to return a church like this one to its 'original form', whatever that might be.

Plate 11.9

Ruins of Roman town of Glanum, near St-Rémy-de-Provence, France (see also Plate 6.1). This site dates back to at least the 6th century BC. The tallest walls (behind the visitors) are the remains of the Curia (the assembly hall for the local Senate) built in the Gallo-Roman era (late 1st century BC to 3rd century AD), while the foreground ruins were houses from the earlier Hellenistic age (2nd to 1st century BC). Modern excavations began in 1921.

Photo: Graeme Aplin

Plate 11.10

St-Etienne-du-Mont, place Ste-Geneviève, Paris, France. This eclectic church contains a shrine to the patron saint of Paris, Ste-Geneviève. Some parts of the structure are Gothic, others Renaissance; the central rose window is medieval, while the belfry tower dates from the 16th century.

Photo: Graeme Aplin

Natural heritage

The administration of national parks in France comes under the Ministry of the Environment. The seven *parcs nationaux* (national parks, shown in Figure 11.2) were established under legislation from 1960; the first park was created in 1963, and the most recent one in 1989. The mission of the Ministry of the Environment is to protect nature, landscapes, and sites; to maintain biodiversity; to allow for public access; and to develop attitudes of respect for nature and its health and equilibrium or sustainability. While there are only seven national parks, there are a very large number of *parcs régionaux* or regional parks (Plate 11.11), and even more local reserves of many kinds.

According to the relevant web site, a national park is defined by the following criteria:

- an exceptional piece of territory—a landscape, ecological, or cultural heritage item
- a legal and social space divided into two zones with specific attributes, central and peripheral
- a group of professionals working together, including those protecting the area, those carrying out research, and those communicating the area's values
- outcomes—protection of nature, landscapes, sites, and biodiversity; making the 'park heritage' available to the present generation and transmitting it to future generations; and participating in the development of attitudes towards nature and sustainability

A national park is thus seen as a place zoned into core and peripheral areas (see Section 5.6); as a group of people working together; and as a series of goals to be worked towards through conservation and protection, public access, and interpretation, all of which jointly make up park management. The Parc national des Pyrénées, for example, created in 1967, has a central zone of 45 707 hectares and a peripheral zone of 206 352 hectares. It employs fifty-two full-time staff and another twenty-eight people seasonally, and has two million visitors per year (for both winter skiing and summer touring and long-distance walking). This park abuts a large Spanish national park and the two are jointly inscribed as a World Heritage property (see Table 11.2).

French national parks (and regional parks and more local equivalents) are seen as dynamic entities, and their management is considered to involve not only protection of the park areas, but also maintaining the ongoing development of traditional activities. Park management does not obliterate development, but contributes to the local economy through management of space, the development of activities and employment, and the creation of an image that promotes environmentally friendly tourism. Box 11.5 describes the Parc naturel régional de Camargue and illustrates many relevant points, including the integration of cultural and natural values, and the continuation of traditional activities.

French World Heritage properties

French sites inscribed on the WHL are overwhelmingly listed for cultural heritage reasons. Over the twenty-year period from 1979 to 2000, twenty-seven properties were inscribed (Table 11.2, Figure 11.2), and only one of these—a site on the island of Corsica—was listed for natural reasons, while the joint French–Spanish site in the Pyrénées was listed for both cultural and natural reasons. The cultural sites include the prehistoric cave paintings of Lascaux and proximate cave systems, Roman ruins such as those at Arles and the Pont du Gard nearby (Plates 3.2 and 11.12), Gothic cathedrals such as Chartres (see Plate 1.2), monastic complexes like Mont-St-Michel (Plate 11.13), and reminders of the opulent lifestyle of the nobility (see Plate 8.4). Finally, a sizeable stretch of the banks of the Seine constitutes perhaps the largest site in any major world city (see Plate 1.9).

Plate 11.11

View north from Col de Guéry in the Monts Dore, Puy de Dôme Département, France. Much of the country in this district in the Massif Central is included in the Parc naturel régional des Volcans d'Auvergne.

Photo: Graeme Aplin

Box 11.5 *Le Parc naturel régional de Camargue*

The park was established in 1970 and includes an area of 86 300 hectares. It has a population of 7400 within its boundaries.

The main objectives of park management are:

- the preservation and integrated management of human activities and the environments on which they impact, of natural areas, and of fauna and flora
- the protection of the whole Camargue area against flooding by the Rhône river, and against marine incursions
- the control and structuring of tourist and recreational developments
- the amelioration of the living conditions of the inhabitants
- the maintenance of the diversity of Camargue landscapes

In 1996, the total area was divided between the following uses:

- 23 per cent as cultivated landscapes—of which about two-thirds was used for rice, just under one-quarter for wheat, and the remainder mainly for hay, sunflowers, vines, and fruit trees
- 51 per cent as natural landscapes—freshwater marshes and woods, reserved for hunting or livestock, or protected for conservation (about 20 000 hectares, or 23 per cent of the total area of the park is protected)
- 2 per cent as urban landscapes—in two towns and a number of hamlets
- 16 per cent as salt marshes, important for bird life
- lagoon and littoral environments
- stream and riparian forest environments
- marine environments

Rice cultivation, fishing, Merino sheep, Camargue horses and cattle (the latter famous for bull-fighting), and salt production (on 11 000 hectares in the south-east) are all important industries.

Source: *Le Parc naturel régional de Camargue*, Bibliothèque de Travail Fondée par Célestin Freinet, Mouans Sartoux.

Figure 11.2

French national parks and World Heritage properties

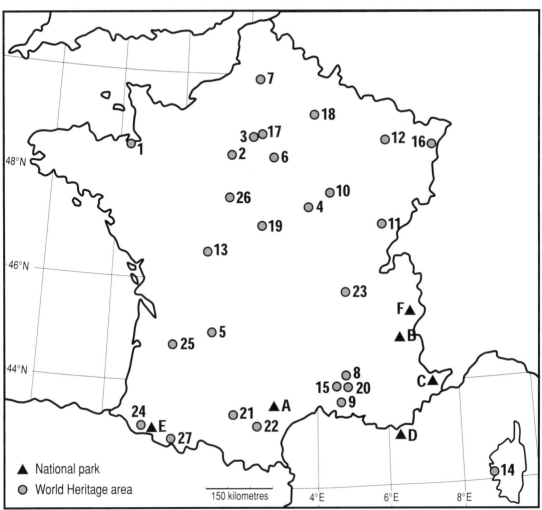

Key:

World Heritage areas

1–27: see Table 11.2.

National parks

A   Les Cévennes

B   Les Ecrins

C   Le Mercantour

D   Port-Cros

E   Les Pyrénées

F   La Vanoise

Table 11.2

French World Heritage properties

Property	Criteria (see Appendix 1 for key)	Date of inscription (and of enlargements)	Brief description and reasons for inscription (from World Heritage List)
1 Mont-Saint-Michel and its Bay	C i, iii, vi	1979	Perched on a rocky islet in the midst of vast sand flats exposed to powerful tides between Normandy and Brittany is the 'Wonder of the West', a Gothic-style Benedictine Abbey dedicated to the archangel Saint Michael, and the village that grew up in the shadow of its great walls. Built between the 11th and 16th centuries, the abbey is an extraordinary technical and artistic tour de force, having to adapt to the problems posed by the unique natural conditions of the site.
2 Chartres Cathedral	C i, ii, iv	1979	Partly built starting in 1145 and reconstructed twenty-six years later after the fire of 1194, Chartres Cathedral is a reference point of French Gothic art. A vast nave (in pure ogival style), porches presenting admirable sculptures from the middle of the 12th century, and sparkling 12th- and 13th-century stained-glass windows, all in remarkable condition, make it a masterpiece.
3 Palace and Park of Versailles	C i, ii, vi	1979	The principal residence of the kings of France from Louis XIV to Louis XVI, the Versailles Palace, embellished by several generations of architects, sculptors, decorators, and landscape architects, has for more than a century provided Europe with the very model of a royal residence.
4 Vézelay, Church and Hill	C i, vi	1979	Shortly after its foundation in the 9th century, the Benedictine monastery acquired the relics of St Mary Magdalene and since then has been an important place of pilgrimage. St Bernard preached the Second Crusade there in 1146 and Richard the Lion-Hearted and Philippe Augustus met there to leave for the Third Crusade in 1190. The Madeleine of Vézelay, a monastic 12th-century church, is a masterpiece of Burgundian Romanesque art, by virtue of its architecture as well as its capitals and sculpted portal.
5 Decorated Grottoes of the Vézère Valley	C i, iii	1979	The Vézère Valley contains 147 prehistoric sites dating to the Palaeolithic era and twenty-five decorated caves. It is particularly interesting from an ethnological and anthropologic, as well as aesthetic point of view, with its cave paintings, especially those of the Lascaux Cave, whose discovery in 1940 was an important date in the history of prehistoric art. Hunting scenes depicted contain about 100 animal figures, remarkable for their detail, the richness of their colours, and their life-like quality.

Property	Criteria (see Appendix 1 for key)	Date of inscription (and of enlargements)	Brief description and reasons for inscription (from World Heritage List)
6 Palace and Park of Fontainebleau	C ii, vi	1981	Used by the kings of France from the 12th century, the hunting residence of Fontainebleau, at the heart of a vast forest in the Île-de-France, was transformed, enlarged, and embellished in the 16th century by François I, who wanted to make a 'New Rome' of it. Surrounded by an immense park, the palace, of Italian inspiration, combines Renaissance and French artistic traditions.
6A¹ Château and Estate of Chambord	C i	1981	Constructed in the midst of a vast forest in the Loire valley, the Château of Chambord is a unique masterpiece of the French Renaissance which associates traditional medieval forms with classical Italian structures in an extremely imaginative way.
7 Amiens Cathedral	C i, ii	1981	Amiens Cathedral, in the heart of Picardy, is one of the largest 'classic' Gothic churches of the 13th century. The coherence of its plan, the beauty of its three-tier interior elevation, and the arrangement of an extremely scholarly sculptural program (on its principal façade and on the wing of the southern transept) are striking features.
8 Roman Theatre and its Surroundings and the 'Triumphal Arch' of Orange	C iii, vi	1981	Situated in the Rhône valley, the ancient theatre of Orange, with its 103-metre long façade, is one of the best preserved of all the great Roman theatres. Built between 10 and 25 AD, during the reign of Augustus, the Roman arch is one of the most beautiful and most interesting provincial triumphal arches known today, decorated with bas-reliefs commemorating the establishment of the Pax Romana.
9 Roman and Romanesque Monuments of Arles	C ii, iv	1981	Arles is a good example of the adaptation of an ancient city to medieval European civilization, with its impressive Roman monuments, of which the earliest—the Arena, the Roman Theatre, and the Cryptoportica (subterranean galleries)—date back to the 1st century BC. During the 4th century Arles saw a second golden age, attested to by the baths of Constantine and the necropolis of Alyscamps. In the 11th and 12th centuries, Arles once again became one of the most attractive cities in the Mediterranean. Within the city walls, Saint Trophime, with its cloister, is one of the major monuments of Romanesque art of Provence.
10 Cistercian Abbey of Fontenay	C iv	1981	This stark Burgundian monastery, founded in 1119 by Saint Bernard, with its church, cloister, refectory, sleeping quarters, bakery, and ironworks, is a wonderful illustration of the ideal of self-sufficiency in the earliest communities of Cistercian monks.

	Name	Criteria	Year	Description
11	Royal Saltworks of Arc-et-Senans	C i, ii, iv	1982	The Royal Saltworks of Arc-et-Senans, near Besançon, was created by Claude Nicolas Ledoux. Its construction, begun in 1775 during the reign of Louis XVI, is the first important achievement of industrial architecture, reflecting the ideal of progress of the Enlightenment. This vast, semi-circular edifice was conceived to permit a rational and hierarchical organisation of work and was to have been followed by the building of an ideal city (ultimately never realised).
12	Place Stanislas, Place de la Carrière and Place d'Alliance in Nancy	C i, iv	1983	Nancy, the temporary residence of a king without a kingdom—Stanislas Leszczynski, who later became the Duke of Lorraine—is paradoxically the oldest and most typical example of a modern capital where an enlightened monarch proved to be conscious of the needs of the public. Constructed between 1752 and 1756 by a brilliant team under the direction of the architect Héré, this was a project of extreme coherence which succeeded perfectly in linking the desire for prestige with the king's concern for functionality.
13	Church of Saint-Savin sur Gartempe	C i, iii	1983	Known as the 'Romanesque Sistine Chapel', the Abbey of Saint-Savin contains many beautiful 11th- and 12th-century mural paintings, which are still in remarkably pure condition.
14	Cape Girolata, Cape Porto, Scandola Nature Reserve and the Piana Calanches in Corsica	N ii, iii, iv	1983	The nature reserve, part of the Regional Natural Park of Corsica, occupies the Scandola Peninsula, an impressive, porphyritic rock mass. The vegetation is an example of scrubland and the reserve is the habitat of seagulls, cormorants, and sea eagles. The clear waters, with islets and inaccessible caves, host a rich marine life.
15	Pont du Gard (Roman Aqueduct)	C ii, iii, iv	1985	The Pont du Gard was built shortly before the Christian era to allow the aqueduct of Nîmes, almost fifty kilometres long, to cross the Gard River. The hydraulic engineers and Roman architects who conceived this bridge, which is almost fifty metres high over three levels—the longest measuring 275 metres—created a technical as well as artistic masterpiece.
16	Strasbourg—Grande Île	C i, ii, iv	1988	Surrounded by two arms of the Ill, the 'Grande Île' (Big Island) is the historic centre of the Alsatian capital which, within a restricted area, contains an outstanding complex of monuments. The Cathedral, the four ancient churches, and the Palais Rohan—former residence of the prince-bishops—far from appearing as isolated monuments, form a district which is very characteristic of a medieval town, and representative of the evolution of Strasbourg from the 15th to 18th centuries.
17	Paris, Banks of the Seine	C i, ii, iv	1991	From the Louvre to the Eiffel Tower or the Place de la Concorde to the Grand and Petit Palais, the evolution of Paris and its history can be seen from the river. The Cathedral of Notre Dame and the Sainte Chapelle are architectural masterpieces while Haussmann's wide squares and avenues influenced late 19th and 20th-century urbanism the world over.

Property	Criteria (see Appendix 1 for key)	Date of inscription (and of enlargements)	Brief description and reasons for inscription (from World Heritage List)
18 Cathedral of Notre Dame, Former Abbey of Saint-Remi and Palace of Tau in Reims	C i, ii, vi	1991	The outstanding handling of new architectural techniques in the 13th century, and the harmonious marriage of sculpted decoration with architecture, has made Notre Dame in Reims one of the master-pieces of Gothic art. The former abbey has conserved its very beautiful 9th-century nave, in which lie the remains of the Archbishop Saint Remi (440–533), who instituted the Holy Anointing of the kings of France. The Tau Palace, former archiepiscopal palace, important in holy ceremonies, was almost entirely reconstructed in the 17th century.
19 Bourges Cathedral	C i, iv	1992	Admired for its proportions and the unity of its design, the Cathedral of Saint Stephen of Bourges, constructed between the late 12th and late 13th centuries, is one of the great masterpieces of Gothic art. Its tympanum, sculptures, and stained-glass windows are particularly striking. Apart from its architectural beauty, it attests to the power of Christianity in medieval France.
20 Historic Centre of Avignon	C i, ii, iv	1995	This city of southern France was the seat of the papacy in the 14th century. The Palais des Papes, an austere-looking fortress lavishly decorated by Simone Martini and Matteo Giovanetti, dominates the city, the surrounding ramparts, and the remains of a 12th-century bridge over the Rhône. On the square beneath this outstanding example of Gothic architecture, the Petit Palais and the Romanesque Cathedral of Notre-Dame des Doms complete an exceptional group of monuments bearing witness to the eminent role played by Avignon in Christian Europe in the 14th century.
21 Canal du Midi	C i, ii, iv, vi	1996	This 360-kilometre network of navigable waterways linking the Mediterranean and the Atlantic through 328 structures—locks, aqueducts, bridges, tunnels etc.—is one of the most remarkable civil engineering feats of modern times. Built between 1667 and 1694, it opened the way for the Industrial Revolution. The care taken in its design by creator, Pierre-Paul Riquet, and the harmony he achieved with the surroundings turned a technical achievement into a work of art.
22 The Historic Fortified City of Carcassonne	C ii, iv	1997	Since the pre-Roman period, a fortified settlement has existed on the hill where Carcassonne now stands. In its present form it is an outstanding example of a medieval fortified town, with massive defences encircling the castle, its associated houses, streets, and the fine Gothic cathedral. Carcassonne is also of exceptional importance because of the long campaign of restoration carried out by Viollet-le-Duc, one of the founders of the modern science of conservation.

23	Historic Site of Lyons	1998	C ii, iv	The long history of Lyons, which was founded by the Romans as the capital of the Three Gauls in the 1st century BC and which has continued to play a major role in the political, cultural, and economic development of Europe since that time, is vividly illustrated by its urban fabric and by its many fine historic buildings from all periods.
24	Routes of Santiago de Compostela in France	1998	C ii, iv, vi	Santiago de Compostela was the greatest of all goals for countless thousands of pious pilgrims converging there from all over Europe throughout the Middle Ages. To reach Spain, pilgrims had to pass through France, and the group of important historical monuments included in this inscription on the World Heritage List mark out the four routes taken to this end.
25	The Jurisdiction of Saint-Emilion	1999	C iii, iv	Viticulture was introduced to this fertile region of Aquitaine by the Romans, and intensified in the Middle Ages. The Saint-Emilion area benefited from its location on the pilgrimage route to Santiago de Compostela. Many churches, monasteries, and hospices were built there from the 11th century onwards. It was granted the special status of a jurisdiction during the period of English rule in the 12th century. It is an exceptional landscape devoted entirely to wine-growing, with many fine historic monuments in its towns and villages.
26	The Loire Valley between Sully-sur-Loire and Chalonnes	2000	C i, ii, iv	The Loire Valley is an outstanding cultural landscape of great beauty, containing historic towns and villages, great architectural monuments (the châteaux), and cultivated lands formed by many centuries of interaction between their population and the physical environment, primarily the river Loire itself. The site includes the Château and Estate of Chambord, which was previously inscribed on the World Heritage List in 1981 (see site 6A).
27[2]	Pyrénées-Mount Perdu	1997, 1999	N i, iii; C iii, iv, v	This outstanding mountain landscape, which spans the contemporary national borders of France and Spain, is centred around the peak of Mount Perdu, a calcareous massif that rises 3352 metres. The site, with a total area of 30 639 hectares, includes two of Europe's largest and deepest canyons on the Spanish side and three major cirque walls on the more abrupt northern slopes with France, classic presentations of these geologic landforms. But the site is also a pastoral landscape reflecting an agricultural way of life that was once widespread in the upland regions of Europe. It has survived unchanged into the 20th century only in this part of the Pyrénées, providing exceptional insights into past European society through its landscape of villages, farms, fields, upland pastures, and mountain roads.

Notes: [1] The Château and Estate of Chambord is now part of the Loire Valley between Sully-sur-Loire and Chalonnes (site 26 in this table).

[2] A property that falls within both France and Spain.

Plate 11.12

Pont du Gard, a French World Heritage property. Built by the Romans, approximately 20–10 AD, the upper level is forty metres above the river and 275 metres long (see also Plate 3.2).

Photo: Graeme Aplin

Plate 11.13

Mont-St-Michel, a French World Heritage property. A monastic settlement built between the 11th and 16th centuries, it draws nearly a million visitors each year.

Photo: Graeme Aplin

11.4   Italy

Introduction

Italy is renowned for its cultural heritage from all periods, from the pre-Etruscan through the Roman period to the present. It also has a wide range of significant natural heritage sites, most obviously in alpine and mountainous areas, but it also is the home of important wetlands and the notorious, isolated volcano of Vesuvius.

Cultural heritage

Italian cultural heritage sites seem to have been conserved for a long time, largely by private individuals, local or possibly regional councils, and, crucially, by the Roman Catholic Church. Legislation in 1974 instituted the Ministry of Cultural Property and the Environment, but in late 1998, heritage functions, including 'landscape management' were transferred to a new Ministry of Cultural Property and Activities. Two relevant bodies exist within the new Ministry: a Central Office of Architectural, Archaeological, Artistic and Historical Properties (UCBAAAS) and a Central Office of Environmental and Landscape Properties (UCBAP). UCBAAAS is responsible for the management and development of national government properties and for the oversight of properties under the control of the regions, more local levels of government, and private bodies and individuals. Major effort goes into reaching negotiated agreements with these other bodies (such as the State Railways and Poste Italiane) to ensure coordinated management of financial resources. UCBAAAS contains two important institutes: an Institute for Restoration and an Institute for Cataloguing and Documentation, and the latter performs a role similar to the three United Kingdom Royal Commissions (see Section 11.2). A database of cultural sites is available through the Internet (see list of web sites in Appendix 2). UCBAP is concerned with broader historical and cultural landscape issues as one aspect of its environmental concerns. It is also the coordinating body for management of Italy's World Heritage properties (discussed later in this Section).

There are a number of 'Superintendents' who are responsible for regional implementation of national programs, and for coordination between the various levels of government. In regions that have considerable heritage to manage, superintendents may be quite specialised, such as the Archaeological Superintendent of Rome, but in less well endowed regions, they may cover the whole spectrum of UCBAAAS and UCBAP concerns. Although agreements between levels of government are negotiated, the basic responsibility for the majority of the national sites (with the exception of the most major ones) remains with the lower levels of government, even though the bulk of the financial input may come from national sources. One recent and very large national initiative involved using national lottery earnings to finance restoration of 263 sites of national importance to coincide with the Christian Jubilee Year in 2000. There is a possibility that this initiative using lottery earnings will continue as a series of triennial programs.

The important role of the Catholic Church has already been mentioned. In 1987 the *Fondo Edifici di Culto* (FEC, loosely translated as the Religious Properties Fund) was created under the Cultural Affairs section of the Ministry of Justice and Culture, to intervene and assist the Church in the conservation of heritage buildings and sites, although the role of the state had been increasing for many decades prior to that. The FEC list includes a relatively small number of churches (see for example Plate 11.14), basilicas and other religious buildings, a castle, a forest, the estate of Monreale, and a small number of other properties. The FEC also provides a Heritage Administration Division that assists with many other religious buildings, and a Conservation and Restoration of Religious Properties Division that provides technical advice and assistance.

Plate 11.14

Chiesa di Santa Croce,
Florence, Italy. This Gothic
church, started in 1294,
contains the tombs of
many famous people,
including Michelangelo,
Galileo, and Machiavelli,
and early 14th-century
frescoes by Giotto. The
neo-Gothic marble façade
was added in 1863.

Photo: Graeme Aplin

Natural heritage

The major agency concerned with natural heritage at the national level in Italy
is the Nature Conservation Service (SCN), which falls within the Ministry of
the Environment. The four areas of concern of the SCN are:

- conservation and development of the natural environment and the faunal
  and floral heritage
- promotion and coordination of activities in scientific and technical research
  and experimentation concerned with aspects of the management of the
  environment and of natural species
- initiatives in environmental education in the field of protected areas
- other functions within the competence of the ministry concerning national
  parks, marine reserves, wetlands, and other protected areas, and the
  management of flora and fauna

In Italy as a whole, more than 2.5 million hectares are under conservation
management, more than 1.8 per cent of the surface area. These areas contain
5599 species of flora, 3255 species of vertebrates and 54 167 invertebrate
species, 199 of which are thought to be at risk of extinction. Protected areas are
seen to help in the conservation of biodiversity, of individual species, of
landscape values, and of hydrological and ecological equilibrium that would
otherwise be gravely compromised. In late 1997, the First National Conference
on Protected Areas, organised by the Ministry of the Environment, heard an
outline of government policy development which would guide future activities.
In particular, it acknowledged the need for guaranteed technical assistance for
reserve managers, further augmentation of the amount of protected land, and a
system-wide policy.

Based on a law of 1991, Italy has a number of types of protected areas (Box 11.6). There are twenty-five national parks (*parchi nazionale*; Figure 11.3), five of which are referred to as 'historical parks' because they existed prior to the first 'modern' park legislation, which dates from 1988. Another twelve were gazetted under laws of 1988 and 1991, and eight between 1994 and 1998 under more recent legislation. Of those eight, five are specifically protected for 'environmental landscape' reasons. Each park is operated by a park board, and is required to have a plan of management and to actively involve the local community. Plans can use a series of four zones as appropriate:

a   an 'integral reserve' (core) zone in which environmental conservation is paramount

b   a 'generally oriented reserve' zone in which virtually all development is prohibited, but pre-existing traditional productive activities can continue

c   an 'area of protection' in which traditional methods of organic agriculture, agro-silvo-pastoral activity, fishing and collecting of natural products, and traditional craftsmanship are all allowed as long as they are in harmony with park criteria and management aims

d   an 'area for economic and social promotion', which is more extensively modified by human activity, providing this is compatible with the park plan and aims, and looks to contribute to improvement of the socio-cultural life of the local community and the greater enjoyment of the park by visitors

This is an extension of the simpler zoning system used in Australian national parks (see Section 5.6), and it specifically caters for a greater range of human activities than the one in Australia.

Box 11.6 Italian protected natural heritage areas

Legislation passed in 1991 defined the classification of protected natural areas according to fixed criteria, and established an official directory of such areas. The types of protected natural areas are as follows:

• **National Parks**—terrestrial, fluvial, lacustrine, or marine areas containing one or more intact ecosystems, or ones partially altered by human activity, or one or more geological, geomorphological, or biological formations, of international or national importance for natural, scientific, aesthetic, cultural, educational, or recreational values requiring state intervention to ensure their conservation for present and future generations

• **Regional and Inter-regional Natural Parks**—terrestrial, fluvial, and lacustrine areas, and eventually parts of the sea close to the coast, of natural and environmental value which constitute, within one or more neighbouring regions, a homogeneous system characterised by the natural assets of the sites, and by landscape and aesthetic values, and the traditional culture of the local population

• **Nature Reserves**—terrestrial, fluvial, lacustrine, or marine areas containing one or more naturally occurring species of flora and fauna, or one or more ecosystems, important for biodiversity or the conservation of genetic resources. Nature Reserves may be at the national or regional level according to the natural elements represented.

• **Wetlands of International Importance**—areas of marsh, swamp, mudflats, or natural or artificial water, permanent or temporary, including marine zones with a low-water depth of not more than six metres, whose characteristics are considered of international importance according to the Ramsar Convention

• **Other natural protected areas**—other areas (environmental 'oases', suburban parks, etc.) not falling within the preceding classes. These areas are either under public management and constituted under regional law, or under private management, instituted with formal public measures or through contracts, concessions, or equivalent forms.

- **Special protection zones**—designated under a particular law and constituting a territory suitable for the extension and/or geographical localisation of the conservation of a species of bird, or connected with the conservation of wild birds
- **Special conservation zones**—designated under a particular law and containing a natural area, geographically defined and of limited area, which:
  a contains a terrestrial or aquatic area distinguished by geographical, abiotic, or biotic characteristics, natural or semi-natural, and which contributes in a significant way to the conservation or restoration of a type of natural habitat or a species of wild flora or fauna of the Palearctic zone through protection of Alpine, Appenine, or Mediterranean environments
  b is designated by the state by means of a regulation, administrative act, and/or contract which contains measures to conserve or restore, in a satisfactory state of conservation, the natural habitat or population of the species for which the natural area is designated

Source: *Servizio Conservazione della Natura* web site http://www.scn.minambiente.it/strutture/sysarpro/corpo.htm (accessed 3 November 1999).

Italian World Heritage properties

There are thirty-four Italian World Heritage properties (one is a joint Italy-Holy See property) and all but one are listed for purely cultural heritage reasons (Table 11.3 and see Figure 11.3). These cultural sites include the prehistoric rock drawings of Valcamonica; a number of major archaeological sites, including a Greek colony of the sixth century BC, other pre-Roman sites and many Roman ruins, including those in Rome itself (Plate 11.15) and those at Pompei (Plate 11.16). A number of historic urban areas in settlements of various sizes are also listed, including Florence, Venice, Siena (Plate 11.17), and Pisa (see Plate 4.9). More unusual inscriptions include the Padua botanic gardens, the church containing Leonardo da Vinci's *The Last Supper*, a 19th-century industrial 'company town', and a strip of the beautiful Amalfi coast. The sole 'natural' site, inscribed in November 2000, consists of the volcanic Aeolian Islands, including Isola Volcano and Isola Stromboli.

Plate 11.15

The Colosseum, Rome, an Italian World Heritage property. Inaugurated in 80 AD, it could hold up to 55 000 people.

Photo: Graeme Aplin

Figure 11.3

Italian national parks and World Heritage properties

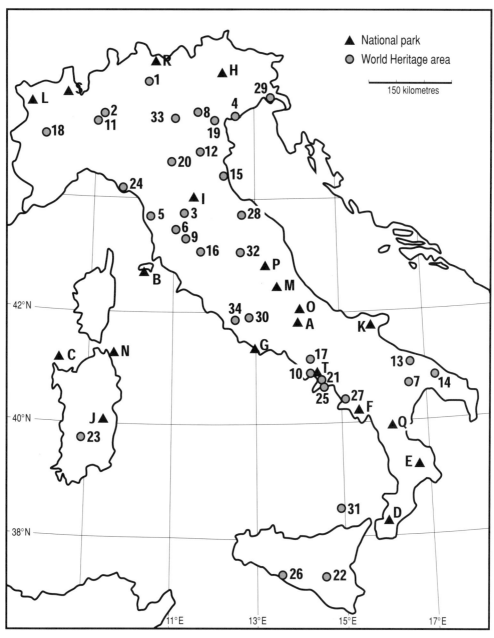

Key:

World Heritage areas

1–34: see Table 11.3.

National parks

A Abruzzo

B Arcipelago Toscano

C Asinara

D Aspromonte

E Calabria

F Cilento

G Circeo

H Dolomiti Bellunesi

I Foreste Casentinesi

J Gennargentu e Golfo di Orosei

K Gargano

L Gran Paradiso

M Gran Sasso e Monti della Laga

N Maddalena

O Maiella

P Monti Sibillini

Q Pollino

R Stelvio

S Val Grande

T Vesuvio

Plate 11.16

Street in Pompeii, Campania, an Italian World Heritage property. This Roman town was 'frozen' by ash from an eruption of Vesuvius in 79 AD. Excavations from 1748 to the present have revealed much about the daily life of Pompeii's inhabitants.

Photo: Carolynne Paine

Plate 11.17

Siena, Tuscany, Italy: rooftops of the old city with, on the right, the Duomo or cathedral (1136–1382) and its belltower (1313). Siena is one of several Italian cities and towns whose historic cores have been inscribed on the World Heritage List.

Photo: Margaret Dudgeon

Table 11.3

Italian World Heritage properties

	Property	Criteria (see Appendix 1 for key)	Date of inscription (and of enlargements)	Brief description and reasons for inscription (from World Heritage List)
1	Rock Drawings in Valcamonica	C iii, vi	1979	Valcamonica, in the Lombardy plain, has one of the greatest collection of prehistoric petroglyphs to be found—more than 140 000 signs and figures carved in rock over a period of 8000 years, depicting themes of agriculture, navigation, war, and magic.
2	Church and Dominican Convent of Santa Maria delle Grazie with *The Last Supper* by Leonardo da Vinci	C i, ii	1980	An integral part of the architectural complex built in Milan beginning in 1463 and reworked at the end of the 15th century by Bramante, the rectory of the convent of Saint Mary of the Graces still has on its northern wall a master-piece without equal—*The Last Supper*, painted between 1495 and 1497 by Leonardo da Vinci, whose work heralded a new era in the history of art.
3	Historic Centre of Florence	C i, ii, iii, iv, vi	1982	Built on the site of an Etruscan settlement, Florence, the symbol of the Renaissance, assumed its economic and cultural predominance under the Medici in the 15th and 16th centuries. Six hundred years of extraordinary artistic creativity can be seen above all in its 13th-century cathedra.—the Santa Maria del Fiore—the Santa Croce Church, the Uffizi Palace, and the Pitti Palace, which are the work of artists such as Giotto, Brunelleschi, Botticelli, and Michelangelo.
4	Venice and its Lagoon	C i, ii, iii, iv, v, vi	1987	Founded in the 5th century and spread over 118 small islands, Venice became a major maritime power in the 10th century. It is, as a whole, an extraordinary architectural masterpiece in which even the smallest of its buildings contains the works of some of the world's greatest artists such as Giorgione, Titian, Tintoretto, Veronese, and others.
5	Piazza del Duomo, Pisa	C i, ii, iv, vi	1987	On a vast lawn, the Piazza del Duomo houses a group of monuments known the world over. The Piazza contains four of the masterpieces of medieval architecture that considerably influenced monumental art in Italy from the 11th to the 14th centuries—the cathedral, the baptistry, the campanile (the 'Leaning Tower'), and the cemetery.
6	Historic Centre of San Gimignano	C i, iii, iv	1990	'San Gimignano delle belle Torri' is situated in Tuscany, fifty-six kilometres south of Florence. It served as an important relay point for pilgrims on the Via Francigena to and from Rome. The patrician families, who controlled the city, built some seventy-two tower houses (up to fifty metres h gh) as symbols of their wealth and power. Only fourteen have survived but San Gimignano has retained its feudal atmosphere and appearance. The city also contains masterpieces of 14th- and 15th-century Italian art.

Property	Criteria (see Appendix 1 for key)	Date of inscription (and of enlargements)	Brief description and reasons for inscription (from World Heritage List)
7 I Sassi di Matera	C iii, iv, v	1993	This is the most outstanding and intact example of a troglodyte settlement in the Mediterranean region, perfectly adapted to its terrain and ecosystem. The first inhabited zone dates from the Palaeolithic period, while later settlements illustrate a number of significant stages in human history.
8 City of Vicenza and the Palladian Villas of the Veneto	C i, ii	1994, 1996	The great architect Andrea Palladio (1508–1580) not only created the image of Vicenza but also designed summer villas and houses for aristocrats, which are scattered throughout the Veneto region. As with his urban buildings, these country houses had a decisive influence on the development of architecture.
9 Historic Centre of Siena	C i, ii, iv	1995	Siena is the embodiment of a medieval city. Its inhabitants, transposing their rivalry with Florence to the area of urban planning, pursued a Gothic dream throughout the centuries by preserving the appearance their city had acquired between the 12th and 15th centuries. During this period Duccio, the Lorenzetti brothers and Simone Martini were shaping the paths of Italian—and, more broadly, European—art. The entire city, converging on the masterpiece of urban planning that is the Piazza del Campo, was devised as a work of art incorporated into the surrounding landscape.
10 Historic Centre of Naples	C ii, iv	1995	From the Neapolis founded by Greek settlers in 470 BC to the city of today, Naples has received and retains the stamp of the cultures that emerged one after the other in the Mediterranean Basin and in Europe. These layers of influence and its continuing role in history have made the site unique, containing such remarkable monuments as the Santa Chiara Church and the Castel Nuovo, to name but two.
11 Crespi d'Adda	C iv, v	1995	Crespi d'Adda is an outstanding example of the 19th and early 20th century 'company towns'. These were villages in Europe and North America built by enlightened industrialists to meet a worker's every need. The site is still remarkably intact and partly in industrial use, although changing economic and social conditions pose a threat to its continued survival.
12 Ferrara, City of the Renaissance and its Po Delta	C ii, iii, iv, v, vi	1995, 1999	Ferrara grew up around a ford over the River Po, where between the 14th and 16th centuries the Dukes of Este carried out extensive land reclamation and building projects, which give this area a unique character and link it intimately with the city of Ferrara, seat of the Este family. The city became an intellectual and artistic centre that attracted the greatest minds of the Italian Renaissance in the 15th and 16th centuries. Piero della Francesca,

No.	Name	Year	Criteria	Description
13	Castel del Monte	1996	C i, ii, iii	Jacopo Bellini, and Mantegna decorated the palaces of the House of Este. The humanist concept of the ideal city came to life here in the quarters built after 1492 by Biagio Rossetti according to the new principles of perspective. The completion of this project marked the birth of modern town planning and its subsequent development.
				The location, the mathematical and astronomical precision of its layout, and its perfect shape reflect the symbolic ambition which inspired Emperor Frederick II when he built this southern Italian castle in the 13th century. A unique piece of medieval military architecture, Castel del Monte is a completely successful blending of classical antiquity, the Islamic Orient, and northern European Cistercian Gothic.
14	The Trulli of Alberobello	1996	C iii, iv, v	The *trulli*, limestone dwelling houses in the southern Italian region of Puglia, are remarkable examples of drywall (mortarless) construction, a prehistoric building technique still in use in this region. These structures, dating from as early as the mid-14th century, were constructed using roughly worked limestone boulders collected from neighbouring fields. Characteristically, they feature pyramidal, domed, or conical roofs built up of corbelled limestone slabs. Although rural *trulli* can be found throughout the Itria Valley, their highest concentration is in the town of Alberobello, where there are over 1500 structures in the quarters of Monti and Aja Piccola.
15	Early Christian Monuments and Mosaics of Ravenna	1996	C i, ii, iii, iv	Ravenna was the seat of the Roman Empire in the 5th century and then of Byzantine Italy until the 8th century. It has a unique collection of mosaics and early Christian monuments. All eight buildings—the Mausoleum of Galla Placidia, the Neonian Baptistery, the Basilica of Sant'Apollinare Nuovo, the Arian Baptistery, the Archiepiscopal Chapel, the Mausoleum of Theodoric, the Church of San Vitale, the Basilica of Sant'Apollinare in Classe—were constructed in the 5th and 6th centuries. All show great artistic skill, including a wonderful blend of Greco-Roman tradition, Christian iconography, and oriental and western styles.
16	Historic Centre of the City of Pienza	1996	C i, ii, iv	It was in the Tuscan town of Pienza that Renaissance urban ideas were first put into practice after Pope Pius II decided in 1459 to renovate his birthplace. The architect chosen, Bernardo Rossellino, applied the principles of his mentor Leone Alberti and built the extraordinary Pius II Square, around which are built the Piccolomini Palace, the Borgia Palace, and the cathedral with its purely Renaissance exterior and an interior in the late Gothic style of south German churches.

Property	Criteria (see Appendix 1 for key)	Date of inscription (and of enlargements)	Brief description and reasons for inscription (from World Heritage List)
17 18th-Century Royal Palace at Caserta with the Park, the Aqueduct of Vanvitelli, and the San Leucio Complex	C i, ii, iii, iv	1997	The monumental complex at Caserta, created by Carlo Borbone in the mid-18th century to rival Versailles and Madrid, is exceptional for the way in which it brings together a sumptuous palace and its park and gardens, as well as natural woodland, hunting lodges, and an industrial establishment for the production of silk. It is an eloquent expression of the Enlightenment in material form, integrated into, rather than imposed upon, its natural landscape.
18 Residences of the Royal House of Savoy	C i, ii, iv, v	1997	When Emmanuel-Philibert, Duke of Savoy, moved his capital to Turin in 1562, he began a series of building projects, carried on by his of buildings successors, to demonstrate the power of the ruling house. This complex of high quality, designed and decorated by the leading architects and artists of the time, radiates out into the surrounding countryside from the Royal Palace in the 'Command Area'of' Turin to include many country residences and hunting lodges.
19 Botanical Garden (Orto Botanico), Padua	C ii, iii	1997	The first botanical garden in the world was created in Padua in 1545. It still preserves its original layout—a circular central plot, symbolic of the world, surrounded by a ring of water. Subsequently additional elements have been included, both architectural (ornamental entrances and balustrades) and practical (pumping installations and greenhouses). It continues to serve its original purpose as a source of scientific research.
20 Cathedral, Torre Civica, and Piazza Grande, Modena	C i, ii, iii, iv	1997	The magnificent 12th-century cathedral at Modena is a supreme example of Romanesque art, the work of two great artists (Lanfranco and Wiligelmo). With its associated piazza and the soaring tower, it testifies to the strength of the faith of its builders and to the power of the Canossa dynasty who commissioned it.
21 Archaeological Areas of Pompei, Ercolano, and Torre Annunziata	C iii, iv, v	1997	When Vesuvius erupted on 24 August 79 AD it engulfed the two flourishing Roman towns of Pompeii and Herculaneum, as well as the many rich villas in the area. Since the mid-18th century these have been progressively uncovered and made accessible to the public. The vast expanse of the commercial town of Pompeii contrasts with the restricted but better preserved remains of the holiday resort of Herculaneum, whilst the superb wall paintings of the Villa Oplontis at Torre Annunziata give a vivid impression of the opulent life-style of the wealthier citizens of the early Roman Empire.
22 Villa Romana del Casale	C i, ii, iii	1997	Roman exploitation of the countryside is symbolised by the villa, the centre of the large estate upon which the rural economy of the Western Empire was based. In its 4th-century AD form, the Villa Romana del Casale is one of the most luxurious examples of this type of monument. It is especially noteworthy for the wealth and quality of the mosaics which decorate almost every room, and which are the finest still *in situ* anywhere in the Roman world.

23	Su Nuraxi di Barumini	C i, iii, iv	1997	During the late 2nd millennium BC, in the Bronze Age, a special type of defensive structure, known as *nuraghi*—for which no parallel exists anywhere else—developed on the island of Sardinia. The complex consists of circular defensive towers in the form of truncated cones built of dressed stone, with corbel-vaulted internal chambers. The complex at Barumini, which was extended and strengthened in the first half of the 1st millennium under Carthaginian pressure, is the finest and most complete example of this remarkable form of prehistoric architecture.
24	Portovenere, Cinque Terre, and the Islands (Palmaria, Tino, and Tinetto)	C ii, iv, v	1997	The Ligurian coastal region between Cinque Terre and Portovenere is a cultural landscape of high scenic and cultural value. The form and disposition of the small towns and the shaping of the landscape surrounding them—overcoming the disadvantages of a steep and broken terrain—graphically encapsulate the continuous history of human settlement in this region over the past millennium.
25	Costiera Amalfitana	C ii, iv, v	1997	The Amalfi coastal strip is one of great physical beauty and natural diversity. It has been intensively settled by human communities since the early Middle Ages. It contains a number of towns such as Amalfi and Ravello which contain architectural and artistic works of great significance, and its rural areas demonstrate the versatility of its occupants in adapting their utilisation of the terrain to suit its diversity, from terraced vineyards and orchards on the lower slopes to wide upland pastures.
26	Archaeological Area of Agrigento	C i, ii, iii, iv	1997	Founded as a Greek colony in the 6th century BC, Agrigento became one of the leading cities of the Mediterranean world. Its supremacy and pride are demonstrated by the remains of the magnificent Doric temples that dominate the ancient town, much of which remains intact under latter-day fields and orchards. Selected excavated areas throw light on the later Hellenic and Roman town and on the burial practices of its palaeochristian inhabitants.
27	Cilento and Vallo di Diano National Park with the Archeological sites of Paestum and Velia, and the Certosa di Padula	C iii, iv	1998	The Cilento area is a cultural landscape of exceptional quality. Dramatic chains of sanctuaries and settlements along its three east–west mountain ridges vividly portray the historical evolution of the area as a major route for trade and for cultural and political interaction during the prehistoric and medieval periods. It was also the boundary between the Greek colonies of Magna Grecia and the indigenous Etruscan and Lucanian peoples, and so preserves the remains of two very important classical cities, Paestum and Velia.
28	Historic Centre of Urbino	C ii, iv	1998	Urbino is a small hill town that experienced an astonishing cultural flowering in the 15th century, attracting artists and scholars from all over Italy and beyond, and influencing cultural developments elsewhere in Europe. Owing to its economic and cultural stagnation from the 16th century onwards, its Renaissance appearance has been remarkably well preserved.

Property	Criteria (see Appendix 1 for key)	Date of inscription (and of enlargements)	Brief description and reasons for inscription (from World Heritage List)
29 Archaeological Area and the Patriarchal Basilica of Aquileia	C iii, iv, vi	1998	Aquileia, one of the largest and wealthiest cities of the early Roman Empire, was destroyed by Attila in the mid-5th century. Most of it still remains unexcavated beneath fields, and as such it constitutes the greatest archaeological reserve of its kind. Its Patriarchal Basilica, an outstanding building with an exceptional mosaic pavement, also played a key role in the evangelisation of a large region of central Europe.
30 Villa Adriana (Tivoli)	C i, ii, iii	1999	Villa Adriana, an exceptional complex of classical buildings created in the 2nd century AD by the Roman Emperor Hadrian, reproduces the best elements of the material cultures of Egypt, Greece, and Rome in the form of an 'ideal city'.
31 Isole Eolie (Aeolian Islands)	N i	2000	The Aeolian Islands provide an outstanding record of volcanic island-building and destruction, and ongoing volcanic phenomena. Studied since at least the 18th century, the islands have provided the science of vulcanology with examples of two types of eruption (Vulcanian and Strombolian) and thus have featured prominently in the education of geologists for more than 200 years. The site continues to enrich the field of vulcanology.
32 Assisi, the Basilica of San Francesco and Other Franciscan Sites	C i, ii, iii, iv, vi	2000	Assisi, a medieval city built on a hill, is the birthplace of Saint Francis, closely associated with the work of the Franciscan Order. Its medieval art masterpieces, such as the Basilica of San Francesco and paintings by Cimabue, Pietro Lorenzetti, Simone Martini, and Giotto, have made Assisi a fundamental reference point for the development of Italian and European art and architecture.
33 City of Verona	C ii, iv	2000	The historic city of Verona was founded in the 1st century BC. It particularly flourished under the rule of the Scaliger family in the 13th and 14th centuries and as part of the Republic of Venice between the 15th and 18th centuries. Verona has preserved a remarkable number of monuments from antiquity, the medieval, and Renaissance periods, and represents an outstanding example of a military stronghold.
34[1] Historic Centre of Rome, the Properties of the Holy See in that City Enjoying Extraterritorial Rights and San Paolo Fuori le Mura	C i, ii, iv, vi	1980, 1990	Founded, according to legend, by Romulus and Remus in 753 BC, Rome was initially the centre of the Roman Republic, then of the Roman Empire, and it then became the capital of the Christian World in the 4th century. The World Heritage Site, extended in 1990 to the walls of Urban VIII, includes some of the major monuments of Antiquity such as the Augustus Mausoleum, the Hadrian Mausoleum, the Pantheon, the Marcus Aurelius Column, as well as the religious and public buildings of Papal Rome.

Note: [1] A property that falls within both Italy and the Holy See.

11.5   Spain

Introduction

Spain has many heritage sites similar to those found in France and Italy, from prehistoric cave art, through Greek and Roman colonies, to Romanesque and Gothic cathedrals, and 20th-century architecture. A major historical difference, however, stems from the long Moorish settlement of large sections of the country. The geography is also different. While Spain shares the Pyrénées with France and has other extensive mountainous areas, large areas of the country consist of semi-arid upland plateaus. Spain also has a number of islands for which it has administrative responsibilities, falling within the Balearic and Canary Island groups.

Cultural heritage

Cultural heritage is administered at the national level by the Sub-Directorate for Protection of the Historical Heritage (*Protección del Patrimonio Histórico*) of the Arts and Cultural Assets Directorate, which falls within the Ministry of Education and Culture. This sub-division is responsible for:

* producing and updating the Register of Assets of Cultural Interest (*Bienes de Interés Cultural*) and an Inventory of Moveable Objects
* evaluating items of interest for possible registration
* drawing up plans for the conservation and preservation of the Spanish Historical Heritage
* investigating and studying methods and techniques of conservation and preservation
* maintaining relevant archives and documentation
* cooperating with public (including provincial and city) bodies and private entities

The Spanish Historical Heritage is a list of items that are judged to possess historical, artistic, palaeontological, archaeological, ethnographic, scientific, or

Plate 11.18

Monasterio de la Oliva, Navarra, Spain. This small Cistercian monastery was built in the 12th century; it has a simple church, a 13th-century chapterhouse, and 15th-century cloisters.

Photo: Graeme Aplin

Plate 11.19

The 11th-century fortified
Moorish Palacio de la
Alfajería, Zaragoza,
Aragon, Spain. A courtyard
surrounds a sunken garden
and a small mosque.

Photo: Graeme Aplin

technical interest of national importance. They are included in the Heritage
Bibliography and Documentation, as well as on the Register of Assets of
Cultural Interest, of which they form a sub-set. The web site of the Sub-
Directorate for Protection of the Historical Heritage maintains that the history
of listings date back more than a hundred years. Two examples, found by the
author on a visit in 1999 were the Monasterio de la Oliva, listed in 1880 (Plate
11.18), and the Moorish Palacio de la Aljaferia in Zaragoza (Plate 11.19),
which was listed in 1931.

Groups of items or precincts can also be listed, such as the 'Historic
Artistic Area of the Old Quarter' in Hondaribbia. Listed in 1963, the
upper (old) town is protected by 15th-century walls, and contains narrow,
cobbled streets and alleys. As well as permanent listing (*código definitivo*),
there is the possibility of a restraining category (*anotación preventiva*). Legal
protection is granted to those items in the highest category on the register.
Many heritage buildings, including former castles, monasteries, and
palaces, are now completely or partially used as *paradors*, a network of
government-run hotels. It must also be stressed that, as in France and Italy,
much of the management, conservation, and restoration of both cultural
and natural heritage items is the responsibility of regional and municipal
governments, often with financial and other assistance from the national
government agencies.

Natural heritage

Legislation passed in 1989 on Conservation of Natural Spaces and of Native
Flora and Fauna established four categories of reserve: Parks, Nature Reserves,
Natural Monuments, and Protected Landscapes, many of which are
administered at provincial and communal levels. Eleven national parks
(*Parques Nacionales*) are administered by the national government (Figure
11.4), and of these, six are in mainland Spain and five on its islands (the

Balearics and Canaries). According to the legislation, a national park is:

> a natural area little transformed by human occupation and exploitation which, by reason of the beauty of its landscapes, the representativeness of its ecosystems, or the uniqueness of its flora, fauna or geomorphological formations, possesses important ecological, aesthetic, educational and scientific values whose conservation merits priority attention.

However, we must bear in mind that 'little transformed by human occupation and exploitation' might mean transformed to a significantly greater degree than would be acceptable in an Australian national park. Each national park has a 'Director–Conservator', assisted by specialised personnel in five major areas: conservation, public use, works and maintenance, security, and administration. Public and institutional participation is encouraged,

Figure 11.4

Spanish national parks and World Heritage properties

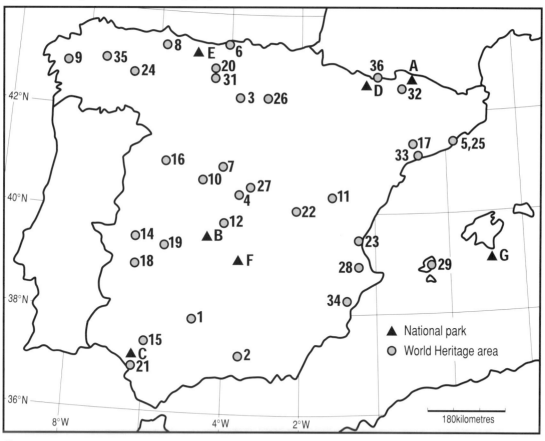

Key:

World Heritage areas

1–36: see Table 11.4.

National parks

A   Aigües Tortes y Estany de Sant Maurici

B   Cabañeros

C   Doñana

D   Ordesa y Monte Perdido

E   Picos de Europa

F   Las tables de Daimiel

G   PN Marítimo-Terrestre del Archipiélago de Cabrera

including that of people owning/occupying land within the park (again quite a different situation to that in Australia). National parks are normally zoned as follows: Reserved Zone (closed to the public); Zone of Restricted Use; Zone of Moderate Use; and Zones of Special Use (containing services essential for the park's operation and for visitors).

Spanish World Heritage properties

Spain has thirty-five World Heritage properties and one shared with France (the Pyrénées). The Pyrénées are listed for both natural and cultural reasons, as is Ibiza, a small island in the Balearic group. Two of Spain's national parks are listed for natural reasons: Garajonay on one of the Canary Islands, and Doñana in Andalusia on the mainland. Nevertheless, Spanish World Heritage properties are predominantly listed because they meet one or more of the cultural criteria (Table 11.4 and Figure 11.4). Cultural properties include the highly significant prehistoric art site of Altamira; Roman gold mines (Las Médulas); a number of monasteries; and Moorish sites in Granada and Tereul. Barcelona boasts one of the few World Heritage properties anywhere to honour the work of a late 19th and early 20th century architect, the brilliant but decidedly eccentric Antoni Gaudí (Plate 11.20). An English-language web site (see Appendix 2) introduces a group of historic Spanish cities with World Heritage status (Ávila, Cáceres, Córdoba, Cuenca, Salamanca, Santiago de Compostela, Segovia, and Toledo).

Plate 11.20

House in the Parc Güell development (1910–14) designed by Antoni Gaudí, one of a group of sites in Barcelona, Spain, which collectively form a World Heritage property.

Photo: Graeme Aplin

Table 11.4

Spanish World Heritage properties

	Property	Criteria (see Appendix 1 for key)	Date of inscription (and of enlargements)	Brief description and reasons for inscription (from World Heritage List)
1	Historic Centre of Cordoba	C i, ii, iii, iv	1984, 1994	Cordoba's glorious period began in the 8th century when, conquered by the Moors, some 300 mosques, innumerable palaces and public buildings were constructed to rival the splendours of Constantinople, Damascus and Baghdad. In the 13th century, under Ferdinand III the Saint, Cordoba's Great Mosque was turned into a Cathedral and new defensive structures, particularly the Alcazar de los Reyes Cristianos and the Torre Fortaleza de la Calahorra, were erected.
2	Alhambra, Generalife, and Albayzin, Granada	C i, iii, iv	1984, 1994	Rising above the modern lower town, the Alhambra and the Albayzin placed on two adjacent hills, form the medieval part of Granada. To the east of the Alhambra fortress and residence are the magnificent gardens of the Generalife, the former rural residence of the Emirs who ruled this part of Spain in the 13th and 14th centuries. The Albayzin, a residential quarter, is a rich repository of Moorish vernacular architecture, into which the traditional Andalusian architecture blends harmoniously.
3	Burgos Cathedral	C ii, iv, vi	1984	Begun in the 13th century, at the same time as the great cathedrals of the Île-de-France, and completed in the 15th and 16th centuries, Our Lady of Burgos sums up Gothic architecture in all its beauty with a unique collection of reredos, tombs, choir, stalls, stained glass, etc.
4	Monastery and Site of the Escurial, Madrid	C i, ii, vi	1984	Built at the end of the 16th century on a plan in the form of a grill, the instrument of the martyrdom of Saint Lawrence, the Escurial Monastery sits on an exceptionally beautiful site in Castile. The austere style of its architecture, a break with previous styles, had a considerable influence on Spain for more than half a century. It was the retreat of a mystic King and was, in the last years of Philippe II's reign, the centre of the greatest political power of the time.
5	Parque Güell, Palacio Güell and Casa Mila, Barcelona	C i, ii, iv	1984	Truly universal works in view of the diverse cultural sources from which they are inspired, the creations of Antoni Gaudí (1852–1926) in Barcelona represent an eclectic as well as very personal architectural style which led to new styles, not only as regards architectural style but also for gardens, sculpture, and all forms of decorative art.

Property	Criteria (see Appendix 1 for key)	Date of inscription (and of enlargements)	Brief description and reasons for inscription (from World Heritage List)
6 Altamira Cave	C i, iii	1985	This prehistoric site in the province of Santander was inhabited in the Aurignacian period and then in the Solutrean and Magdalenian periods. Most of the stone implements and, in particular, the famous paintings in the great chamber, in ochre, red, and black tones and depicting a variety of wild animals—bisons, horses, fawns and wild boars—date from this latter period.
7 Old Town of Segovia and its Aqueduct	C i, iii, iv	1985	The Roman aqueduct of Segovia, probably built around 50 AD, is remarkably well preserved. This impressive construction, with its two tiers of arches, forms part of the setting of the magnificent historic city of Segovia, where one can also visit the Alcazar, begun around the 11th century, and the 16th-century Gothic cathedral.
8 Monuments of Oviedo and the Kingdom of the Asturias	C i, ii, iv	1985, 1998	In the 9th century the flame of Christianity was kept alive in the Iberian peninsula in the tiny Kingdom of the Asturias, where an innovative form of pre-Romanesque architectural style was created, which was to play a significant role in the development of the religious architecture of the peninsula. Its highest achievements can be seen in the churches of Santa Maria del Naranco, San Miguel de Lillo, Santa Cristina de Lena, the Cámara Santa, and San Julián de los Prados, in and around the ancient capital city of Oviedo. Associated with them is the remarkable contemporary hydraulic engineering structure known as La Foncalada.
9 Old Town of Santiago de Compostela	C i, ii, vi	1985	This famous pilgrimage site in the north-west of Spain became a symbol in the Spanish Christians' struggle against Islam. Destroyed by the Moslems at the end of the 10th century, it was completely rebuilt in the following century. The Old Town of Santiago forms one of the world's most beautiful urban areas with Romanesque, Gothic, and Baroque buildings. The oldest monuments are grouped around St James' tomb and the Cathedral which contains the remarkable Pórtico de la Gloria.
10 Old Town of Avila with its Extra-muros Churches	C iii, iv	1985	Founded in the 11th century to protect the Spanish territories from the Moors, this 'City of Saints and Stones,' the birthplace of Saint Theresa and the burial ground of the Great Inquisitor Torquemada, has kept its medieval austerity. This purity of form can still be seen in its Gothic cathedral and its fortifications which, with eighty-two semi-circular towers and nine gates, are the most complete in Spain.

11	Mudejar Architecture of Teruel	C iv	1986	Remains of an era when, until the 15th century, Christian, Jewish, and Moslems lived in harmony, the four towers of Teruel—especially San Salvador and San Martin, built respectively at the end of the 12th and the beginning of the 13th centuries—form a characteristic complex of mudéjar architecture following the Reconquest. The Christian churches used the structure and decor of Almohades minarets, adapting them to their new functions.
12	Historic City of Toledo	C i, ii, iii, iv	1986	Successively a Roman municipium, the capital of the Visigothic kingdom, a fortress of the Emirate of Cordoba, an outpost of the Christian kingdoms fighting the Moors and, in the 16th century, the temporary seat of the supreme power under Charles V, Toledo is the keeper of more than two millennia of history. Its masterpieces are the product of heterogeneous civilisations in an environment where the existence of three major religions—Judaism, Christianity, and Islam—was a major factor.
13	Garajonay National Park	N ii, iii	1986	Laurel forest covers some 70 per cent of the park located in the centre of the Island of La Gomera in the Canary Islands archipelago. The presence of springs and numerous streams assures a lush vegetation resembling that of the Tertiary period which, due to climatic changes, has largely disappeared from southern Europe.
14	Old Town of Caceres	C iii, iv	1986	The city's history of battles between Moors and Christians is reflected in its architecture which is a blend of Roman, Islamic, Northern Gothic, and Italian Renaissance styles. From the Moslem period remain about thirty towers, of which the Torre del Bujaco is the most famous.
15	Cathedral, Alcazar and Archivo de Indias, in Seville	C i, ii, iii, vi	1987	Together these three buildings comprise a remarkable monumental complex at the heart of Seville. The Cathedral and the Alcazar are an exceptional testimony to the civilisation of the Almohades as well as of Christian Andalusia, dating from the reconquest of 1248 to the 16th century and thoroughly imbued with Moorish influences. The Giralda minaret, masterpiece of Almohad architecture, next to the cathedral with five naves, is the largest Gothic edifice in Europe, and contains the tomb of Christopher Columbus. The ancient Lonja, which became the Archivo de Indias, contains valuable documents from the archives of the colonies in the Americas.

Property	Criteria (see Appendix 1 for key)	Date of inscription (and of enlargements)	Brief description and reasons for inscription (from World Heritage List)
16 Old City of Salamanca	C i, ii, iv	1988	This ancient university town north-west of Madrid was first conquered by the Carthaginians in the 3rd century BC. It then became a Roman settlement before being ruled by the Moors until the 11th century. The University, one of the most ancient in Europe, reached its height during Salamanca's Golden Age. The city's historic centre has important Romanesque, Gothic, Moorish, Renaissance, and Baroque monuments. The Plaza Mayor, with its galleries and arcades, is particularly impressive.
17 Poblet Monastery	C i, iv	1991	Located in Catalonia, this Cistercian abbey, one of the largest in Spain, surrounds its 12th-century church. The majestic severity of the monastery, which is associated with a fortified royal residence and contains the pantheon of the kings of Catalonia and Aragon, is an impressive sight.
18 Archaeological Ensemble of Mérida	C iii, iv	1993	The colony of Augusta Emerita, which became present-day Mérida in the Estremadura, was founded in 25 BC, at the end of the Spanish Campaign, and was the capital of Lusitania. The remains of the old city, complete and well-preserved, include, in particular, a large bridge over the Guadiana, an amphitheatre, a theatre, a vast circus, and an exceptional water supply system. It is an excellent example of a provincial Roman capital during the Empire and in the years following.
19 Royal Monastery of Santa Maria de Guadalupe	C iv, vi	1993	The monastery, an exceptional illustration of four centuries of Spanish religious architecture, symbolises two significant events in world history that occurred in 1492: the reconquest of the Iberian peninsula by the Catholic kings, and Christopher Columbus' arrival in the Americas. Its famous statue of the Virgin became a powerful symbol of the Christianisation of much of the New World.
20 The Route of Santiago de Compostela	C ii, iv, vi	1993	Proclaimed the first European Cultural Capital by the Council of Europe, this is the route, from the French–Spanish border, which was—and still is—taken by pilgrims to Santiago de Compostela. Some 1800 buildings along the route, both religious and secular, are of great historic interest. The route played a fundamental role in facilitating cultural exchanges between the Iberian peninsula and the rest of Europe during the Middle Ages. It remains a testimony to the power of Christian faith in people of all social classes and all over Europe.

	Name	Year	Criteria	Description
21	Doñana National Park	1994	N ii, iii, iv	Located in Andalusia, Doñana National Park occupies the right bank of the Guadalquivir River at its estuary on the Atlantic Ocean. It is notable for the great diversity of its biotopes, especially lagoons, marshlands, fixed and mobile dunes, scrub woodland, and 'maquis'. It is home to five threatened bird species. It is one of the biggest heronries in the Mediterranean region and is the wintering site for more than 500 000 water fowls each year.
22	Historic Walled Town of Cuenca	1996	C ii, v	Built by the Moors on a defensive position in the heart of the Caliphate of Córdoba, Cuenca is a very well-preserved fortified medieval city. Conquered by the Castilians in the 12th century, it became a royal town and bishopric rich with major buildings, such as Spain's first Gothic cathedral, and the famous *casas colgadas* (hanging houses), suspended from sheer cliffs overlooking the Huécar River. Admirably making the most of its location, the city crowns the magnificent countryside surrounding it.
23	La Lonja de la Seda de Valencia	1996	C i, iv	Built between 1482 and 1533, this group of buildings, originally used for trading in silk (hence its name, The Silk Exchange), has, especially in its strikingly grandiose *Sala de Contratación* (Contract or Trading Hall), always been a place of commerce. A masterpiece of Late Gothic, it illustrates the power and wealth of a major Mediterranean mercantile city of the 15th and 16th centuries.
24	Las Médulas	1997	C i, ii, iii, iv	In the 1st century AD the Roman Imperial authorities began to exploit the gold deposits of this region in north-west Spain, using a technique based on the utilisation of hydraulic power. After two centuries of working the deposits, the Romans withdrew, leaving a devastated landscape. Since there was no subsequent industrial activity, the dramatic traces of this remarkable ancient technology are everywhere visible, in the form of sheer faces in the mountainsides and vast areas of tailings, now in use for agriculture.
25	The Palau de la Música Catalana and the Hospital de Sant Pau, Barcelona	1997	C i, ii, iv	These are two of the finest contributions to the architecture of Barcelona by the Catalan Art Nouveau architect Lluís Domènech i Montaner. The Palau de la Música Catalana is an exuberant steel-framed structure full of light and space, and decorated by many of the leading designers of the day. The Hospital de Sant Pau is equally bold in its design and decoration, while at the same time perfectly adapted for the needs of the sick.

Property	Criteria (see Appendix 1 for key)	Date of inscription (and of enlargements)	Brief description and reasons for inscription (from World Heritage List)
26 San Millán Yuso and Suso Monasteries	C ii, iv, vi	1997	The monastic community founded by St Millán in the mid 6th century became a place of pilgrimage, and a fine Romanesque church was built in honour of the holy man, which still survives at the Suso site. It was here that the first literature was produced in the Castilian tongue, from which one of the most widely spoken languages in the world today is derived. In the early 16th century the community was housed in a fine new monastery, Yuso, below the older complex, and continues in active use up to the present day.
27 University and Historic Precinct of Alcalá de Henares	C ii, iv, vi	1998	Alcalá de Henares was the first planned university city in the world, founded by Cardinal Ximénez de Cisneros in the early 16th century. It was the original model for the Civitas Dei (City of God), the ideal urban community which Spanish missionaries brought to the Americas, and also for universities in Europe and beyond.
28 Rock-Art of the Mediterranean Basin on the Iberian Peninsula	C iii	1998	The late prehistoric rock-art sites of the Mediterranean seaboard of the Iberian peninsula form an exceptionally large group in which the way of life in a critical phase of human development is vividly and graphically depicted in paintings that are unique in style and subject matter.
29 Ibiza, Biodiversity and Culture	N ii, iv; C ii, iii, iv	1999	Ibiza gives an excellent example of the interaction between the marine and coastal ecosystems. The dense prairies of oceanic *Posidonia* (sea grass), an important endemic species found only in the Mediterranean basin, contain and support a diversity of marine life. Ibiza preserves considerable evidence of its long history. The archaeological sites at Sa Caleta (settlement) and Puig des Molins (cemetery) testify to the important role played by the island in the Mediterranean economy in protohistory, particularly during the Phoenician–Carthaginian period. The fortified Upper Town (Alta Vila) is an outstanding example of Renaissance military architecture, which had a profound influence on the development of fortifications in the Spanish settlements of the New World.
30 San Cristóbal de La Laguna	C ii, iv	1999	San Cristóbal de La Laguna (on the Canary Islands) has two nuclei, the original unplanned Upper Town, and the Lower Town, the first ideal 'city-territory' laid out according to philosophical principles. Its wide streets and open spaces contain a number of fine churches and public and private buildings from the 16th to 18th centuries.

31	Archaeological Site of Atapuerca	C iii, v	2000	The caves of the Sierra de Atapuerca contain a rich fossil record of the earliest human beings in Europe, from nearly one million years ago and extending up to the current day. They represent an exceptional reserve of data, the scientific study of which provides priceless information about the appearance and the way of life of these remote human ancestors.
32	Catalan Romanesque Churches	C iii, iv	2000	The narrow Vall de Boí valley, is situated in the high Pyrénées, in the Alta Ribagorça region and is surrounded by steep mountains. Each village in the valley contains a Romanesque church, and is surrounded by a pattern of enclosed fields. There are extensive seasonally used grazing lands on the higher slopes.
33	The Archaeological Ensemble of Tárraco	C ii, iii	2000	Tárraco (modern-day Tarragona) was a major administrative and mercantile city in Roman Spain and the centre of the Imperial cult for all the Iberian provinces. It was endowed with many fine buildings, and parts of these have been revealed in a series of exceptional excavations. Although most of the remains are fragmentary, many preserved beneath more recent buildings, they present a vivid picture of the grandeur of this Roman provincial capital.
34	Palmeral of Elche	C ii, v	2000	The Palmeral of Elche, a landscape of groves of date palms, was formally laid out, with elaborate irrigation systems, during the Arab occupation of much of the Iberian peninsula, starting in the 8th century AD. However, there is evidence that their origins are much older, dating back to the Phoenician and Roman settlement of the region. The Palmeral is a unique example of Arab agricultural practices on the European continent.
35	The Roman Walls of Lugo	C iv	2000	The walls of Lugo were built in the later part of the 2nd century to defend the Roman town of Lucus. The entire circuit survives intact and is the finest example of late Roman fortifications in western Europe.
36[1]	Pyrénées-Mount Perdu	N i, iii; C iii, iv, v	1997, 1999	This outstanding mountain landscape, which spans the contemporary national borders of France and Spain, is centred around the peak of Mount Perdu, a calcareous massif that rises 3352 metres. The site, with a total area of 30 639 hectares, includes two of Europe's largest and deepest canyons on the Spanish side and three major cirque walls on the more abrupt northern slopes with France, classic presentations of these geologic landforms. But the site is also a pastoral landscape reflecting an agricultural way of life that was once widespread in the upland regions of Europe. It has survived unchanged into the 20th century only in this part of the Pyrénées, providing exceptional insights into past European society through its landscape of villages, farms, fields, upland pastures, and mountain roads.

Note: [1] A property that falls within both France and Spain.

11.6   Ireland

Introduction

The Republic of Ireland has a remarkable amount of heritage accessible to visitors for such a small nation. These span time from the prehistoric, through the early Celtic Christian period, to the Anglo-Norman and later English occupations of much of the country. Despite the often tragic history of the nation, it seems that all of this heritage is displayed without any particular rancour or bitterness. There is also considerable natural heritage, including some stunningly beautiful scenery in the west. Unusually, at least for the group of countries dealt with thus far, the one national government agency administers and cares for all heritage, natural and cultural, with minimal involvement by lower levels of government.

Cultural and natural heritage

The government body responsible for major cultural and natural heritage sites in the Republic of Ireland used to be the Office of Public Works (OPW), the function of which is equivalent to the Public Works Department in Australia. In July 1996, following the passage of the *Heritage Act 1995,* responsibility for all types of heritage was brought under a new body called Dúchas—The Heritage Service, within the Department of Arts, Heritage, Gaeltacht and the Islands. (*Dúchas* is translated in Irish–English dictionaries as 'heritage, birthright, patrimony, native place, natural state and homeland'.) The Act also established the Heritage Council as an independent body with 'a statutory responsibility to propose policies and priorities for the identification, protection, preservation and enhancement of the national heritage'. It is actively involved in the planning process when heritage issues are involved.

Cultural heritage of national significance is administered under the *National Monuments Act 1930* and amendments made in 1954, 1987, and 1999. Preservation orders can be made under the Act if any national monument appears endangered, transferring its control to the Dúchas. Wildlife conservation and protection, and the management of nature reserves, come under the *Wildlife Act 1976*, and the management of national parks under the *State Authorities, Development and Management Act 1993.* The OPW was originally responsible for national monuments, national parks and gardens, wildlife, and inland waterways. All of these functions have now been transferred to Dúchas, which has three major divisions: National Parks and Wildlife; National Monuments and Historic Properties; and Waterways. Dúchas also maintains the National Inventory of Architectural Heritage, the Archaeological Survey of Ireland, and the Inventory of Natural Heritage Areas in Ireland. These three 'registers' notify owners, developers, and local government of the importance of sites and may provide the basis for planning decision or legal action.

Sites administered by Dúchas cover a wide range of types. A small group are designated as National Historic Monuments (including Castletown House, Plate 11.21), but others include prehistoric sites (such as the Dromberg Stone Circle, Plate 11.22), Anglo-Irish castles, and Celtic monastic sites such as Glendalough (Plate 2.8). Many of the sites are open to the public, and the service operates some very good visitor centres at sites such as Glendalough and Brú na Bóinne (Newgrange). Nevertheless, the group of sites administered by Dúchas is still relatively restricted, and much of the practical conservation of built heritage beyond this lies with local planning laws and regulations, as it does in Australia and in the United Kingdom.

Dúchas is responsible for managing all lands reserved for conservation purposes, including national parks and nature reserves, totalling approximately 80 000 hectares in March 1998. According to their publication, *Dúchas The Heritage Service: A Guide*:

> National parks exist to conserve natural plant and animal communities and scenic landscapes which are both extensive and of national importance and, under conditions compatible with that purpose, to enable the public to visit and appreciate them.[2]

According to the IUCN criteria, national parks in Ireland fall into Category 2 ('National Park'): 'protected area managed mainly for ecosystem protection and recreation'. In contrast, national parks in the United Kingdom fall into Category 5 ('Protected Landscape/Seascape'): 'protected area managed mainly for landscape/seascape conservation and recreation'. This means that Irish national parks have some human activity unrelated to the parks' key roles, and some permanent residents within their boundaries, but these aspects are certainly less prominent than they are in the United Kingdom. In late 1999 there were six national parks (Figure 11.5): Killarney, Connemara, Glenveagh, Wicklow Mountains, Mayo, and The Burren (Plate 11.23).

The main voluntary organisation involved in heritage in Ireland is An Taisce—The National Trust for Ireland. It was founded in 1948 'to advance the conservation and management of Ireland's natural and built environment in manners which are sustainable'. Thus, it was active before there was any major government involvement in the heritage area. An Taisce has about 5000 members, and carries out the following functions: provision of advice on environment-related and heritage-related policy; lobbying the government and other bodies; input to development plans; reviewing planning applications and environmental impact assessments; and providing educational programs.

Plate 11.21

Castletown House, Celbridge, Co. Kildare, Ireland. This Palladian house, 1722–32, with interiors from the second half of the 18th century is an example of a cultural heritage site administered by Dúchas.

Photo: Graeme Aplin

Plate 11.22

Drombeg Stone Circle
(c.150 BC), Co. Cork,
Ireland, administered by
Dúchas.

Photo: Graeme Aplin

Figure 11.5

Irish national parks and World Heritage properties

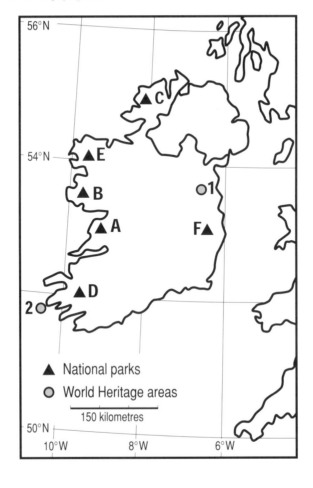

Key:

World Heritage areas

1–2: see Table 11.5.

National parks

A The Burren

B Connemara

C Glenveagh

D Killarney

E Mayo

F Wicklow Mountains

Irish World Heritage properties

By the end of 2000 there were only two properties in the Republic of Ireland that were inscribed on the WHL (Table 11.5): the Archaeological Ensemble of the Bend of the Boyne and Skellig Michael, an ancient monastic complex on a rocky island. Dúchas is responsible for administering and protecting these sites.

Plate 11.23

Limestone pavement, The Burren National Park, Co. Clare, Ireland. This is a typical surface scene on the vast limestone plateau of The Burren. There are very few trees, but many smaller rare and/or endemic plants. These are now under threat from cattle grazing the area.

Photo: Graeme Aplin

Table 11.5

Republic of Ireland World Heritage properties

Property	Criteria (see Appendix 1 for key)	Date of inscription (and of enlargements)	Brief description and reasons for inscription (from World Heritage List)
1 Archaeological Ensemble of the Bend of the Boyne	C i, iii, iv	1993	This is the largest and most important expression of prehistoric megalithic art in Europe, with its concentration of monuments with social, economic, and funerary functions.
2 Skellig Michael	C iii, iv	1996	This monastic complex, perched, since about the 7th century, on the steep sides of the rocky island of Skellig Michael a dozen kilometres off the coast of south-west Ireland, illustrates the very spartan existence of the first Irish Christians. The extreme remoteness of Skellig Michael has until recently discouraged visitation allowing thus an exceptional state of preservation.

11.7   The European Union

Since European unity began, increasing attempts have been made to achieve a degree of uniformity—in many areas, including heritage conservation—across member states by the centralised, and increasingly powerful, European body. Initially the group of nations forming this body was called the EC, but following the Maastricht Treaty, this was superseded by the EU, which includes fifteen European nations (in mid-2001). The EU has provided considerable financial support to important conservation projects (see for example Plate 3.2), and a number of EC and EU instruments have been concerned with various aspects of heritage, including *75/65/EEC: Commission Recommendation of 20 December 1974 to Member States concerning the protection of the architectural and natural heritage*; and, more recently, the *Council Directive 92/43/EEC of 21 May 1992 on the conservation of natural habitats and of wild fauna and flora.*

The EU has also been responsible for a number of heritage programs across its member states. One recent example was *Natura 2000*, a plan to preserve biodiversity by maintaining or re-establishing a state of conservation favourable to preserving natural habitats and habitats of flora and fauna of particular concern to the Community (significant at a scale between the national and the global). Lists of important sites have been drawn up and divided among a number of biogeographical regions in order to achieve a coverage of all important ecosystem types. After a false start in 1996, the project eventually got underway in August 1997. The EU relied on national cooperation and nomination of sites. The first list drawn up in early 1998 contained 543 proposed sites, representing 901 490 hectares, or 1.6 per cent of the land surface of EU member states.

The effect of EU involvement is that member states have a further level of heritage concern imposed between the national and global levels. Just as all national governments have to take into consideration global treaties and conventions (see Chapter 8), many European nations must also take into account EU directives and instruments, and administer them within their own national territory. National laws often need to be passed or amended to allow national compliance with supra-national demands.

Notes

[1]   Apart from anything else, the depth and breadth of coverage are severely limited by the author's restricted personal experience in these countries; a limited and in some cases virtually non-existent command of the languages involved; and the availability of information.

[2]   Dúchas (1998) *Dúchas The Heritage Service: A Guide,* Dublin, p. 14.

Further Reading

Updated information on changes to legislation and bureaucratic structures is available at the web site associated with this book, at http://www.es.mq.edu.au/courses/REM/heritage.htm.

Antoine, S. (1987) *Promouvoir le Patrimoine Français pour l'An 2000*, Caisse Nationale des Monuments Historiques et des Sites, Paris.

Bailey, R. (ed.) (1994) *Eyewitness Travel Guides: France*, Dorling Kindersley, London.*

Béghain, P. (1998) *Le Patrimoine: Culture et Lien Social*, Presses de Sciences Politique, Paris.

Botting, D. (2000) *Escape to Wild France: A Travellers Guide*, Interlink Books, New York.

Botting, D. (2000) *Wild Britain: A Travellers Guide*, Interlink Books, New York.

Bown, D. (1996) *Eyewitness Travel Guides: Italy*, Dorling Kindersley, London.*

Bown, D. (1996) *Eyewitness Travel Guides: Spain*, Dorling Kindersley, London.*

Brennan, E (ed.) (1990) *Heritage: A Visitor's Guide*, The Office of Public Works/Stationery Office, Dublin.

Bromwich, J. (1993) *The Roman Remains of Southern France: A Guidebook*, Routledge, London.

Busselle, M. (1997) *Discovering Spain: A Comprehensive Traveller's Guide Featuring the National Parador Hotels*, Pavilion Books, London.

Constable, N. & Farrington, K. (1997) *Ireland*, Sunburst Books, London.

Delaforce, P. (1995) *The Nature Parks of France*, Windrush Press, Moreton-in-Marsh.

Department of Arts, Culture and the Gaeltacht (1996) *A Report Submitted to the Minister for Arts, Culture and the Gaeltacht and the Minister for the Environment by the Inter-Departmental Working Group on Strengthening the Protection of the Architectural Heritage*, Stationery Office, Dublin.

Dúchas (1998) *Dúchas The Heritage Service: A Guide*, Department of Arts, Culture, Gaeltacht and the Islands, Dublin.

English Heritage (1999) *The English Heritage Visitor's Handbook 1999–2000*, English Heritage, London.

Gerard-Sharp, L. & Perry, T. (1995) *Eyewitness Travel Guides: Ireland*, Dorling Kindersley, London.*

Grunfeld, F. V. (2000) *Wild Spain: A Travellers Guide*, Interlink Books, New York.

Hedgecoe, J. & Souden, D. (1997) *England's World Heritage*, English Heritage/Collins & Brown, London.

Historic Scotland (no date) *Historic Scotland: The Sites to See—A Guide to over 300 Historic Sites Spanning 5000 Years*, Historic Scotland, Edinburgh.

Larkham, P. J. (1996) *Conservation and the City*, Routledge, London.

Leapman, M. (1995) *Eyewitness Travel Guides: Great Britain*, Dorling Kindersley, London.*

National Trust (1999) *The National Trust Handbook for Members and Visitors 1999*, National Trust, Bromley, Kent.

National Trust for Scotland (1999) *Guide to Scotland's Best: Descriptions and Colour Photographs of all National Trust for Scotland Properties Open to the Public*, NTS, Edinburgh.

Scarre, C. (1998) *Exploring Prehistoric Europe*, Oxford University Press, New York.

Note: * The guidebooks in this series are of particular relevance because of their accurate and thorough treatment of heritage sites, many of which have superb illustrations.

CHAPTER 12

Regulatory Frameworks and Approaches to Heritage: Some Other Countries

12.1   Introduction

This chapter follows in the same pattern as the previous one, but deals with the approaches to heritage recognition and protection of countries outside Australia and Europe. Obviously the coverage can be only partial, and can no more than highlight a few key issues related to the general themes of this book and to earlier chapters. Again, material presented here should be seen as illustrating the issues discussed in Chapters 1 to 8.

The nations represented in this chapter—New Zealand, the USA, South Africa, China, and Thailand—are very diverse. Like Australia, the first three were formerly English colonies, heavily influenced by European settlers. However in South Africa (unlike the other two) the majority population is non-European, and this has had a noticeable effect on heritage perceptions and management procedures. It should also be noted that South Africa has only very recently begun to construct a comprehensive heritage management system, something that could not be done under the previous political situation when a powerful minority tried to impose the heritage of Europeans, and predominantly Afrikaaners, on the whole of the nation's population, something the majority clearly never accepted. On the other hand, China and Thailand have never been colonies in the accepted sense, although each of these nations has pockets of built and cultural heritage influenced by Europeans. The Asian nations are touched on quite briefly, mainly due to limitations in the availability of official literature and web sites in English.

12.2   New Zealand

Background

New Zealand (NZ) is similar to Australia in many aspects of its general historical and cultural background (see Section 9.2), but is quite different in political terms. It is not a federation and, although regional governments do have a strong role in planning, including heritage planning and management, the regions are nowhere near as strong or autonomous as the Australian states. The Māori role in national and local politics and administration has been longer established and is more formalised and embedded in law than the Aboriginal role in Australia. NZ is also noteworthy in that, in 1991, it brought many Acts of Parliament dealing with environmental issues, including heritage issues, under one consolidated act, the *Resource Management Act 1991* (RMA), a model that has since been followed to a large degree by Australia (see Section 9.6).

Heritage management

The key Acts for NZ heritage management are the RMA (as amended—especially Part VIII); the *Historic Places Act 1993*; the *Conservation Act 1987*; the *Reserves Act 1977*; and the *National Parks Act 1980*. Cultural heritage places are listed by the non-government New Zealand Historic Places Trust (NZHPT), which plays a similar role to the National Trusts in Australia and the United Kingdom. However, unlike the situation in those countries, it is the official listing body for much cultural heritage and its role is enshrined in legislation: it was set up under the *Historic Places Act 1954* and more recently has been given legislative backing in Part VIII of the RMA. The NZHPT has an eleven-member Board and an eight-member Māori Heritage Council, and receives about three-quarters of its funding from the government. Like the Trusts in Australia and the United Kingdom, it also has members and manages properties, many of which are open to the public (see for example Plates 4.1 and 4.2) and which provide additional revenue. As well as maintaining the register, the NZHPT owns about 60 properties, provides conservation advocacy and advice, and oversees archaeological sites.

The RMA also recognises the following 'heritage protection authorities': the Minister for Conservation, the Minister for Māori Affairs, local authorities (generally the regional councils), and other approved 'bod[ies] corporate having an interest in the protection of any place'. In September 1999, the administration of the NZHPT and the Historic Places Act were transferred from the Department of Conservation to the new Ministry for Culture and Heritage, introducing a more obvious division between cultural and natural heritage.

Under the RMA, heritage orders may be made to protect:

a any place of special interest, character, intrinsic or amenity value or visual appeal, or of special significance to the *tāngata whenua* (traditional owners) for spiritual, cultural, or historical reasons; and

b such area of land (if any) surrounding that place as is reasonably necessary for the purpose of ensuring the protection and reasonable enjoyment of that place.

For these purposes, a place may be of special interest by having special cultural, architectural, historical, scientific, ecological, or other interest. If a heritage order is made over land in a district plan, consent from the relevant heritage protection authority must be obtained before undertaking any development likely to affect the heritage values. Listings on the NZHPT-maintained register in 1997 comprised 4676 buildings (see for example Plate

12.1), 1012 archaeological sites, 90 historic areas, 12 *waahi tapu* (sacred sites), and 4 *waahi tapu* areas.[1] Heritage areas include the Art Deco business district of Napier, while many buildings in central Dunedin are listed and are now well preserved (Plate 12.2).

Plate 12.1

Old Parliament House (1876), Wellington, New Zealand: section of main façade of what is the second largest wooden building in the world, made to simulate stone.

Photos: Helen Dimas

Plate 12.2

The Norman-Gothic First Presbyterian Church (1868–73), Dunedin, Otago, New Zealand. The soaring spire is particularly notable. Dunedin has many other fine public buildings dating from the late 19th century, often built from dark volcanic stone.

Photo: Graeme Aplin

The Department of Conservation (DOC)—also known by its Māori name, *Te Papa Atawhai*, which very appropriately means 'to care for a treasure chest'—was set up in 1987 under the Conservation Act, and is dedicated to:

- protecting New Zealand's natural and historic heritage
- providing opportunities for people to use and enjoy the lands and waters under its care—but carefully and with respect
- acting as a voice for conservation in the community and in government

The activities of the DOC include conserving biodiversity, caring for the coast, catering for recreation and tourism, managing protected lands, and servicing the NZHPT. More specifically, the DOC administers national, maritime, and forest parks, farm parks, wilderness areas, more than a thousand reserves of different kinds (for example, scenic reserves), marginal strips around lakes and rivers, and other protected areas—in all covering almost one-third of the country. It also promotes the protection of natural and historic values on privately owned land, in conjunction with semi-independent bodies such as the NZHPT and the Queen Elizabeth II National Trust for Open Space in New Zealand (*Nga Kairauhi Papa*). The latter acts as a permanent trustee to protect privately owned land under covenants, and, by late 1991, this amounted to over 100 000 hectares. The DOC also has responsibility for historic sites on conservation properties.

In certain cases, private trusts are also important. One example is the Otago Peninsula Trust, formed in 1972 to protect the royal albatross colony on Taiaroa Head. The Trust now allows public access to a visitor centre, which has very informative static and audio-visual displays. Visitors in small groups are taken by guides, under strictly enforced conditions, into the fenced-off reserve and to an observatory overlooking the colony's breeding grounds. Numbers of visitors are strictly limited by the requirement that tickets must be pre-purchased in Dunedin.

There are thirteen national parks in NZ (Figure 12.1). Many of these are on the rugged West Coast of the South Island, forming an almost continuous sweep of protected areas along the length of the coast, which includes NZ's largest World Heritage property. The highest peak in the Southern Alps, Mount Cook, and a number of major glaciers, including the Tasman Glacier, are included in Aoraki/Mount Cook National Park (Plate 12.3), while two large, well-known glaciers that are relatively easy to visit, the Franz Josef and the Fox, are included in the Westland/Tai Poutini National Park (Plate 12.4). Key features of the late 1999 Draft Management Plan for the Westland/Tai Poutini National Park are given in Box 12.1. The World Heritage property that covers the area of the two parks (and others) is mentioned again in the next section. Two key North Island national parks—Egmont National Park and Tongariro National Park—conserve extensive areas of volcanic landscapes centred on dormant and very recently active volcanoes.

Box 12.1 Westland/Tai Poutini National Park—Draft Management Plan

The Preface to this Plan indicates the framework within which it was drawn up and is thus worth quoting at some length.

> The management plan for Westland/Tai Poutini National Park has been reviewed in accordance with the procedures set out in Section 47 of the National Parks Act 1980 ... This draft management plan has been

prepared by the West Coast Conservancy of the Department of Conservation in consultation with the Canterbury Conservancy, representatives from Te Rūnanga o Ngāi Tahu, the West Coast/Tai Poutini Conservation Board, the Canterbury Conservation Board and other interested groups and individuals.

The plan acknowledges mana whenua[1] and tāngata whenua[2] status of Ngāi Tahu over their ancestral lands and waters within the park … This requires the Department to give effect to the Ngāi Tahu Claims Settlement Act 1998, the Ngāi Tahu Deed of Settlement 1997 and the principles of the Treaty of Waitangi, to the extent that they are not inconsistent with the principles of the National Parks Act 1980.

The primary objectives of the draft management plan are:

- To preserve in their natural state in perpetuity the landscape, natural ecological systems, and natural features of Westland/Tai Poutini National Park.
- To retain the essential character of Westland/Tai Poutini National Park as a natural area of great beauty, diversity, and value for the benefit, use, and enjoyment of the general public to the extent that this is compatible with Objective 1.
- To give effect to the principles of the Tiriti o Waitangi/Treaty of Waitangi to the extent that they are not inconsistent with the National Parks Act 1980.

A number of sub-objectives flow from these objectives:

- To exterminate all plant and animal pests in the park as far as possible.
- To preserve the park's heritage of places, artefacts and archaeological sites.
- To permit a level of commercial use to occur within the park to the extent that it is compatible with the primary objectives …

Notes: [1]   *mana whenua*: 'customary rights and authority over land'
       [2]   *tāngata whenua*: 'traditional owners'

Source: West Coast *Tai Poutini* Conservancy (1999), *Westland/Tai Poutini National Park Management Plan: Draft*, Department of Conservation/*Te Papa Atawhai*, Hokitika, pp. 5, 36–7.

Plate 12.3

Hochstetter Icefall, on the east face of Mount Tasman (3498 metres) in the Mount Cook Range, Mount Cook National Park, South Canterbury, New Zealand. The icefall feeds onto the Tasman Glacier. The whole of the park is included in the Te Wahipounamu–South West New Zealand World Heritage property.

Photo: Graeme Aplin

Plate 12.4

Franz Josef Glacier,
Westland National Park,
Westland, New Zealand, is
also included in the Te
Wahipounamu-South West
New Zealand World
Heritage property.

Photo: Graeme Aplin

Despite the unified act and the over-arching role of the DOC, there is still a division made between natural and cultural heritage that reveals a particular way of looking at the environment, one that separates humans and nature and is culturally specific:

> At a deeper level the heritage split can be seen to mirror the separation of humankind and nature in Western, Enlightenment philosophy. A Eurocentric or Anglo-American influence, and an imperialist viewpoint, may also be seen in the museum-like attitude to cultural objects and a conception of 'untouched' nature.[2]

Problems arose in the application of the division between 'natural' and 'cultural' heritage in the case of the West Coast of the South Island and its nomination for World Heritage listing because of the close identification between Māori people and their land: 'What emerged was a strong sense of the significance of cultural activity and culturally mediated landscapes as determinants of heritage at the local level'.[3] The local people took their case to UNESCO and the WHCom and tried to take out an injunction in the New Zealand courts against the inscription because they felt it should be a 'cultural park', and not inscribed for purely natural reasons.[4]

New Zealand World Heritage properties

New Zealand has three World Heritage properties (see Table 12.1), one on each of the main islands (Figure 12.1) and a third consisting of a number of sub-Antarctic islands. Tongariro National Park, in the volcanic zone of the North Island, was in 1993 the first property in the world to be inscribed on the WHL under the revised criteria concerning cultural landscapes (see Section 8.3). As well as its physical attributes as an outstanding volcanic landscape with three major peaks (recognised in the initial 1990 inscription on the basis of natural criteria), the area has great cultural and spiritual significance for the Māori people. In 1986, Fjordland National Park and the combined Aoraki/Mount Cook and Westland national parks were separately inscribed. These were combined and Mount Aspiring National Park added in 1990 to become the very extensive Te Wahipounamu/South West New Zealand World Heritage property (Plates 12.3 and 12.4). All of these South Island inscriptions were solely on the basis of natural criteria, despite pleas from Māoris to also recognise them as cultural landscapes.

Figure 12.1

New Zealand national parks and World Heritage properties

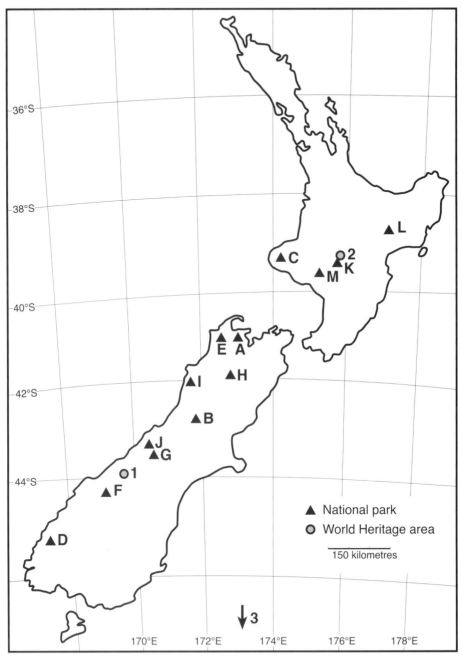

Key:

World Heritage areas

1–3: see Table 12.1.

National parks

A Abel Tasman	C Egmont	I Paparoa
B Arthur's Pass	D Fiordland	J Tongariro
	E Kahurangi	K Urewera
	F Mount Aspiring	L Westland
	G Mount Cook	M Whanganui
	H Nelson Lakes	

Table 12.1

New Zealand World Heritage properties

Property	Criteria (see Appendix 1 for key)	Date of inscription (and of enlargements)	Brief description and reasons for inscription (from World Heritage List)
1 Te Wahipounamu–South West New Zealand	N i, ii, iii, iv	1990	In south-west New Zealand, this park offers a landscape shaped by successive glaciations into fjords, rocky coasts, towering cliffs, lakes, and waterfalls. Two-thirds of the park is covered with southern beech and podocarps, some of which are over 800 years old. The kea, the only alpine parrot in the world, lives in the park, as does the rare and endangered takahe, a large flightless bird.
2 Tongariro National Park	N ii, iii; C vi	1990, 1993	In 1993 Tongariro became the first property to be inscribed on the World Heritage List under the revised cultural criteria describing cultural landscapes. The mountains at the heart of the park have cultural and religious significance for the Māori people and symbolise the spiritual links between this community and its environment. The park contains active and extinct volcanoes, a diverse range of ecosystems and highly scenic landscapes.
3 New Zealand Sub-Antarctic Islands	N ii, iv	1998	The New Zealand Sub-Antarctic Islands consist of five island groups (the Snares, Bounty Islands, Antipodes Islands, Auckland Islands, and Campbell Island) in the Southern Ocean, south-east of New Zealand. The islands, lying between the Antarctic and Sub-tropical Convergences and the seas, have a high level of productivity, biodiversity, wildlife population densities, and endemism among birds, plants, and invertebrates. They are particularly notable for the large number and diversity of pelagic seabirds and penguins that nest there. There are 126 bird species in all, including forty seabirds of which five breed nowhere else.

12.3 United States of America

Background

In a sense, the USA led the modern movement to conserve and protect natural heritage areas by setting up the Yellowstone National Park in 1872. Although not actually called a 'National Park' for its first few years of existence, it was in fact, if not in name, the world's first national park. It is ironic and disturbing that Yellowstone now finds itself on the LWHD (see Table 8.2, and Box 12.5). The US National Park Service (NPS) was founded in 1916 as a federal bureau in the Department of the Interior. It now cares for 378 areas covering 83 million hectares across forty-nine states, the District of Columbia, American Samoa, Guam, Puerto Rico, Saipan, and the Virgin Islands. These areas are deemed to be of national significance and are protected under various Acts of Congress. They range in size from the huge 5.34 million hectare Wrangell–St Elias National Park in Alaska to the 0.008 ha Thaddeus Kosciuszko National Memorial in Pennsylvania. Not all are natural heritage areas, and they go under a variety of titles apart from 'National Park' (see Box 12.2 and the next two parts of this Section). The *National Park Service Organic Act 1916* gives the mission of the NPS as being to:

> … promote and regulate the use of the … national parks … which purpose is to conserve the scenery and the natural and historic objects and the wild life therein and to provide for the enjoyment of the same in such manner and by such means as will leave them unimpaired for the enjoyment of future generations.

Box 12.2 United States National Parks Service—System Units

The major types of reserve administered by the United States National Parks Service are as follows (the number of reserves of each type, as it stood in November 1998, are given in parentheses):

National Park (55)
Generally a large natural place with a wide variety of attributes, including significant historic assets. Hunting, mining, and consumptive activities are not permitted.

National Monument (73)
The *Antiquities Act 1906* authorised the president to declare landmarks, structures, and other objects of historic or scientific interest situated on lands owned or controlled by the government to be National Monuments (see Box 12.3 for examples). These were transferred to the NPS in 1933.

National Preserve (16)
Areas having characteristics associated with National Parks, but in which public trapping, hunting, or oil and gas exploration and/or extraction are allowed to continue. Many National Preserves would qualify as National Parks if sport hunting were discontinued.

National Historic Site (77)
Usually contains a single historical feature directly associated with its 'subject' (see Box 12.3 for examples).

National Historic Park (38)
Generally applies to historic reserves that extend beyond single properties or buildings (see Box 12.3 for examples).

National Memorial (28)

Commemorative of a historic person or episode, but it need not occupy a site historically connected with that person or episode.

National Battlefield (24)

Includes the formerly distinct National Military Park category.

National Cemetery (14)

These are burial places for US service personnel and some others of national importance.

National Recreation Area (19)

Twelve NRAs are centred on large reservoirs and emphasise water-based recreation, while five others are near major population centres and combine scarce open space with historic resources and natural areas that can provide recreation for large numbers of people.

National Seashore (10)

Some of these areas are developed and others remaining relatively primitive. Hunting is generally permitted.

National Lakeshore (4)

All on the Great Lakes, they closely parallel National Seashores.

National River (9*)

There are several variants, including National River and Recreation Area, National Scenic River, and Wild River.

National Parkway (4)

Parkland paralleling a roadway to allow for scenic motoring along a protected corridor, often connecting cultural sites.

National Trail (3*)

National Scenic Trails and National Historic Trails are linear parklands authorised under the *National Trails System Act 1968* and used for walking, cycling and horse-riding.

There are also other minor categories, and some sites, such as the White House, have unique names that fall outside any category.

Note: * The numbers given are not always totals for the category, as some sub-types fall in the web site's 'other' category.

Source: National Parks Service web site: http://www.nps.gov/.

According to the NPS web site (see list in Appendix 2), a proposed conservation area will be considered nationally significant if it meets all four of the following criteria:

- it is an outstanding example of a particular type of resource
- it possesses exceptional value or quality in illustrating or interpreting the natural or cultural themes of [the United States] heritage
- it offers superlative opportunities for recreation, for public use and enjoyment, or for scientific study
- it retains a high degree of integrity as a true, accurate, and relatively unspoiled example of the resource

The Federal Government can also become involved in heritage matters in other ways, notably through appropriation Bills passed by Congress to provide finance for conservation projects of all types; for example the fiscal year 2001 Interior Appropriations Bill significantly boosted federal spending on land acquisition, conservation, urban parks, and historic preservation. Under this Bill (if it survives, following the election of George W. Bush), the Land Conservation, Preservation and Infrastructure Improvement Trust Program provides a large amount—ranging from US$1.6 billion in 2001 to US$2.4 billion in 2006—for land conservation, preservation, and maintenance. Of this, US$160 million will be earmarked annually for urban and historic preservation programs, and US$35 million in 2001 for the Save America's Treasures program. Other funds will go to the states and to native tribes for historic preservation of objects important to them.

Like Australia, the USA is a dynamic federation where the national government, component states, and local government play complementary roles in many areas, including heritage. Each state has its own system of protected areas, both natural and cultural, to complement the federal NPS-managed system, although the federal NPS is stronger than its Australian counterpart. As in the case of virtually all other nations (and discussed in Chapters 9 to 12), the choice of which level of government is charged with managing a particular protected site depends on the scale at which that site is perceived to be significant. In the sections that follow we will look at cultural and natural heritage deemed to be significant at the national level, and then the system in place in California will be taken as one example of a US state structure.

Cultural heritage

The NPS is involved in cultural, specifically historic (Plates 12.5, 12.6, and 12.10), sites as well as natural sites. In 1933, an Executive Order transferred sixty-three national monuments from other federal agencies to the NPS, and an Act of 1970 declared that the NPS system should include 'superlative natural, historic, and recreation areas in every region'—it was to be a genuine national system. In addition to the general criteria mentioned in the previous section, cultural areas administered by the NPS 'may be districts, sites, structures, or objects that possess exceptional value or quality in illustrating or interpreting [the US] heritage and that possess a high degree of integrity of

Plate 12.5

The Harpers Ferry National Historical Park, managed by the National Parks Service, is located in West Virginia, USA, at the junction of the Shenandoah and Potamac rivers.

Photo: Graeme Aplin

location, design, setting, materials, workmanship, feelings and association'. This should be compared with criteria listed in Box 1.4 (Register of the National Estate in Australia), in Box 6.1 (for NSW), and in Section 8.3 (relating to World Heritage). Some specific examples of cultural sites in the USA are included in Box 12.3.

Plate 12.6

The Alamo, San Antonio, Texas, USA. Originally the chapel of a Spanish mission founded in 1718, the Alamo gained prominence as a Texan icon after the war for Texan independence from Mexico in 1836. The small force of Texan defenders of the Alamo were overwhelmed after two weeks of fierce resistance, 150–180 dying in the face of superior Mexican forces. Texas gained its independence later that year.

Photo: Graeme Aplin

Box 12.3 Some examples of US National Monuments, National Historic Sites, and National Historic Parks

The examples briefly described below were selected to illustrate the range of sites and types of significance covered by the NPS categories of National Monuments, National Historic Sites, and National Historic Parks.

National Monuments

Buck Island Reef NM, Virgin Islands

This small island is nearly encircled by a coral reef: the reserve has an area of 71 hectares of land and 285 hectares of seabed. There are two marked underwater trails to guide snorkellers, scuba-divers, and glass-bottomed boats through the reef ecosystem. There is also a hiking trail through tropical vegetation to the top of the island for views of the reef and other islands. Other facilities include picnic areas. The island is a rookery for the endangered brown pelican and a nesting place for three species of sea turtles. Access is by charter boat.

George Washington Birthplace NM, Virginia

Washington was born here in 1732 in a modest plantation house on the creek's bank. The original house was destroyed by fire in 1779 (brick foundations remain), and was replaced by a Colonial Revival 'memorial house' in the 1930s. The NPS now operates the 223-hectare grounds as a working colonial-era farm. The Washington family cemetery, a visitor centre, picnic grounds, nature trails, and a Potomoc River beach are also part of the site.

Lava Beds NM, California

The rugged terrain of this 18 850 hectare reserve was formed by eruptions of the Medecine Lake shield volcano. It is characterised by numerous lava-tube caves, lava flows, and cinder cones. Prehistoric Indians left glyphs on the soft rock, and the Modoc Indians used the area as a 'fortress' during the Modoc Wars against the US Army in 1872–73. There is excellent bird watching in spring and autumn. Facilities include forty-one campsites, hiking trails, and picnic areas.

Little Bighorn Battlefield NM, Montana

This reserve is the site of one of the battles that is not only important in American history, but has also become part of its folklore. Lt. Col. George Custer and over 200 men of the Seventh Cavalry died here in June 1876, during an attack on a large camp of Sioux and Cheyenne Indians. Exhibits include battle artefacts and some of Custer's personal belongings. Tours are conducted. This site was declared a National Cemetery in 1879 and a National Monument in 1946.

Statue of Liberty NM, New York

The Lady Liberty statue on this small island in New York Harbour was a gift of France in 1886. It has greeted millions of immigrants and others arriving in the USA by ship and remains an unmistakable symbol of the city. There is a museum of the statue's history, while a lift takes visitors to the observation deck at the top of the pedestal. It is also possible to climb to the top of the crown. This is a World Heritage property, and was extensively restored for its centennial in 1986.

National Historic Sites

Andersonville NHS, Georgia

Officially known as Fort Sumter, this infamous Civil War prison camp, established near Atlanta in 1864, was the largest one of the Confederate forces. More than a quarter of the 45 000 Union soldiers held there died, mostly from disease caused by overcrowding and a poor water supply. A driving tour of the 200-hectare site takes visitors past earthworks, the remains of escape tunnels, and a large number of headstones of those buried there. The National Prisoner of War Museum was opened in 1998.

Fort Laramie NHS, Wyoming

Fort Laramie, then known as Fort William, was established as a fur-trading post in 1834 and is considered to be the first permanent European settlement on the northern plains. It later became an important stopping place for overland immigrants on the Oregon Trail and the Mormon Trail, a major army post, and site of treaty negotiations with the Plains Indians. The Pony Express, the Trans-Continental Telegraph, and the Deadwood Stage all passed through. It now has an excellent living-history museum and retains many original buildings, several of which have been painstakingly restored.

Knife River Indian Villages NHS, North Dakota

Hidatsa, Mandan, and Arikara Indians built earth lodges, some with diameters of up to 12 metres, at this site at the junction of the Knife and Missouri rivers. The 711-hectare site preserves historical and archaeological remnants of the culture and agricultural lifestyles of the Northern Plains Indians. Over fifty archaeological sites span the 8000 years of occupation. Trails pass the mounds and depressions of the original villages.

Saugus Iron Works NM, Massachusetts

Industrial America is said to have begun here in the 1640s with the establishment of a technologically advanced ironworks on the banks of the Saugus River. It was the first integrated ironworks in North America. Water-powered iron-making technology is explained in an open-air museum, which includes reconstructed buildings, blast furnace, forge, and rolling mill, and an indoors museum. The original Iron Works House survives.

Vanderbilt Mansion NM, New York

This extravagant 54-room Italian Renaissance-style mansion in Hyde Park, built in 1898, has retained the appearance of the days of Frederick Vanderbilt, grandson of railroad magnate Cornelius. Guides give an introductory talk before visitors are free to tour the fully furnished house at their leisure. This is the most intact of the type of estate constructed by 19th-century industrialists. There are also magnificent views from the house and grounds.

National Historic Parks

Chaco Culture NHP, New Mexico

This World Heritage property is one of the most important North American archaeological sites, situated at the hub of ceremony, trade, and administration in the prehistoric south-west. The 27-kilometre-long canyon has seventeen multi-storeyed Great Houses and 400 smaller dwellings from the Puebloan culture. The site dates from 850–1250 and includes the continent's largest excavated prehistoric building. Five self-guided trails explore the major structures. It is still part of the sacred homeland of the Pueblo, Hopi, and Navajo Indians.

Dayton Aviation Heritage NHP, Ohio

This reserve consists of four separate sections and is dedicated to Dayton's significant place in the history of flight. The Wright Cycle Company Shop preserves the Wright Brothers' last shop in the city; here, in the 1890s, they made bicycles, operated a printing works, and researched for their flying machine. The site of their earlier shop is nearby. The Wright Brothers Aviation Centre in the Carillon Historical Park has on display the 1905 Wright Flyer III, the world's first practical aeroplane, while Huffman Prairie Flying Field is where the brothers tested the plane and established the first permanent flying school. The site also honours Paul Dunbar, a famous African-American writer, whose works the Wrights printed.

Harpers Ferry NHP, West Virginia

This site, at the junction of the Potomac and Shenandoah rivers, covers 1012 hectares reserved for both natural and historical values. A major federal armory and arsenal was established here in the 1790s to take advantage of the site's water-power potential. In 1859 John Brown, an anti-slavery leader, and twenty-one others took the arsenal at Harpers Ferry; Brown was captured, tried, and hanged in 1859. The trial added to North–South tensions in the lead-up to the Civil War. Brown is also remembered in the song 'John Brown's Body'. Much of the historic interpretation at the site revolves around this incident. The town changed hands eight times during the Civil War. There are also many other important historical associations. Historic buildings now house museums, restaurants, and souvenir shops (see Plate 12.5).

Klondike Gold Rush NHP, Alaska

This park includes fifteen restored buildings scattered around the centre of Skagway, a port that was a staging centre for the 1898 gold rush. A museum is dedicated to this dash for wealth, while exhibits and videos in the Visitor Center (in a former railroad depot) tell of the rigours of the Chilkoot Trail. More than fifty historic buildings are included in the Skagway Historic District, some of which are also in the NHP. The park also administers the Chilkoot Trail and part of the White Pass Trail, two routes to the goldfields.

Valley Forge, Pennsylvania

In extremely difficult conditions in the winter of 1777–78, George Washington's ragbag of troops was trained to become a disciplined force that took part in the War of Independence. Interpretation of those events involves a film, reconstructed huts, Washington's headquarters, and well-preserved fortifications. The Valley Forge Historical Society Museum displays Washington memorabilia.

Source: National Parks Service web site and various guidebooks.

Cultural resources that have national, state, or local significance may be listed by the NPS on the National Register of Historic Places (NRHP), which means they are considered worthy of preservation and of special consideration in planning for federal projects. The NRHP, in its present form, was established under the *National Historic Preservation Act 1966*, which also set up the Advisory Council on Historic Preservation. Nationally significant sites, including historic districts, may be designated as national historic landmarks, and Congress may authorise financial or technical assistance for such sites even when they remain under state, local, or even private control. State and local governments may apply for grants through the NPS for historic preservation and acquisition, or for the development of recreational and visitor facilities. Before they can be listed on the NRHP, properties must satisfy an 'integrity test' and they must first be considered by the relevant local and state government agencies that comment on proposals (unless, of course, one of these agencies is the originator).

The National Trust for Historical Preservation (NTHP), formed in 1949, is an NGO (but which has a charter granted by Congress). Its mission statement states that it 'provides leadership, education and advocacy to save America's diverse historic places and revitalize [US] communities'. It is thus similar to the National Trusts in Australia and in the United Kingdom, and it is usually known simply as the National Trust. It owns and operates twenty historic sites across the USA. It also operates the Community Partners Program (CPP), which seeks to promote the use of historic preservation as a tool to revitalise historic neighbourhoods (or precincts) at all scales through 'preservation-based community development'. Grants, loans, and assistance obtaining historic housing tax credits are provided, as is technical assistance with conservation projects. Since 1979, there has been a Rural Heritage Program, which includes small towns in its field of interest. One of the NTHP's most important and influential programs has been the *Main Street Program*, the role of which is outlined in Box 12.4.

Box 12.4 United States National Trust for Historic Preservation Main Street Program

---

Since 1980, the NTHP's National Main Street Center has been helping communities revitalise their historic or traditional commercial or business districts. The program was developed to preserve historically and architecturally significant commercial architecture and the broader fabric of these areas that have value to their communities on so many levels, including their streetscape value, especially in mid-sized towns and smaller cities. Very real economic benefits have frequently flowed from the work done, although that is not the primary focus of the program.

According to the NTHP's web site (see list in Appendix 2):

The Main Street program is designed to improve all aspects of the downtown or central business district, producing both tangible and intangible benefits. Improving economic management, strengthening public participation, and making downtown a fun place to visit are as critical to Main Street's future as recruiting new businesses, rehabilitating buildings, and expanding parking. Building on downtown's inherent assets—rich architecture, personal service, and traditional values and most of all, a sense of place—the Main Street approach has rekindled entrepreneurship, downtown cooperation and civic concern. It has earned national recognition as a practical strategy appropriately scaled to a community's local resources and conditions. And because it is a locally driven program, all initiative stems from local issues and concerns.

The Main Street Four Point Approach focusses on design by enhancing physical appearance through rehabilitation and appropriate new construction; organisation, through building consensus and cooperation between groups involved; promotion and marketing; and economic restructuring. Combined with this are eight approaches that can be encapsulated in the following words or phrases: comprehensive; incremental; self-help; public–private partnership; identifying and capitalising on existing assets; quality; change; and action-oriented.

A recent article in *Time* reported in very positive terms on projects in Burlington (population c. 27 000) and Fort Madison (population 11 618). The author sees the Main Street program as a chance to save, or reinstate, the character and individuality of towns and to allow them to distinguish themselves from the amorphous blandness of United States towns. And, in the process, some significant cultural heritage is being saved; for example:

One day in Fort Madison, while rehabbing a storefront, a workman peeled back an atrocious-looking aluminium façade and found carved wooden columns and stained-glass windows beneath. Several townsfolk heard the news and strolled over to celebrate the discovery of the buried treasure.

Sources: NTHP's web site: http://www.nthp.org/; S. Lopez, 'The battle of Downtown', *Time*, 10 July 2000, pp. 54–6).

The NTHP now publishes an annual list of 'America's Eleven Most Endangered Historic Places', and has had considerable success in drawing attention to, and in some cases saving, listed sites. In 2000 the list included a group listing for 'Historic Neighbourhood Schools' (often situated in inner city areas where declining local populations meant they were no longer needed); the extremely important George Washington and American Revolution site of the

Valley Forge National Historic Park (which suffered from the ravages of time and weather); and the Santa Anita Racetrack near Los Angeles (an unusual Art Deco complex threatened by unsympathetic redevelopment and upgrading).

Natural heritage

The NPS manages a range of different reserves which protect natural heritage to varying degrees. These include fifty-five national parks (see for example Figure 12.2 and Plates 4.4, 12.7, and 12.11), national lakeshores, national preserves, national rivers, national scenic trails, national seashores, national wild and scenic rivers, and many other conservation areas. Box 12.2 shows the number of each type of reserve and lists some reasons why natural areas might be deemed worthy of conservation at the federal level, provided they also satisfy the more general standards quoted above in the first part of Section 12.3: briefly, to be an outstanding example, to have exceptional values, to offer major opportunities for public use or scientific study, and to retain a high degree of integrity. In order to achieve the mission statement (quoted at the beginning of Section 12.3), the NPS follows a set of guiding principles that include:

- providing the best possible service to visitors
- collaborating with other levels of government, including Native American governments, and private organisations and businesses
- involving citizens in NPS decision-making
- educating visitors and others about heritage
- integrating social, economic, environmental, and ethical considerations into decision-making and management
- adopting a management philosophy based on creativity, results, and accountability
- conducting research and using the results of it
- sharing information and expertise with other land managers

Plate 12.7

Mount McKinley, the highest mountain in the USA at 6194 metres, in Denali National Park, Alaska, USA. The road shown is the route of the shuttle bus into the heart of the Park. The tundra-type vegetation in the foreground is home to a number of mammal species, large and small.

Photo: Stephanie Aplin

Figure 12.2

United States national parks and World Heritage properties in the forty-eight contiguous states

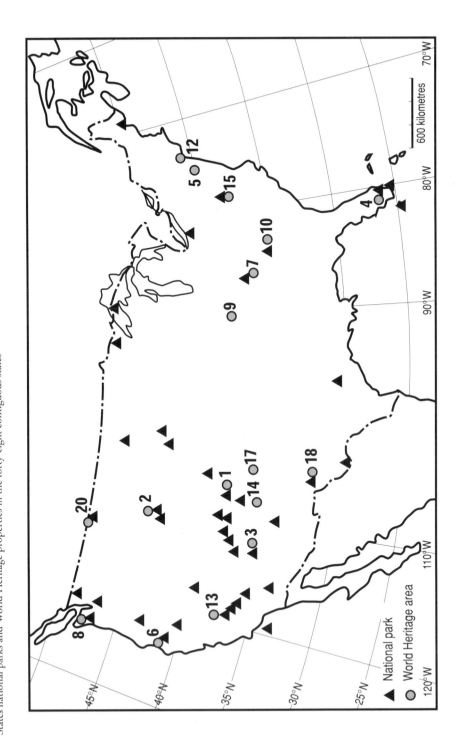

Key:

1–20: World Heritage areas—see Table 12.2.

Denali National Park illustrates a number of points. Alaska's oldest national park, Denali includes many mountains, including Mount McKinley (Plate 12.7), and numerous large glaciers in the Alaska Range. The area covers over 2.4 million hectares, encompassing a complete sub-Arctic ecosystem and containing a number of large mammal species. It was established in 1917 as Mount McKinley National Park, and in 1976 was designated as an international Biosphere Reserve (see Section 8.5). In 1980 the original area was declared a wilderness area and incorporated into an enlarged reserve that was renamed Denali National Park. The major uses of the park are sightseeing, wildlife viewing, mountaineering, and hiking, and in 1999 it had 1 130 643 visitors. The total area now includes the central Denali National Park Wilderness, which has sections of the national park on either side, and the Denali National Preserve in two outlying sections. (Box 12.2 describes these different types of reserve.) An area adjacent to the park on the main highway is designated as Denali State Park. The wilderness area is somewhat unusual as it includes the single public road into the national park as well as two visitors' centres, two ranger stations, six campgrounds, and a number of picnic areas. At the end of the road, deep in the heart of the national park, but just beyond the Wilderness, there is an airstrip. However, while the road is public, access for visitors is generally by shuttle bus.

The National Parks Conservation Association (NPCA), a non-government parks 'watchdog' organisation, sees serious threats to Denali from road and resort development and from a proposal to open about 800 000 hectares of the wilderness area to snowmobiles. As is the case for many parks in the USA, there is a serious conflict between conservation aims, and visitor facility and recreational aims. In 2000, the NPCA included Denali on its List of Ten Most Endangered National Parks. Outside Denali National Park, the NPCA is also lobbying for new areas to be given protection, and for some existing conservation areas to be extended. It is also working with the NPS to clarify priorities and construct strategic business plans.

Example of heritage management at the state level: California

California is discussed here briefly as an example of state involvement in heritage protection and management in the USA. The key department is the California Department of Parks and Recreation, and within it, California State Parks (Cal-Parks) and its California Office of Historic Preservation (COHP).

In July 2000, the Cal-Parks System included 266 properties, most of which are classified as one of the following: state beach, state historic park, state historical monument, state park, state recreation area, state reserve, state seashore, state vehicular recreation area, or wayside campground. Sections of these may be further classified as cultural preserve, natural preserve, or state wilderness. These designations run in close parallel to those of the NPS at the national level (see Box 12.2). The state vehicular recreation areas are managed separately from other units, not surprisingly, given the very different and possibly incompatible objectives involved. The state wilderness areas within the Cal-Parks System are part of a wider California Wilderness Preservation System. Management plans are required for all units.

The COHP coordinates many activities to encourage and enable the preservation of historical and cultural heritage resources (Plates 12.8 and 12.9). It seeks the input of individuals, communities, and local government in the processes of identification and assessment, and any proposal for listing requires comment from the relevant local authority. Proposals for the inclusion of Californian properties on the NRHP require comment from the COHP (acting on behalf of the state). The COHP maintains an information base—the Californian Historical Resources Information

Plate 12.8

Reconstructed interior of a miner's hut in the Californian gold town of Columbia, USA which was once the second largest town in the state. Columbia State Historic Park has preserved the town and it is one of the best kept reminders of the Californian gold rushes of the 1840s.

Photo: Graeme Aplin

Plate 12.9

Corner of 2nd and K Streets in Old Sacramento, California, USA, showing the boardwalk pavements in an historic precinct between the river and the modern city. The area preserves many historic buildings, which are re-used for visitor-oriented activities (most are restorations, some are reconstructions). The corner building is the restored Bank Exchange Building (built in 1853, later used as a saloon).

Photo: Graeme Aplin

System—and three state programs for listing properties: the California Historical Landmark Program for items of state-scale significance, established in 1931 and now containing over 1000 items; the California Point of Historical Interest Program for places of more local significance, established in 1959; and the 1992 California Register of Historical Resources Program which combines the functions of the two earlier programs for more recent listings. Native American communities are involved whenever their concerns are likely to be relevant. Listing on the NHRP, and to varying degrees on the state programs, provides access to tax incentives and deductions and federal and state grants and loans, but also places requirements to gain approvals for certain works and development activities. The COHP (in conjunction with the another Californian agency—the State Historical Resources Commission) has also been involved in producing a revised Comprehensive Statewide Historic Preservation Plan.

United States World Heritage properties

There are eighteen US World Heritage properties and two joint US–Canadian properties (Table 12.2 and Figure 12.2). The joint properties are both inscribed for natural reasons—one consists of a number of parks on the Canadian–Alaskan border, and the other is a pair

Plate 12.10

Independence Hall (built 1732 to the 1750s), Philadelphia, Pennsylvania, a United States World Heritage property. The Declaration of Independence (1776) and the United States Constitution (1787) were signed in this building.

Photo: Graeme Aplin

of adjacent parks on a mountainous section of the main US–Canadian border. Eight of the US properties were inscribed for cultural reasons, and they range in age from the early Anasazi Indian dwellings of Mesa Verde and a Chaco culture centre, the pre-Colombian Mississippi civilisation site of Cahokia Mounds, and the adobe settlement of Pueblo de Taos, to the Statue of Liberty and the Jefferson-designed buildings of 'Monticello' and the University of Virginia. Also included in this group is a building that is one most deeply entrenched in US history and the national psyche: Independence Hall in Philadelphia (Plate 12.10). Natural sites include some of the best known US national parks: Yellowstone, Grand Canyon (Plate 12.11), Everglades, Redwood, Mammoth Cave, Olympic, Great Smoky Mountains, Yosemite (Plate 4.4), and Carlsbad Caverns. Two island sites are also inscribed—the Hawaii Volcanoes National Park and a historic site in Puerto Rico. It is interesting to note that the Cahokia Mounds property is a State Historic Site, administered by the State of Missouri rather than by a federal agency.

Two of the natural properties, the Everglades and Yellowstone, are included in the LWHD (Table 8.2, Section 8.4), showing that World Heritage can be endangered by development in a wealthy country, as well as by wars, civil unrest, and poverty in less-wealthy nations. Indeed, one of the dangers said to be threatening Yellowstone is 'visitor pressure' (Box 12.5).

Plate 12.11

Grand Canyon, Grand Canyon National Park, Colorado, a United States World Heritage property. Maricopa Point on the South Rim, near the village, is in the left foreground.

Photo: Richard Aplin

Table 12.2

United States World Heritage properties

	Property	Criteria (see Appendix 1 for key)	Date of inscription (and of enlargements)	Brief description and reasons for inscription (from World Heritage List)
1	Mesa Verde	C iii	1978	A great concentration of Anasazi Indian dwellings, built from the 6th to the 12th centuries, can be found on the Mesa Verde plateau in south-west Colorado, at an altitude of more than 2600 metres. Some 3800 sites have been recorded, including villages built on the plateau, and imposing cliff-side sites, built of stone and comprising more than 200 houses.
2	Yellowstone	N i, ii, iii, iv	1978	In a vast natural forest in Wyoming, Yellowstone National Park covers more than 9000 square kilometres. An impressive collection of geothermal phenomena can be observed there, including more than 3000 geysers, fumaroles, and hot springs. Established in 1872, Yellowstone is equally known for its wildlife, such as grizzly bears, wolves, bison, and wapiti.
3	Grand Canyon National Park	N i, ii, iii, iv	1979	Carved out by the Colorado River, the Grand Canyon, nearly 1500 metres deep, is the most spectacular gorge in the world. Located in the state of Arizona, it cuts across the Grand Canyon National Park. Its horizontal strata retrace the geological history of the past two billion years. Prehistoric traces also remain of human adaptation to a particularly harsh environment.
4	Everglades National Park	N i, ii, iv	1979	This site at the southern tip of Florida has been called 'a river of grass flowing imperceptibly from the hinterland into the sea'. The exceptional variety of its water habitats has made it a sanctuary for a considerable number of birds and reptiles, as well as for threatened species such as the manatee.
5	Independence Hall	C vi	1979	The Declaration of Independence and the Constitution were signed in this hall in the heart of Philadelphia, in 1776 and 1787 respectively. Since then, the universal principles set forth in these two documents of fundamental importance to American history have continued to guide lawmakers all over the world.
6	Redwood National Park	N ii, iii	1980	A region of coastal mountains bordering the Pacific Ocean north of San Francisco, Redwood National Park is covered with a magnificent forest of sequoia—redwood—trees, which are the tallest and most impressive in the world. The marine and land life are equally remarkable, in particular the sea lions, bald eagle, and the endangered California brown pelican.

Property	Criteria (see Appendix 1 for key)	Date of inscription (and of enlargements)	Brief description and reasons for inscription (from World Heritage List)
7 Mammoth Cave National Park	N i, iii, iv	1981	Mammoth Cave National Park, located in the state of Kentucky, contains the largest network of natural caves and underground passageways in the world, characteristic examples of limestone formations. The park and its underground network shelter a varied flora and fauna, including a number of endangered species.
8 Olympic National Park	N ii, iii	1981	Located in the north-west corner of Washington state, Olympic National Park is dominated by Mount Olympus (2428 metres high), which gave the park its name. A great variety of landscapes and ecosystems can be found there, with a great wealth of marine life along its rocky coast, forests of giant conifers in the valleys where huge herds of wapiti roam, and craggy peaks overhanging some sixty active glaciers.
9 Cahokia Mounds State Historic Site	C iii, iv	1982	About 15 kilometres north of St Louis (Missouri), Cahokia provides the most complete source of information on pre-Colombian civilizations in the regions of the Mississippi. It is a striking example of a pre-urban sedentary structure that allows for the study of a kind of social organisation about which no written traces exist.
10 Great Smoky Mountains National Park	N i, ii, iii, iv	1983	Stretching over more than 200 000 hectares, this exceptionally beautiful park is home to more than 3500 plant species, and almost as many trees as in all of Europe (130 natural species). Many endangered animal species can also be found there, including what is probably the greatest variety of salamanders in the world. Relatively untouched, it gives an idea of temperate flora before the influence of humankind.
11 La Fortaleza and San Juan Historic Site in Puerto Rico	C vi	1983	A vital strategic point in the Caribbean Sea, the defensive structures built over four centuries (15th to 19th) to protect the city and the Bay of San Juan have left a rich display of European military architecture adapted to the harbours of the American continent.
12 The Statue of Liberty	C i, vi	1984	Made in Paris by the French sculptor Bartholdi, with help on the metalwork from Gustave Eiffel, this symbolic monument to liberty was a gift from France on the centenary of American independence. Standing at the entrance of New York Harbor it has welcomed millions of immigrants to the United States of America since it was inaugurated in 1886.
13 Yosemite National Park	N i, ii, iii	1984	Located in the heart of California, Yosemite National Park, with its 'hanging' valleys, many waterfalls, cirque lakes, polished domes, moraines, and U-

No.	Name	Criteria	Year	Description
				shaped valleys, offers a view of all kinds of granite reliefs fashioned by glaciation. At 600 to 4000 metres high, a great variety of flora and fauna can also be found here.
14	Chaco Culture National Historical Park	C iii	1987	This national park, in north-west New Mexico, contains the most important remains of the Chaco culture, which was at its height between about 1020 and 1110. It was characterised by a very elaborate system of urban dwellings surrounded by villages and linked by a network of roads.
15	Monticello and University of Virginia in Charlottesville	C i, iv, vi	1987	Excellent examples of Neoclassicism, seen in the relationship of the buildings with nature and the blending of functionalism and symbolism, the mansion of Monticello and the University of Virginia reflect the design of their architect, Thomas Jefferson (1743–1826), who was strongly influenced by the Enlightenment.
16	Hawaii Volcanoes National Park	N ii	1987	Two of the most active volcanoes in the world, Mauna Loa (4170 metres high) and Kilauea, tower over the Pacific Ocean at this site. Volcanic eruptions have created a continually changing landscape, and the lava flows reveal surprising geological formations. Rare birds and endemic species can be found there, as well as forests of giant ferns.
17	Pueblo de Taos	C iv	1992	Situated in the valley of a small tributary of the Rio Grande, this adobe settlement consists of dwellings and ceremonial buildings, representing the culture of the Pueblo Indians of Arizona and New Mexico.
18	Carlsbad Caverns National Park	N i, iii	1995	In the state of New Mexico, this karstic network comprises eighty-one currently recognised caves. Among this high concentration of caves, outstanding because of their size and the profusion, diversity and beauty of mineral formations, the Lechuguilla cave stands out, forming an underground laboratory where geological processes can be studied in a virtually intact setting.
19*	Tatshenshini-Alsek/Kluane National Park/Wrangell-Saint Elias National Park and Reserve and Glacier Bay National Park	N ii, iii, iv	1979, 1992, 1994	These parks comprise an impressive complex of glaciers and high peaks on either side of the frontier between Canada and the United States of America (Alaska). These spectacular natural landscapes are home to many grizzly bears, caribou, and Dall sheep.
20*	Waterton Glacier International Peace Park	N ii, iii	1995	These two National Parks were designated by law the world's first International Peace Park in 1932. Located on the Canada–USA border and offering outstanding scenery, the parks are exceptionally rich in plant and mammal species as well as in alpine and glacial features.

Note: * A property that falls within both the USA and Canada.

Box 12.5 Yellowstone National Park—World Heritage in Danger

Yellowstone National Park, established in 1872, was inscribed on the WHL in 1978 under all four natural criteria, and on the LWHD in 1995. The park is situated in a vast natural forest in Wyoming; it covers more than 9000 square kilometres; contains an impressive collection of geothermal phenomena, including more than 3000 geysers, fumaroles, and hot springs; and is also well known for its wildlife, such as grizzly bears, wolves, bison, and wapiti.

Yellowstone was inscribed on the LWHD mainly because of concerns that adjacent mining operations might compromise the values of the park by threatening the watershed ecology of the Yellowstone River. Other issues included sewage leakage and waste contamination; the unconsidered and illegal introduction of non-native lake trout, which are competing with the endemic Yellowstone cut-throat trout; road construction; and year-round visitor pressures (more than three million visitors annually). Threats to the bison population are apparent in proposals to slaughter large numbers of them as a control measure to eradicate brucellosis in the herds, perceived as a threat to cattle in the surrounding area. Finally, there are fears that groundwater extraction inside and outside the park may adversely affect the geothermal features.

The US authorities noted that all of these concerns would be thoroughly analysed and measures taken to mitigate any negative impact. The gold, silver, and copper-mining project, located about four kilometres from the park's boundary, was under consideration in the early to mid-1990s. Park authorities were concerned that mining would pollute rivers flowing into Yellowstone to the detriment of wildlife, especially as toxic waste would also have to be stored in the area. In September 1996, however, the US President announced the successful conclusion of efforts to achieve a satisfactory resolution of the mining issue with a mutually agreed trade of land valued at US$65 million that fully removed this potential threat. Other progress was reported to the WHCom, particularly the control of the spread of the brucellosis through the elaboration of the Interim Bison Management Plan and the creation of a State–Federal interagency committee, the Greater Yellowstone Brucellosis Committee, which allows for the participation of concerned cattle owners.

The question of visitor pressure appears unresolved. In 2000 the National Parks Conservation Association included Yellowstone on its List of Ten Most Endangered National Parks because the winter season brings 1000 snowmobiles into the park daily. These machines shatter the peace that so many people see as part of the national park experience, as well as creating atmospheric pollution. In addition, noise and traffic congestion in all seasons detract from the visitor experience.

Sources: National Parks Conservation Association and World Heritage Committee web sites: http://www.npca.org/flash.html and http://www.unesco.org/whc/; M. R. Peterson (1997), 'Yellowstone', *World Heritage Review*, No.5, pp. 68–78.

12.4 South Africa

Background

It is not surprising, given the nation's history, that a comprehensive approach to heritage at the national level is relatively new in South Africa. Prior to the end of the apartheid regime, the European—and particularly the Afrikaaner—heritage was imposed as the national heritage despite the fact that it was the heritage of a minority group. The power wielded by the minority was reinforced by an imposed definition of heritage, and other definitions of heritage were ignored or downgraded by those with political power. Despite this, or perhaps because of it, the heritage of many indigenous African, and Indian, or groups was kept alive and vibrant by members of those groups, especially, but not solely, in the 'homelands' and in Black suburbs like Soweto. Active conservation of their heritage gave these people a very real sense of group identity, and conservation of heritage was a crucial ingredient in keeping up morale at times of severe oppression. The preservation of heritage concentrated on song, dance, art, and folk traditions, but certain locations and even buildings were also perceived as being important.

The bureaucracy of the apartheid era preserved sites and buildings important to the hegemonic group, but few others (although some provincial governments with important non-European constituencies, above all in the 'homelands', also preserved elements of indigenous African heritage). Natural heritage received greater national attention than cultural heritage, and its conservation has extended in a more seamless fashion into the post-apartheid period. This is probably largely because wildlife conservation, and the essential concurrent preservation of habitat and landscape, has always been viewed as a major earner of foreign currency through tourism. Game parks were also recognised as part of the essential national identity. It is only since the end of apartheid that Black cultural and built heritage has been recognised as part of the national identity by the national government and all provincial governments. In 1999, the first South African properties were inscribed on the WHL, and three key pieces of legislation were passed. When reading the description of the heritage system in South Africa, it is important to realise that South Africa is a functional federation, more like Australia or the USA than the United Kingdom in its political structure.

New legislation of 1999

Three key Acts were passed by the South African Parliament in 1999: the *National Heritage Resources Act 1999* (NHRA); the *National Heritage Council Act 1999*; and the *World Heritage Convention Act 1999*. The first two of these set up an integrated, post-apartheid national framework for heritage recognition and conservation, while the third gave legislative recognition to the World Heritage process and led the way for the inscription of the first South African World Heritage properties.

The NHRA sets out its purposes as follows:

> To introduce an integrated and interactive system for the management of the national heritage resources; to promote good government at all levels, and empower civil society to nurture and conserve their heritage resources so that they may be bequeathed to future generations; to lay down general principles for governing heritage resources management throughout the Republic; to introduce an integrated system for the identification, assessment and management of the heritage resources of South Africa; to establish the South African Heritage Resources Agency together with its Council to co-ordinate and promote the management of heritage resources at national level; to set norms and maintain essential national standards for the management of heritage resources in the Republic and to protect heritage resources of national significance; to control the export of nationally significant heritage objects and the import into the Republic of cultural property illegally exported from foreign countries; to enable the provinces to establish heritage authorities which must adopt powers to protect and manage certain categories of heritage resources; to provide for the protection and management of conservation-worthy places and areas by local authorities; and to provide for matters connected therewith.

Three elements are particularly worthy of further note. First, the NHRA consistently makes reference to *heritage resources*. Heritage is a resource like other things that can be used. It must thus be valued, managed, and conserved as all resources should be. As a resource, heritage can be, and often is, commodified and commercialised (Section 3.6), but even if it is not, it has very real values and non-economic uses for the nation and its people. Secondly, the NHRA aims to 'empower civil society to nurture and conserve' heritage, implying quite correctly that the identification and conservation of heritage is not something that can be left solely to bureaucracies, but which must involve all citizens. Thirdly, the purposes refer to nationally significant items being managed by the national agency, but also highlight that provincial and local levels of government must be enabled to play their role in heritage matters. Like Australia, South Africa encourages and, indeed, needs all three levels of government to be involved.

The NHRA applies primarily to cultural heritage, as becomes clear in the definition of the *national estate* in Box 12.6, but includes landscapes with cultural significance and geological sites of scientific or cultural importance. It also includes items of moveable heritage. The definitions and criteria for inclusion on the national estate list have not only much in common with those for other nations, including Australia (see Boxes 1.4 and 6.1) and for World Heritage (Section 8.3), but also have some features peculiarly adapted to the South African context.

Box 12.6 Definition of the South African National Estate

Those heritage resources of South Africa which are of cultural significance or other special value for the present community and for future generations must be considered part of the national estate …
… the national estate may include:
a places, buildings, structures and equipment of cultural significance;
b places to which oral traditions are attached or which are associated with living heritage;
c historical settlements and townscapes;
d landscapes and natural features of cultural significance;
e geological sites of scientific or cultural importance;
f archaeological and palaeontological sites;
g graves and burial grounds, including ancestral graves, royal graves and graves of traditional leaders, graves of victims of conflict, graves of designated individuals, and historical graves and cemeteries;
h sites of significance relating to the history of slavery in South Africa;
i specified types of moveable objects.
… a place or object is to be considered part of the national estate if it has cultural significance or other special value because of:
a its importance in the community, or pattern of South Africa's history;
b its possession of uncommon, rare or endangered aspects of South Africa's natural or cultural heritage;
c its potential to yield information that will contribute to an understanding of South Africa's natural or cultural heritage;
d its importance in demonstrating the principal characteristics of a particular class of South Africa's natural or cultural places or objects;
e its importance in exhibiting particular aesthetic characteristics valued by a community or cultural group;
f its importance in demonstrating a high degree of creative or technical achievement at a particular period;
g its strong or special association with a particular community or social group for social, cultural or spiritual reasons;
h its strong or special association with the life or work of a person, group or organisation of importance in the history of South Africa; or
i its significance in the history of slavery in South Africa.

Source: adapted slightly from the *National Heritage Resources Act 1999*, Section 3, Chapter 1.

The National Heritage Council Act has as its sole purpose the setting up of the National Heritage Council. According to the Act, the objects of the council are:

- to develop, promote, and protect the national heritage for present and future generations
- to coordinate heritage management
- to protect and promote the content and heritage which reside in *orature* [i.e. oral tradition] in order to make it accessible and dynamic
- to integrate living heritage with the functions and activities of the Council and all other heritage authorities and institutions at national, provincial, and local level
- to promote and protect indigenous knowledge systems, including but not limited to enterprise and industry, social upliftment, institutional framework and liberator! processes
- to intensify support for the promotion of the history and culture of all South African peoples and particularly to support research and publication on enslavement in South Africa

Again, this indicates a role well beyond the immoveable heritage that forms the focus for this book. It also reinforces some of the particularly South African focuses evident in Box 12.6, notably oral traditions, the need to include the heritage of all groups, and the place of slavery in national history. Bringing slavery into the heritage mainstream is a form of cultural catharsis a little like the open portrayal of the English occupation of Ireland (see Section 11.6).

The final important piece of legislation passed in 1999 that relates to heritage was the World Heritage Convention Act. The purposes of the Act are:

> To provide for: the incorporation of the World Heritage Convention into South African law; the enforcement and implementation of the World Heritage Convention in South Africa; the recognition and establishment of World Heritage Sites; the establishment of Authorities and the granting of additional powers to existing organs of state; the powers and duties of such Authorities, especially those safeguarding the integrity of World Heritage Sites; where appropriate, the establishment of Boards and Executive Staff Components of the Authorities; integrated management plans over World Heritage Sites; land matters in relation to World Heritage Sites; financial, auditing and reporting controls over Authorities; and to provide for incidental matters.

South African World Heritage sites will be discussed later in this section.

Cultural heritage

Following the passage of the NHRA in 1999, the South African Heritage Resources Agency (SAHRA) became the key national agency concerned with cultural heritage items of all types. Prior to that time, the National Monuments Council oversaw the listing of buildings as National Monuments. These were quite numerous and listing was not necessarily reserved for the 'grand and imposing' houses and public buildings—for example, in the medium-sized town of Montagu in Cape Province there were fourteen houses denoted as National Monuments in one street alone. In this way, South African National Monuments are similar to sites on the Australian RNE (see Section 9.3). Objects on the list are varied, and include a 250-year-old fruit-bearing citrus tree at Citrusdal. In addition to the system of National Monuments, some provinces, including KwaZulu-Natal, Transkei, and Ciskei, had similar agencies of their own. In 1996 the White Paper on Arts, Culture and Heritage recognised an imbalance in the list of National Monuments due to the predominance of 'European' sites and recommended that the National Monuments Council be reconstituted as a broader National Heritage Council. The Acts of 1999 stemmed in large part from this White Paper.

One of the general principles of the NHRA is that identification, assessment, and management of heritage resources must 'take account of all relevant cultural values and indigenous knowledge systems'. The state of affairs in post-apartheid South Africa has led to the scope of heritage being widened, which is part of the move to assert the rights of non-European South Africans, and strengthen the identity and pride of the various groups. Under the new system, heritage items are graded on a three-step scale: Grade I items are of national significance (*national heritage sites*); Grade II are significant 'within the context of a province or a region' (*provincial heritage sites*); and Grade III are other heritage resources worthy of conservation. National level functions (including Grade I sites) are the responsibility of SAHRA, while provincial heritage authorities and local authorities have more local responsibilities, including Grade II and Grade III sites respectively. This three-tier system seems to have replaced the previous list of National Monuments, which may foreshadow a similar move in Australia, with the revision of the RNE now under consideration (see Section 9.6).

The NHRA makes provision for protected areas, which are defined as 'such area of land surrounding a national heritage site as is reasonably necessary to ensure the protection and reasonable enjoyment of such site, or to protect the view of and from such site' (also known as the curtilage—see Section 6.4). These areas are protected by a range of legal provisions. Provisional protection may be granted to areas under threat while they are still under investigation for permanent listing.

Heritage registers are to be compiled at national and provincial levels, and possible heritage listings must be considered by a planning authority whenever any town or regional planning scheme or spatial development plan is considered, or at the instigation of a provincial heritage resources agency. An inventory of heritage resources is to be provided by each provincial authority. As well as specific safeguards for heritage-listed items, special permission is needed to demolish or alter any structure that is more than sixty years old. There are special provisions relating to archaeological and palaeontological sites, and to burial grounds and graves. Financial assistance may be made available to conserve and restore listed objects, and heritage agreements can be entered into with private owners or other authorities. In addition, national, provincial, and local authorities must cater for the presentation and interpretation of heritage items where appropriate.

Natural heritage

South Africa has a relatively long history of natural heritage reserves, including national parks (Figure 12.3), national forests, nature reserves and other reserves (wilderness areas, game reserves, and wildflower reserves) in addition to private game parks. Different reserves are managed by different levels of the three tiers of government. At the national level, the responsible department is the

Department of Environmental Affairs and Tourism (DEA&T). Given the importance of natural-area tourism in South Africa, this is undoubtedly far from an accidental grouping. A key focus area for the DEA&T is the 'promotion of conservation and development of natural and cultural resources for sustainable and equitable use'. The emphasis is clearly on natural heritage rather than cultural heritage, remembering, of course, that the two are rarely separable in South Africa. More particularly, the Chief Directorate of Biodiversity and Heritage has a section dealing with Cultural and Local Natural Resources Management. DEA&T emphasises the need for a national system for managing biodiversity and conservation areas, and the need to facilitate the 'participation of marginalised and local people and groups in cooperative management, equitable use and benefit sharing'.

South African National Parks (SANP or SANPARKS) is a statutory body allied to, but separate from, DEA&T, which has responsibility for conservation areas of national importance. A further group of areas is the responsibility of provincial government agencies and local authorities, and an important role is played by privately owned game parks (see Box 12.7). The Vision of SANP is that 'national parks will be the pride and joy of all South Africans', while their Mission is 'to acquire and manage a system of national parks that represent the indigenous wildlife, vegetation, landscapes and significant cultural assets of South Africa for the pride and benefit of the nation'. Each government department and agency in South Africa has a 'Transformation Mission', recognising the need to better serve the whole nation in the post-apartheid era; for SANP that is to 'transform an established system for managing the natural environment to one which encompasses cultural resources, and which engages all sections of the community'. The implication of this is that national parks and other conservation areas are now to be seen as the homes of indigenous peoples (marginalised under apartheid), as well as areas of natural heritage and biodiversity conservation. Throughout the 20th century, however, one eye has been firmly on the tourism potential of such conservation areas.

In late 2000 there were eighteen national parks (Figure 12.3), including the recently proclaimed Kgalagadi Transfrontier Park in the Kalahari Desert, shared with Botswana. The parks range in size from the giant Kruger National Park of nearly two million hectares (the forerunner of which was set up in 1898), to much smaller, more localised parks.

Kruger, like many other national parks, caters for large numbers of visitors, and contains many different standards of accommodation, good roads, wildlife viewing areas, guided tours of many types, and wilderness trails (for which small groups are accompanied by experienced, but armed, guides). According to the park's web site, when booking 'preference is given to written applications received 13 months in advance', and these bookings are confirmed nearly a year in advance. Numbers of visitors are therefore limited and the total demand cannot be met, certainly not at popular times of year. Kruger contains approximately 250 known cultural heritage sites, including 130 rock art sites and stone ruins at Thulamela Hill and Masorini.

Each province also has its agency to manage conservation areas, two of which are the KwaZulu-Natal Nature Conservation Services (*Ezemvelo KZN Wildlife* or KZNNCS) and Cape Nature Conservation. KwaZulu-Natal was the first province to establish a game reserve after a vote in its *Volksraad* (People's Council) in 1889: the Pongola Game Reserve was established on the

Figure 12.3

South African national parks and World Heritage properties

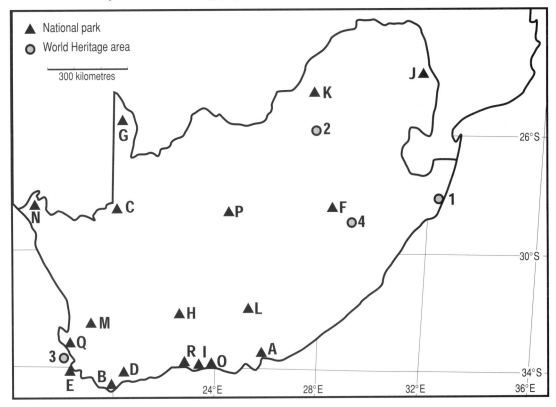

Key:

World Heritage areas

1–4: see Table 12.3.

National parks

A	Addo Elephant	
B	Agulhas	
C	Augrabies Falls	
D	Bontebok	
E	Cape Peninsula	
F	Golden Gate Highlands	
G	Kgalagadi Transfrontier Park (Kalahari)	
H	Karoo	
I	Knysna National Lake Area	
J	Kruger	
K	Marakele	
L	Mountain Zebra	
M	Namaqua	
N	Richtersveld	
O	Tsitsikamma	
P	Vaalbos	
Q	West Coast	
R	Wilderness	

Swaziland border in 1894. KZNNCS now employs over 4000 people, manages a large number of reserves, including the well-known Hluhluwe Umfolozi Park, and is responsible for the Greater St Lucia Wetland Park World Heritage property (see Table 12.3). It has played a leading role in wildlife conservation and, in particular, in bringing the white rhinoceros back from the brink of extinction. In fact, numbers of many species are increasing within its reserves so rapidly that it conducts an annual auction of wildlife to private reserve managements. Cape Nature Conservation (CNC) carries out a similar role in the Western Cape, managing twenty-nine conservation areas, including many featuring the unique *fynbos* vegetation (Plate 12.12). Both provincial agencies emphasise visitor facilities and management as well as conservation aims.

Plate 12.12

Fynbos vegetation below Table Mountain, Cape Town, South Africa. The fynbos is typical vegetation of the Cape Floral kingdom, unique to the south-western Cape. Proteas are a key family of the fynbos.

Photo: Peter Curson

The KZNNCS provides a definition of *wilderness* which contrasts strongly with the traditional Australian one, and which is worth quoting at length.

> The Wilderness philosophy is a broad and complex concept. However in its essence wilderness is the embracing of the singular spirit of primitive peoples and of an unmodernised era where silence and solitude, timelessness and unspoilt wildness, free from the impingement of modern technology pervades. In wilderness man [*sic*] is subservient, finding his unobtrusive niche amongst the flora and fauna, the rocks and stones and all creation around him. Here man [*sic*] seeks to harmonise with the natural world, to utilise and not exploit, to enjoy yet not spoil, to understand though not in order to act destructively, to learn and grow without attempting to dominate, to contribute, yet not for selfish gain.
>
> Less than one per cent of our country's land surface is proclaimed wilderness, a sad indication of the priorities of modern man [*sic*]. KZNNCS has set aside areas in some of our parks that are managed according to stringent wilderness principles in an attempt to preserve wilderness for future generations to visit. It would be unacceptable if our grandchildren were only able to read about wilderness, what it was like, but never able to experience it.[5]

Humans are an integral part of wilderness under this definition, but only under very strict conditions. Wilderness is seen as having definite value that makes it worth preserving in its own right, regardless of economic returns.

Private game parks play a key role in South Africa, probably to a greater extent than in any other nation. The desire to view the South African wildlife is so great among foreigners—and, to some extent, local South Africans—that they are willing to pay high prices to view it in comfort and safety. Some of the private reserves certainly offer extremely high standards of accommodation and service, but at correspondingly high prices. This is a clear case of the commodification and commercialisation of natural heritage. Box 12.7 describes a small number of such ventures.

Box 12.7 Private wildlife parks in South Africa

South Africa is notable for the role played by private wildlife parks. These private reserves are complementary to the National Parks operated by SANPARKS and tend, for obvious reasons, to be in the more remote and more arid parts of the country. A few of these parks will be mentioned below.

The *Shamwari Game Reserve*, approximately 70 kilometres north of Port Elizabeth, is in the relatively less remote Eastern Cape. Covering an area of 140 square kilometres, it is the largest private reserve in the province, and is also the only one there where visitors can see all of the 'big five'—lions, black rhinoceros, buffalo, leopards, and elephants. The owner of a ranch in this undulating hill country gradually bought several neighbouring farms and gradually re-introduced wildlife. The reserve offers luxury accommodation and ranger-led game-viewing drives in open vehicles, but at a very considerable price.

Much further north-east in the province of KwaZulu-Natal (north of Durban), the large 296-square-kilometre grassland *Itala Game Reserve* was established in 1972. Over time, thirteen farms have been consolidated to form this popular wildlife sanctuary. The main camp has forty self-catering chalets, and the central area includes a restaurant, store, and coffee shop. There are also three exclusive bush camps, but don't expect to exactly 'rough it', or to find cheap tent sites! Well maintained roads run through the park and guided walks are offered.

A number of private reserves are located along the western boundary of the Kruger National Park. An agreement reached in the early 1990s led to the removal of the Kruger boundary fence and herds of animals now roam freely between the various reserves. Again, luxury and exclusiveness mark the reserves, rather than low-budget, low-key ecotourism. These reserves serve a useful purpose of another type, by forming a buffer zone between the densely populated areas to the west and Kruger National Park.

The *Tswalu Private Desert Reserve* is a particularly ambitious project and is South Africa's largest private reserve at 750 square kilometres. It is in the Kalahari Desert dune area near the Botswana border. A wealthy British citizen bought and amalgamated twenty-six cattle farms, and had 800 kilometres of fencing and concrete dams and farmsteads removed. Over 7000 head of cattle were sold off in the process. Over 4700 animals from twenty-two species have been re-introduced, including lions, black rhinoceros, leopards, cheetahs, buffalo, zebras, giraffes, and a number of antelope species. The exclusive resort has its own tarred airstrip. Development has cost over 54 million rand [approximately A$13.5 million].

Source: *Eyewitness Travel Guides: South Africa*, Dorling Kindersley, London, 1999, pp. 186, 230–1, 275, 303.

South African World Heritage properties

The four existing South African World Heritage properties are listed in Table 12.3 and mapped in Figure 12.3. The Greater St Lucia Wetland Park is an extremely important and highly varied wetland area on the east coast. The group of fossil hominid sites has provided crucial evidence of the evolution of *Homo sapiens*. Robben Island is an important natural coastal site, and was nominated for protection by the South African Natural Heritage Programme for its significance as a seabird breeding site, but it is in fact inscribed on the WHL under cultural criteria because of historical reasons important to modern South Africa. Although Nelson Mandela is not mentioned by name in the official World Heritage short description (Table 12.3), he inevitably springs to mind in this context. The latest inscription, made in November 2000, is the Ukhahlamba–Drakensberg Park, inscribed for a mix of natural and cultural reasons (Table 12.3) and administered by KZNNCS.

In late 2000, the South African World Heritage Site Committee announced that it would nominate the Cape Floral Kingdom for inscription in the following year. This is one of the world's six floral kingdoms, and the only one limited to such a small area.

Table 12.3

South African World Heritage properties

	Property	Criteria (see Appendix 1 for key)	Date of inscription (and of enlargements)	Brief description and reasons for inscription (from World Heritage List)
1	Greater St Lucia Wetland Park	N ii, iii, iv	1999	The ongoing fluvial, marine, and aeolian processes in the site have produced a variety of landforms including coral reefs, long sandy beaches, coastal dunes, lake systems, swamps, and extensive reed and papyrus wetlands. The interplay of the park's environmental heterogeneity with major floods and coastal storms and a transitional geographic location between sub-tropical and tropical Africa has resulted in exceptional species diversity and ongoing speciation. The mosaic of landforms and habitat types creates superlative scenic vistas. The site contains critical habitat for a range of species from Africa's marine, wetland, and savannah environments.
2	Fossil Hominid Sites of Sterkfontein, Swartkrans, Kromdraai, and Environs	C iii, vi	1999	These fossil hominid sites have produced abundant scientific information on the evolution of modern man [sic] over the past 3.5 million years, on his way of life, and on the animals among which he lived and on which he fed. The landscape also preserves many features of that of prehistoric man.
3	Robben Island	C iii, vi	1999	Robben Island was used at various times between the 17th and the 20th century as a prison, a hospital for socially unacceptable groups, and a military base. Its buildings, and in particular those of the late 20th century, such as the maximum security prison for political prisoners, bear witness to the triumph of democracy and freedom over oppression and racialism.
4	Ukhahlamba–Drakensberg Park	N iii, iv; C i, iii	2000	The spectacular natural landscape of the Drakensberg Park contains many caves and rock-shelters with a wealth of paintings made by the San people over a period of 4000 years. They depict animals and human beings, and represent the spiritual life of this people, who no longer live in their original homeland.

A number of intact, protected areas of unique vegetation (fynbos), including Table Mountain in Capetown (Plate 12.12), are to be included in the Cape Floral Kingdom. Other areas include existing nature reserves, wilderness areas and public land within the Cape Peninsula Protected Natural Environment, centred on the Cape Peninsula National Park, formerly the Cape of Good Hope Nature Reserve. The issue of unified management will have to be addressed if the nomination is to be successful.

12.5   Thailand

Background

Thailand is one of the few nations in Asia to have retained its independence through the colonial period of the 16th to mid-20th centuries. Thai cultural heritage is therefore largely indigenous, rather than externally imposed. Over ninety per cent of Thais are Theravada Buddhists, and therefore related religious architecture (Plate 12.13) looms large in the inventory of built heritage sites. This heritage spans eleven centuries of various branches of Buddhist worship, including the Theravada tradition. Ancient national capitals are an important part of Thai cultural heritage, and feature as World Heritage properties. Natural heritage is also important with many conservation areas, including a number of national marine parks (Box 12.8). Thais are intensely proud of their heritage, but are also building a thriving tourist industry around it.

Plate 12.13 (A)

Wat Phra Keo, adjacent to the Royal Palace, Bangkok, Thailand: (A) Temple or Chapel Royal *(bot)* of the Emerald Buddha (B) one of the 178 panels in the extensive gallery, which together form a mural depicting the story of Rāmakien. Frequent restoration of this mural is necessary because of the damaging effects of the hot, humid climate.

Photo: Graeme Aplin

Plate 12.13 (B)

Photo: Graeme Aplin

Heritage management

Built heritage sites of national significance are generally under the management of the Thai Fine Arts Department (TFAD). Many of the temples and other buildings are built of wood and contain extensive murals, and because of the punishing tropical climate, much conservation and restoration has been necessary (Plate 12.13B). Isolated or less used sites are also prone to invasion by fast-growing vegetation (Plate 12.14). The TFAD has a list of cultural heritage sites, including, for example, sixty-six ruins within the walls of the far northern town of Chiang Saen and another seventy-nine nearby. More concentrated areas have been designated as historical parks; these include two of Thailand's World Heritage properties (see below). The TFAD has also taken part in conservation work on sites that fall outside the mainstream Thai tradition, such as on the Khmer temple at Phimai, where restoration began in 1925.

Plate 12.14

Head of Buddha surrounded by roots of tropical trees, Ayutthaya, Thailand. Vegetation grows rapidly in tropical areas and frequently invades and severely damages neglected heritage sites. This head has probably been dislodged from its original location.

Photo: Robert Wells

Thai National Parks (Figure 12.4) are managed by the Royal Forest Department under the *National Park Act 1961*. The Department is also in charge of wildlife conservation under the *Wildlife Preservation and Protection Act 1992*. The first Thai national park, Khao Yai National Park, was gazetted in 1962. There are now over 100 officially recognised parks, which include at least sixty national parks, many wildlife sanctuaries, and a number of national marine parks (Box 12.8). National parks vary greatly in size, ranging from the largest, the 2920-square-kilometre Kaeng Krachan National Park, to one of the smallest, the Khao Kitchakut National Park at 59 square kilometres, and preserving some spectacular waterfalls in the now rare lowland forest. Some are extremely popular with Thais and tend to have entrance roads lined with souvenir shops and other small-scale commercial enterprises.

Box 12.8 Thailand's National Marine Parks

A number of National Marine Parks have been established on the Gulf of Thailand Coast and on the Andaman Sea coast of far south-western Thailand. As well as aiming to conserve marine ecosystems, their goal is usually also to conserve coastal and island landscapes and ecosystems.

Ko Chang National Marine Park, south-east of Bangkok, covers an area of about 650 square kilometres, two-thirds of which is sea. The park also includes about fifty islands; some of the smaller ones are expensive, privately owned resorts. The largest, mountainous island, Ko Chang, was developing a lower key, more generally accessible tourist infrastructure in the 1990s. Thai-Chinese farmers first settled on the island in the mid-19th century, and since then most of the island's wildlife has been destroyed, although some species of small mammals and many species of birds, reptiles, and amphibians have survived. Visitors can experience many good, clean beaches, inland hiking, snorkelling, and fishing. Fishing remains the main industry, apart from tourism, for the residents.

Angthong National Marine Park is a stunning group of small, rugged islands that is easily accessible from the popular tourist resort area of Ko Samui, on the eastern coast of Thailand's narrow peninsula, yet it has remained teeming with wildlife. Unlike Ko Chang, the forty islands in this park are virtually uninhabited. These islands are in such a pristine state largely because they were the exclusive preserve of the Royal Thai Navy until the National Marine Park was declared in 1980. As there is very little accommodation and few other facilities on the islands, most visitors come on day trips from Ko Samui. All of the accommodation and visitor facilities are concentrated near the Park Headquarters on the largest island, Ko Wau Talab. Visitors, including many snorkellers, are mainly attracted by beautiful white sand beaches, lush tropical forests, and corals. Terrestrial and marine wildlife is abundant. Leopard cats, squirrels, long-tailed macaques, sea otters, dusky langurs, and pythons can all be encountered, as can at least forty bird species. One of the most noteworthy birds is the edible-nest swiftlet, whose nests are used in bird-nest soup, an Asian delicacy. The nests now fetch large sums of money and collectors were endangering the survival of the species on the islands. A government licence is now needed to collect the nests, allowed only between February and April and in September, and many key nesting sites are protected by armed guards.

Tarutao National Marine Park is situated on the western side of the narrow peninsula, and its fifty-one islands are the most south-westerly in the nation. The archipelago extends over 1490 square kilometres. Tarutao was declared Thailand's first National Marine Park in 1974, after the British Navy, in the 1960s, had curbed the activities of pirates operating from the islands. The Park is said to have some of the best dive sites in the world, with ninety-two species of coral-reef fish, and perhaps a quarter of the world's fish species in surrounding waters. Off-shore sightings of sperm and minke whales, dugongs and dolphins are common. There is also much terrestrial wildlife on the islands, including deer, wild pigs, macaques, otters and turtles; sea turtles are also quite common. The larger islands are covered with semi-evergreen rainforest, and the largest, Ko Taratuo, reaches an elevation of 708 m. There is only a limited amount of accommodation on the islands, and few other visitor facilities. Ferries cannot safely reach the islands during the monsoon season, so visitor access is limited to the mid-November to mid-May period. A smaller island, Ko Adang, is home to a community of sea gypsies, displaced from two other islands by Park authorities when the Park was created. Relations between the authorities and the sea gypsies remain strained.

Source: *Eyewitness Travel Guides: Thailand*, Dorling Kindersley, London, 1997, pp. 312–13, 330–1, 376.

Figure 12.4

Thai national parks and World Heritage properties

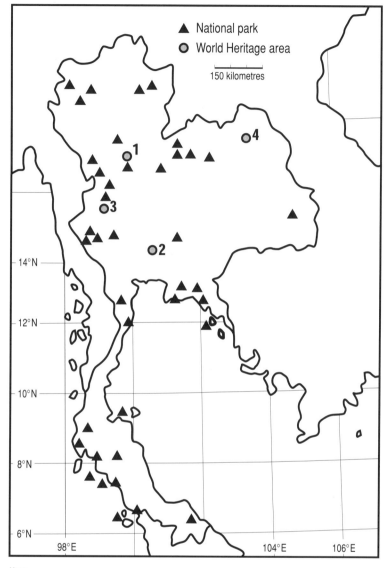

Even though the National Park Act quite explicitly forbids many human activities, including 'occupying or possessing land' and taking wildlife, there are large numbers of people living off the land in Thai national parks and other reserves. This is particularly true of some of the hill tribes in the mountainous interior and near the Burmese, Laotian, and Cambodian borders. Thai national parks are thus possibly closer to European ones than to Australian ones in this respect, even if this situation is unintentional.

Thai World Heritage properties

Thailand has four World Heritage properties, all inscribed in 1991–92 (Table 12.4 and Figure 12.4). Two of these—at Sukhotai and Ayutthaya (Plate 12.15)— are former national capitals that are now historical parks within which extensive restoration work has been undertaken by the TFAD. The others comprise an archaeological site of great importance in the earliest stages of the human history of South-East Asia, and an extensive and largely intact forest wilderness area on the Burmese border.

Plate 12.15

Wat Phra Si Sanphet, Ayutthaya Historical Park World Heritage property, Thailand. Ayutthaya was the Thai capital from approximately 1350, but especially from the mid-16th century, until the 18th century. Many architecturally and historically significant buildings remain and a number have been restored. Wat Phra Si Sanphet was built during the 15th century as a state temple; the three chedis on the left contained the ashes of kings, precious Buddha images, and royal regalia. Partial restoration occurred in the 20th century, but many of its treasures are now in museums.

Photo: Robert Wells

12.6 China

Background

China has an immensely old cultural heritage and an impressive natural heritage that represents a wide range of geographic zones. As literature and web sites in English on the Chinese framework for heritage protection are extremely rare, the following sections are impressionistic, and based mainly on information gleaned from two short trips to China and from what English-language literature is available. One thing that strikes the visitor is the range of historical and cultural experiences that have been incorporated into the accepted list of Chinese cultural heritage sites. For example, despite the Chinese Communist dislike of all religions, Buddhist temples (Plate 12.16) and Confucian sites are included, as well as buildings from the days of Shanghai's foreign concessions (Plate 12.17 and Box 12.9), despite the immense ill-feeling towards those foreigners at the time and since.

Table 12.4

Thailand's World Heritage properties

Property	Criteria (See Appendix 1 for key)	Date of inscription (and of enlargements)	Brief description and reasons for inscription (from World Heritage List)
1 Historic Town of Sukhotai and Associated Historic Towns	C i, iii	1991	Capital of the first Kingdom of Siam in the 13th and 14th centuries, a number of notable monuments, which illustrate the beginnings of Thai architecture, can be seen in Sukhotai.
2 Historic City of Ayutthaya and Associated Historic Towns	C iii	1991	Founded in about 1350, Ayutthaya became the second Siamese capital after Sukhotai. It was destroyed by the Burmese in the 18th century. The remains, characterised by its *prang* or reliquary towers, and gigantic monasteries, give an idea of its past splendour.
3 Thungyai-Huai Kha Khaeng Wildlife Sanctuaries	N ii, iii, iv	1991	Stretching over more than 600 000 hectares along the Myanmar border, the sanctuary, which is relatively intact, contains examples of almost all the forest types of continental South-East Asia. It is home to a very diverse array of animals, including 77 per cent of the large mammals (especially elephants and tigers), 50 per cent of the large birds and 33 per cent of the land vertebrates to be found in this region.
4 Ban Chiang Archaeological Site	C iii	1992	Considered the most important prehistoric settlement so far discovered in South-East Asia, Ban Chiang was the centre of a remarkable phenomenon of human cultural, social, and technological evolution. The site presents the earliest evidence of farming in the region and of the manufacture and use of metals.

Box 12.9 Historic buildings of Shanghai

The following information provides a brief impression of the scope of built heritage listings in Shanghai. It is very difficult to gain an accurate understanding of how many, and which, buildings are officially listed by the Shanghai Provincial (Municipal) Government, or by the national agencies. The following account is taken from a listing compiled by the Shanghai Municipal Tourism Administration. The list includes six categories of buildings: ancient constructions; buildings on the Bund; former residences of prominent figures; religious constructions; residential constructions; and public constructions. It should be noted that the list covers a greater area than the continuous urban area of Shanghai proper.

A Ancient constructions

These include a 9th-century stella (memorial column); a 10th-century pagoda; a site where a famous 17th-century painter 'wrote poems and drank wine'; the famous 16th-century Yu Yuan Garden in central Shanghai; remains of the 16th-century city wall; a five-arched, humpback 16th-century bridge; and a 13th-century Confucian temple.

B Buildings on the Bund

These represent the late 19th-century and early 20th-century period when Shanghai was the centre for European and US interests in much of China. As well as former banks and other commercial buildings, such as those shown in Plate 12.17, listed buildings include the Shanghai Mansions, an Early-Modern high-rise apartment block which is now a hotel; the 1917 Russian Consulate; the steel bridge over Suzhou Canal; and the famous Peace Hotel built in 1929.

C Former residences of prominent figures

These buildings illustrate associational significance and provide some interesting examples of adaptive re-use. The former homes of Sun Yat-sen, Zhou Enlai, and Chiang Kai-shek are included, and the last of these is now the Middle School of the Shanghai Conservatorium. The house where the First National Congress of the Communist Party of China was held in secret in 1921 is also included. Another large, European-style house began as the American Country Club, became the home of Sun Yat-sen's son, and is now the Shanghai Biochemical Research Institute. The enormous Gothic residence of a Mr Muller ('King of Horse-racing') is now the office of the Shanghai Committee of the Chinese Communist Youth League.

D Religious constructions

Despite the notably anti-religious policies of the Communist Government, a number of buildings in this category are noted in this publication and actively preserved by the Municipal Government. They include Buddhist temples and monasteries; three Roman Catholic cathedrals; the 14th-century Songjiang Mosque; a Russian Orthodox church; a Daoist temple; and a Christian Community Church.

E Residential constructions

Several 'lane housing' groups from different periods are included, along with larger residential complexes comprising quite extensive groupings of three- to four-storey apartment blocks. Some very large and luxurious private homes are also listed, generally built in various European and American architectural styles; many of these are now used as 'guest houses' (luxurious visitor accommodation), consulates, or government agency offices.

F Public constructions

This extremely varied group includes two 1920s–30s high-rise apartment blocks, now hotels; the 1934 Park Hotel, once the tallest building in the Far East; commercial buildings, including a number of department stores; the Great World Entertainment Centre, a recreation complex; the Shanghai Library (originally the Shanghai Race Course Club); the Grand Cinema (1933); the China Coin Works, a Classical building from 1929; the Yangshupu Water Plant built in an English castle style in 1881; Jiaotong University, built in 1896; at least two schools; the main Post Office and Supreme People's Court buildings; a Jewish-Russian hall which served Second World War refugees; and, intriguingly, an old-style timber, steel and cement 'electric wire pole' on Sichuan Road.

Source: Shanghai Municipal Tourism Administration (1996), *A Tour of Shanghai's Historical Architecture*, Henan Fine Arts Publishing House, Shanghai.

It is apparent that heritage items, cultural or natural, can be listed and managed at a number of scales in China, as is the case in most countries. Box 12.10 shows this through discussion of the listing history of the components of the Suzhou Gardens World Heritage property (see Plate 12.18). Commune, municipal, provincial, and national authorities are all involved in one way or another. All are now taking advantage of the tourism potential of heritage items, from both domestic and foreign visitors.

Plate 12.16

Grounds of Ling Yin (Soul's Retreat) Buddhist temple complex, Hangzhou, Zhejiang Province, China: the Buddhist carvings in the Feilefeng Grottoes are 500 to 800 years old, a national cultural heritage item under protection.

Photo: Graeme Aplin

Plate 12.17

The Bund, Shanghai, China with mainly 1920s and 1930s commercial and government buildings. Those shown include on the left, the Dongfen Hotel (1910, formerly the Shanghai Club), second from right, the former Shanghai Municipal People's Government building (1923) and, on the right, the Shanghai Customs House (1927).

Photo: Graeme Aplin

Box 12.10   History of protection of the classical Suzhou gardens

---

In December 1997, the Classical Gardens of Suzhou were inscribed on the World Heritage List. This property consisted of four of the best known gardens in Suzhou: the Humble Administrator's Garden, the Lingering Garden, the Master-of-Nets Garden, and the Mountain Villa with Embracing Beauty. In late 1998, the State Council of the People's Republic of China agreed to nominate five more gardens, and these were added to the World Heritage List in November, 2000. These additional gardens are: the Canglang Pavilion, the Lion Forest Garden, the Garden of Cultivation, the Couple's Garden Retreat, and the Retreat and Reflection Garden. These gardens had previously been given various heritage recognitions within China as follows:

1 *The Humble Administrator's Garden* and the *Lingering Garden* (or the Garden to Linger In) were listed as cultural relics of national importance in 1961.
2 *The Master-of-Nets Garden* was listed as a cultural relic of national importance in 1982.
3 *The Mountain Villa with Embracing Beauty* was listed as a cultural relic of national importance in 1988.
4 *The Canglang Pavilion* was listed in 1982 as a cultural relic under the protection of Jiangsu Province.
5 *The Lion Forest Garden* does not appear to have been previously listed at provincial or national level.
6 *The Garden of Cultivation* was listed as a cultural relic under the protection of Jiangsu Province in 1995.
7 *The Couple's Garden Retreat* was also listed as a cultural relic under the protection of Jiangsu Province in 1995.
8 *The Retreat and Reflection Garden* was listed in 1988 as a cultural relic under the protection of Jiangsu Province.

Source: *The Classical Gardens of Suzhou, the World Heritage*, CiP/SJPC, 2000.

Heritage management

In terms of natural heritage, the top level of conservation in China is given to a national forest park (NFP), under the control of the National Forestry Administration, which makes it similar to the structure in Thailand. These parks are by no means entirely forest, nor concerned with forests as a timber resource. A recent (2000) list oriented at the ecotourist includes 120 conservation areas, the great majority of which are designated as NFPs, but some as forest parks and others as nature reserves. Some are also designated as national scenic areas, and many contain extensive Buddhist temple complexes (especially on mountain peaks), and/or tourist infrastructure. The Longsheng Hot Springs NFP contains a major summer resort and spa centre, while the Mulanweichang NFP is on the ecotone between forest and grassland. Yet another form of reserve is the historical site. Figure 12.5 maps the nature reserves and the Biosphere Protection Zones, fourteen of the latter being Biosphere Reserves and thus China's contribution to the Man and Biosphere Program (see Section 8.5).

Large numbers of cultural heritage buildings and sites are also protected by the various levels of government. A small number of examples will be presented here to indicate the range of features represented.

- The Banpo archaeological site near Xian was discovered in 1953 and extensively excavated over the following few years to reveal the remains of a Neolithic village and large numbers of artefacts from that period. In 1961 the site was declared a Historical Monument and Cultural Relic under state protection by Shaanxi Province. In 1958 the on-site Banpo Museum was opened to provide protection from weather for the diggings and to allow controlled visitor access. Extensions were being built in 2001.
- At Yancheng, near Changzhou, are the ruins of a town built 2500 years ago with three city walls and three moats. Although few buildings remain, the defensive works are in a good state of preservation under state protection.

Figure 12.5

Chinese Biosphere Protection Zones, Nature Reserves, and World Heritage properties

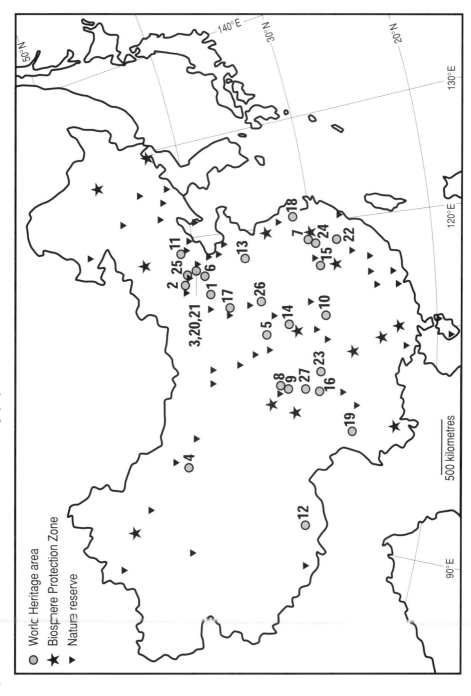

Key:
World Heritage areas
1–27: see Table 12.5.

Source: based, in part, on *China's National Forest Parks* (1999) China National Tourism Administration, Beijing, p. 44.

- The Liuhe Pagoda, or Pagoda of Six Harmonies, in Hangzhou was built on Mount Yuelun in 970 and rebuilt in the 1150s. It was placed under state protection in 1961 as a major relic.
- The Municipality of Shanghai has recognised more than 1400 buildings of historical and scientific value within its confines and offers varying degrees of protection over them (see Plate 12.17 and Box 12.9).
- The Stone Pagoda of the Temple of Soul's Retreat and nearby rock carvings of Buddhas and other Buddhist figures (see Plate 12.16) outside Hangzhou are under provincial protection as a key cultural relic.

Chinese World Heritage properties

The Chinese Government has taken enthusiastically to the concept of World Heritage for a number of possible reasons: genuine pride in Chinese heritage and national achievements over many centuries, if not millennia; a desire to be seen as a good world citizen; the possibility of foreign aid to restore and conserve inscribed properties and to provide conservation advice; and the perceived tourist spin-off of inscriptions. The Chinese National Tourism Administration certainly produces some beautifully illustrated (but not always well translated) literature on its World Heritage properties.[6]

Table 12.5 lists the twenty-seven Chinese World Heritage properties, which are mapped in Figure 12.5, and some of which are illustrated in Plates 12.18, 12.19, and 12.20. The first six properties were inscribed in 1987, the last four in November 2000. Three of these properties were inscribed for natural reasons alone, although each of the three is known as a 'Scenic and Historic Interest Area'. Jiuzhaigou was selected in 1982 as one of the Top State Scenic Areas in China. This area has a population of ethnic Tibetan farmers within its borders, and giant pandas also inhabit the valley; in 1997 it also became a Biosphere Reserve. China's first NFP, Zhangjiajie, is also included on the WHL—in 1988 it, too, was recognised as one of the Top State Scenic Areas. In its central, easily accessible scenic area, there are a town and a number of temples. Other more obvious sites for inclusion are the Great Wall, Forbidden City (Plate 12.20), and Summer Palace, but also the site of the important archaeological and anthropological find of Peking Man *(Sinanthropus pekinensis)* at Zhoukoudian; ancient Buddhist art sites at the Mogao Caves and Dazu; the temple, cemetery, and family mansion of Confucius at Qufu; the site of the first Buddhist temple in China at Mount Emei, still one of the holiest places for Buddhists; and the exceptionally well preserved 14th-century city of Pin Yao. The inclusion of the Potala Palace at Lhasa (in 1994, with extensions in 2000) could be interpreted as an attempt to legitimise Chinese incorporation of Tibet. The Classical Gardens of Suzhou are described in Box 12.10 (see also Plate 12.18). The Mausoleum of the First Qin Emperor is the site of the famous terracotta warrior statues. Unfortunately these statues have been at serious risk of deterioration; a recent newspaper article heralded 'Terracotta warriors "seriously ill"'.[7] A three-year conservation program is now planned, with Belgian assistance, to prevent the build-up of mould on the statues.

Plate 12.18

The central lake of the Garden of the Humble Administrator, Suzhou, Jiangsu Province, China. Begun in 1509, it is one of a series of classical Suzhou gardens that jointly constitute a World Heritage property.

Photo: Graeme Aplin

Plate 12.19

The Summer Palace, a Chinese World Heritage property. Situated 10 kilometres north-west of central Beijing, it was begun in 1153 and many of its component buildings were rebuilt in 1888. It has an extensive classical Chinese garden, which incorporates a large artificial lake.

Photo: Diane Callender

Plate 12.20

The Gate of Supreme Harmony at the Forbidden City or Palace Museum, Beijing, China, which was the imperial palace of the Ming and Qing dynasties, construction taking place in 1406–20. The Palace Museum is a World Heritage property.

Photo: Diane Callender

Table 12.5

People's Republic of China World Heritage properties

	Property	Criteria (see Appendix 1 for key)	Date of inscription (and of enlargements)	Brief description and reasons for inscription (from World Heritage List)
1	Mount Taishan	N iii; C i, ii, iii, iv, v, vi	1987	The sacred Mount Tai has been the object of an imperial pilgrimage for nearly 2000 years, and the artistic masterpieces contained within it are in perfect harmony with the natural landscape. It has always been a source of inspiration to Chinese artists and scholars, and symbolises ancient Chinese civilisations and beliefs.
2	The Great Wall	C i, ii, iii, iv, vi	1987	In about 220 BC, under Qin Shin Huang, sections of fortifications which had been built earlier were joined together to form a united defence system against invasions from the north. Construction continued up to the Ming Dynasty (1368–1644), when the Great Wall became the world's largest military structure. Its historic and strategic importance is matched only by its architectural value.
3	Imperial Palace of the Ming and Qing Dynasties	C iii, iv	1987	Seat of supreme power for over five centuries, the Forbidden City, with its landscaped gardens and many buildings whose 9000 rooms contain furniture and works of art, constitutes a priceless testimony to Chinese civilization during the Ming and Qing dynasties.
4	Mogao Caves	C i, ii, iii, iv, v, vi	1987	Situated at a strategic point along the Silk Route, at the crossroads of trade as well as of religious, cultural, and intellectual influences, the 492 cells and cave sanctuaries in Mogao are famous for their statues and wall paintings, spanning 1000 years of Buddhist art.
5	Mausoleum of the First Qin Emperor	C i, iii, iv, vi	1987	No doubt thousands of statues still remain to be unearthed on this archaeological site, not discovered until 1974. Qin, the first unifier of China, who died in 210 BC, is buried, surrounded by the famous terracotta warriors, at the centre of a complex designed to mirror the urban plan of the capital, Xianyan. The figures, all different, with their horses, chariots, and weapons, are masterpieces of realism and also hold great historical interest.
6	Peking Man Site at Zhoukoudian	C iii, vi	1987	Scientific work at the site, 42 kilometres south-west of Beijing, is still underway. So far, it has led to the discovery of the remains of *Sinanthropus pekinensis*, who lived in the Middle Pleistocene era, along with various objects, and the remains of *Homo sapiens sapiens*, dating as

No.	Site	Date	Criteria	Description
				far back as 18 000 to 11 000 BC. The site is not only an exceptional reminder of the human societies of the Asian continent very long ago, but also illustrates the process of evolution.
7	Mount Huangshan	1990	N iii, iv; C ii	Huangshan, known as 'the loveliest mountain of China', was acclaimed through art and literature during a good part of Chinese history (the Shanshui 'mountain and water' style of the mid-16th century). Today it holds the same fascination for visitors, poets, painters, and photographers who come in pilgrimage to this enchanting site, renowned for its magnificent scenery made up of many granite peaks and rocks emerging out of a sea of clouds.
8	Jiuzhaigou Valley Scenic and Historic Interest Area	1992	N iii	Stretching over 72 000 hectares in the northern part of Sichuan Province, the jagged Jiuzhaigou Valley reaches a height of more than 4800 metres, therefore comprising a series of diverse forest ecosystems. Its superb landscapes are specially interesting for their series of narrow conic karst landforms and spectacular waterfalls. Some 140 bird species also inhabit the valley, as well as a number of endangered plant and animal species, including the giant panda and the Sichuan takin.
9	Huanglong Scenic and Historic Interest Area	1992	N iii	Situated in the north-west part of Sichuan province, the Huanglong valley is made up of snow-capped peaks and the eastern-most of all the Chinese glaciers. In addition to its mountain landscape, diverse forest ecosystems can be found, as well as spectacular limestone formations, waterfalls, and hot springs. The area also has a population of endangered animals, including the giant panda and the Sichuan golden snub-nosed monkeys.
10	Wulingyuan Scenic and Historic Interest Area	1992	N iii	A spectacular area stretching over more than 26 000 hectares in China's Hunan Province, the site is distinguished by more than 3000 narrow sandstone pillars and peaks, many over 200 metres high. Between the peaks lie ravines and gorges with streams, pools, and waterfalls, some forty caves, as well as two large natural bridges. In addition to the striking beauty of its landscape, the region is also noted for the fact that it shelters a number of endangered plant and animal species.
11	The Mountain Resort and its Outlying Temples, Chengde	1994	C ii, iv	The Mountain Resort, the Qing Dynasty's summer palace, in Hebei Province, was built between 1703 and 1792. It is a vast complex of palaces and administrative and ceremonial buildings. Temples of various architectural styles and Imperial gardens subtly blend into a landscape of

Property	Criteria (see Appendix 1 for key)	Date of inscription (and of enlargements)	Brief description and reasons for inscription (from World Heritage List)
			lakes, pasture land, and forests. In addition to its aesthetic interest, the Mountain Resort is a rare historic vestige of the final development of feudal society in China.
12 The Potala Palace, Lhasa and the Jokhang Temple Monastery	C i, iv, vi	1994, 2000	The Potala Palace, an administrative, religious, and political complex, is built on the Red Mountain in the centre of the Lhasa Valley, at an altitude of 3700 metres. The complex comprises the White Palace and the Red Palace, with their ancillary buildings. The Potala, winter palace of the Dalai Lama since the 7th century AD, symbolises Tibetan Buddhism and its central role in the traditional administration in Tibet. The beauty and originality of its architecture, its ornate decoration and its harmonious integration in a striking landscape add to its historic and religious interest.
13 Temple and Cemetery of Confucius and the Kong Family Mansion in Qufu	C i, iv, vi	1994	The temple, cemetery, and family mansion of Confucius, the great philosopher, politician, and educator of the 6th–5th century BC, is located at Qufu, in Shandong Province. The temple built in his commemoration in 478 BC, destroyed and reconstructed over the centuries, today comprises more than 100 buildings. The cemetery contains Confucius' tomb, and the remains of more than 100 000 of his descendants. The small house of the Kong Family has become a gigantic aristocratic residence, of which 152 buildings remain. This complex of monuments at Qufu has maintained its outstanding artistic and historic character due to the devotion of successive Chinese emperors over more than 2000 years.
14 Ancient Building Complex in the Wudang Mountains	C i, ii, vi	1994	The Complex consists of palaces and temples forming the nucleus of secular and religious buildings exemplifying the architectural and artistic achievements of the Yuan, Ming, and Qing dynasties of China. Situated in the scenic valleys and on the slopes of the Wudang mountains in Hubei Province, the site, built as an organised complex during the Ming Dynasty (14th–17th century), contains Taoist buildings from as early as the 7th century, and represents the highest standards of Chinese art and architecture over a period of nearly 1000 years.
15 Lushan National Park	C ii, iii, iv, vi	1996	Mount Lushan, in Jiangxi, is one of the spiritual centres of Chinese civilisation. Buddhist and Taoist temples, along with landmarks of Confucianism, where the most eminent masters taught, blend well into a strikingly beautiful landscape which has inspired countless artists who developed the aesthetic approach to nature found in Chinese culture.

16	Mount Emei Scenic Area, including Leshan Giant Buddha Scenic Area	N iv; C iv, vi	1996	The first Buddhist temple in China was built here in the first century in very beautiful surroundings atop Mount Emei. The addition of other temples turned the site into one of the main holy places of Buddhism. Over the centuries, the cultural treasures grew in number. The most remarkable was the Giant Buddha of Leshan, carved out of a hillside in the eighth century and looking down on the junction of three rivers. At 71 metres high, it is the largest Buddha in the world. Mount Emei is also notable for its very diverse vegetation, ranging from subtropical to subalpine pine forests. Some of the trees are more than 1000 years old.
17	Ancient City of Ping Yao	C ii, iii, iv	1997	Ping Yao is an exceptionally well preserved example of a traditional Han Chinese city, founded in the 14th century. Its urban fabric is an epitome of the evolution of architectural styles and town planning in Imperial China over five centuries. Of special interest are the imposing buildings associated with banking, for which Ping Yao was the centre for the whole of China in the 19th and early 20th centuries.
18	Classical Gardens of Suzhou	C i, ii, iii, iv, v	1997, 2000	Classical Chinese garden design, which seeks to recreate natural landscapes in miniature, is nowhere better illustrated than in the gardens in the historic city of Suzhou. They are universally acknowledged to be masterpieces of the genre. Dating from the 16th–18th centuries, the gardens reflect the profound metaphysical importance of natural beauty in Chinese culture in their meticulous design.
19	Old Town of Lijiang	C ii, iv	1997	The Old Town of Lijiang, which adapted itself harmoniously to the uneven topography of this key commercial and strategic site, has retained an historic townscape of high quality and authenticity. Its architecture is noteworthy for the blending of elements from several cultures that have come together over many centuries. Lijiang also possesses an ancient water-supply system of great complexity and ingenuity that is still functioning effectively.
20	Summer Palace, an Imperial Garden in Beijing	C i, ii, iii	1998	The Summer Palace in Beijing, which was first built in 1750, largely destroyed in the war of 1860, and restored on its original foundation in 1886, is a masterpiece of Chinese landscape garden design, integrating the natural landscape of hills and open water with man-made [sic] features such as pavilions, halls, palaces, temples, and bridges into a harmonious and aesthetically exceptional whole.
21	Temple of Heaven—an Imperial Sacrificial Altar in Beijing	C i, ii, iii	1998	The Temple of Heaven, founded in the first half of the 15th century, is a dignified complex of fine cult buildings set in gardens and surrounded by historic pine woods. In its overall layout and in that of its individual buildings, it symbolises the relationship between earth and heaven which

Property	Criteria (see Appendix 1 for key)	Date of inscription (and of enlargements)	Brief description and reasons for inscription (from World Heritage List)
			stands at the heart of Chinese cosmogony, and also the special role played by the emperors within that relationship.
22 Mount Wuyi	N iii, iv; C iii, vi	1999	Mount Wuyi is the most outstanding area for biodiversity conservation in south-east China and a refuge for a large number of ancient, relict species, many of them endemic to China. The serene beauty of the dramatic gorges of the Nine Bend River, with its numerous temples and monasteries, many now in ruins, provided the setting for the development and spread of neo-Confucianism, which has been very influential in the cultures of East Asia since the 11th century. In the 1st century BC a large administrative capital was built at nearby Chengcun by the Han Dynasty rulers. Its massive walls enclose an archaeological site of great significance.
23 The Dazu Rock Carvings	C i, ii, iii	1999	The steep hillsides in the Dazu area contain an exceptional series of rock carvings dating from the 9th to 13th centuries. They are remarkable for their high aesthetic qualities, for their rich diversity of subject matter, both secular and religious, and for the light they shed on everyday life in China during this period. They provide outstanding evidence of the coming together of Buddhism, Taoism, and Confucianism in a harmonious synthesis.
24 Ancient Villages in Southern Anhui—Xidi and Hongcun	C ii, iv, v	2000	The two traditional villages of Xidi and Hongcun preserve to a remarkable extent the appearance of non-urban settlements of a type that largely disappeared or was transformed during the last century. Their street plan, their architecture and decoration, and the integration of houses with comprehensive water systems are unique surviving examples.
25 Imperial Tombs of the Ming and Qing Dynasties	C i, ii, iii, iv, vi	2000	The Ming and Qing imperial tombs are natural sites modified by human influence, carefully chosen according to the principles of geomancy (Fengshui) to house numerous buildings of traditional architectural design and decoration. They illustrate the continuity over five centuries of a world view and concept of power specific to feudal China.
26 Longmen Grottoes	C i, ii, iii	2000	The grottoes and niches of Longmen contain the largest and most impressive collection of Chinese art of the late Northern Wei and Tang Dynasties (316–907). These works, entirely devoted to the Buddhist religion, represent the high point of Chinese stone carving.
27 Mount Qincheng and the Dujiangyan Irrigation System	C ii, iv, vi	2000	Construction of the Dujiangyan irrigation system began in the 3rd century BC, and still controls the waters of the Minjiang River and distributes it to the fertile farmland of the Chengdu plains. Mount Qincheng was the birthplace of Taoism, which is celebrated in a series of ancient temples.

12.7   Conclusion

The brief treatments of a small number of nations and their approaches to heritage identification and conservation in this chapter can do no more than illustrate, and hopefully reinforce, the more general material of Chapters 1 to 8. Naturally, each nation's heritage is worth more than one weighty tome in its own right; many such tomes, frequently magnificently illustrated, undoubtedly exist, though often not in English. Many readers have, I imagine, travelled to these and many other nations, while others plan to do so in the future. You will be able to add your own observations on heritage, based on personal experience.

Notes

1. *The State of New Zealand's Environment 1997*, Ministry for the Environment, Wellington, 1997.
2. Pocock, D. (1997) 'Some reflections on world heritage', *Area*, 29/3, p. 261.
3. Kirby, V. (1996) 'Landscape, heritage and identity: Stories from New Zealand's West Coast', in Hall, C. M. & McArthur, S. (eds) *Heritage Management in Australia and New Zealand: The Human Dimension* (2nd edn), Oxford University Press, Melbourne, p. 239.
4. ibid., p. 238.
5. KwaZulu-Natal Nature Conservation Service web site at http://www.rhino.org.za.
6. *China New Millennium—China's World Heritages*, China National Tourism administration, 1999; *The Art of Chinese Gardens*, China National Tourism administration, 1999.
7. Schauble, J., 'Terracotta warriors "seriously ill"', *Sydney Morning Herald*, September 2000.

Further Reading

Updated information on changes to legislation and bureaucratic structures is available at the web site associated with this book, at http://www.es.mq.edu.au/courses/REM/heritage.htm.

Bown, D. (1997) *Eyewitness Travel Guides: California*, Dorling Kindersley, London.*

Brett, M., Johnson-Barker, B. & Renssen, M. (1999) *Eyewitness Travel Guides: South Africa*, Dorling Kindersley, London.*

Butche, R. D. (1997) *Exploring Our National Historic Parks and Sites*, Roberts Rinehart, Niwot, CO.

Chang, K-C. (1986) *The Archaeology of Ancient China*, Yale University Press, New Haven, CT.

China National Tourism Administration (1998) *China's National Forest Parks: Highlights*, CNTA, Beijing.

China National Tourism Administration (1999) *The Art of the Chinese Gardens*, CNTA, Beijing.

China National Tourism Administration (1999) *China: New Millennium—China's World Heritages*, CNTA, Beijing.

Cohen, J. L. & Cohen, J. A. (1986) *China Today and Her Ancient Treasures*, Abrams, New York.

Cornwel-Smith, P. (ed) & Bown D. (1997) *Eyewitness Travel Guides: Thailand*, Dorling Kindersley, London.*

Everhart, W. C. (1972) *The National Park Service*, Praeger, New York.

Herr, P. B. (1991) *Saving Place: A Guide and Report Card for Protecting Community Character*, National Trust for Historic Preservation, Boston.

Hoover, M. B., Rensch, H. E. & Rensch, E. G. (1966) *Historic Spots in California* (3rd edn), Stanford University Press, Stanford, CA.

Knobel, J. (1999) *The Magnificent Natural Heritage of South Africa*, Sunbridge Publishing, Llandudno, South Africa.

Memon, P. A. (1993) *Keeping New Zealand Green: Recent Environmental Reforms*, University of Otago Press, Dunedin.

National Geographic Society (1996) *National Geographic Guide to America's Historic Places*, National Geographic Society, Washington D.C.

National Geographic Society (1997) *National Geographic Guide to the State Parks of the United States*, National Geographic Society, Washington D.C.

National Geographic Society (2001) *National Geographic Guide to the National Parks of the United States* (3rd ed), National Geographic Society, Washington D.C.

Ombler, K. (2001) *National Parks and Other Wild Places of New Zealand*, New Holland Publishers, London.

Pope, D. & Pope J. (1993) *Mobil New Zealand Travel Guide: North Island* (8th edn), Reed Books, Auckland.

Pope, D. & Pope J. (1993) *Mobil New Zealand Travel Guide: South Island, Stewart Island and the Chatham Islands* (6th edn), Reed Books, Auckland.

Reader's Digest (Australia) (1992) *Wild New Zealand* (revised edn), Reader's Digest, Sydney.

Reader's Digest (1988) *America's Historic Places: An Illustrated Guide to Our Country's Past*, Reader's Digest Association, Pleasantville, NY.

Stuart, C. & Stuart, T. (1997) *Guide to Southern Africa Game and Nature Reserves*, Passport Books, Chicago.

Tunbridge, J. E. & Ashworth, G. J. (1996) *Dissonant Heritage: The Management of the Past as a Resource in Conflict*, Wiley, Chichester, particularly Chapter 8: 'Southern Africa: dissonant heritage as the "Black Man's Burden"?', pp. 223–62.

Williams, D. A. R. & Nolan, D. (1997) *Environmental and Resource Management Law in New Zealand*, Butterworths, Wellington.

Note: * The guidebooks in this series are of particular relevance because of their accurate and thorough treatment of heritage sites, many of which are superbly illustrated.

CHAPTER 13

Heritage: Conserving the Best of the Past and Present for the Future

This is not intended to be a traditional concluding chapter, although it does attempt to draw together the threads of the arguments that have run through the book. In particular, it briefly revisits the themes outlined in the Introduction, though not always in an explicit manner. It is more discursive than most concluding chapters in academic works. This is because it also attempts to convey the author's enthusiasm for the subject matter as illustrated by some particular travel experiences, chiefly in France. It is hoped that readers will react by reflecting on their own experiences, both in travel and in everyday life at and near home. This act of reflection should broaden the reader's appreciation of heritage and should encourage active involvement in heritage preservation. It may also indirectly enrich future travel and other experiences because of a greater awareness of heritage as an important part of the natural, built, and cultural environments. This chapter is thus as much a beginning as a conclusion; as much forward-looking as backward-looking. Heritage enriches all our lives by heightening our sense of place, our sense of time and our connection with our personal and group pasts, and our sense of belonging to a nation, and to many groups in and beyond that nation. Our heritage helps make us who we are. And it can also be hugely satisfying and enjoyable.

13.1 What is heritage?

To paraphrase a popular song: 'Heritage is a many splendoured thing', and in many cases heritage holds our fascination because of its splendour. But not all heritage could be described as splendid. The very concept of heritage is ambiguous and both its definition and the meaning of individual heritage items are contested. And, in some cases, it is the very ordinariness or representativeness of heritage, natural or cultural, that is fascinating, and certainly frequently more personally rewarding. Such 'ordinary' heritage gives us an insight into everyday life in the past or in a different country, or into some aspect of the natural environment. In other words, it heightens our sense of place and our connection with our environment.

Some heritage is historical in nature. We all have a feeling, to a greater or lesser extent, of nostalgia for the past. While some aspects of that nostalgia will be personal, and probably even trivial, other aspects that are shared with others will be part of our group heritage, and thus deemed worthy of conservation and management. This connection with the past is real and important. Perhaps calling these important reminders of the past *heritage* has the advantage of getting away from the often negative, cloyingly sweet connotations of *nostalgia*.

Other aspects of our heritage are not connected with the past at all. There are important elements of the present to which we also feel strong ties, and which we feel must be protected for our generation and future generations. This is the case for most natural heritage, as its history is less important than it is for cultural or built heritage. Typically, there are also strong scientific and environmental reasons for conserving key natural heritage sites.

Having said that, the cultural and natural heritage of a site are commonly inseparable and that interconnection can be a key part of both the fascination and the value of a site. Problems can arise when natural and cultural heritage are administered by separate bureaucratic departments. In many countries, indigenous heritage is treated as a separate category again. In the author's view, this need not be the case. Indigenous heritage should be seen as part of cultural heritage, and its protection should be closely integrated with natural heritage through the concept of *country*, the term that Australian Aboriginal people use to describe the environment in which they live, and with which they have a strong spiritual connection. The WHCom has recognised this unity between natural and cultural heritage in the creation of the category of World Cultural Landscapes (see Section 8.3). Ideally, that recognition of unity would be the norm. As with any heritage item, there must, however, be the proviso that the sensitivities of the people intimately connected with the particular item of heritage must be taken into account. A division between mainstream cultural heritage and indigenous heritage frequently seems to reflect a division between mainstream society and indigenous society—and, sadly, in Australia, and in several other nations, it reflects that division quite accurately. In 2001, however, there is a glimmer of hope that these divisions are beginning to disappear in Australia. It is evident that natural and cultural heritage merge more obviously and imperceptibly in the eyes of indigenous peoples than they do for European-Australians or European-North Americans (Chapters 7 and 9). To European-Europeans, on the other hand, the perception of the connection between the natural and the cultural lies somewhere between those extremes, as centuries or even millennia of occupation of landscapes has effectively blurred the distinction (Chapter 11).

Heritage is probably a key ingredient in anyone's enjoyment of travel, both within Australia and overseas, even if 'heritage' never appears in their letters or emails home, or in their travel diaries. Much popular travel writing does not explicitly refer to heritage either, and the term is not all that common in guidebooks, even though they are usually full of references to heritage sites. Nonetheless, heritage is a key component of the tourist industry, both on the international and domestic levels. There are certain places tourists want to visit, and many cultures and landscapes they wish to experience.

Plate 13.1 (like many of the other images shown in this book) shows an icon of world tourism, but many tourists also love—and may even prefer—to experience lesser known sites, to get off the beaten track (see, for example, Plate 13.2). Much of the deep satisfaction of such 'low-key' experiences comes from sharing, however inadequately and briefly, the heritage of other peoples and other cultures, and from learning about other people and other places. A high standard of interpretation and presentation of heritage items becomes crucial in this context if visitors are likely to be from other places and other cultures (see Chapter 2). Interpretation must be effective, but also both accurate and sensitive to cultural issues. Much of the burgeoning global tourism industry is, in one way or another, dependent to some extent on heritage, as are more local recreation and travel. While, in one sense the world has become smaller, and more accessible, we are also much more aware of its splendid natural and cultural diversity.

Plate 13.1

A section of the Egyptian World Heritage property known as 'Memphis and its Necropolis with the Pyramid Fields'. Inscribed in 1979, it was one of the original World Heritage sites. The Sphinx is seen in front of one of the Pyramids of Cheops at Giza.

Photo: Kevin McCracken

Plate 13.2

Street scene in Orcival, a small town in the Puy de Dôme Département of the Massif Central region of France, with the 12th-century Auvergne Romanesque Basilique d'Orcival.

Photo: Graeme Aplin

Of course, heritage status brings both advantages and disadvantages. Tourism, and commercialisation and commodification more generally, provide financial resources and draw attention to heritage sites, thus assisting conservation efforts (see Chapter 3). On the other hand, the well-publicised heritage status of a site may mean that visitors put great stress on it. The mere existence of modern life and the growth and development of modern society can also have a negative impact on heritage. Heritage items cannot be isolated from the rest of society, nor should they be, but effective heritage management is crucial. To borrow from another well-known phrase: 'The price of heritage is eternal vigilance'. The benefits of preserving key items of heritage are very real, on individual and community levels, even if those benefits cannot always be given a monetary value. Where political debate is dominated by materialist economic rationalists, these values may not always be understood. People say that anything worth preserving is worth fighting to preserve. Heritage is worth the fighting to preserve, and not only in the sense of a defensive action. It also requires vigorous positive and proactive promotion.

13.2   Whose heritage?

Personal preferences and differences of character and personality mean that people view heritage in vastly different and infinitely varied ways. Indeed, this helps to make the world a more interesting, meaningful and rewarding place. It is also important that all people feel that their heritage is included and taken seriously. The heritage of a group or community plays a major role in establishing and maintaining a sense of identity, pride, and self-worth. Recognition of heritage and group morale often go hand in hand. Excluding or marginalising a group's heritage can have the effect of marginalising the group, and reducing their sense of pride and identity. The heritage of any nation, as it is defined and regulated, and at least partially managed and financed by the national government, should be inclusive. No group in the community should be excluded because another group controls the machinery of government. On the other hand, heritage should never be seen to be appropriated by another group. If it is to be incorporated into a broader national heritage, as it should be in preference to being excluded, the group who most directly 'owns' the specific heritage should have a role at all stages of its identification, listing, conservation, interpretation, and management.

Hence the question 'Whose heritage is it?' may well require a number of answers at different scales: in the case of a World Heritage property, for example, it might be owned in various ways by a local indigenous group, then a more broadly defined local community, then a state or region, then a nation, then humankind. Each level in this hierarchy should be prepared to consider the desires and needs of lower or more specific levels. They should defer to their knowledge and experience, and be sensitive to their feelings, beliefs, and culture. Only rarely, and usually for reasons of cultural or spiritual sensitivity, will a group or community not be pleased to have an element of their heritage recognised as significant at higher levels. But, at the same time, it is important for that group to feel they are retaining ownership in the cultural and intellectual sense. They want to feel that they matter, and that their feelings and specific knowledge are being taken seriously. Their inclusion in the heritage processes must be real, not just token, or for commercial, revenue-raising reasons alone.

13.3 Scale revisited: local to global significance

The previous section implies that heritage is defined at all spatial scales and political levels from the personal through the local to the district, regional, national, and global levels. Apart from the very personal scale, all are within the scope of this book. We have dealt with personal perceptions and reactions to heritage, of course, but generally in the sense of a number of individuals combining to give heritage items a meaning and importance beyond the purely personal.

While many of the examples of European heritage in this book have focussed on sites inscribed on the WHL, those in this Section illustrate the range of scales relevant to a selection of sites in France. Among the most memorable places visited on a trip to France in 1999 was Orcival (see Plate 13.2), a small town in the rugged Massif Central region. In late March, outside holiday season and with snow still on the higher country nearby, there were few tourists around. A visit to the Basilica was very moving. Somehow, the simple, relatively dark interior appealed more than those of Gothic cathedrals like Chartres (see Plate 1.2). It was more intimate, and more at one with the community it still serves. On reflection, this represents a common reaction of heritage lovers to buildings and landscapes in general, and there is often a preference for the small-scale over the grandiose. The Orcival Basilica is not a World Heritage property, and may or may not be listed and protected on a more local scale. It probably features in relatively few tourist guidebooks available to foreigners. But apparently Orcival is overrun by French visitors in high season. From all accounts pedestrians can hardly move and there are constant traffic jams in the narrow streets. Orcival is thus of heritage importance on the local and regional scales, and perhaps on the national scale, but certainly not on the global scale like the Pyramids.

Orcival is almost entirely 'of a piece', with a consistent architectural style, or set of related styles, and its buildings are almost universally constructed of local stone. Little seems out of place or intrusive. Yet Orcival is still home to a living community, as evidenced by the active local primary school, the local older men leisurely drinking coffee outside the café, and the women doing their food shopping in the small shops in the main square. The town created such an impression because the community of people on the one hand, and the assemblage of buildings and spaces on the other, were so beautifully interwoven.

Claude Monet's house and garden at Giverny (Plate 13.3), not far from Paris, is certainly on the route of the international tourist, and it presents an excellent example of associational significance. While it is not a World Heritage site, it is in a real sense part of the heritage of anyone from the European cultural tradition who has even a vague interest in paintings, and certainly part of the heritage of those who have enjoyed Monet's impressionist paintings of the gardens and their waterlilies. Like many other places associated with famous people, there are aspects of the site with which visitors feel an immediate affinity. The gardens are beautiful in their own right, and could be enjoyed for that reason alone, but the association with such well-known paintings, many of which are in famous galleries, adds to the enjoyment of a visit.

Still in France, the Camargue, a vast area of wetlands in the Rhône Delta, is not a World Heritage property either, but it is a Biosphere Reserve, a Ramsar Wetland of International Significance (see Section 8.5), and an

Plate 13.3

Claude Monet's house and garden, Giverny, Eure, France, the site of Monet's famous waterlily garden.

Photo: Graeme Aplin

Important Zone for the Protection of Birds in France (*Zone Important pour la Conservation des Oiseaux en France* or ZICO), a site covered by an EC directive of 1979. The Camargue is a regional park, rather than a national park, but it is also recognised as important on a global level for its biophysical attributes. Most people generally do not consider swamps to be beautiful, yet the Camargue is nonetheless fascinating and certainly of great heritage significance—particularly because of the bird life it nurtures. The presence of wild flamingos at the Camargue was particularly appealing to an Australian visitor, as was the intricate patchwork of land uses, both commercially productive and conservation-oriented (see Box 11.5). And then there is the traditional lifestyle maintained by some of the approximately 7500 residents within the reserve boundaries, including the *gardiens* (cowboys) and the operators of the *mas* (farms). As in the examples given above, visitor pressures are immense, especially in summer, and in holiday periods generally. For example, the small town of les Saintes-Maries-de-la-Mer sees its population grow from approximately 2000 to a summer high of 25 000. Active management, including visitor management, and interpretation are thus essential. In this case these roles are played in part by an extremely good visitor centre.

13.4   Conservation and management

Monet's house and garden are maintained, managed, and opened to the public by a private foundation, with visitors paying to enter. This is but one method of funding the upkeep of a heritage site, natural or cultural. Sometimes individuals or local community groups will fund their own heritage conservation efforts, perhaps without even being aware of it, especially if it is simply a case of constructively using and maintaining heritage sites. When government agencies fund heritage conservation and management, as taxpayers, we all pay. Some sites, of course, are obviously both larger in scale and involve a more complex pattern of ownership, and thus there is a need for government involvement at the local, regional, or even national level, even if individual buildings or parcels of land that are key parts of the heritage precinct are privately owned and managed. Carcassonne, shown in Plate 13.4, is one example of a site with such a structure of involvement.

Carcassonne also illustrates a number of other points. It is one of the most complete and intact fortified medieval towns in the world, and is a World Heritage property that could be described as both splendid and monumental. It was comprehensively restored in the late 19th century, and in the eyes of some commentators, it was over-restored. This raises the controversial issues of originality and authenticity. Critics argue that architect–historian Eugène Viollet-le-Duc over-restored the town fortifications and castle in the 19th century, striving too much for originality and authenticity, and having too little regard to organic change and the patina of age. This factor does not deter visitors, and Carcassone is extremely crowded in high season, largely with French people, as it is not a world tourist icon in the same sense as the Pyramids. It has its quota of cafes, restaurants, hotels, and souvenir shops to cater for those crowds, but all are in keeping with the general urban landscape and the ambience of the town. It is, however, on a completely different scale in size and complexity than the Monet property, and demands very different approaches to management and conservation.

Plate 13.4

Porte Narbonnaise (1280) and medieval city ramparts, Carcassonne, Aude, France, restored in the 19th century.

Photo: Graeme Aplin

Re-use of heritage buildings is one aspect of the commodification and commercialisation of heritage (see Section 3.6). One of the beauties of travel is that it is sometimes possible to stay or dine in heritage surroundings, and heritage buildings are often re-used as accommodation or restaurants. The Moulin de Cierzac, near Cognac in western France (Plate 13.5), was a 17th-century water-powered flour mill before its conversion into a rather up-market hostelry, and it represents a very successful example of adaptive re-use of a building that might otherwise have been lost. From many of the guest-room windows, there is a view of the former water-races that once brought water to the waterwheels that have unfortunately been removed. The considerable architectural and aesthetic values of the building have been conserved, even if the full industrial archaeological values have not.

Plate 13.5

17th-century Moulin de Cierzac, Cierzac, Charente, south of Cognac, French heritage accommodation.

Photo: Graeme Aplin

The scale and nature of interpretation for visitors will depend on the sites involved. In small-scale examples or on private properties, interpretation will be limited. Sites that cater for large numbers of visitors, however, frequently employ excellent techniques to explain their significance and heritage values to visitors. Attracting and catering for those visitors serves both to justify conservation in a political sense and contribute to the funds required to carry out the maintenance and conservation. When all these aspects are taken into account, it becomes clear that active management of the best possible kind is essential.

Education is an important aspect of many heritage sites. Although the practical details of heritage education go beyond the central concerns of this book, in many cases education is a central aspect of successful interpretation. The Beamish outdoor museum north of Durham, England illustrates the value of the educative function of heritage interpretation in its broadest sense, even though the buildings have been relocated and the 'village' is artificial. One section of the park is a rebuilt village street, using old buildings relocated from various sites in the area (see Plate 6.13). There are houses, shops (Plate 13.6), a bank, a motor garage and other typical village buildings. Even though the site is artificial and highly commodified, it was obvious that the two busloads of British pensioners visiting on the same day as the author gained immensely from being able to experience this heritage site. Comments included: 'I remember those'; 'We had one of them'; 'Aunty Mabel's sitting room looked just like this, except her carpet was navy blue'; 'I haven't seen one of those since I was at school in 1927'. They were enthusiastic and enjoying immersing themselves in *their* heritage. In this case, heritage merged education with entertainment, as it so often does.

Plate 13.6

Relocated general store, Beamish, the North of England Open Air Museum, north of Durham, England. The store displays a full range of foods and other goods as they would have been available in 1913.

Photo: Graeme Aplin

13.5 Final conclusions

It is common at the end of a book to 'close the circle' and take readers back to the beginning, in this case to Plate 1.1. Outside a small village south of Cognac, France, insignificant directional signs point to *le dolmen*. With only a vague idea as to what a *dolmen* was, it was thrilling for an Australian visitor to find at the end of the narrow dirt track a small and local, but nonetheless impressive, prehistoric burial site, quite literally in the middle of operative vineyards. (Where in France isn't!) It was, in a sense, a personal discovery, and a thrill for that very reason. While the Sistine Chapel, the prehistoric cave paintings of Lascaux, or the Grand Canyon can have the same effect, it is often the unexpected encounter with heritage that touches people most deeply. But it is the smaller, less-significant sites that, almost by definition, hold most significance for local communities, and are the type of heritage most people are first likely to encounter. In many cases, the sites are part of those communities and rate little explicit mention, but they would be sadly missed if lost. Undoubtedly there would be heated and prolonged battles if anyone suggested they be removed.

This concluding chapter has been something of a meandering, personal account of heritage, which in a way represents the nature of heritage. Heritage means so many things to different people. By this stage readers will have concluded that the author is enthusiastic about preserving heritage for both the present generation—so we can enjoy it as the British pensioners enjoyed the Beamish outdoor museum—and for future generations. The working definition of heritage in this book has been 'those things that we value and feel are worth preserving for present and future generations'. This differs from many other definitions in that it makes no mention of the past. Much cultural heritage does have a clear historical aspect, but some very modern architecture can be said to have heritage values, and to be worth preserving (see Plate 6.2 and Plate 11.20 for examples). Some recent events are already recognised as having heritage significance—hundreds of thousands of Australians have their own heritage items from the Sydney 2000 Olympic Games, and they are already undoubtedly part of our community and national psyche, and some heritage sites will emerge. In addition, natural heritage sites are often worth preserving for many reasons regardless of any history those sites might have.

Heritage helps locate ourselves socially, spatially, and temporally, and is a key ingredient of our personal, group, community, and national identities. It helps us to locate ourselves at various scales and relate to others at each of those scales. Ultimately, global heritage helps us relate to humankind in general, and to place our own experiences in the tapestry of human endeavour, as well as in the tapestry of ecosystems and natural environments. The way a group's heritage is treated by those in power affects their sense of self-worth, their perceptions of their place in the world, and their perceptions of their future.

The 'sense of place' and 'sense of time' that are brought by heritage not only contribute to group identities, but they also play a major role in the tourism industry. Most people do not want to travel somewhere that resembles their home environment (despite stories of British and American travellers, in particular, cocooning themselves in the familiar). Most travellers want to 'get a feeling' for a place, to immerse themselves in its atmosphere, and to learn about different times, places, cultures, and environments. Heritage plays a major role in giving those experiences, both for actual visitors and for virtual visitors, through travel writing, photographs, television and video, and, increasingly, web sites and other electronic media. The preservation of heritage protects the particular character of places and is a barrier against universal, globalised blandness.

However, heritage cannot always save itself. In a sense, it often does, because heritage items continue to be both useful and used, and hence are cared for by owners and occupiers, or are generally accepted as valuable, and hence cared for by public agencies. But the many different perceptions of the value of heritage in general, and of individual heritage items in particular, mean that there are also many contentious cases where development, demolition, or radical alteration is proposed for an item that others see as significant and wish to conserve. Therefore it is imperative that heritage values are recognised and clearly stated when decisions are being made. Even when there is general agreement about conserving a heritage item, it must be actively managed in an ongoing way. Conservation is an active process that does not simply happen— it has to be made to happen. And someone has to pay for it to happen. While we cannot, and should not, try to save everything, the effort and expense of saving well-chosen heritage items are definitely worthwhile.

Heritage is both intensely personal and intensely political. In effect, these two elements go hand in hand, as heritage is hotly contested because we each have our own views on what represents heritage, and what is worth conserving. Different groups in society have their own heritage, which may or may not be integrated into a larger national heritage. The sub-group's heritage can be recognised, appreciated, ignored, sensitively incorporated, appropriated, or denigrated. How a group's heritage is perceived and dealt with by a government or hegemonic group is intimately related to the political relationships in any given nation. Because heritage is so personal, inappropriate political actions regarding heritage can be extremely hurtful—or extremely positive and reinforcing. All of us, even those who prioritise personal wealth and present circumstances, value our own heritage, want others to value it, and want to share the heritage of others.

Key to World Heritage criteria used in the tables in this book

Criteria for the inclusion of cultural properties

A monument, group of buildings or site... which is nominated for inclusion in the World Heritage List will be considered to be of outstanding universal value for the purposes of the Convention when the Committee finds that it meets one or more of the following criteria and the test of authenticity. Each property nominated should therefore [meet one or more of the following criteria]:

Ci represent a masterpiece of human creative genius

Cii exhibit an important interchange of human values, over a span of time or within a cultural area of the world, on developments in architecture or technology, monumental arts, town planning, or landscape design

Ciii bear a unique or at least exceptional testimony to a cultural tradition or to a civilisation which is living or which has disappeared

Civ be an outstanding example of a type of building or architectural or technological ensemble or landscape which illustrates a significant stage or significant stages in human history

Cv be an outstanding example of a traditional human settlement or land use which is representative of a culture or cultures, especially when it has become vulnerable under the impact of irreversible change

Cvi be directly or tangibly associated with events or living traditions, with ideas, with beliefs, or with artistic and literary works of outstanding universal significance (a criterion used only in exceptional circumstances, or together with other criteria)

Criteria for the inclusion of natural properties

A natural heritage property... which is submitted for inclusion in the World Heritage List will be considered to be of outstanding universal value for the purposes of the Convention when the Committee finds that it meets one or more of the following criteria and fulfils the conditions of integrity set out below. Sites nominated should therefore [meet one or more of the following criteria]:

Ni be outstanding examples representing major stages of the earth's history, including the record of life, significant ongoing geological processes in the development of landforms, or significant geomorphic or physiographic features

Nii   be outstanding examples representing significant ongoing ecological and biological processes in the evolution and development of terrestrial, fresh water, coastal and marine ecosystems and communities of plants and animals

Niii   contain superlative natural phenomena or areas of exceptional natural beauty and aesthetic importance

Niv   contain the most important and significant natural habitats for *in situ* conservation of biological diversity, including those containing threatened species of outstanding value from the point of view of science or conservation

Source: extracts from the Operational Guidelines for the Implementation of the World Heritage Convention, Part I. Establishment of the World Heritage List.

Relevant web sites

The following list roughly follows the sequence in Chapters 8 to 12 and covers most of the agencies referred to in the text. Many of these sites have useful links to other relevant sites. Visual material relating to many specific heritage sites is often available.

The URLs were all correct at the time of most recent 'road-testing', late August 2001. Many had, however changed over a short period prior to that, a good indication of just how fluid such things can be. Therefore, the author cannot guarantee that all of the URLs will be current at the time of reading. However, all of the sites listed in the appendix will be updated where necessary and available through links from the web site that complements the book, at http://www.es.mq.edu.au/courses/REM/heritage.htm. In addition, as noted in Chapters 9 to 12, government and bureaucratic structures are liable to change frequently, and the web site will also include relevant updates on such changes.

World Heritage

UNESCO: http://www.unesco.org/
World Heritage Commission/Committee/Convention: http://www.unesco.org/whc/
List of World Heritage properties: http://www.unesco.org/whc/heritage.htm
Brief descriptions of WH properties: http://www.unesco.org/whc/brief.htm
MAB Biosphere Reserves: http://www.unesco.org/mab/wnbr.htm
IUCN: http://www.iucn.org/
ICOMOS: http://www.icomos.org/
ICCROM: http://www.iccrom.org/
Ramsar Convention: http://www.ramsar.org/
Biodiversity Convention: http://www.iisd.ca/biodiv.html
UNEP World Conservation Monitoring Centre: http://www.unep-wcmc.org/
World Commission on Protected Areas (of IUCN): http://wcpa.iucn.org/
Asia-Pacific Focal Point for World Heritage Managers: http://www.heritage.gov.au/apfp/

Australia (federal)

Australian Heritage Directory: http://www.heritage.gov.au/
Environment Australia: http://www.ea.gov.au/
Environment Australia heritage site: http://www.ea.gov.au/heritage/
Australian Heritage Commission: http://www.ahc.gov.au/heritage/
Infoterra Australia heritage pages: http://www.ea.gov.au/sdd/library/infoterra/heritage.html
Register of the National Estate: http://www.ahc.gov.au/heritage/register/index.html
Biodiversity pages, EA: http://www.ea.gov.au/biodiversity/
Parks and reserves pages, EA: http://www.ea.gov.au/parks/

Australia's World Heritage: http://www.ea.gov.au/heritage/awh/worldheritage/index.html
Kakadu National Park:
>   http://www.ea.gov.au/heritage/awh/worldheritage/sites/kakadu/index.html
>   (Use the search facility on the EA home page and type in "Kakadu" for further information.)

New legislation, EPBC Homepage: http://www.ea.gov.au/epbc/index.html
New heritage legislation:
>   http://www.ahc.gov.au/heritage/infores/publications/newheritage.html
>   (You can find more related material by using the search facility for "heritage" at http://www.aph.gov.au/legis.htm/)

Australian Heritage Bibliography (formerly HERA):
>   http://www.ahc.gov.au/heritage/infores/HERA/index.html

Australia ICOMOS: http://www.icomos.org/australia/
Natural Heritage Trust: http://www.nht.gov.au/
Aboriginal and Torres Strait Islander Commission:http://www.atsic.gov.au/default_ns.asp

New South Wales

Department of Urban Affairs and Planning: http://www.duap.nsw.gov.au/
NSW Heritage Office: http://www.heritage.nsw.gov.au/
State Heritage Inventory: (Use link from NSW Heritage Office site.)
Historic Houses Trust: http://www.hht.nsw.gov.au/
National Parks and Wildlife Service: http://www.npws.nsw.gov.au/
State Forests of NSW: http://www.forest.nsw.gov.au/
Heritage education site: http://www.teachingheritage.nsw.edu.au/

Australian Capital Territory

Environment and Heritage Gateway: http://www.act.gov.au/environ/
Heritage Unit: http://www.act.gov.au/environ/heritage/
Parks: http://www.act.gov.au/environ/parksres.html
ACT Heritage Council: http://www.act.gov.au/environ/heritage/hertc.htm
Aboriginal heritage: http://www.act.gov.au/environ/heritage/abrhp.html

Northern Territory

Department of Lands, Planning and Environment: http://www.lpe.nt.gov.au/
Heritage branch of DLPE: http://www.lpe.nt.gov.au/heritage/
Heritage Register: http://www.lpe.nt.gov.au/heritage/register/list/
Aboriginal Areas Protection Authority: http://www.nt.gov.au/aapa/
Parks and Wildlife Commission: http://www.nt.gov.au/paw/
NT Heritage Trail: http://www.lpe.gov.au/heritage/trail/

Queensland

Department of the Environment Protection Authority: http://www.env.qld.gov.au/
Cultural heritage: http://www.env.qld.gov.au/environment/culture/
Aboriginal Heritage: http://www.env.qld.gov.au/environment/culture/aboriginal/
National Parks: http://www.env.qld.gov.au/environment/park/
Queensland Heritage Register: http://www.env.qld.gov.au/environment/culture/registers
Heritage trails: http://www.heritagetrails.qld.gov.au/

South Australia

Department for Environment and Heritage: http://www.environment.sa.gov.au/
Heritage section of DEH: http://www.environment.sa.gov.au/heritage/
Heritage SA: http://www.environment.sa.gov.au/heritage/heritage.html
State Heritage Register: http://www.environment.sa.gov.au/heritage/register.html
National Parks and Wildlife SA: http://www.environment.sa.gov.au/parks/
Aboriginal Heritage Branch: http://www.dosaa.sa.gov.au/projects/#Section_1.Section_3

Tasmania

Department of Primary Industries, Water and Environment: http://www.dpiwe.tas.gov.au/
Tasmanian Parks and Wildlife Service: http://www.parks.tas.gov.au/
Cultural Heritage Branch, TPWS:
    http://www.parks.tas.gov.au/manage/culther/culther.html
Aboriginal Heritage Section:
    http://www.parks.tas.gov.au/manage/culther/abher/abher.html
Historical Heritage Section:
    http://www.parks.tas.gov.au/manage/culther/histher/histher.html

Victoria

Department of Natural Resources and Environment: http://www.nre.vic.gov.au/
Heritage Council of Victoria: http://www.heritage.vic.gov.au/
Parks Victoria: http://www.parkweb.vic.gov.au/
Aboriginal Affairs, Heritage Branch: (Use link on DNRE home page.)

Western Australia

Department of Conservation and Land Management: http://www.calm.wa.gov.au/
Heritage Council of WA: http://www.heritage.wa.gov.au/
Heritage Register: http://register.heritage.wa.gov.au/quicksearch.html
Department of Indigenous Affairs: http://www.aad.wa.gov.au/
National parks: http://www.calm.wa.gov.au/national_parks/

Australian voluntary organisations

Australian Council of National Trusts: http://www.nationaltrust.org.au/
National Trust of Australia (ACT): http://www.act.nationaltrust.org.au/
National Trust of Australia (NT): http://www.northernexposure.com.au/trust.htm
National Trust of Australia (NSW): http://www.nsw.nationaltrust.org.au/
National Trust of Australia (Qld): http://www.nationaltrustqld.org/
National Trust of Australia (Tas): http://www.tased.edu.au/tasonline/nattrust/
Nature Conservation Council of NSW: http://www.nccnsw.org.au/
National Parks Association of NSW: http://www.npansw.org.au/

United Kingdom

English Heritage: http://www.english-heritage.org.uk/
English Nature: http://www.english-nature.org.uk/
Historic Scotland: http://www.historic-scotland.gov.uk/sw-frame.htm

Cadw Welsh Historic Monuments: http://www.cadw.wales.gov.uk/
The Castles of Wales: http://www.castlewales.com/home.htm
RCAHMS: http://www.rcahms.gov.uk/
National Monuments Record (RCHME):
http://www.english-heritage.org.uk/knowledge/nmr/index.asp
RCAHMW: http://www.rcahmw.org.uk/
Environment Agency: http://www.environment-agency.gov.uk/
Scottish Natural History: http://www.snh.org.uk/
Council for National Parks (with links to all UK National Park Authorities.):
   http://www.cnp.org.uk/
National Trust: http://www.nationaltrust.org.uk/main/
National Trust for Scotland: http://www.nts.org.uk/
The Landmark Trust: http://landmarktrust.org.uk/

France (mainly in French)

Direction de l'architecture et du patrimoine: http://www.culture.gouv.fr/culture/da.htm
Centre des monuments nationaux: http://www.monuments-france.fr (English version
   available)
Lascaux caves (in English): http://www.culture.gouv.fr/culture/arcnat/lascaux/en/vide.htm/
Ministry of Land Management and the Environment: http://www.environnement.gouv.fr/
National parks:
   http://www.environnement.gouv.fr/actua/cominfos/dosdir/DIRNP/parcnat.htm
National parks: http://vosdroits.service-public.fr/ARBO/070505-FXENV113.html
Regional natural parks (in English):
   http://www.parcs-naturels-regionaux.tm.fr/lesparcs/index-en.html

Italy (in Italian)

Ministry of Cultural Property and Activities: http://www.beniculturali.it/index.as
Storio del Fondo Edifici di Culto: http://www.cittadinitalia.it/fec/index_fec.html
Divisione Conservazione e Restauro Degli Edifici di Culto:
   http://www.mininterno.it/culti/divconse.htm
Ministry of the Environment: http://www.minambiente.it/Sito/home.asp
Nature Conservation Service (SCN): http://www.scn.minambiente.it/

Spain (mainly in Spanish)

Secretary of State for Culture: http://www.mcu.es/homemcu.html
Fine Arts, Museums and Heritage: http://www.mcu.es/bbaa/index.html
World Heritage Cities of Spain (in English):
http://www.cyberspain.com/ciudades-patrimonio/ihome.htm
Ministry of the Environment: http://www.mma.es/
National Parks Network: http://www.mma.es/parques/lared/
National parks: http://www.gorp.com/gorp/location/europe/sp_park/sp_park.htm

Ireland

Heritage of Ireland site: http://www.heritageireland.ie/
Department of Arts, Heritage, Gaeltacht and the Islands: http://www.irlgov.ie/ealga/
Dúchas – The Heritage Service: http://www.heritagedata.ie/

Heritage Council: http://www.heritagecouncil.ie/mainpage.html
An Taisce, The National Trust of Ireland: http://www.antaisce.org/

European Union

Eurosite (network of organisations involved in natural heritage):
    http://www.eurosite-nature.org/
Council of European Heritage: http://www.european-heritage.net/
EU Nature Protection: http://europa.eu.int/comm/environment/nature/
Natura 2000: http://europa.eu.int/comm/environment/nature/natura.htm

New Zealand

Department of Conservation: http://www.doc.govt.nz/index.htm
NZ World Heritage: http://www.doc.govt.nz/cons/world.htm
National Parks: http://www.doc.govt.nz/rec/np.htm
Historic conservation: http://www.doc.govt.nz/cons/histry/histry.htm
Historic Places Trust: http://www.historic.org.nz/

USA

National Parks Service ('ParkNet'): http://www.nps.gov/
National Register of Historic Places: http://www.cr.nps.gov/nr/
National Trust for Historic Preservation: http://www.nthp.org/
National Parks Conservation Association: http://www.npca.org/flash.html
California State Parks: http://parks.ca.gov/homepage/default.asp
Office of Historic Preservation, CSP: http://www.ohp.parks.ca.gov/

South Africa

Department of Environmental Affairs and Tourism:
    http://www.environment.gov.za/
Parks SA: http://www.parks-sa.co.za/
Cape Nature Conservation: http://www.capenature.org.za/
KwaZulu-Natal Nature Conservation Services: http://www.rhino.org.za/
1996 White Paper on Arts, Culture and
    Heritage:http://www.dacst.gov.za/arts_culture/artculwp.htm

Thailand

Royal Forestry Department: http://www.forest.go.th/default_e.asp
Sri Thep Historic Park: http://www.srithep.fineart.go.th/en.htm
World Heritage: http://www.fineart.go.th/subworld.html
Ayutthaya: http://ayothaya.com/english.html

China

Chinese World Heritage properties: http://worldheritagefoundation.com/
Suzhou gardens: http://www.szgarden.com.cn/en/yl.htm

INDEX

Abomey   173
Aboriginal and Torres Strait Islander Heritage Protection
    Amendment Act 1987 (Cth)   230
Aboriginal and Torres Strait Islander Heritage Protection Bill 1998
    (Cth)   205
Aboriginal Areas Protection Authority (NT)   223
Aboriginal Australians   12, 24–5, 26, 94, 141–2, 143–4,
    145–6, 147, 150, 151–2, 182, 199, 201–3, 223, 224–5, 226,
    227–8, 231, 236
Aboriginal Heritage Act 1972 (WA)   231
Aboriginal Heritage Act 1988 (SA)   226
Aboriginal Land Rights (Northern Territory) Act 1976 (Cth)
    223
Aboriginal Relics Act 1975 (Tas)   226
Aboriginal Sacred Sites Act 1989 (NT)   223
ACT Planning Authority   222
adaptation and adaptive re-use   52, 73, 131, 134–7, 355
additions   129
Advisory Council on Historic Preservation (USA)   309
Aeolian Islands   270, 278
aesthetics   118, 122, 127
Afghanistan   3, 32, 170
Africa (see also individual nations)   169, 170, 172, 182, 183
Agrigento   277
Air and Ténéré Natural Reserves   174
Albania   173
Alberobello   275
Alcalá de Henares   288
Alice Springs Desert Park   102
Alpine National Park   228
Altamira cave   282, 284
alterations   129
Amalfi   270, 277
Amiens   262
An Taisce—The National Trust for Ireland   291
Angkor Wat   173
Angthong National Marine Park   332
Aoraki/Mount Cook National Park   299, 300
apartheid   320–1, 325
appropriation   24, 147
Aquileia   278
Arc-et-Senans   263
archaeological sites   9, 24, 46, 113, 114, 128, 218, 219, 224,
    231, 257, 270, 338
architectural significance   117–18
architectural styles   118–20, 121
areas of outstanding natural beauty   245
Arles   258, 262
Asia (see also individual nations)   169, 182, 183
assessing significance   120–1
Assisi   278
associational significance   118
Atapuerca   289
audio-visual materials   45
Australia (see also individual states, territories and cities)   1,
    16, 19–20, 24–7, 56, 60, 88, 90, 96, 114, 141–2, 145, 147,
    152, 166, 167, 168, 169, 170, 176, 178, 181–237, 239, 255,
    296, 297, 306, 321, 350
Australian Capital Territory   221, 222
Australian Conservation Foundation   167

Australian Council of National Trusts   235
Australian Federal Government   181–2, 183, 184, 185–90,
    196–99, 202–9, 211
Australian federation   181–2
Australian Fossil Mammal Sites   192
Australian Heritage Commission   107, 185, 187–90
Australian Heritage Commission Act 1975 (Cth)   187–8, 224
Australian Heritage Council   208–9
Australian ICOMOS Charter for the Conservation of Places of
    Cultural Significance (see Burra Charter)
Australian Nature Conservation Agency   187, 205
Australian Natural Heritage Charter   67, 75, 107–8
Australia Post   185–6
Austria   169
authenticity   25, 129–30, 166
Avebury   250, 252
Avignon   264
Ávila   282, 284
Avoca (Ireland)   118
Ayutthaya   10, 331, 334, 335

Bahla Fort   174
Balearic Islands   279, 281, 282
Ban Chiang Archaeological Site   335
Bangkok   330–1
Banpo archaeological site   338
Barcelona   282, 283, 287
barriers, protective   101, 134, 147–8, 149
Barumini   277
Basques   25, 114, 142
Bath   252
Beijing   340, 341, 342, 345
Belgium   169
Bendigo   186
Benin   173
Bermuda   254
Bern   239–40
biodiversity   12, 86–7, 96, 176–7, 178, 184, 190, 222, 299
Biodiversity Advisory Council   205
Biosphere Protection Zones   338, 339, 340
Biosphere Reserves   176, 194, 205, 313, 353
Blaenavon   170, 250, 254
Blenheim Palace   250, 252
Blue Mountains, Greater   35, 85, 167, 190, 193, 218
Botany Bay National Park   219
Botswana   325
Bourges   264
Brazil   173
brochures   34, 44–5
Brú na Bóinne   291, 293
building applications   216
buildings   1, 10, 25, 50, 52, 77, 113–38
Bulahdelah State Forest   70
Bulgaria   173
Bunjil's Cave   148
Bunratty Castle   9, 53, 137
Burgos   283
Burra Charter   67–74, 75, 107, 131–2
Burren National Park   291, 293
Butrint   173

Cáceres   282, 285
Cadw Welsh Historic Monuments   243, 244
Cahokia Mounds State Historic Site   316, 318
Cairngorms   249
Caisse Nationale des Monuments Historiques et des Sites   34, 256
California   313–15
California Historical Landmark Program   315
California Office of Historic Preservation   313–15
California Point of Historical Interest Program   315
California Register of Historical Resources Program   315
California State Parks   313–14
California Wilderness Preservation System   314
Californian Historical Resources Information System   314–15
Cambodia   173
Canada   50, 114, 142, 169, 315–16, 319
Canal du Midi   170, 264
Canary Islands   279, 281, 282, 288
Canberra   53
Canowindra   124–5
Canterbury   250, 253
Cape Floral Kingdom   327, 328, 330
Cape Nature Conservation (S Af)   325–6
Cape Peninsula National Park   330
Cape Province   323, 325–7
Cape Town   327
Carcassone   264, 355
Carlsbad Caverns National Park   319
Carnac   24
Caserta   276
Castel del Monte   275
Castlemaine   234
castles of Wales   250, 252
Castletown House   290–1
Catalan Romanesque Churches   289
cave paintings   7, 9, 24, 145, 147–8, 258, 261, 270, 279, 282
cemeteries   128
Central African Republic   173
Central Eastern Australian Rainforest Reserves   191
Central Office of Architectural, Archaeological, Artistic and Historical Properties (Italy)   267
Central Office of Environmental and Landscape Properties (Italy)   267
Chaco Culture National Historical Park   316, 319
Chan Chan Archaeological Zone   175
change   80–1, 129–30, 256
Charlottesville   316, 319
Chartres   8, 10, 258, 261, 353
Château de Chambord   166, 262
Chengde   343
Chester   242
Chiang Saen   331
Chillagoe   128–9
China   34, 36, 45, 127, 296, 334, 336–46
Chitzén Itzá   10, 164
Christmas Island National Park   221
Cilento and Vallo di Diano National Park   277
Ciskei   324
Cirrusdal   323
Cognac   355–6, 357
Columbia (California)   314
commercialisation   53, 56–7, 58–9, 138, 352
commodification   12, 15, 53, 56–7, 138, 352
Commonwealth Heritage List   208–9
Community Partners Program (USA)   310
compatible use   73
compensation   224, 226
Comprehensive Statewide Historic Preservation Plan (California)   315
Congo, Democratic Republic of   173–4
Connemara National Park   291

conservation   4, 52, 67–82, 86–7, 96, 108, 131–3, 147, 150, 354–5
Conservation Act 1987 (NZ)   297, 299
conservation agreements   209, 219, 223
conservation areas   224
Conservation and Land Management Act 1984 (WA)   230
conservation plans   75, 132–3, 172
conservation zone   26, 50
contents   67
context and contextual significance   121–6
Convention on Biological Diversity   176, 178, 187, 204, 205
Convention on International Trade in Endangered Species   205
Convention on Wetlands of International Importance (see Ramsar Convention)
Conwy   243
Córdoba   282, 283
Cornish   142
corridors   94
Corsica   258, 263
Côte d'Ivoire   173
Council for National Parks (UK)   245, 249
Council of Australian Governments   205
Cradle Mountain–Lake St Clair National Park   103–4
Crespi d'Adda   274
criteria   18–21, 115–19, 163–5, 212, 322
Croatia   172
Cuenca   282, 287
Culloden Field   250
cultural landscapes   143, 169, 170
Cultural Record (Landscapes Queensland and Queensland Estate) Act 1987 (Qld)   224, 225
cultural tourism   62
curtilage   68, 122–3, 127, 324

data requirements   120–1, 131–3, 143–4
Dazu   340, 346
definitions   13–15, 163–5, 349–52
Denali National Park   311, 313
Department of Aboriginal Affairs (WA)   231
Department of Conservation (NZ)   299
Department of Conservation and Land Management (CALM) (WA)   101, 231
Department of Environmental Affairs and Tourism (S Af)   325
Department of National Heritage (UK)   242
Department of Natural Resources and the Environment (Vic)   184
Department of the Environment (UK)   242, 244
Department of the Environment Protection Agency (Qld)   224
Department of Urban Affairs and Planning (NSW)   211, 213, 216–17, 220
design guidelines   216
designated landscape area   225
development applications   216, 235
development control guidelines   216
developmentalism   25, 183, 222
Direction de l'Architecture et du patrimoine   256
Directorate of Architecture and Heritage (France)   256
disabilities   33, 40
Djoudj National Bird Sanctuary   175
documentation of heritage   27, 74–5
Doñana National Park   282, 287
Drombeg Stone Circle   290, 292
Drum Castle   255
Dublin   12
Dubrovnik   172
Dúchas—The Heritage Service (Ireland)   290–3
Dujiangyan   346
Dunedin   298, 299
Durham   137, 251, 356–7

Earth Sanctuaries 96
economics 3, 17, 49–65, 81, 183
ecosystems 12, 70, 85–8, 98–9
ecotourism 60–1, 109–10
Ecotourism Association of Australia 44, 109–10
Ecuador 174
Edinburgh 12, 77, 250, 253
education 33, 35, 38, 42, 101, 103, 356
Egmont National Park 299
Egypt 351
endangered species 87–8, 89, 96
Endangered Species Protection Act 1992 (Cth) 205
England 10, 24, 73, 128, 137, 142, 164, 170, 241, 242–3, 244–7, 250, 255
English Heritage 242–4, 247
English Nature 245
entertainment 35, 37, 42
entry charges 58
Environment Act 1995 (UK) 245
Environment Australia 185–7
Environment and Heritage Service (Northern Ireland) 244
Environment Planning and Assessment Act 1979 (NSW) 213, 216–17
Environment Protection and Biodiversity Conservation Act 1999 (Cth) 196, 206, 209
environmental services 86
erosion 98
Ethiopia 174
Europe (see also individual nations) 24–7, 169, 239–94
European Union 55, 255, 294
Everglades National Park 175, 316, 317
exotic fauna 99

fabric 52, 69, 73, 129, 131–2
façadism 134, 135
farmland and farms 8, 9, 10
Ferrara 274
Finland 170
fire 99–100, 103
Fjordland National Park 301
Flinders Ranges National Park 225
flora and fauna 9, 11, 12, 69, 70, 84–5, 86–8, 93–4, 96, 268, 290
Florence 268, 270, 273
Fondo Edifici di Culto 267–8
Fontainebleau 262
Fontenay 262
Fountains Abbey 251
France 7–8, 9, 10, 14, 16, 24, 25, 53, 55, 60, 72, 130, 135, 137, 166, 168, 170, 239–40, 255–66, 351, 353–4
Franklin–Lower Gordon Wild Rivers National Park 197, 199
Fraser Island 192, 204
Friends of National Parks (UK) 249

game parks 321, 324, 327–8
Garajonay National Park 282, 285
Garamba National Park 173
gardens 127, 270, 337, 338, 341
Gartempe 263
geographic information systems (GIS) 103
Germany 164, 170, 239
Giant's Causeway 250, 251
Giverny 353–4
Glanum 114, 257
Glen Coe 249
Glendalough 46, 291
Glenveagh National Park 291
Global Strategy (World Heritage) 170–2, 178
Globe Theatre 73
Gordes 240
Gordon-below-Franklin Dam Project 197
Goslar 164, 170, 239
Gough Island 254

government funding 26, 49, 55–6, 96, 187, 217, 226, 267, 305–6, 310, 324, 354–5
Grampians National Park 11, 98, 149, 228–30
Granada 282, 283
Grand Canyon National Park 316, 317, 357
Great Barrier Reef 87, 191, 204
Great Smoky Mountains National Park 316, 318
Great Wall 340, 342
Greater St Lucia Wetland Park 326, 328, 329
grouped heritage items 123–6
guides 36, 41, 43–4
Guinea 173

Hadrian's Wall 246–7, 250, 252
Hampi 174
Hangzhou 337, 340
Harpers Ferry National Historical Park 306
Hawaii Volcanoes National Park 316, 319
Heard and McDonald Islands 192
Henderson Island 253
heritage—cultural (built) 1, 4, 14, 113–38, 154, 163, 165, 166, 183–4, 206–9, 213–17, 224, 225, 226, 227, 239, 241, 242–5, 256–7, 267–8, 279–80, 290–1, 297–9, 306–11, 314–15, 321, 323–4, 330, 334, 338, 340
ethnic 17
global (see also World Heritage) 10, 12
immovable 113
indigenous 1, 3, 14, 24–5, 36, 114, 140–52, 185, 205–6, 217–18, 222, 223, 225, 226, 230, 231, 239, 297, 306, 321, 324, 350
mixed cultural and natural 154, 169, 170, 190, 350
movable 1, 12, 113
national 3, 14, 16–17, 24, 114, 140–2, 184, 206–9, 239
natural 1, 4, 14, 83–110, 154, 164–6, 184, 186–7, 190, 206, 217–20, 221, 222, 223, 224, 226, 227–8, 230, 245–6, 249, 257–8, 259, 268–70, 280–2, 290–1, 299–301, 311, 313–14, 321, 324–8, 330, 338–9
non-material 1–2, 12, 113
Heritage Act 1977 (NSW) 212, 217
Heritage Act 1978 (SA) 225
Heritage Act 1992 (Qld) 224
Heritage Act 1993 (SA) 225
Heritage Act 1995 (Ireland) 290
Heritage Act 1995 (Vic) 227
heritage agreements 225, 226, 230
Heritage Amendment Act 1998 (NSW) 217
Heritage Assistance Program (NSW) 217
Heritage Buildings Protection Act 1990 224
Heritage Conservation Act 1991 (NT) 222
Heritage Council (ACT) 222
Heritage Council (Ireland) 290
Heritage Council (NSW) 17, 75, 115–16, 118, 211–14, 216, 217
Heritage Council (NT) 222–3
Heritage Council (Qld) 224
Heritage Council (Tas) 226
Heritage Council of Western Australia 230
Heritage Council Victoria 227
Heritage Inventory (Vic) 227
Heritage Inventory Program (NSW) 115–16
Heritage Objects Act 1991 (ACT) 222
Heritage of Western Australia Act 1990 (WA) 230
Heritage Office (NSW) 14, 17, 211–14, 220–1
Heritage Places Register (ACT) 222
heritage plans 75
heritage precincts 50, 298
Heritage Register (Qld) 224
Heritage South Australia 225
Hill End–Tambaroora 126
Hindmarsh Island 143
Historic Buildings Act 1981 (Vic) 227
Historic Buildings Council (Vic) 227
Historic Buildings Register (Vic) 227

Historic Houses Trust (NSW)   55, 212
Historic Places Act 1993 (NZ)   297
Historic Scotland   244
historic sites and reserves   218–19, 223, 227, 304
Historical Cultural Heritage Act 1995 (Tas)   226
history   2, 15, 121
Hluhluwe Umfolozi Park   326
Holy See (see Italy, Vatican)
Hondaribbia   280
Honduras   174
Hongcun   346
Hope Inquiry into the National Estate   187
Huanglong   343
Hydro-Electric Commission (Tas)   197

Ibiza   282, 288
Iceland   170
Ichkeul National Park   175
identity   2, 4–5, 16, 37–8
Iguacu National Park   173
Illawarra   126
Imperial Tombs of the Ming and Qing Dynasties   346
India   174
indigenous peoples (see also particular groups)   3, 12, 14, 24, 114, 169, 325
industrial archaeology   128–9, 170, 356
information technology   42, 46
Institution of Engineers   235, 236
integrity test   306–7, 309
Intergovernmental Agreement on the Environment   196
Interim Biogeographic Regionalisation   88
interim conservation orders   217, 222, 230, 280
interim preservation orders   227
International Centre for the Study of the Preservation and Restoration of Cultural Property (ICCROM)   167, 168, 172
International Charter for the Conservation and Restoration of Monuments and Sites   75
International Council on Sites and Monuments (ICOMOS)   75, 131, 167, 168, 172
International Union for the Conservation of Nature and Natural Resources (IUCN)   75, 94–5, 107, 167, 168, 172, 220
interpretation   15, 30–47, 101, 144–6, 356
Inventory of Movable Objects (Spain)   279
Ireland, Republic of   9, 12–13, 24, 25, 46, 53, 118, 127, 137, 169, 290–3
Ironbridge   128, 170, 250, 251
Israel   170
Itala Game Reserve   328
Italy (including Holy See)   63, 81, 266–78

Jenolan Caves   40–1, 167, 218, 236
Jerusalem   163, 170, 174
Jervis Bay National Park   221
Jiuzhaigou Valley   340, 343
Jordan   170, 174

Kaeng Krachan National Park   332
Kahuzi–Biega National Park   173
Kakadu National Park   77, 103, 146, 166, 170, 176, 190, 191, 195, 197, 199–203, 204, 221
Kanangra–Boyd National Park   35, 85, 167
Kgalagadi Transfrontier Park   325
Khao Kitchakut National Park   332
Khao Yai National Park   332
Killarney National Park   291
Ko Chang National Marine Park   332
Kosciuszko National Park   101
Kotor   175
Kromdraai   329
Kruger National Park   325
Ku-ring-gai Chase National Park   33, 58, 146, 148–50
KwaZulu–Natal   324, 325–7

KwaZulu–Natal Nature Conservation Services (S Af)   325–7, 328

Lahore   174
Lake District National Park   246
Lake Pedder   197
land clearing   92
Land Conservation Council (Vic)   228
Land Conservation, Preservation and Infrastructure Improvement Trust Program (USA)   306
Land and Environment Court (NSW)   216, 217
Land (Planning and Environment) Act 1991 (ACT)   222
Land for Wildlife   97
Landcare   97
Lands Act 1933 (WA)   230
landscape conservation area   126
landscape protection zone   26
landscapes   1, 8, 11, 50, 85–7, 122, 126
language   33, 40, 45
Las Médulas   282, 287
Lascaux Caves   9, 24, 145, 258, 261, 357
Leshan Giant Buddha   345
Lhasa   340, 344
Liguria   277
Lijiang   345
listing proposals   74–5, 120–1, 143–4
Liverpool (UK)   250
local approvals policy   216
local environment plans   212, 216
local government   4, 181, 213–17, 224, 225, 226, 227, 231, 237, 242, 244
Local Government Act 1962 (Tas)   226
Local Government Act 1993 (NSW)   216–17
Local Government (Planning and Environment) Act 1990 (Qld)   224
local heritage studies   214–16
Loch Lomond   249
Loire Valley   166, 265
London   73, 243, 250, 253, 254
Longmen Grottoes   346
Longsheng Hot Springs National Forest Park   338
Lord Howe Island   191
Los Angeles   311
Lugo   289
Lushan National Park   344
Lyons   265

Macchu Picchu   10
Macquarie Island   193
Madrid   283
Main Street Program (US)   123, 310
maintenance   71, 147, 150
Maldon   126
Mali   174
Mammoth Cave National Park   316, 318
Man and the Biosphere Programme   175, 338
management   4, 38, 43, 67–82, 97–107, 131–4, 146, 177, 203, 220, 258, 297–301, 325, 354–5, 358
management plans   4, 75–6, 100, 102–7, 166, 172, 201, 220, 223, 231, 240, 249, 299–300, 314, 320
Manas Wildlife Sanctuary   174
Manovo–Gounda St Floris National Park   173
Maoris   297, 301
marine parks   104–5, 330
market segmentation   32–3, 65
marketing   4, 12, 33, 53, 65
Matera   274
Mayo National Park   291
meanings, contested   2, 4, 30–1
Melbourne   124–5, 135, 227, 234
Memphis   351
Mérida   286
Mesa Verde   316, 317

Mexico   10, 164
Milan   270, 273
mines and mining   128–9, 170, 197, 199–203, 225
Ministry of Cultural Property and Activities (Italy)   267
Ministry for Culture and Heritage (NZ)   297
Ministry of the Environment (France)   257
Ministry for Maori Affairs (NZ)   297
Minnamurra National Park   101
minority groups   2, 14, 25, 37–8, 114, 140–52
Modena   276
Mogao Caves   340, 342
Monasterio de la Oliva   279
Mont-Saint-Michel   258, 261, 266
Montagu   323
Monument Valley Tribal Park   143, 144
Mount Aspiring National Park   301
Mount Emei   340, 345
Mount Huangshan   343
Mount Nimba Nature Reserve   173
Mount Qincheng   346
Mount Taishan   342
Mount Wuyi   346
Mulanweichang National Forest Park   338
multiple use of natural areas   109
museums   2, 113, 128, 129, 137

Nancy   263
Napier   298
Naples   274
Naracoorte   192
national estate   187–9, 232–5, 322
National Estate Grants Program   187–8
national forest park   338
National Heritage Convention   207
National Heritage Council (S Af)   323–4
National Heritage Council Act 1999 (S Af)   321
National Heritage List   208–9
National Heritage Resources Act 1999 (S Af)   321–4
National Heritage Strategy   207–8
national historic monuments (Ireland)   290
National Historic Preservation Act 1966 (USA)   309
National Monument Record (UK)   242, 244
national monuments   290, 307–8, 323–4
National Monuments Act 1930 (Ireland)   290
National Monuments Council (S Af)   323–4
National Park Act 1961 (Thailand)   332, 333
National Park Service (USA)   304–6
National Park Service Organic Act 1916 (USA)   304
national parks   8–9, 12, 24, 25, 26, 49, 55, 102, 184, 218–20,
   224, 227, 230, 241, 245–9, 257–8, 260, 269, 271, 280–1,
   290–2, 299–301, 304, 311–13, 324–6, 332–3
National Parks Act 1975 (Vic)   227–8
National Parks Act 1980 (NZ)   297
National Parks Association   235, 249
National Parks Conservation Association (USA)   313, 320
National Parks and Nature Conservation Authority (WA)   230
National Parks (Scotland) Act 2000   249
National Parks and Wildlife Act 1970 (Tas)   226
National Parks and Wildlife Act 1972 (SA)   226
National Parks and Wildlife Act 1974 (NSW)   219
National Parks and Wildlife Council (Tas)   226
National Parks and Wildlife Service (NSW)   75, 150, 167,
   185, 211, 213, 217–20
National Register of Historic Places (USA)   309, 314
National Reserves System Cooperative Program   88
National Strategy for the Conservation of Australia's
   Biodiversity   204–5
National Threatened Species Strategy   205
National Trust (UK)   247, 250, 255, 297, 309
National Trust of Australia   22–3, 75, 118, 121, 124, 126,
   211, 224, 227, 297, 309
National Trust for Historic Preservation (US)   123, 309–11
National Trust for Ireland (see An Taisce)

National Trust for Scotland   77, 249, 250, 255
National Wilderness Inventory   95–6
Native Americans   143, 144, 306, 315, 316
Natural Heritage Trust   190
Nature Conservation Service (Italy)   268
nature reserves and refuges   218–19, 224, 245, 267, 291, 339
Navajo Nation   143, 144
Netherlands   169
New Forest   245
New South Wales   14, 17, 24, 55, 56, 70, 89–92, 101, 104–5,
   115–16, 117, 123–5, 126, 136, 148–50, 167, 185, 190, 205,
   211–21, 232–4
New South Wales Heritage Database   211–12, 218, 220
New South Wales Heritage Management System   213
New York   316, 318
New Zealand   68, 69, 135, 296–303
New Zealand Historic Places Trust   297, 299
New Zealand Sub-Antarctic Islands   303
Newcastle (NSW)   22–3, 121, 123–4, 126, 129
Newgrange   24, 291
Niger   174
Norfolk Island National Park   221
North of England Open Air Museum   137, 356–7
Northern Ireland   241, 244, 250
Northern Territory   77, 90, 102, 145–6, 166, 170, 183, 190,
   195–6, 204, 221, 222–3
Northumberland National Park   246–7, 250

Oberon   117
Office of Public Works (Ireland)   290
off-reserve conservation   96
Okapi Wildlife Reserve   173
Old Sydney Town   138
Olympic Games   17, 33, 141, 151, 358
Olympic National Park   316, 318
Oman   174
Operational Guidelines (World Heritage Committee)   166–7
Orange (France)   262
Orcival   351, 353
originality   25, 130
Orkney   250, 254
Otago Peninsula Trust   299
Oviedo   284
'ownership' of heritage   140–1, 143–8, 352

Padua   270, 276
Pakistan   174
Palmeral of Elche   289
paradors   280
Parc national des Pyrénées   258
Parc natural régional de Camargue   258–9, 353–4
Parc régional des Volcans d'Auvergne   259
parchi nazionale   269
parcs nationaux   257–8, 260
Paris   26–7, 53, 72, 130, 135, 137, 168, 256–7, 258, 263
park authorities (UK)   245–6, 249
Parks and Wildlife Commission (NT)   102, 223
Parks Australia   185, 204, 205, 221, 223
parques nacionales   280–1
perceptions of heritage   2, 4–5, 7–12, 23–7
permanent conservation orders   217
Peru   10, 175
pests   99
Philadelphia   315, 316, 317
philosophies   4, 18
Phimai   331
Pienza   275
Ping Yao   340, 345
Pisa   81, 270, 273
planning   122–3, 143–4, 216–17, 222, 227, 235, 291
Planning and Development Act 1966 (SA)   225
Planning and Environment Court (Qld)   224
Planning Environment Act 1987 (Vic)   227

Plitvice Lakes National Park   172
Poblet Monastery   286
Poland   172
politics   16–17, 32, 140–2, 352, 358
Pompei   270, 272, 276
Pongola Game Reserve   325–6
Pont du Gard   55, 258, 263, 266
Powerscourt   127
precinct, heritage   123–5
prehistoric sites   7, 9, 24–5, 164, 250, 260, 279, 282, 292
presentation   4, 30–47, 144–6
preservation   4, 71, 131
preservation orders   290
private ownership   3, 26, 50–2, 78–9, 96, 131
Protección del Patrimonio Histórico   279
protected landscapes   280
public access   76
public awareness   34–5
public involvement   102
Pueblo de Taos   316, 319
Puerto Rico   316, 318
Purnululu National Park   230
Pyrénées   258, 265, 279, 282, 289

Queen Elizabeth II Trust for Open Space in NZ   299
Queensland   87, 90–2, 128–9, 136, 183, 224–5
Queensland Parks and Wildlife Service   224
Qufu   340, 344

Rammelsberg Mines   164, 170
Ramsar Convention   177, 187
Ramsar sites   176, 177, 194, 205, 353–4
Ravenna   275
reconstruction   72–3, 131–2
recreations   102
Redwood National Park   316, 317
Regional Forests Agreements   88, 218
Register of Assets of Cultural Interest (Spain)   279–80
Register of Government Buildings (Vic)   227
Register of Heritage Places (WA)   230
Register of the National Estate   20–1, 184, 187–90, 208–9, 224, 307, 323
Register of the National Fund for Historic Monuments and Sites (France)   34, 256
Register of the Queensland Estate   224
Register of Sacred Sites (NT)   223
Registrar of Aboriginal Sites (WA)   231
Reims   264
Religious Properties Fund (Italy)   267–8
relocation   8, 10, 137
remote and natural areas   227
representativeness   10, 20–21
research   39–40, 79, 143–4
reserves   88–94, 221, 245, 269–70, 280, 304–5, 307–9, 313
Reserves Act 1977 (NZ)   297
Residences of the Royal House of Savoy   276
Resource Management Act 1991 (NZ)   297
restoration   72, 131
Rio Platano Biosphere Reserve   174
Riversleigh   192
Robben Island   328, 329
rock art sites   147–50, 288, 325
Rome   63, 270, 278
Routes of Santiago de Compostela   265, 286
Royal Australian Institute of Architects   235, 236
Royal Commission on the Ancient and Historical Monuments of Scotland   244–5
Royal Commission on the Ancient and Historical Monuments of Wales   244
Royal Commission on the Historical Monuments of England   244
Rural Heritage Program (USA)   310
Russian Federation   170
Rwenzori Mountains National Park   175

Sacramento   314
Saint-Emilion   265
St Kilda (Scotland)   252
Saintes-Maries-de-la-Mer   354
Salamanca   282, 286
Salonga National Park   174
San Antonio   307
San Cristóbel de la Laguna   288
San Gimignano   273
San Juan   318
San Millán Monasteries   288
Sangay National Park   174
Santa Maria de Guadalupe   286
Santiago de Compostela   282, 284
Saudi Arabia   170
Save America's Treasures (USA)   306
scale   2, 20–1, 353–4, 356
Scotland   12, 77, 241, 244–5, 249, 250, 255
Scottish Natural Heritage   245, 249
Segovia   282, 284
sense of place, sense of time   5, 122, 358
Seville   285
Shamwari Game Reserve   328
Shanghai   334, 336, 337, 340
Shark Bay   192
shipwrecks   129
Siena   270, 272, 274
significance   19, 68, 115–19
signs   34, 35, 36–7, 41, 43, 77
Simen National Park   174
Sites and Monuments Records (UK)   242, 244
Sites of Special Scientific Interest   245
Skellig Michael   293
social context   4–5, 30, 42, 80, 358
Solitary Islands Marine Park   104–5
South Africa   62, 94, 96, 142, 296, 320–30
South African Heritage Resources Agency   323–4
South African National Estate   322
South African National Parks   325
South African National Monuments   323
South African Natural Heritage Programme   328
South Australia   143, 221, 225–6
South Downs   245
South West New Zealand   300–1, 303
south-western Tasmania (see Tasmanian Wilderness)
Sovereign Hill   138
Soweto   320
Spain   7, 24, 25, 114, 142, 258, 279–89
Spanish Historical Heritage   279
Srebarba Nature Reserve   173
State Authorities, Development and Management Act 1993 (Ireland)   290
State Forests of NSW   150, 218
state heritage areas   225
State Heritage Authority (SA)   225
State Heritage Register (NSW)   211–12, 218, 220
State Heritage Register (SA)   225
State Historical Resources Commission (California)   315
state recreation areas   218–19
statement of heritage impact   210
statement of significance   20, 22–3, 115–6, 121
Sterkfontein   329
Stonehenge   24, 164, 243, 250, 252
stop-work orders   222, 230
Strasbourg   26
structures in natural areas   100–1, 103
Studley Royal Park   251
Sub-Directorate for Protection of the Historical Heritage (Spain)   279–80
Sudan   170
Sukhotai   334, 335
Suzhou   127, 338, 340, 341, 345

Swartkrans 329
Switzerland 239–40
Sydney 26, 50–2, 117, 124, 126, 219, 232–4, 235

Tárraco 289
Tarutao National Marine Park 332
Tasmania 103–4, 136, 190, 191, 196, 197, 198–9, 221, 226
Tasmanian Heritage Register 226
Tasmanian Parks and Wildlife Service 226
Tasmanian wilderness 190, 191, 196, 197, 198–9, 204
Tatshenshini–Alesek/Kluane National Park 319
Te Wahipounamu/South West New Zealand 300–1, 303
Terracotta Warriors 340, 342
Territory Parks and Wildlife Conservation Act 1976 (NT) 223
Teruel 282, 285
Thaddeus Kosciuszko National Memorial 304
Thai Fine Arts Department 331, 334
Thailand 10, 296, 330–4, 335
theme parks 8, 10, 356–7
Thungyai–Huai Kha Khaeng Wildlife Sanctuaries 335
Timbuktu 174
Tivoli 278
Toledo 282, 285
Tongariro National Park 169, 299, 301, 303
Torres Strait Islanders 12, 26, 94, 141–2, 182, 224
tourism and recreation 15, 17, 59–65, 85, 108–10, 147, 151–2, 321, 325, 330, 350, 352
Tourism New South Wales 151–2
Tower of London 253
towns and villages, historic 126, 164, 227, 240–1, 256
Tswalu Private Desert Reserve 328
Tunisia 175

Uganda 175
Ukhahlamba–Drakensberg Park 328, 329
Uluṟu–Kata Tjuṯa National Park 145–6, 170, 190, 192, 196, 204, 221
UNESCO Mission to Kakadu National Park 199, 202
uniqueness 20–1
United Kingdom (see also England, Northern Ireland, Scotland and Wales) 25, 126, 181, 241–55, 291, 321
United Nations Educational, Scientific and Cultural Organization (UNESCO) 49, 75, 154, 161, 163, 202, 301
United Nations Environment Programme 178
United States of America 24, 37, 45, 50, 70, 106–7, 142, 143, 144, 169, 175, 181, 182, 304–20, 321
urban conservation areas 123–5, 164
Urbino 277
user-pays principle 57–8

Valcamonica 270, 273
Valencia 287
Valley Forge National Historic Park 311
Valley of the Giants 101
valuing heritage 53–4
Venice 270, 273
Venice Charter 75
Verla 170
Verona 278
Versailles 60, 261
Vézelay 261
Vézère Valley 261
Vicenza 274
Victoria 19–20, 94–5, 97, 98, 124–5, 126, 135, 136, 148–9, 184, 186, 227–30, 234
Victoria Archaeology Survey 230
Victorian Heritage Register 227
Villa Romana del Casale 276
Virunga National Park 172, 173
visitor centres 46–7, 114

visitor management 4, 76–8, 81, 100–2, 134
visitor surveys 39–41
Völklingen 170

Waddesdon Manor 25
Waitangi 68, 69
Wales 25, 170, 241, 243, 244–6, 250, 252
walking tracks 98, 101, 103
Wallsend 123–4
Washington DC 37
Watarrka National Park 223
water pollution 99
Waterton Glacier International Peace Park 319
web sites 34, 46
weeds 99
Wellington 135, 298
Western Australia 101, 136, 183, 205, 221, 230–1
Westland/Tai Poutini National Park 299–301
Wet Tropics of Queensland 105–6, 192, 204
Wicklow Mountains National Park 291
wild and scenic rivers 219
wilderness 12, 25, 26, 35, 85, 94–6, 218–19, 222, 223, 224, 226, 227–8, 241, 299, 313, 327
Wilderness Act 1987 (NSW) 219
Wilderness Advisory Committee (SA) 226
Wilderness Protection Act 1992 (SA) 226
Wilderness Society 235
Wildlife Act 1976 (Ireland) 290
Wildlife Preservation and Protection Act 1992 (Thailand) 332
Wieliczka Salt Mine 172
Willandra Lakes 190, 191
Wollemi pine 84–5, 167
World Heritage (also see specific categories) 154–79
World Heritage Bureau 163, 166–7, 168, 178, 190–204, 239
World Heritage Committee 3, 142, 154, 163, 165–6, 167, 170, 172, 176, 178, 199, 203, 301, 320, 350
World Heritage Convention 154–66, 168, 170, 176, 185, 197, 204
World Heritage Convention Act 1999 (S Af) 321, 323
World Heritage Cultural Landscapes 169, 350
World Heritage in Danger, List of 167, 168, 170, 172–6, 199, 304, 316, 320
World Heritage Fund 161, 167, 172
World Heritage List 9, 26, 75, 154–63, 166, 169–72, 196
World Heritage, national obligations 168–9
World Heritage Properties Act 1983 (Cth) 197, 204
World Heritage sites/properties 10, 26–7, 55, 62, 85, 105–6, 127, 128, 152, 154–61, 164, 166–76, 178, 190–204, 206, 218, 239, 246–8, 250–4, 258, 260–6, 267, 270–8, 281–9, 292–3, 299–303, 315–20, 321, 326, 330, 331, 333–4, 335, 337, 339, 340–6, 351
Wrangell–Saint Elias National Park 304, 319
Wudang Mountains 344
Wulingyuan 343

Xi'an 338, 340, 342
Xidi 346

Yancheng 338
Yellowstone National Park 175, 304, 316, 317, 320
Yemen 175
Yorkshire Dales National Park 10–11, 246
Yosemite National Park 70, 106–7, 316, 318
Yugoslavia 170, 175

Zabid 175
Zaire 172
Zaragoza 280
Zhangjiajie National Forest Park 340
Zhoukoudian 340, 342
zoning 68, 100, 104–6, 177, 200–1, 229, 258, 269, 282